PEP
GUARDIOLA

ANOTHER WAY OF WINNING
The Biography

GUILLEM BALAGUÉ

An Orion paperback

First published in Great Britain in 2012
by Orion
This paperback edition published in 2013
by Orion Books Ltd,
Orion House, 5 Upper St Martin's Lane,
London WC2H 9EA

An Hachette UK company

1 3 5 7 9 10 8 6 4 2

The author and publisher are grateful to Miguel Ruiz for permission
to reproduce all the photographs except page 15 (Getty) and (*below*) page 16
(Press Association); and to Plataforma Editorial for permission to quote from
Todos mis hermanos by Manel Estiarte (Barcelona, 2009)

A CIP catalogue record for this book is available
from the British Library.

ISBN 978-1-4091-2946-2

Printed and bound by CPI Group (UK) Ltd, Croydon, CR0 4YY

The Orion Publishing Group's policy is to use papers that
are natural, renewable and recyclable products and
made from wood grown in sustainable forests. The logging
and manufacturing processes are expected to conform to
the environmental regulations of the country of origin.

www.orionbooks.co.uk

To my brother Gustavo (*culé*),
my sister Yolanda (new-born *culé*),
Luis Miguel García (who will never be *culé*)
and Brent Wilks (who reminds us constantly
football is not about life and death)

CONTENTS

FOREWORD

by Sir Alex Ferguson

I missed out on signing Pep Guardiola as a player back at the time when he realised that his future no longer lay at Barcelona.

Although there wasn't any apparent reason for him to leave his club, we spoke to Guardiola and I thought I had a good chance of getting him: maybe the timing I chose was wrong. It would have been interesting; he was the kind of player that Paul Scholes developed into: he was captain, leader and midfield playmaker in Johan Cruyff's incredible Barcelona Dream Team and displayed a composure and ability to use the ball and dictate the tempo of a game that made him one of the greatest players of his generation. Those were the kinds of qualities I was looking for. I ended up signing Juan Sebastián Verón for that reason. Sometimes, you look back at a really top player and you say to yourself: 'I wonder what it would have been like if he'd have come to United?' That is the case with Pep Guardiola.

I can understand Pep's situation as a player. When you're at a club like Barcelona, you would like to think you have a place for life. So when we approached him he probably thought he still had a future at the club even though he ended up leaving that season. It is a shame, because nothing is for life in football: age and time catch up with you and the day comes when both you and the club have to move on. At the time I thought we were offering Pep a solution, a different road in his career, but it didn't work out. It reminds me of Gary Neville. Having had Gary at Manchester United since he was twelve years old, he became almost like family: like a son, someone you depend upon and trust, who was part of the whole structure of the team. But one day it all finishes. In Pep's case, the realisation that all that was coming to an end must have been difficult. I could understand his doubts, his delay in committing, but it got to a point where we had to look somewhere else and that opportunity disappeared.

One thing I have noticed about Guardiola – crucial to his immense success as a manager – is that he has been very humble. He has never tried to gloat, he has been very respectful – and that is very important. It is good to have those qualities and, looking back, it is apparent that he has been unassuming throughout his career. As a player he was never the type to be on the front pages of the papers. He played his game in a certain way; he wasn't tremendously quick but a fantastic, composed footballer. As a coach he is very disciplined in terms of how his team plays, but whether they win or lose he is always the same elegant, unpretentious individual. And, to be honest, I think it is good to have someone like that in this profession.

However, it seems that he reached a point in his coaching career where he was conscious of the importance of his job at Barcelona while experiencing the demands attached to it. I am sure he spent time thinking, 'How long is it going to last? Will I be able to create another title-winning team? Will I be able to create another European Cup-winning team? Can I maintain this level of success?'

If I had arrived in time to advise him, I would have told Pep not to worry about it: a failure to win the Champions League is not an indictment of his managerial abilities or of his team. I understand the pressure, though: the expectation was so high every time Guardiola's team played, everyone wanted to beat them. In fact, I think he was in a fortunate position in a way, because the only thing he had to worry about was how he was going to break down the opposing team to stop them winning.

Personally, I think it's about keeping going. So, why go? It might be a question of controlling the players, of finding new tactics because teams have started working out Barça's style of play. Or a question of motivating them. In my experience, a 'normal' human being wants to do things the easiest possible way in life. For instance, I know some people who have retired at fifty years old – don't ask me why! So the drive that most people have is different from that of individuals like Scholes, Giggs, Xavi, Messi and Puyol who, as far as I am concerned, are exceptional human beings and motivation is not an issue for them because their pride comes before everything. I am sure Pep's squad was full of the types of characters who were an example to others and a source of motivation: not types who wanted to retire too early.

I know Gerard Piqué from his time here at United. I know his type of personality: off the pitch he can be a laid-back, easy-going guy, but on the pitch he is a winner. He was a winner here and we didn't want the boy to leave, and he is a winner there at Barcelona. The players Pep had under him needed less motivation than most. Perhaps Pep underestimated his motivational abilities? You could see what he consistently achieved with that Barcelona team and you need to have a special talent to keep them competing at that level and with such success for so long. But I am convinced he has enough weapons to do it again. And again and again.

What Guardiola achieved in his four years at the first team of Barcelona betters anything that previous coaches at the Camp Nou have done – and there have been some great ones: van Gaal, Rijkaard and Cruyff to name a few; but Guardiola has taken certain areas to another level – such as pressing the ball – and Barcelona's disciplined style of play and work ethic have become a trademark of all his teams. Pep created a culture where the players know that if they don't work hard, they won't be at the club. Believe me, that is not easy to do.

Whatever Pep's next move may be after he has taken some time out, whether he moves to the Premier League or not, there's always going to be a lot of speculation surrounding his future. He was at a fantastic football club at Barcelona and it is not going to get any better for him wherever he goes. Going to another club will not take any pressure off him or reduce the level of expectation surrounding him. In fact, wherever he goes he is going to have the same experience: he is a manager; he has to decide what is best for his team, about choosing players and their tactics. It is that simple. In that respect it is the same wherever you go, because all managers' jobs come with pressure. I've been successful at Manchester United for many years and it's not without its problems – every hour of every day you have to deal with something. It comes down to the fact that you are dealing with human beings in the world of football. There's a plethora of things to worry about: agents, family, form, injuries, age, profile, ego, etc. If

Pep were to go to another club the questions would be the same as those he has faced so far. The expectation would follow him around.

So, why? Why would he decide to leave? When you asked me before Pep announced his decision, I did say that it would be silly not to see the job through. If you look at Madrid, who won five European Cups in the late fifties and early sixties, there's no reason to think that he couldn't have done the same with Barça. That to me would be a personal motivation if I had that team. And if I were Pep, leaving would have been the most difficult decision to make.

Sir Alex Ferguson
Spring 2012

Rome. 27 May 2009. UEFA Champions League final

It is the eighth minute of the match. Barcelona yet to find their rhythm.
The players are all in the right positions, but none of them willing to bite,
to step forward and pressure the man on the ball. They are playing within
themselves, showing too much respect to Manchester United. Ronaldo
has a shot saved by Víctor Valdés. Another shot. United are getting closer.
Cristiano fires just wide of the post. Centimetres. That's the difference.
Centimetres away from goal.

Centimetres away from changing the way the world judges Pep
Guardiola and his Nou Camp revolution.

Giggs, Carrick, Anderson are moving the ball around at will between
the lines. Something has to be done. Pep leaps from the bench and
barks rapid-fire instructions, his voice carrying to his players above the
cacophony of noise in a packed Olympic stadium in Rome.

Messi is told to take up a position between the United centre backs,
as a false striker – and Eto'o is shifted out wide, to occupy his place on
the right wing. Ferguson, on the bench, impassive. Delighted with the
outcome so far, feels in control.

But the tide changes. Imperceptibly at first. Messi finds Iniesta, who
finds Xavi, who finds Messi. Suddenly, Carrick and Anderson must react
quickly, decide who to mark, which pass to break, space to cover. Giggs
is tied up with Busquets and cannot help.

Iniesta receives the ball in the centre of the pitch. Evra has lost Eto'o and
Iniesta spots the opportunity opening up on the right flank. He dribbles
the ball forward and then, at precisely the right moment, finds Eto'o on
the edge of the box with an incisive, inch-perfect pass. He receives the

ball. Vidić is making a last-ditch attempt to cover him but Eto'o jinks past him, and, in the blink of an eye, relying on his pure assassin's instinct, fires in a shot at the near post.

The destination of that shot, that instant, the culmination of a move, would help convert an idea, a seed planted forty years earlier, into a footballing tsunami that would transform the game for years to come.

PROLOGUE

Pep left Barcelona and all he had shaped because, Sir Alex, he is not like most managers. He walked away because he is, quite simply, not your typical football man.

You could already see it in your first encounter in the dugout, in the Champions League final in Rome in 2009. For that final, Guardiola had made a compendium of his thoughts and applied his club philosophy to everything related to that game, from preparation to tactics, from the last tactical chat to the way they celebrated the victory. Pep had invited the world to join him and his players in the joy of playing a huge European Cup final.

He was confident he had prepared the team to beat you, but, if that was not possible, the fans would take home the pride of having tried it the Barça way and, in the process, of having overcome a dark period in their history. Not only had he changed a negative trend within the club, but he had also, in only twelve months since his arrival, started to bury some powerful unwritten but fashionable commandments that talked about the importance of winning above anything else, the impossibility of reconciling the principle of reaching the highest targets with playing well, producing a spectacle. Or the one that considered obsolete the essential values of sportsmanship and respect. Who came up with those rules, who started the fashion? Since day one of his arrival in the dugout at Barcelona, Pep was willing to go against the tide because that was all he believed in.

But that was then.

By the end of his tenure he was no longer the youthful, eager, enthusiastic manager you met that night in Rome or the following year in Nyon, at the UEFA headquarters, for a rare moment of socialising.

On the day he announced to the world he was leaving his boyhood club after four years in charge of the first team you could see the toll it had taken: it was discernible in his eyes and in his receding hairline, now flecked with grey. But the eyes: it was especially visible if you looked into his eyes. He was no longer as spirited and impressionable as on that morning in Switzerland, when you offered him some words of wisdom and fatherly advice. Did you know that he still talks about that chat, those fifteen minutes with you, as one of the highlights of his career? He was like a star-struck teenager, repeating for days afterwards: 'I was with Sir Alex, I spoke to Sir Alex Ferguson!' Back then, everything was new and exciting: obstacles were challenges rather than insurmountable hurdles.

On that sunny morning in September 2010, at UEFA's modern rectangular building on the shores of Lake Geneva, the annual coaches' conference provided the setting for the first social meeting between yourself and Pep Guardiola since you became coaches. Before that, you scarcely had time to exchange anything more than pleasantries in Rome, and Pep had been looking forward to spending some time in your company, away from the pressures of competition. The conference provided an opportunity for coaches to gossip, discuss trends, whinge and bond as an elite group of professionals who would spend the rest of the year in a state of perpetual solitude, struggling to manage twenty or so egos, plus their families and agents.

Among the guests in Nyon was a certain José Mourinho, the colourful new manager of Real Madrid and reigning European champion with Inter Milan, the team that had knocked Pep's Barcelona out in the semi-final the previous season. Mid-morning, on the first of two days, you arrived at UEFA headquarters in one of a pair of minibuses; the first carrying the Portuguese coach, along with the then Chelsea manager Carlo Ancelotti and Roma's Claudio Ranieri. Guardiola travelled in the second bus, with you. As soon as you entered the building, Mourinho approached the group that had gathered around you, while Guardiola stepped to one side to take it all in: to photograph the moment – always aware of the significance of these events in his own life story. After all, he was surrounded by some of football's great minds, he was there to listen, to watch and to learn. As he has always done.

Pep spent a while on his own, distanced from the conversations that were taking place. Mourinho spotted him out of the corner of his eye and left the group he was in. He greeted Guardiola and shook his hand effusively. The pair smiled. They started talking animatedly for a few minutes and the Werder Bremen coach, Thomas Schaaf, joined in, occasionally managing to catch his colleagues' attention.

It was the last time Pep Guardiola and José Mourinho were to speak on such amicable terms.

The groups entered the main conference hall for the first of the two sessions that day, where you talked about the tactical trends that were used in the previous Champions League campaign, as well as other topics related to the World Cup in South Africa, which Spain had just won. At the end of the first meeting, everyone posed for a group photograph. Didier Deschamps was sitting between Guardiola and Mourinho in the centre of the front row. On the left, you sat next to Ancelotti. There was laughter and banter and it was developing into quite an entertaining day.

Just before the second session, there was time for coffee and you and Guardiola found yourselves together in a seating area with a breathtaking view of Lake Geneva, overlooking clear blue water and the exclusive homes visible on the far shore.

Pep felt humbled in your presence. In his eyes you are a giant of the dugout, but that morning you were an affable Scot who smiled easily – as you often do when out of the limelight. You admired the younger manager's humility, despite the fact that Pep had already won seven titles out of a possible nine at that point – and had the world of football arguing about whether he was implementing an evolution or a revolution at FC Barcelona. The general consensus at the time was that, at the very least, Pep's youth and positivity were a breath of fresh air.

That chat over coffee quickly turned into an improvised lesson between teacher and pupil. Pep enjoys spending time watching and taking in what the legends of football have added to the game. In great detail he recalls van Gaal's Ajax, Milan's achievements with Sacchi.

He could talk to you for ages about both. And he holds winning a European Cup in almost the same esteem as he does his shirt signed by his idol Michel Platini. You are also a member of Pep's particular hall of fame.

As the pupil listened, soaking up every word, his respect for you was transformed into devotion: not only because of the symbolic content of the chat, your vision of the profession. It wasn't just the insight. It was the stature of the man who was doing the talking.

He is in awe of the longevity of your tenure at Manchester United: the resilience and inner strength required to stay in the job for so long. Pep has always thought that the pressures at Barcelona and Manchester must be different. He yearns to understand how one sustains the hunger for success and avoids the loss of appetite that must inevitably follow successive victories. He believes that a team that wins all the time needs to lose to benefit from the lessons that only defeat can bring. Pep wants to discover how you deal with that, Sir Alex; how you clear your mind; how you relate to defeat. You didn't have time to talk about everything, but those issues will be raised next time you cross paths, you can be sure of that.

Pep venerates your composure in both victory and defeat and the way you fight tooth and nail to defend your own brand of football – and you also advised him to keep faithful to who he is, to his beliefs and inner self.

'Pepe,' you said to him – and he was too respectful to correct you about getting his name wrong – 'you have to make sure you don't lose sight of who you are. Many young coaches change, for whatever reason – because of circumstances beyond their control, because things don't come out right at first or because success can change you. All of a sudden, they want to amend tactics, themselves. They don't realise football is a monster that you can only beat and face if you are always yourself: under any circumstance.'

For you, it was perhaps little more than some friendly advice, satisfying a fatherly instinct you have often had for the new faces on the scene. Yet, unintentionally perhaps, you revealed to Pep the secrets of your enduring resilience in the football profession, your need to continue and your strange relationship with the sport, where sometimes you feel trapped and at other times liberated.

Your words came back to him more than once while he was agonisingly deliberating his future. He understands what you were talking about, but, nevertheless, he could not help changing during his four years leading the Barcelona first team. Football, that monster, transformed him.

You warned him against losing sight of his true self, but he changed, partly due to the pressure from a grateful and adoring fanbase, who forgot he was only a football coach; partly because of his own behaviour, eventually being unable to take decisions that would hurt him and hurt his players – the emotional toll ended up being too much, became insurmountable, in fact. It reached the point where Pep believed the only way he could recover some of his true self was to leave behind everything that he had helped create.

It turned out that, as much as he wanted to heed your advice, Pep is not like you, Sir Alex. You sometimes compare football to a strange type of prison, one that you in particular don't to want to escape. Arsène Wenger shares your view and is also incapable of empathising with or understanding Guardiola's decision to abandon a gloriously successful team, with the world's best player at his disposal, adored and admired by all.

On the morning that Pep announced his departure from Barcelona, three days after Chelsea had shocked the football world by dumping them out of the Champions League in the semi-final, Wenger told the media: 'The philosophy of Barcelona has to be bigger than winning or losing a championship. After being knocked out of the Champions League, it may not be the right moment to make this decision. I would have loved to see Guardiola – even going through a disappointing year – stay and come back and insist with his philosophy. That would be interesting.'

Guardiola's mind is often in turmoil, spinning at 100 rpm before every decision – still questioning it even after he's come to a conclusion. He couldn't escape his destiny (as a coach, going back to Barcelona) but he is incapable of living with the level of intensity that would eventually grind him down. His world is full of uncertainty, debate, doubts and demands that he can never reconcile or satisfy. They are ever-present: when he is golfing with his friends; or sprawled on the sofa at home, watching a movie with his partner Cris and their three children; or unable to sleep at night. Wherever he is, he is always working, thinking, deciding, always questioning. And the only way he can disconnect from his job (and the huge expectations) is to sever his ties completely.

He arrived full of life as a novice coach with the B team in 2007. He left as first-team coach, drained, five years – and fourteen titles – later. Don't take my word for it; Pep himself said how exhausted he felt in the press conference when he confirmed that he was leaving.

Remember when, before the 2011 Ballon d'Or event, you were once asked about Pep? You were both at the press conference that coincided with your lifetime achievement award and Pep's recognition as manager of the year. You were frank in your response: 'Where is Guardiola going to go that will be better than at home? I don't understand why he would want to leave all that.'

That same day, Andoni Zubizarreta, the Barcelona director of football and long-time friend of Pep, aware of the influence of that chat in Nyon and the esteem he holds you in, referred to your words in conversation with Guardiola: 'Look what this wise man, Alex Ferguson, full of real-world and football experience, is saying …', to which Pep, having already told Zubi that he was thinking of leaving at the end of that season, replied, 'You bastard. You are always looking for ways to confuse me!'

Sir Alex, just look at the images of Pep when he first stepped up to take charge of Barcelona's first team in 2008. He was a youthful looking thirty-seven-year-old. Eager, ambitious, energetic. Now look at him four years later. He doesn't look forty-one, does he? On that morning in Nyon, he was a coach in the process of elevating a club to new, dizzying heights, of helping a team make history. By the time of your brief chat overlooking Lake Geneva, Pep had already found innovative tactical solutions, but in the following seasons he was going to defend and attack in even more revolutionary ways, and his team was going to win almost every competition in which they took part.

The problem was that, along the way, every victory was one victory closer to, not further from, the end.

A nation starved of contemporary role models, struggling through a recession, elevated Pep into a social leader, the perfect man: an ideal. Scary even for Pep. As you know, Sir Alex, nobody is perfect. And you might disagree, but there are very, very few who can endure the weight of such a burden upon their shoulders.

To be a coach at Barcelona requires a lot of energy and after four years, now that he no longer enjoyed the European nights, now that Real Madrid had made La Liga an exhausting challenge both on and off the pitch, Pep felt it was time to depart from the all-consuming entity he had served – with a break of only six years – since he was thirteen. And when he returns – because he *will* return – isn't it best to do so having left on a high?

Look again at the pictures of Pep, Sir Alex. Does it not now become clearer that he has given his all for FC Barcelona?

Part I

Why Did He Have to Leave?

1
THE 'WHYS'

In November 2011, just before the last training session ahead of the trip to Milan for a Champions League group game, Pep, who was in his fourth year with the first team, asked the players to form a circle. He started to explain the secret that he, Tito Vilanova and the doctors had kept from the squad, but he couldn't articulate what he wanted to say. The enormity of the moment left him lost for words. He was anxious and uncomfortable. His voice wobbled and he moved aside. The doctors took over and explained the gravity of the situation to the players while Pep kept looking at the floor and drinking from his ever-present bottle of water that was supposed to prevent his voice from quavering. It didn't work on that occasion.

The medical staff explained that the assistant manager, Tito Vilanova, Pep's right-hand man and close friend, would have to undergo emergency surgery to remove a tumour from his parotid gland, the largest of the salivary glands – and therefore he would not be able to travel to Italy with them.

Two hours later the Barcelona players left town in a state of shock. Pep appeared distant, isolated, wandering separately from the group, deep in contemplation. The team ended up beating Milan 3–2 at the San Siro to top the Champions League group in a thrilling game in which neither side concentrated on defending, treating the fans to an end-to-end encounter with lots of chances. But, despite the result, Pep remained understandably melancholic.

Life, as the saying goes, is what happens when you are busy making other plans. It is also that thing that slaps you in the face and makes you fall when you think you are invincible, when you forget falling is also part of the rules. Guardiola, who accelerated his inquisition of everything when he found out his friend was ill, went through a similar thought process when he was told that Eric Abidal had a tumour on his liver the previous season. The French left back recovered enough to play a brief part in the second leg of the semi-finals of the Champions League against Real Madrid in what Pep would describe as the 'most emotional night' he could remember at the Camp Nou. Abidal came on in the ninetieth minute, when the game was 1–1 and Barcelona were on the verge of another Champions League final, having beaten Madrid in the first leg. The stadium gave him a powerful standing ovation which was something of a rarity. For Catalans are very much like the English: they have a safety-in-numbers approach to showing their feelings, until a collective wave of public emotion lets them release much of what they innately repress.

Weeks later, Puyol, unbeknown to Pep or anybody in the squad, would give Abidal the captain's armband to allow him to receive the European Cup from Platini. Almost a year later, the doctors would tell the French left back that the treatment had failed and he needed a transplant.

The health problems of Abidal and Vilanova left Guardiola shaken; they hit him very hard. It was an unforeseen, uncontrollable situation, difficult to deal with for someone who likes to predict and micro-manage what happens in the squad and to have a contingency plan when things come out of the blue. But with them he was helpless. There was nothing he could do. Much more than that – the lives of people he felt responsible for were on the line.

After that victory in Milan, Barcelona had to travel to Madrid to play a modest Getafe side. Defeat meant that neither Guardiola nor the team, who dominated that game but failed to make an impact in front of their opponent's goal, could dedicate a victory that night to Tito Vilanova, who was on the road to recovery following a successful operation to remove the tumour.

Barcelona lost the game 1–0 in a cold, half-empty stadium, in the kind of ugly match in which it was becoming increasingly more challenging to inspire a group of players (and also the manager) who had been the protagonists on so many glorious nights. Pep was upset at dropping three points, as their League campaign seemed to be faltering far too early in the season. Real Madrid, who had beaten their city rival Atlético de Madrid 4–1 away, were now five points ahead and they seemed unstoppable, hungry for success and with a burning desire to bring Guardiola's era to an end.

La Liga wasn't the only reason for Pep feeling low – and his appearance after the game worried members of the team. On the flight back to Barcelona, in the early hours of Sunday 27 November 2011, Pep had never looked more isolated, down in the dumps and untalkative: far more bitter than he would have been had it just been a case of dealing with a defeat. There was a space next to him on the plane, an empty aisle seat – and nobody wanted to fill it. It was where Tito Vilanova would have sat.

It would be difficult to pinpoint a lower moment for the Barça coach's morale.

'It would be silly not to see the job through.' That is what Sir Alex Ferguson would have told Pep before he made his decision. But the Manchester United manager might have thought differently had he had seen Pep, alone, on that flight.

Andoni Zubizarreta had witnessed first hand the effect of Tito's illness on Pep; he'd seen it on the trips to Milan and Madrid and in the way the coach behaved at the training ground around those games. It was as if he'd had a puncture and all his energy was leaking out through the hole. He seemed deflated, thinner, stooped, suddenly older and greyer.

Zubi wished now he'd known then what to say to Pep, how to comfort and support him. It might not have changed anything, but the feeling of regret persists.

Of course, Tito pulled through, but that week confirmed Pep's worst fears – he was not ready for more: more responsibility, more searching for solutions, more crisis avoidance and endless hours of work and preparation, more time away from his family.

It confirmed a nagging doubt that had persisted since October, when just after the Bate Borisov Champions League game, he told Zubi and president Sandro Rosell that he didn't feel strong enough to continue for another season: that if he was asked to renew his contract right then, his answer would be 'no'. It was not a formal decision, but he was making his feelings known. The reaction of the club was instant: he would be given time, there was no need to rush.

Zubi, a lifelong friend and colleague, understands Pep's character – and knew that it was best not to put pressure on him. The director of football hoped that Pep's revelation could be attributed to him feeling a little tired, understandably low: something of an emotional rollercoaster that he had seen Guardiola riding on a few occasions when they were team-mates.

Yet Zubizarreta also recalled a meal he had with Pep in his first season with the first team. It was a meeting between friends. Zubi wasn't working for the club at that point and Pep was still very excited about what he was doing with the side and how well everything was being received. His enthusiasm was contagious. Yet he reminded Zubizarreta that his job at Barcelona came with an expiry date. It was a defence mechanism for Pep, because he knew as well as anybody that the club could chew up and spit out managers mercilessly. Pep was insistent that one day he would lose his players, his messages wouldn't carry the same weight, that the whole environment (the media, the president's enemies, talk-show panels, former coaches and players) would be impossible to control in the long term.

A friend of Pep's, Charly Rexach – former player, assistant manager to Johan Cruyff and Barcelona first-team coach, an icon of the Catalan club and legendary public philosopher – always said that a Barcelona manager dedicates only 30 per cent of his efforts to the team: the other 70 per cent is spent dealing with the rest of the baggage that comes with such a huge institution. Pep sensed this when he was a player, but as a coach he quickly experienced that interminable pressure – and that Charly's calculation was correct.

Johan Cruyff, who regularly shared long meals with Guardiola, understood that as well and had already warned Pep that the second year was harder than the first, and the third harder than the second. And if he could relive his experience as boss of the Dream Team, he would have left the club two years earlier. 'Don't stay longer than you should,' Cruyff told Pep on one occasion.

So Zubizarreta knew it was going to be difficult to convince him to stay, but would give it his best shot. The director of football mixed protection with silence, and sometimes a bit of pressure in search of an answer. The answer never came. Guardiola's responses to Zubi's questions about his future were always the same: 'You already know what I'm going through, it is difficult' and 'We'll talk, we'll talk'.

At the start of the 2011–12 season, after the league and the Champions League had been won, Guardiola called a meeting with his players to remind them what every coach has told his successful team since the day football was invented: 'You should know that the story doesn't end here. You must keep on winning.' And the team continued winning silverware: the Spanish Super Cup, the European Super Cup and the World Club Championship in December.

With limited weapons in his armoury due to the absences of Villa and Abidal, and after having built a small squad, Barcelona paid a high price in La Liga for the energy they put into the Copa and the Super Cup (games in which they celebrated wins over Real Madrid). Barcelona's fanbase supported Pep, obsessed as they all were with halting their bitter rival's revival.

In September, the game against AC Milan in the group stage of the Champions League was a turning point and an omen for the season ahead. The Italians drew 2–2 in the last minutes of the game at the Camp Nou – the equaliser the consequence of a poorly defended corner – and Guardiola reached the conclusion that his team had lost its competitive edge and there was a lack of attention being paid to the finer points that had made Barcelona so special. This was followed by a run of relatively poor away form in La Liga, that included that 1-0 defeat to Getafe in November.

Pep periodically asked himself if the players were getting his message the way they were a few years ago; he debated the reasons why the 3-4-3 system he had been using that year wasn't working to plan. He took risks with the line-up, as if he knew that there wouldn't be a fifth season. He sensed that it was getting increasingly difficult to control his players, some of whom could even lose their way in the world of football if they didn't start correcting their bad habits. Dani Alves, who separated from his wife during the summer and made the mistake of returning late from his holidays over Christmas, was given the unexpected surprise of a week off mid-season to clear his mind – an unprecedented move, at least one done so openly, in the history of Spanish football's greats.

Furthermore, there were a couple of occasions when the full back would receive a telling-off in front of his team-mates for not paying attention to tactics, something Pep rarely did. 'A defender, first and foremost you're a defender,' he told him after a game in which he got involved in the attack more than he should have done. The Brazilian, meanwhile, was unimpressed when he was left on the bench. He wasn't the only one. Seeing their distraught faces during games upset Pep. He spoke indirectly to the players who were angry about being left out of the team by praising the behaviour of players such as Puyol and Keita when they weren't starting. 'I'm sure they've called me everything, but the first thing they did when they found out was support the team,' he told them.

Logically, those kinds of problems multiplied as the seasons went by, commonplace in any dressing room. But every conflict, even the most trivial, was chipping away at the bridges Pep had so delicately constructed with his squad.

There were still high points. Barcelona eliminated Real Madrid in the quarter-finals of the cup in February and Guardiola appeared to have gone back to being the Pep of previous seasons: energetic, challenging, inexhaustible. The team was still fighting for every trophy and the board thought that success would convince him to stay, even though his silence on his future had started to become the subject of criticism from some directors who referred to Pep as the 'Dalai Lama' or the 'mystic'. In a way, the club was a hostage to Guardiola's decision.

Little by little, Zubizarreta was trying to find common ground to get Pep to put pen to paper on a new contract. Then, in November, the director of football proposed Tito Vilanova as Pep's successor, an almost logical Plan B, perhaps, but also a tactic to get Pep to visualise his departure and, perhaps, make him think twice about it.

Secretly, the club calculated that Pep's birthday could be the turning point. Two years before, on his thirty-ninth birthday, Pep went with his girlfriend Cris to see the Catalan band Manel. His lack of renewal had become national news and the band, and the audience, changed the words of a song to wish him a happy birthday and demand his signature. The next day, Pep announced he was staying for another year.

By 18 January 2012, on his forty-first anniversary, Tito Vilanova had returned to the team, Barcelona had destroyed Santos in the FIFA Club World Cup final in Tokyo and the club thought the conditions were right for Pep to change his mind. But the confirmation wasn't forthcoming.

Over the course of the following months, up until 25 April 2012 when he announced that his decision was final, both the director of football and the president Sandro Rosell would subtly introduce the conversation even in private dinners.

'So, how are things going?' Sandro asked him at an event in February, surrounded by figures from Catalan politics and society, perhaps not the best moment to raise the issue.

'Now's not the time, President' was Pep's blunt response. He never let his guard down.

Rosell had won the presidential elections in June 2010 after Joan Laporta ended his final permitted term. Months before, Pep had agreed to stay on for a season but wanted the new man in charge to confirm the details. Two weeks after Rosell was voted in the contract had not been signed, agreed, negotiated or even talked about. In the meantime, Dmytro Chygrynskiy, signed the previous season for €25 million, was sold for €15 million back to Shakhtar Donetsk, from where he had originally come. Guardiola was not pleased. He didn't want his centre back to go but the club, he was told, needed to pay wages, having run out of cash, thus shrewdly proving the point that Laporta had left the club in a poor financial state.

The response came quickly. Johan Cruyff, Pep's mentor, returned the medal given to him by Laporta as a President of Honour, a very public gesture that amounted to an official declaration of war between the two presidents. A throwing down of the gauntlet. And Guardiola was going to be placed in the middle of it all.

It was clearly not the beginning of a mutual friendship.

Life in the directors' box had been infernal since Rosell's arrival: false accusations of doping against Barcelona made on national radio; the Champions League semi-finals against Real Madrid and its implications; the future of the manager. But the new president preferred to keep a low profile in contrast to the loquacious Laporta, partly because he felt out of place. Rosell sensed his hands were tied by a club that had elevated to an idol, whether or not he wanted it, the figure of Guardiola, so he had to follow the coach's line in many issues he would have argued against if he had had more authority: the vast number of assistants, the resultant cost and, above all, the signing of Cesc Fàbregas.

When Rosell, who was reluctant to end the feud with his nemesis, brought a civil lawsuit against Laporta for alleged financial maladministration of the club, which could have meant the freezing of Laporta's properties and assets, Pep met the former president for dinner. He watched as his friend, the man who had given him his first coaching job, cried openly. He was about to lose everything and his personal life was falling apart. A few days later Guardiola admitted in a press conference that he felt sorry for Laporta. That was, according to Rosell's acolytes, an 'unpleasant surprise'.

The situation was defused and the civil lawsuit abandoned, but nothing gets forgotten in the Camp Nou!

So it is no wonder Guardiola never had the same level of mutual devotion with Rosell as he had with Laporta. But a president doesn't have to love you. When Rosell was asked in London, after the club had been awarded the Laureus as the World Team of the Year, 'What would happen if Pep left at the end of the season?', the president answered, 'There was life at the club before him and will be after him.'

No, he doesn't have to love you, but it would have been beneficial for the club if it hadn't been so obvious that the two men were on completely different wavelengths.

'Make a list of the things that you would like to do next season. It will help you to reflect and see if what you write down is exactly what you want to do.' Zubizarreta kept trying. He had thought of a good way to make Guardiola reflect on a decision that seemed to be taking form in his mind. Pep laughed: 'It's not the time,' he repeated.

The very light pressure was not working, so it was almost better not even to mention it. Zubi's tactics changed again and the topic hardly ever came up in conversation between the president, the sporting director and the coach from that moment on. It would be up to the manager, whenever he was ready, to tell them what he wanted to do.

There were occasions during the season when Pep would look through a talkative Zubizarreta, a half-smile on his lips perhaps, and his friend would know that the coach was miles away – and that it was the wrong time to talk about that or really anything significant, that there was no way at that point to communicate with Pep.

His players will tell you that, like Zubizarreta himself, they feel they know him pretty well. They recognise the guy who jokes with them, the one who has a presence that makes them sit up and pay attention. A coach whose care for the smallest detail improves them, who can see and communicate the secrets of a game. But they would also say that there is a lot they cannot understand about their boss. They see a complex man with so much on his mind, always mulling things over, excessively so sometimes. Players say they are sure he would love to spend more time with his wife and kids, but he can't, because he dedicates the vast majority of his time to winning games. He lives for that, but sometimes even they wonder: does he overdo it?

For Pep, that excessiveness is exactly what he needs to find that flash of inspiration: that moment when he realises what the next game will be like or discovers how it can be won; that moment that 'gives sense to his profession', as he puts it.

Despite having twenty-four assistants, he worked longer hours than most of them and although the club offered him a unit of experts who could analyse games, he could never bring himself to surrender control of that part of the job. 'For me, the most wonderful thing is planning what is going to happen in each game,' Guardiola has explained. 'Which players I have at my disposal, which tools I can use, what the opposition is like … I want to imagine what will happen. I always try and give the players the security of knowing what they'll encounter. This increases the possibility of doing things well.'

Moving from task to task, from deadline to deadline, is when he feels most alive, totally immersed or dashing between several projects, addicted to the adrenalin rush generated by it. And that way of understanding his profession fulfils and yet consumes him, but it is the only one possible for him and the one pledged to the fans: 'I promise you that we'll work hard. I don't know if we'll win, but we will try very hard. Fasten your seat belts, you are going to enjoy the ride' is what he told them at the presentation of the team in summer 2008.

That work ethic, instilled in him by his parents, is very much part of the Catalan character: saving the soul through industry, effort, honest labour and giving your all to the job. In a suitably symbolic place (the Catalan Parliament), and on being awarded the Nation's Gold Medal, the country's highest accolade for a Catalan citizen, in recognition for his representation of Catalan sporting values, he said in his acceptance speech: 'If we get up early, very early, and think about it, believe me, we are an unstoppable country.'

But at the same time Pep sets impossibly high standards and is beset by a sense of never being quite good enough. Guardiola might look strong and capable of carrying a club and a nation on his shoulders but he is very sensitive about the reaction of the team and about disappointing the fans by not meeting their expectations. Or his own.

He once confided to a close friend: 'I can imagine the most amazing solution to a problem and then sometimes players come out with something better during the game that I hadn't thought of. Then that for me it is like a little defeat, it means I should have found that solution earlier.'

The club, the director of football and the coach try to reduce the element of surprise, of unpredictability, in a game through training and analysing the opposition. Before a game, the manager wants to know which approach to take, but in the end it comes down to the player, it can't be directed and, what's more, there are infinite variables on the pitch. How else can Iniesta's goal at Stamford Bridge in 2009 be explained, when Barcelona seemed to have lost the game? For Pep, that is the wonder of football. And the frustration, too: trying to make something so unpredictable, predictable. No matter how hard he works, he is fighting a losing battle.

'Guardiola loves football,' his friend the film director David Trueba wrote. 'And he loves winning, because that is what the game is about – but particularly by doing justice to the approach. He proposes a system and he only asks for you to trust him, that you are faithful to him. The day he notices players who are uncommitted, apathetic, doubtful, even after an irrelevant training session, he is a sad man, demoralised, willing to leave everything.

'No one should be confused about this,' Trueba continues. 'He is an obsessive professional, who pays attention to detail, knowing that details can decide a game. He reveres the club he works for and has imposed a rule not to be more than a mere piece in the structure, to earn his salary and never ask for as much as a coffee without paying for it. He doesn't aspire to be recognised as an indoctrinator, a guru or a guide. He just wants to be recognised as a coach: a good coach. The other things, the good and the bad, are burdens put on him by a society in need of role models. Perhaps everybody is tired of cheats, of profiteers, of villains, people who impose selfish values, opportunism and selfishness, from the privileged platform of television or the media, business or politics. He belongs to that society. But he dignifies it, in a very simple way, trying to do his job well, helping to make common sense prosper from his place in the public eye, with the same quiet dignity with which a good bricklayer, without anyone looking or applauding, lays bricks.'

'A manager's work is never done,' Pep was often heard saying. But one morning, following one of those evenings in which Pep ('a football freak', *enfermo de fútbol*, as he has lovingly been called by some of his star players) stayed at the training ground watching videos that had already been dissected and analysed by his colleagues, the coaching staff saw him walk across the training ground looking under the weather. The enthusiastic Pep they had seen the previous day had made way for a silent Pep, whose words said one thing and his sunken eyes another. 'What's wrong?' one of his colleagues asked him. 'Yesterday I should have gone to see my daughter in a ballet and

I couldn't go.' 'Why not?' his friend asked, surprised. 'Because I was watching videos of our opponent.'

'Look, every day I think that I'm leaving tomorrow,' Guardiola said publicly two years into the job. 'When you're in charge of something, you always have to bear in mind that you can leave. I work better thinking that I am free to decide my own future. Being tied to a contract for a long time distresses me and this can make you lose your passion. That is why I sign year by year. If I could I would sign only for six months … I have always thought that everything starts from looking for what you really like, which nowadays is the hardest thing to find. Finding that is the essence of everything.'

But that essence, in his last season, was eluding him: he was not even enjoying the big European nights, tormented by his worries and indecision. Should I continue? Is it better for Barcelona for me to carry on or should I look for new messages, new solutions to keep people on their toes? How can I find new ways to give Leo Messi what he needs? And Iniesta and Cesc and Alves? Can I carry on with this for another month, another year? How do young coaches grow old having been successful so early? Wouldn't it be better to find new horizons?

Roman Abramovich had been aware of Guardiola's anxieties for a few years and he wanted to take advantage of the situation. He pursued Pep persistently for two years before he left Barcelona and tried to convince him on many occasions to take the reins at Stamford Bridge. After Ancelotti's departure from Chelsea in the summer of 2011, the owner's pursuit gained momentum. André Villas-Boas was the fourth choice candidate to replace the Italian, behind Guus Hiddink, José Mourinho and Pep, who in February of that year had renewed his contract for another season. In June, just before the start of Guardiola's last season in charge of Barça, Abramovich, working through a middleman, invited Pep to be picked up by private helicopter and whisked away to a meeting on his yacht in Monaco. 'Stop telling me these things. I don't want to meet Roman or I might have my head turned by him' was Pep's polite answer. But Abramovich was going to come back during his final months in charge of Barcelona. On two occasions, he offered Rafa

Benítez a three-month deal to finish the season after the sacking of André Villas-Boas: the Chelsea owner thought he could convince Pep to forget his sabbatical and take over at Stamford Bridge straight after leaving Barcelona.

The Chelsea owner's last offer, before Pep Guardiola disappeared from the public eye at the end of the 2012 season, proposed the appointment of an interim manager for one season to leave the Stamford Bridge door open for Pep a year later, wanting him to design the squad for the 2013–14 season as soon as he was ready.

Chelsea had become the first club to actively try and seduce him. AC Milan, Inter and Bayern Munich would follow.

There was a moment earlier on in the season that was to have an impact upon the squad dynamic for the remainder of the campaign. In the third league game, Pep left Messi on the bench for the game against Real Sociedad in San Sebastián: he thought the player would be tired after returning from duties with the Argentine national team. Leo was spectacularly angry, so much so that his contribution during the few minutes he did play was almost non-existent and he didn't turn up for training the next day. From that day onwards Messi did not miss a game.

Messi's role was something to think about. Pep had created a team that revolved around the diminutive, record-breaking Argentinian and there was an abundance of forwards who had come and gone (Ibrahimović, Eto'o, Bojan; even David Villa had to get used to playing on the wing, although upon his arrival he had been told that he would be Barça's number nine) having been unable to fit in in a style of play that demanded submission to Messi. When the team began to falter, especially in away games, the Argentinian was given more responsibility and Pep selected sides to support him: but that prioritising of Messi reduced others' responsibilities and terrified the younger players.

Messi ended up netting seventy-three goals that 2011–12 season in all competitions. In contrast, the next highest goalscorers were Cesc and Alexis with fifteen each. Pep was creating a goalscoring monster but collectively the team was suffering for it – and he knew he was as responsible for this situation as any of his players. As Johan Cruyff said: 'Guardiola has had to control a lot of egos in the dressing room. It's not surprising that he has run out of energy.'

Pep Guardiola rang one of the world game's leading managers to ask him one question: if you get to a situation where the balance seems broken, what do you do? Do you go or do you change players? He was given the answer that he perhaps didn't want to hear: you change players. That is what Sir Alex Ferguson has always done, but clearly the United manager feels less beholden to his footballers, both morally and emotionally, than Pep, who invested an awful lot of personal feeling into his first experience as a manager. Too much, in fact. Guardiola needed pills to help him sleep and would go for walks with his partner and their children to help him to find some sort of emotional balance.

At one point the team trailed thirteen points behind Madrid. 'What I have done so far doesn't guarantee me anything, if the fans have their doubts they will have their own reasons for that,' he said in one of the most delicately poised moments of the season. The statistics were still impressive, but less so than in the previous three seasons: the team was losing its competitive edge and Pep felt it was his fault. After the defeat to Osasuna in Pamplona (3–2) in February, he said: 'We've made too many mistakes. I didn't know how to answer the questions before they were asked. I failed. I didn't do my job well enough.'

But in fact Pep had one trick left up his sleeve. He followed Johan Cruyff's example by employing reverse psychology in admitting publicly that Barcelona were 'not going to win this league'. It had the desired affect. Players, suspicious that the manager was thinking of leaving them, wanted to show that they were still up for the challenge, still hungry. Barcelona clawed back some ground on Madrid, getting to within four points of their rivals but it was too little too late. Defeat to their bitter rivals at the Camp Nou in May effectively handed the title to Mourinho and the old enemy.

There were uncharacteristic complaints about the referee from Pep in various press conferences during the last few months of the season: a search for excuses that revealed how Guardiola was perhaps losing his focus.

Pep struggled to accept a fact of life: that after a period of unprecedented success (thirteen titles in his first three years with the first team), there must inevitably be a slump. If you win all the time, there's less desire to carry on winning. He tried to prevent this inevitable cycle by putting in longer shifts and making huge sacrifices. Even taking care of himself dropped down his list of priorities, and health problems were ignored until they became debilitating, such as the slipped disc that incapacitated him for few days in March.

The coaching staff's analysis was that mistakes weren't being made during the team talks – they were still based on in-depth studies of their rivals and delivered with the same enthusiasm and charisma as ever – but, rather, in their execution. But there were question marks over Pep's faith in first-team newcomers from La Masía. Tello (who started on the wing against Real Madrid at the Camp Nou in what was a key victory for Mourinho's team) and Cuenca (in the eleven against Chelsea in the return leg of the semi-finals of the 2012 Champions League) were expected to produce the same level of performance as Cesc, Alexis or Pedro, who were left out in one of the two games.

Could Barcelona afford to leave that sort of talent on the bench? Was Pep too close to the squad to actually see the wood for the trees?

These were pivotal decisions that affected the outcome of the season and Guardiola's judgement in replacing experienced internationals with near-debutantes in season-defining games raised more than a few eyebrows. It also had a negative impact on the confidence of the youngsters selected and the older players dropped.

José Mourinho watched it all from Madrid with a wry smile. The impact of Mourinho and his destabilising strategies is irrefutable even though Pep will always deny it. When asked what he remembered of the previous Clásicos on the eve of his last as coach, Pep lowered his voice: 'I don't have fond memories, of either the victories or the defeats. There are always reasons that aren't related to the game that have made a lot of things incomprehensible to me.' Really? He couldn't remember even the 2–6 demolition at the Bernabéu? The 5–0 in Mourinho's first Clásico, described by many as the best performance in the history of the game? There was enormous pressure, not just from Mourinho but from Madrid's sporting press who went as far as insulting Pep and suggesting Barcelona's performances were enhanced by drugs. For a sensitive soul like Pep it was enough to wipe out even the best memories.

As the season was reaching the end, the decision about his future became unmovable – he was going to leave the club that was one of the most admired on the planet courtesy of his leadership. He just had to find the right way to tell the club. And the players. And the fans. But how? If they won the Champions League everything would be much easier.

While he finalised the details of his departure, he decided not to share his decision with anyone, not even his parents.

2
THE DECISION

Before he made an official announcement, the biggest hint that Guardiola gave about his future was inadvertently revealed in a chat with an Italian journalist, in his third year with the first team, in an interview that was to feature in a DVD on the history of Brescia; but Pep, who normally doesn't do 'on-the-record', one-to-one interviews but making an exception here was betrayed and his quotes were leaked to Italian national television. It wasn't so much an evaluation of his personal situation, but the description of an historic constant, applicable not just to Barcelona but to the majority of great clubs. 'In order to be in a great institution for four years,' Guardiola said, 'you must have a lot of courage. The players get tired of you and you get tired of the players; the press gets tired of you and you get tired of the press, seeing the same faces, the same questions, the same things. In the end, you must know when the time comes, in the same way that I understood that when I was a player and said, "Look, it's time for me to leave".'

It turns out that Pep now felt the time had come for him to leave as a manager, too.

Just after Chelsea qualified for the Champions League final after drawing 2–2 (winning 3–2 on aggregate) in Barcelona playing with ten men for almost an hour, Guardiola met the president, Sandro Rosell, at the Camp Nou. 'Come and see me at my house tomorrow morning, President,' the coach said.

Pep also talked to his assistant, Tito Vilanova, telling him that, as Vilanova already suspected, he was not going to continue. Guardiola also surprised him with a prediction. 'I think they are going to propose that you take over,' he said. 'And I will back you up with whatever decision you take.' Unbeknown to Vilanova, his name had first been proposed in a conversation between Zubizarreta and Guardiola the previous November. 'Do you think Tito can replace you if you decide to leave?' the director of football asked. 'For sure' was Pep's answer even though he had no idea if his friend was going to take the job – or if Zubizarreta was being serious.

At 9 a.m. the following day, Pep Guardiola held a meeting at his house with Sandro Rosell, Andoni Zubizarreta, Tito Vilanova and vice-president Josep Maria Bertomeu. It was then that he broke the news to the club hierarchy that he would not continue at FC Barcelona.

The meeting lasted for three hours as Pep explained his reasons for calling it a day. 'You know all those things we have been talking about during the season? Nothing has changed. I am leaving. I have to leave,' Pep told them. The defeat to Real Madrid and the loss against Chelsea weren't the cause, but both had served as the catalyst for the chain of events.

The following day he told his parents and, although his mother, Dolors, believed that her son's 'health comes first', she also felt that her 'heart shrank' on hearing the news. He needed, according to Dolors, 'a place of rest and relaxation'. That is also how his father, Valentí, saw it: his son felt 'overwhelmed by so much responsibility towards the members, the fans and the club'. His dad – according to Ramón Besa in *El País* – understood and even predicted the outcome, having said back in September, when Guardiola received the Gold Medal from the Catalan Parliament, that 'as soon as the tributes start pouring in, it's time to start packing your bags'.

As journalist Luis Martín, also from *El País*, discovered, many tried to change Pep's mind in the two days leading up to the formal public announcement. SMS messages from Valdés, Iniesta, Xavi, and especially Messi, flooded his inbox. Even Vilanova asked him to reconsider. Zubizarreta ended up having a crazy idea, one of those forlorn hopes that you have to express even when you already know the answer: 'There's a vacancy in one of the youth teams. Why don't you take it? What you like most of all is training the kids, isn't it?' Pep looked at him, trying to work out what was behind the question. He answered him with the same sense of ambiguity: 'God, that could be a good idea.' The two friends laughed.

Two days after announcing his departure to the president, it was time to tell the players.

Nobody in the squad was sure of the outcome. Following the Champions League semi-final defeat to Chelsea, Carles Puyol, waiting around after the match to give a urine sample for a routine drugs test, saw that Pep was stalling his arrival at the press conference. He thought it was a positive sign. So he told a team-mate: 'He will tell us this week he is staying, you will see. He doesn't want to leave us now.' Puyol, as he now admits, doesn't have a future as a clairvoyant. After the Champions League game, the players were given two days off. They had heard the rumours and knew about the meeting with Rosell but were unsure about what was going to happen.

The morning papers came with headlines which confirmed that nobody outside the club had a clear idea of what was about to take place; the front page of *Mundo Deportivo* split its front page in two, one half with the headline 'Pep to leave' and the other with 'Pep to stay'. The majority of players thought that the meeting before training was merely to receive confirmation that Guardiola was staying. 'He seems all right,' they said to each other. They were hoping he had managed to shake off his fears and doubts and stay a bit longer, even one more season.

Only a handful of people knew for sure what was going to be said. The players gathered in the dressing room at the training ground. There were no jokes, just a low murmur of conversation which turned to silence once Pep walked in and started speaking. As the players were being told, Sky Sports News reported his decision. What he revealed was a shock. The Barcelona manager was departing.

'You're the best and I'm proud of you all. But now I have not got the energy to continue and it is time to leave. I'm drained.' He appeared relaxed but his voice betrayed his emotions. He was using the same tricks that were so common to him when he wanted to show them where the weakness of the rival team was: he was trying to convince them it was the best that could happen and to do so he dwelt on his players' feelings. 'Around October I told the president that the end of my time as manager was close. But I couldn't tell you then because it would have been problematic. Now it is definite. The next manager to come in will give things that I can no longer give. He will be strong. It would have been a risk for me to continue because we would have hurt each other. I think a lot of you all, and I would never forgive myself. There have been many moves that I have imagined that you have made a reality. So I will leave with the feeling of having done the job well, of having fulfilled my duty. This club has an unstoppable power, but I am the third coach in its history with the most number of games played – in just four years. What we have done has been exceptional because Barcelona coaches don't last long. And we have lasted this long because we have won. But while that was happening, my strength was disappearing. I am leaving as a very happy man. The president has offered me another position but I need to be away from it all if I want to recharge again.'

There was further silence after those words were spoken. So he continued. 'I wanted to tell you now that we are out of the big competitions so I have time to say goodbye to everyone – and call you individually into the office to thank you personally. I don't want applause or anything, so … let's get to training.'

And Pep clapped his hands together to emphasise that the talk was over; it was an order to get up and move on. In less than a quarter of an hour, the history of the club had received a definitive twist. Players were confused, bewildered.

Pep asked very little of his footballers that day on the training ground. He knew that he had dealt them a bitter blow. For the players running out on to the pitch, that session represented the first steps on the road to healing. For Pep, it represented the beginning of the end of a journey that had begun around three decades earlier, in a sleepy little Catalan village called Santpedor.

Part II

From a Santpedor Square to the Camp Nou Dugout

Main square of the village of Santpedor. Almost any given morning in 1979

As you approach Pep's childhood home in Santpedor, there is a striking view across the immense valley in which the village is situated. The air is fresh but it carries the smell of the dry earth. Looming on the horizon, the rocky outline of Montserrat, Catalonia's striking iconic 'serrated' mountain, soars up out of the valley like a giant cardboard cut-out, providing a majestic backdrop for the sleepy Catalan village situated seventy kilometres from Barcelona.

One of the first buildings you come across on the outskirts of this village of only 7,500 inhabitants is the new home of Guardiola's parents – built by Pep's father, a bricklayer – a modern, three-storey edifice just off the main road, in an area dotted with new-build properties. As you head towards the centre of Santpedor, a few dilapidated factories remind you of the village's more recent industrial past and provide a stark contrast to the medieval archways. Santpedor is the kind of village where people greet one another in the streets, whether they know each other or not. And those who do know each other stop for a chat about the same topics, as any other day. The broad roads start to merge into narrow labyrinths, centuries-old streets winding their way towards Santpedor's two main squares, the Plaça Gran and the Plaça de la Generalitat. The latter also used to be known as the Plaça de Berga, but now it is more commonly referred to as 'the square where Guardiola was born'.

On any given morning in 1979, a skinny eight-year-old boy would come out of number 15 Plaça de la Generalitat and walk the few steps towards the centre of the square with a football under his arm. Known to the locals as 'Guardi', the kid, with spindly legs like twigs, would call out for his friends, including a girl named Pilar, to join him. He would kick the ball against the wall until enough of his mates had arrived for a kickabout.

PlayStations didn't exist back then and there were hardly enough cars on the roads to justify traffic lights or to pose any real danger to a bunch of kids engrossed in a game of street football. Pep would play before going to school, on his way home from school. He'd take the ball everywhere to have a kickabout at breaktime, at lunchtime, in the cobbled streets, around the fountains. He was even known to practise football during family dinners and his mother would tire of berating him, 'Leave that ball alone for five minutes and get yourself over here!' Like so many kids and so many mothers in towns and villages all over the world.

Back then everything was much more relaxed; there was less 'protocol', less 'bureaucracy', as Guardiola puts it. You'd go down to the square with the football and you'd play until it was too dark to see the ball: it was that simple. You didn't need to go to a proper pitch or organise matches, nor set a time to play. There were no goalposts or nets, and nor were there signs warning kids that they couldn't play ballgames either.

A metal garage door served as the goal and there were always arguments over who would be the keeper. Pilar never wanted to be the goalie; she had quite a kick and a good first touch – and for more than a decade the women's team in a neighbouring village would enjoy the benefits of her hours of practice with Pep and the gang.

There were always disputes about who got to have Pep in their team. The tactics were clear: give him the ball so that he could control the game. All his friends were aware that he was better than the rest, that he had something that the others didn't have. In the end, to avoid arguments, it was decided that Pep would be the one to choose the two teams – so that they were of more or less equal ability – and it also meant that from an early age, without hesitation, Pep assumed his role as a leader.

And when, in one of those street football games that might last the whole of Saturday or Sunday, one of the kids damaged something in the square with a wild shot, a smile from Pep would always get him and the rest of his friends out of trouble.

Nowadays, cars can drive through the square and even park in the centre. It's no longer a place where kids can play.

When Pep returned to Barcelona to coach the reserve team, brief getaways to Santpedor and long walks in the surrounding countryside became a regular occurrence. Reflective to the point of bordering on meditation, Pep also made numerous trips to his village when he was debating about making the jump from the reserves to the first team. Although it was hardly seen during the four years that he was changing the football world as coach of the best team on the planet, his presence is felt in various corners of the village. The football stadium bears his name; his photograph adorns several bars; there is a plaque on a stone in the centre of the square dedicated to FC Barcelona by the local supporters club, which, by the way, has gained one hundred additional members in the past four years. The popularity of grass-roots football has grown to such an extent that the handball teams have dwindled. The children from the village only want to play football. And they will proudly tell you that they are from Pep Guardiola's village: Santpedor.

So, there's a bit of Pep in Santpedor, but there's also clearly a lot of Santpedor in Pep. The whispered conversations you hear around here are in Catalan, along with signs and street names. The *senyera* – the Catalan flag – hangs from many balconies and graffiti on several abandoned buildings echo people's sentiments for their nation and their strong sense of Catalan identity. The vilage even had the honour of being named 'Carrer de Barcelona', a medieval Catalan distinction with all the privileges and taxes that came with it. Santpedor was a 'road to Barcelona', the capital of Catalonia and Guardiola's life-changing destination.

Pep is a very proud Catalan. An educated and courteous individual, he takes after his parents, the Guardiolas and the Salas, who are like any other parents in the village: modest and respectable. They sowed the seed. Or was it sown originally by Santpedor?

Pep's friend David Trueba thinks both of them did: 'Nobody has paid any attention to the fundamental fact that Guardiola is a bricklayer's son. For Pep, his father, Valentí, is an example of integrity and hard work. The family he has grown up with, in Santpedor, has instilled old values in him, values from a time in which parents didn't have money or property to hand down to their children, just dignity and principles. When it comes to analysing or judging Guardiola, you must bear in mind the fact that underneath the elegant suit, the cashmere jumper and the tie, is the son of a bricklayer. Inside those expensive Italian shoes there is a heart in espadrilles.'

When Pep thinks back to his childhood in the village, to his parents, to the long games in the square, he doesn't recall a specific moment, but a feeling: happiness. Joy in its purest, most simple form. And that sensation comes back to him whenever he returns to visit his parents, or his auntie Carmen or uncle José, or any of the relatives still living in Santpedor, and sits with them in the village square: until a legion of admirers gatecrashes his privacy and the moment is lost.

Back when he was a kid, and the sun had set on that village square, the young Pep would head home and set the ball in a corner of his bedroom, a modest space decorated by little more than a poster featuring Michel Platini: the face of football when Guardiola was ten years old. Guardiola had never seen him play – in those days television did not show much international football – but he had heard his dad and grandad talk about the ability of the Juventus player, his leadership and his aura. All that Pep knew about Platini were those wise words of his elders and that poster of the elegant Frenchman – caressing the ball, head up, surveying the pitch and picking his next pass. The attraction was instant. Five years later, a young Camp Nou ball boy named Pep Guardiola would earnestly try to get Platini's autograph at the end of a match – but in failing he ended up learning a key lesson. That story will be told later.

A good student in his days at the village convent school, Pep was known as a *tros de pa* – a bit of bread, as they say in Catalan, 'a well-behaved child' – soaking up knowledge, always willing to help in church. Just about the closest Guardi came to rebellion was disappearing early on the odd occasion his dad asked him to help out with some bricklaying. He always looked as if butter wouldn't melt in his mouth, an asset on the occasions he was asked to play the role of an angel in the village nativity plays.

Pep moved to a Catholic school a few miles from home, La Salle de Manresa, when he was seven: his first exodus. It was a strict environment and he had to adapt quickly to his new surroundings and teachers – Brother Virgilio was responsible for teaching him his first words in English, a language he now switches to with ease whenever questioned at a Champions League press conference in front of the world's media. As well as Italian, and, of course Catalan and Spanish. Oh, and French, too.

At La Salle his personality traits continually emerged and developed: self-demanding, blessed with a natural charm and obsessed with football; but, above all else, Pep proved to be an excellent listener and, like a sponge, absorbed knowledge from everyone around him, especially his elders. He was a bit taller and thinner than most, perhaps a consequence of the fact that he never stood still – or so his mother thinks – and he was still the first player to be picked by the football captains and frequently the sole participant in one of his favourites games: keepy-uppy. He played that by himself, because there was no point in competing: he couldn't be beaten.

During one of those games at La Salle he was spotted by a couple of scouts from Club Gimnàstic de Manresa – the 'wiry lad's' leadership and passing ability easily caught the eye. With the blessing of his dad, Valentí, he began training at Gimnàstic two or three times a week and some key principles were quickly instilled in him: 'Don't stamp on anybody but don't let anybody stamp on you; keep your head high; two-touch football; keep the ball on the ground.' If the golden thread to success is coaching, Pep had started off in the ideal academy.

Perhaps it was only natural that a kid from Pep's village would support Barcelona, considering there was only one fan of Espanyol, their rivals from across the city. That Espanyol fan also happened to be Pep's grandad and there was even an Espanyol poster hanging on the walls of the family home in his honour. But his elder's preference didn't influence Pep's sporting allegiance: 'My grandad was the nicest person in the world and had such a huge heart that burst out of his chest. He had an enormous sense of compassion so he almost felt compelled to support the smaller team, the underdog. In our village there was not a single Espanyol fan apart from him.'

A team-mate of his at Gimnàstic had a relative who was a season-ticket holder at FC Barcelona and Pep asked him if he could borrow it to see a game at the Camp Nou one day. In 1981 a ten-year-old Pep set foot in the imposing stadium for the very first time to watch FC Barcelona take on Osasuna in La Liga. The street leading up to it was a river of people waving Barcelona flags and Pep experienced 'an incredible feeling' of joy, of excitement, of being a part of something big, an epiphany. As he sat in row seven of the north stand, just off to one side behind the goal, he muttered to his friend, as thousands of kids before him must have done: 'I would pay millions to play on that pitch one day.'

In fact, while he was with Gimnàstic, Pep played in a few friendlies against the FC Barcelona academy sides, which provided him with some valuable lessons regarding his own and his team's limitations: he was the best player in that Gimnàstic side but he sensed there were many more kids like him, or even better, wearing the blue and red shirt of FC Barcelona.

It was around this time, and without his eleven-year-old-son knowing it, that Valentí filled in a form published in a sports paper offering kids the opportunity to take part in trials organised by Barça.

'Barcelona want to see you,' his dad told him few days later, to his son's amazement. Of course, he went to the trial: nervous, still very lightweight. He played badly. And he knew it. A sleepless night followed. He was asked to return for a second day but he was no better. At the trial, Pep was played in an attacking wide position and he lacked the pace and strength to excel. He was given one more chance, invited back for a third day. The coach moved him into central midfield where, suddenly, Pep was a magnet for the ball, directing the forward play and dictating tempo. He'd done enough. Barcelona decided they wanted him to join them.

His dad kept that information to himself until he was sure it was in his son's best interests. Valentí, and Pep's mum, Dolors, were worried that those daunting and stressful trips to Barcelona were unnerving their son, who returned home quieter than usual, apprehensive and unable to eat properly. After discussing it with his wife, Valentí decided to reject Barcelona's offer. They believed that Pep was too young to move to La Masía, too naïve to live on his own away from his family, not yet strong enough to compete or to cope.

In the years following that trial with Barcelona, football remained a key part of the Guardiola family routine with constant trips to Manresa and throughout the region for league games and friendlies with Pep promoted to captain of the Gimnàstic side. The dream of Barça, it seemed, had been forgotten.

A couple of years later, FC Barcelona made another phone call to the Guardiola household. Valentí picked up the receiver and listened to their offer.

'We have to talk,' he told his son after a training session with Gimnàstic. The family gathered around the dinner table, Valentí, Dolors and their thirteen-year-old son, Pep. Dad tried to explain, as best he could to a young teenage boy, that there was life beyond the village and the Catholic school; he tried to prepare him for what he should expect if he left home; that his studies were a priority; that a move to Barcelona would expose Pep to an entirely new level of obligations, responsibility and expectation. Up until that moment in Pep's life, football had been little more than a game, but, as Valentí told his son, he now had the opportunity to transform his life and make a living out of the sport he loved at the club he adored.

Pep took his father's words on board and understood what was at stake: he had already made up his mind that if Barcelona didn't come back for him, he would abandon his dream of becoming a professional footballer because he couldn't take any further rejection. But Barça *had* called. The decision was made. Pep Guardiola was going to leave home and all that was familiar behind him: he was going to move to the big city, he was going to give his all to become a professional footballer, he was going to pursue his dream of playing for FC Barcelona.

A kid jumping on a bunk bed in La Masía, Barcelona.
An early August evening, late 1980s

Soon after receiving the call, Pep, together with his parents and brother Pere, visited Barcelona's facilities at La Masía, the old farm that housed the young academy players from outside Barcelona. Lying on top of one of the bunk beds, Pep opened the window of the room he would share with four other lads and could barely contain his excitement as he shouted, 'Wow, Mum, look! Every day I'll be able to open this window and see the Nou Camp!'

When he moved to La Masía he left behind the Platini poster that adorned his room – consciously or not, football had moved into another dimension. Yet, for Pep, it was still a game. He doesn't look back on his early days at the club as a time of emotional hardship, although he admits it was difficult to leave behind everything he knew, including all his friends, at just thirteen years old. From one day to the next, family ties were broken, new relationships had to be forged. Occasionally, at night, he would go down to the ground floor of the old farmhouse to use the payphone to chat with his parents, but, unlike many of the kids who suffered terrible homesickness because of the distances separating them from their families, Pep's calls were less frequent because most weekends he would return to his village, just an hour away. He describes it now as an eye-opening time, full of novelties and discoveries and some absences that helped him mature: he grew up and developed quickly. The distance separating him and his team-mates from family and friends was going to make them resilient.

His father doesn't remember it like that: 'The lad phoned us up in tears; he used to break our hearts.'

Memory likes to play tricks. His life as a manager, tense, exhausting, created a curious effect: his young life seems to have been rewritten and Pep has started to look back on those days with a mixture of melancholy and envy for the lost innocence of it all. Clearly he has now forgotten the most painful parts, the good memories blotting out the bad, but a decade ago he wrote that he sometimes felt 'helpless' at 'The Big House', which is how the Barça headquarters was known to the kids. The club had given him and the other youngsters everything they required, but 'especially the affection and peace of mind to know that whenever I needed them, they were always nearby to stop my problems getting in the way of my dreams. And that fact – that they're there for us – is so important to me that I'll always be grateful to them and I'll never be able to repay them.'

Their day started with a breakfast that consisted of yogurts, cereals, toast, jam and milk. Unlike other kids of their generation, the youngsters at La Masía shared a television with an automatic timer that clicked off at eleven o'clock every night. Apart from daily training sessions, there were distractions far more eye-opening than anything their TV was showing before the watershed. After dark, and despite the curfew, Pep and his room-mates would gather at the window to be entertained by one of the rituals of the residence: spying on the nightly comings and goings of the prostitutes who plied their trade up and down the street that leads to the gates of La Masía. With time, their presence became 'part of the furniture'.

The bedtime tears of some of the kids also became a part of the nightly soundtrack, but Pep quickly grasped that crying didn't make him feel any better; they were living the dream after all. Far better to focus on the job in hand, which in his case included a programme of physical improvement as his mentors could see the potential, but were worried about his slight frame.

He talked and talked football during the long coach journeys travelling to games all over Catalonia, the homeland that he got to know so well in those teenage years. He continually learnt from everything he saw around him, from other teams, from coaches, from older team-mates. On one occasion, he asked a couple of his colleagues to repeat a free-kick routine he had seen the B side perform the previous weekend. The move led to a goal and their coach asked, 'Whose idea was that? And where did you pick that up?' 'From the grown-up players,' responded a fifteen-year-old Pep Guardiola. La Masía: a footballing university campus where players and coaches mixed.

'The kids only want to play football, live football, and La Masía allows you to do it,' Pep recalls. 'Any time of day was ideal to get the ball and have a kickabout or to go and see how the others trained. Occasionally, when I'm asked to do a talk in La Masía, I use the following example: each night when you are going to sleep, ask yourselves if you like football or not; ask yourselves if right then, you'd get up, grab the ball and play for a bit.' If ever the answer is 'no', then that is the day to start looking for something else to do.

There were other benefits to living in the football school. The Masía kids had the opportunity to become privileged spectators in the Nou Camp by handing out club leaflets on match days or, after a long waiting list, becoming ball boys. There is a picture of a young Pep on the pitch, gleefully clapping alongside a couple of Barcelona players with Terry Venables carried aloft on their shoulders in celebration after the final whistle the night FC Barcelona beat Gothenburg to reach the European Cup final in 1986.

Pep learnt an unexpected lesson as a ball boy when the teenager waited for his idol Michel Platini to come out for the warm-up before a Barcelona–Juventus game. He had been dreaming about it for weeks, his first chance to see his childhood hero in the flesh, and he had a cunning plan to secure Platini's autograph: pen and paper tucked away in his pocket, Pep planned to pounce on the French star as he walked across the pitch to join his team-mates in the warm-up on the far side – he knew it was the only chance he was going to get without getting into trouble. Cabrini, Bonini, Brio jogged out, then Michael Laudrup. But no Platini. It transpired that the French superstar didn't always come out with the team to do some stretching. 'Ah,' Pep thought, 'so not all players are treated as equals; it turns out they're not all the same.' The pen and paper stayed in his pocket, unused.

The Platini poster that hadn't accompanied him to La Masía stayed on the wall of his bedroom in Santpedor for a few years, but gradually another player, this one far more accessible, took centre stage: Guillermo Amor, future midfielder of the Johan Cruyff side, four years older than Pep and also resident at La Masía.

'At the time, when I started to pay attention to everything that you did, I was thirteen years old,' Pep wrote a decade ago in reference to Amor, in his autobiography *My People, My Football*. 'I didn't just follow every one of your games, but also the training sessions; I paid attention to your attitude, because you faced everyone as if your life depended on it. I used to have my practical football lessons at 7 p.m. on an adjacent pitch; but I used to turn up two hours earlier, so I could listen in on the theory class on pitch number 1: seeing how you carried yourself, how you encouraged your team-mates, how you asked for the ball, how you listened and how you earned the respect of everyone around you. I pay tribute to you today for every one of those moments you gave us back then at La Masía on pitch number 1, during mealtimes, in the dressing room, throughout the holidays, away at hotels and even on television.'

When Amor returned from away games with the B team – a side that also included Tito Vilanova, Pep's future assistant and successor in the Camp Nou dugout – Guardiola would pester him for the score and details of how they'd got along. 'We won,' would be the standard answer. Over the next few years, Amor, who embodied all the values instilled in players at the club right through to the first team, became like a big brother to Pep, who intuitively understood that the club is not only about the bricks and mortar of the stadium or training facility, but mostly about the footballing DNA shared by Guillermo and others like him. So when Pep took his first major decisions as a Barcelona manager, selling Ronaldinho and Deco or approving Amor's appointment as director of youth football, he did so with a desire to return the focus of influence in the dressing room to home-grown players.

Guardiola remained a lanky teenager with little muscle mass, the opposite of the ideal footballer's stature. But great art is always born of frustration and since he lacked the pace and strength to overcome the opposition, he substituted physical power with the power of the mind: instinctively developing a sense of spatial awareness that was second to none. He was capable of leaving behind three players with one pass, widening or narrowing the field at will, so that the ball always travelled more than the player. Usually when children start to play football, they want to learn to dribble. Guardiola didn't: he learnt how to pass the ball.

La Masía, a word also used to generically describe the Barcelona youth system, was and still is rich in talent – the product of promoting, for more than three decades, a style of football now celebrated around the world. 'Some think it is like the Coca-Cola recipe,' says the Catalan journalist Ramón Besa, 'some sort of secret, winning formula.' In fact, it's no secret at all; it is, simultaneously, a simple yet revolutionary idea: possession, combining, defending by attacking and always looking for a way to the opposition goal; finding the best talent without physical restrictions as the key element of the selection of players. Add to that the commitment to technical quality and ensuring that the kids develop an understanding of the game. It is a philosophy based on technique and talent: nothing more, nothing less. 'I have never forgotten the first thing they told me when I came to Barça as a little boy,' says the Barcelona midfielder Xavi Hernández. 'Here, you can never give the ball away.'

The Barcelona model is the consequence of a club that always favoured good football (in the 1950s the Catalan club recruited the Hungarians Ladislao Kubala, Sándor Kocsis and Zoltán Czibor, key members of the best national team in the world at that time) and also of the revolutionary ideas brought to the club by two men: Laureano Ruíz and Johan Cruyff. Laureano was a stubborn coach who, in the 1970s, introduced a particular brand of training to Barcelona based upon talent and technique, and by his second season at the club had managed to convince all the junior teams follow suit. Under Cruyff, dominating the ball became the first and most important rule. 'If you have the ball, the opposition doesn't have it and can't attack you,' Cruyff would repeat daily. So the job became finding the players who could keep possession and also doing a lot of positional work in training.

On top of that, La Masía, as all good academies should, develops players and human beings and instils in them a strong sense of belonging, of identity, as Xavi explains: 'What is the key to this Barcelona? That the majority of us are from "this house" – from here, this is our team, but not just the players, the coaches too, the doctors, the physios, the handymen. We're all *culés*, we're all Barça fans, we're all a family, we're all united, we all go out of our way to make things work.'

Despite the fact that, since 2011, the old farmhouse no longer serves as a hall of residence, the revolution that started there three decades ago continued and reached its zenith with the arrival of Guardiola as first-team coach as he put his faith in La Masía's finest 'products'. It is, as the Catalan sports writer and former Olympian Martí Perarnau puts it, 'a differentiating factor, an institutional flag and a structural investment' – and it is one that pays dividends as well. In 2010, it became the first youth academy to have trained all three finalists for the Ballon d'Or in the same year, with Andrés Iniesta, Lionel Messi and Xavi Hernández standing side by side on the rostrum.

'I had the best years of my life at La Masía,' Pep recalls. 'It was a time focused upon the singular most non-negotiable dream that I have ever had: to play for Barça's first team. That anxiety to become good enough for Johan Cruyff to notice us cannot be put into words. Without that desire, none of us would be who we are today. Triumph is something else. I am talking about loving football and being wanted.'

Even though Pep managed to overcome his lack of physical strength and got himself noticed, the final step was missing: the call-up to the first team. But when Johan Cruyff needed a number four, a player to direct the team in front of the defence, the Dutch coach wasn't deterred by Pep's slight physique. He called him up because he sensed that he could read the game and pass the ball.

On that day in May 1989, Pep had to drop everything, including a girl he was just getting to know, grab his kit and travel with the first team to a friendly in Banyoles. Suddenly, unexpectedly, he had made his senior Barcelona debut. He was eighteen years old. If he'd hoped that the girl would be impressed with his new status, the same could not be said of Cruyff who was distinctly underwhelmed by Pep's debut performance. 'You were slower than my granny!' the coach told him at half-time; but Pep grew to understand Cruyff's methods when it came to chastising his players: 'When he attacked you most and when you were at your worst was when he helped you most. But since it was my first experience with a coach, who was so important to me, that affected me enough for me never to forget it.'

'Slower than my granny' – those words marked the beginning of one of the most enduring and influential football relationships in history.

A training session. Nou Camp. Late morning, winter 1993

According to the principles Johan Cruyff introduced to Barcelona, coaches should lead by example: play football, be on the field during training and teach, because there is nothing better than stopping the game, correcting and instructing, explaining why someone needed to pass to a certain player, move to a particular position or change an element of their technique. That's how Carles Rexach, Cruyff's assistant for eight years at Barcelona, explains it: 'One word from Johan during a training drill is worth more than a hundred hours of talks at the blackboard.'

It is a training style that Pep emulates and applies today in his training sessions; but for a young player, Cruyff could be so imposing that it was difficult to talk to him. His iconic status and his absolute conviction in his methods and ideas often created a near-authoritarian way of communicating.

On a sunny but cold day on the pitch sandwiched between La Masía and the Camp Nou, Cruyff decided to target Guardiola. 'Two legs!' he shouted at his pupil. And Laudrup and the others laughed. 'Two legs, two legs!' The coach was trying to get Pep to lose his fear of his left foot. If he received the ball with his left foot, he could, with a slight touch, switch it to the right one, then hit a pass. And vice versa. The problem for Pep was that he didn't feel comfortable. 'Two legs, kid!' Cruyff kept shouting.

Johan Cruyff was the person who had the greatest influence on Guardiola: as the coach who was with Pep the longest (six years), and the one for whom Pep has the greatest affection and respect. Cruyff was also the man who gave him the opportunity to play in the Barcelona first team, the one who believed in him at a time when he was looking for exactly the kind of player that Pep came to be – a passer of the ball positioned in front of the defence who could provide the platform from which every Barcelona attack would begin. He also taught his players how to mark an opponent, teaching them to focus on a rival's weaknesses – while accentuating what you were good at, to fight the battles you could win, in other words. It was a revelation for Pep, who lacked the physique to beat a tall, powerful, central midfielder in the air – so he learnt, under Cruyff, to avoid jumping with his rival, but to wait instead. Cruyff's theory was: 'Why fight? Keep your distance, anticipate where he'll head the ball and wait for the bounce. You'll be in control while he's jumping around.'

But it wasn't all that easy for Pep, not in the beginning. After making his debut against Banyoles, eighteen months passed before Guardiola had the opportunity to play with the first team again although his performances with the B side were not going completely unnoticed. Then, in the summer of 1990, Barcelona were looking for a central midfielder as Luis Milla, who regularly filled that role, signed for Real Madrid – and Ronald Koeman was injured. Cruyff and his assistant Charly Rexach proposed that the club move for Jan Molby of Liverpool. The president asked for alternatives and Rexach suggested Guardiola. Cruyff had little recollection of Pep's disappointing debut and decided to go and see him play.

Unfortunately, on the day Cruyff dropped in on the B team, Pep spent the entire match on the bench. 'You tell me he's good; but he didn't even play!' he shouted to Rexach. 'I asked who was the best in the youth team. Everyone told me it was Guardiola but he didn't even warm up. Why not if he is the best?'

Cruyff was incensed. They told him Pep wasn't that strong physically and that other, bigger or more dynamic, quicker players were occasionally preferred in his position; to which Cruyff replied: 'A good player doesn't need a strong physique.'

That argument led to the type of decision that has helped shape the recent history of the club.

The first day he was summoned again to train with the Dutch coach, Pep arrived early, eager. He opened the door of the changing room where he found a couple of players alongside the boss and Angel

Mur – the team physio who was also an inadvertent conductor of the Barcelona principles, history and ideas. Pep kept his head down as he walked in. He stood still and waited for instructions. 'This is your locker. Get changed,' Cruyff told him. Not another word.

On 16 December 1990, Pep, then nineteen years old, made his competitive La Liga debut against Cádiz at the Camp Nou – in a match for which his mentor, Guillermo Amor, was suspended. Minutes before kick-off Pep suffered an attack of nerves: sweating profusely, his heart racing at a thousand miles an hour. 'My palms were sweating and I was really tense.' Thankfully it didn't occur on this occasion, but on other occasions his body had been known to betray him completely and he'd even been known to throw up before a big game. 'He really lived it, too much, even,' remembers Rexach. At nineteen, Pep Guardiola lined up alongside Zubizarretta, Nando, Alexanco, Eusebio, Serna, Bakero, Goiko, Laudrup, Salinas and Txiki Beguiristain – a collection of names that would soon become synonymous with one of the most glorious periods in the club's history. The players who would come to be remembered for ever beat Cádiz 2–0 that day.

That competitive debut marked some kind of a watershed moment for the club: a before and after in Barcelona's history. Although Laureano Ruíz was the first coach to take the steps towards the professionalisation of grass-roots football at Barça, it was Cruyff who really went on to establish the big idea, the philosophy – and no player epitomises that transition better than Guardiola. Pep was the first of a legacy who has become a quasi-sacred figure at Barça: the number four (derived from the number five in Argentina, the midfielder in front of the defence who has to defend but also organise the attack). It is true that Luis Milla played that role at the beginning of the Cruyff era, but it was Guardiola who elevated it to another level.

Pep only played three first-team games in that debut season but the following year Cruyff decided to position the lanky Guardiola at the helm of this historic team and, in doing so, established a playing model and defined a position. The figure of Barcelona's number four has evolved at the same rate as global football has edged towards a more physical game, and La Masía has gone on to produce players like Xavi, Iniesta, Fàbregas, Thiago Alcantara and even Mikel Arteta, proving that Guardiola's legacy endures.

'Guardiola had to be clever,' Cruyff says today. 'He didn't have any other choice back then. He was a bit like me. You must have a lot of technique, move the ball quickly, avoid a collision – and to avoid it you must have good vision. It's a domino effect. You soon get a sharp eye for detail, for players' positions. You can apply this when you are a player and a coach, too. Guardiola learnt that way – thanks to his build – and he was lucky enough to have had a coach who had experienced the same thing.'

Once established in the first team, the best piece of advice Rexach gave Pep is one that he likes to repeat to his midfielders today: 'When you have the ball, you should be in the part of the pitch where you have the option of passing it to any one of the other ten players; then, go for the best option.'

Guardiola has said on numerous occasions that if he was a nineteen-year-old at Barcelona today, he would never have made it as a professional because he was too thin and too slow. At best, he likes to say, he'd be playing in the third division somewhere. It might have been true a decade ago and perhaps even true at many other top clubs today, but not at FC Barcelona; not now. His passing range and quick thinking would fit wonderfully into the team he coached – and his leadership skills must not be forgotten either; as it soon became evident in his playing career; he didn't just pass the ball to his teammates, he talked to them constantly.

'Keep it simple, Michael!' shouted a twenty-year-old Guardiola on one occasion to Laudrup, the international superstar. The Danish player had tried to dribble past three players too close to the halfway line, where losing the ball would have been dangerous. 'That *was* simple,' Michael replied with a wink. But he knew the kid was right.

Just seven months after his debut, Pep was not only one of the regulars, but also a leading player with immense influence in, at least up until recent times, the best Barça team in history: Cruyff's Barcelona won four consecutive La Liga titles between 1991 and 1994.

In the 1991–92 season, Barcelona had qualified for the European Cup final to be played against Sampdoria at Wembley, something that for Pep, both as a *culé* and player, represented the culmination of a dream. The club had never won that trophy.

The night before, in the last training session in London before the game, striker Julio Salinas and Pep were arguing about the number of steps up to the famous balcony where the cup was collected at the old stadium. 'There's thirty-one steps, I'm telling you,' argued Pep, for whom accuracy was important as he has a weakness for football mythology and rituals. Salinas, who loved winding Pep up, got a kick out of disagreeing with him. Zubizarreta, the keeper, couldn't bear to hear them squabbling any longer: 'The best way to resolve this is to win the game tomorrow! When we go up the steps to collect the cup, you can bloody well count them then, OK?'

Seventeen months after his debut, on 20 May 1992, Guardiola, as expected, found himself in the line-up of the European Cup final. Before heading out on to the pitch, Johan Cruyff gave his players a simple instruction: 'Go out there and enjoy yourselves.' It was a statement that embodies an entire footballing philosophy and was central to Cruyff's principles; yet for others, its simplicity, ahead of such a key game, might be considered an insult to the coaching profession.

As Barcelona fans, players and directors were celebrating wildly after Ronald Koeman fired home a free-kick in the final moments of the second half of extra time, at least one person wearing a Barça shirt had something else on his mind amidst the chaos and euphoria. As the stadium erupted while one by one the Barcelona players held aloft the trophy known as 'Old Big Ears', Zubi sidled up to Guardiola and said: 'You were wrong, son, there's thirty-three of them. I just counted them one by one.'

'*Ciutadans de Catalunya, ja teniu la copa aquí*' (Catalans, you have the cup here), cried Pep Guardiola from the balcony of the Generalitat Palace in Barcelona that houses the offices of the Presidency of Catalonia. It was no accident that Barcelona's returning heroes presented their first European trophy to the city on the exact spot from where, almost fifteen years earlier, the former Catalan president Josep Tarradellas had used a similar expression to announce his return from exile (*'Ciutatans de Catalunya, ja soc aquí'*, 'I am finally here'). Guardiola, a Catalan referent of the team, of the club, understood the significance of FC Barcelona's coronation as a European superpower and its role now clearly established as an iconic symbol of the nation.

'That night at Wembley was unforgettable: my greatest memory. It turned into a party that carried on through the following Liga matches,' remembers Guardiola. Just a few days later, Barcelona, led in midfield by the young Pep, won an historic league title in truly dramatic fashion. On the final day of the season, Real Madrid travelled to Tenerife as league leaders needing a win to secure the title, something that many saw as a foregone conclusion. Yet after taking a 2–0 lead in the first half, a shambolic second-half collapse saw Madrid lose the match and, with it, surrendered the league trophy to their rivals in Barcelona.

Cruyff was transforming a club that had, before 1992, been successful on the domestic front yet had failed to impose itself upon the European stage and established Barcelona as a genuine international power. In fact, Cruyff did more than set a unique footballing model in motion: he challenged Barcelona fans to confront their fears, to overcome the sense of victimisation that had been a constant feature of the club's identity since the beginning of the century. This team, a collection of brilliant individual talents such as Ronald Koeman, Hristo Stoichkov, Romário, Michael Laudrup, Andoni Zubizarreta, José Mari Bakero and Pep Guardiola pulling the strings in midfield, combined to become synonymous with beautiful, yet effective, fast and free-flowing football that became universally known as the Dream Team.

The year 1992 continued to be a magical one for Pep as a footballer and, not long after the European Cup success, he found himself celebrating a gold medal win at the Barcelona Olympic Games. Yet, Guardiola has bitter-sweet memories of the experience with the national team: 'It passed me by like sand slips through your fingers,' he recalls.

The Spanish Olympic football squad convened almost a month before the tournament at a training camp some 700 kilometres from Barcelona, near Palencia in northern Spain, where, according to Pep, he behaved 'like a complete idiot. I say it that clearly because that is just how I feel when I remember that I was distant and made myself an outsider from the group. I didn't show any intention of integrating, nor sharing in the solidarity that team members who have a common objective must show. My team-mates, despite being kind, would have at the very least thought that I was full of myself: a fool. In the end, when I woke up from my lethargy, I ended up enjoying playing football with a team full of excellent players: guys with whom I managed to forge strong, consistent friendships that have lasted until this day. The friendship, a triumph, as much as the gold medal we won.' Some of the players in that Olympic Spanish side – Chapi Ferrer, Abelardo, Luis Enrique (then at Real Madrid), Alfonso and Kiko – would go on to form the backbone of the senior national team throughout the following decade.

That summer Guardiola earned a reputation for being a little strange, a bit different from your average player: a label that, within certain football circles, he has been unable to lose. If the distance he placed between himself and the rest of the national squad upset some, his intensity in games and training frightened others, distancing him even further from those who had little interest in understanding the game. José Antonio Camacho, his national coach for three years, shares that view. 'I saw Guardiola as a mystical type of person. The way he dressed – always in black – he was sometimes very quiet, constantly analysing things, thinking things over: why we won, why we lost, why he'd lost the ball. Sometimes his obsessiveness was excessive.'

That same year, his talent for making the right pass, for setting the rhythm of a game, touching the ball a thousand times a match and never for more than a second each time, his belief in the style of play Cruyff had imposed, did not go unnoticed internationally and he was awarded the Trofeo Bravo for the most promising European footballer in 1992.

His rise had been meteoric: he had become recognised as a world-class player in the two years since making his debut. Even more league trophies immediately followed, one after another, but then came the first big slip-up, one that would teach him something more than any victory. It was 18 May 1994: the all-powerful Dream Team was the bookmakers' favourite in the European Cup final against Fabio Capello's Milan in Athens. The 4–0 defeat served up a slice of humble pie for Barcelona, a lesson in the dangers of becoming overconfident, complacent even, and made all the more bitter because the reason for the defeat was neither defensive nor tactical – it was mental, it was down to a lack of preparation: 'All of us thought that we were playing against a gang. We went out there convinced that we were the better team and they put four past us. Their superiority was so great that I just wanted the game to be over,' Pep wrote years later.

After the golden era of 1990–94, Cruyff found it increasingly difficult to find new solutions and motivational tools to counter the team's problems, leading to the Dutchman making some strange decisions during his last two seasons at the club. One in particular revealed Pep's sensitivity. When the goalkeeper Zubizarreta, a captain, a leader, a man whom Guardiola considered a brother, was told by Cruyff he had to leave the club, Pep was devastated. He held it together until the night the squad gathered in a restaurant to pay tribute to the man they knew fondly as 'Zubi'. Pep disappeared and was found, tucked away in a corner, in tears. Only Zubi was able to console him.

By 1994, Guardiola was established as the figure who orchestrated Barça's play. 'My role was to move the ball around the pitch for my team-mates to finish off the move,' he says. The departure of Zubizarreta had made Guardiola the new leader, in charge of carrying out Cruyff's instructions on and off the pitch.

Even if sometimes, albeit rarely, he forgot what his role involved. He understood football as a team sport, but his genuine appreciation of the game made him an unconditional admirer of the best. His adoration was particularly reserved for the magical players capable of transforming a game into a spectacle. When Romário joined the club, Cruyff wanted the Brazilian to accompany him and Pep, the captain, for dinner. The coach was stunned by the admiration, the reverence even, that Pep showed towards the newcomer. In fact, such was his fawning adoration of the new star that when Romário disappeared to the bathroom, Cruyff had to remind Pep to stop acting like a star-struck fifteen-year-old.

Unfortunately, the quality of the squad had deteriorated since that fateful night in Athens. With eleven trophies, Cruyff was Barcelona's most successful manager (Pep would surpass him) and he still is the club's longest serving; however, in his final two years until his departure in 1996, he failed to deliver any silverware and underwent a very public and acrimonious falling-out with club president, Josep Lluís Núñez.

In his final season in charge (1995–96), Cruyff signed Luís Figo from Sporting Lisbon but results on the pitch did not improve substantially enough. The end was on the cards as soon as it became mathematically impossible for Barça to win the league: something that happened with two games remaining, just after they had been knocked out of the UEFA Cup by Bayern Munich in the semi-finals and beaten by Atlético de Madrid in the Copa del Rey final. Cruyff's relationship with President Núñez had become untenable and it all came to a head on 18 May, just before the final training session ahead of FC Barcelona's final home game against Celta Vigo when, following an extremely heated discussion between Cruyff and vice-president Joan Gaspart in the coach's office at the Camp Nou, the man who had led Barcelona to the most successful period in their history was sacked.

The Dutchman would not have continued beyond the end of that season, but had wanted to see out the rest of the campaign and leave with some dignity in the summer. The falling-out denied him that opportunity and his discovery that the club had already made a move to appoint Sir Bobby Robson as his successor heaped further humiliation upon him. Guardiola preferred, during that convulsive period, to act like most players would do – watch from a distance as everything fell apart.

In the first game of the post-Cruyff era, the Nou Camp was filled with banners supporting the Dutch coach, thanking him for all the success he had brought to the club. The club was divided between supporters of Cruyff and those of Núñez. In the end, even the man who had changed the history of Barcelona cracked under the intense pressure at the club, the behind-the-scenes conflicts and his deteriorating relationship with the board. Cruyff was gone, yet one of his most enduring legacies remained in the form of Pep Guardiola, a spindly young central midfielder who became both icon and embodiment of the philosophies that the Dutchman had set in motion.

After Cruyff came Sir Bobby Robson, a jovial sixty-three-year-old manager who rapidly earned the nickname 'Grandad Miquel' (the star of an advertisement for cheap wine) among the senior players. Robson never grasped the Spanish language or his players, but he suffered unfair comparisons to the Dutch master, whose shadow would have eclipsed anybody.

One of Sir Bobby Robson's first training sessions at the Nou Camp. Late morning, 1996

One morning soon after his arrival, Sir Bobby Robson used a piece of chalk to scrawl his tactics on the dressing-room floor, with José Mourinho duly translating Robson's English into Spanish. The players looked on and exchanged bewildered glances with each other as the old man knelt down before them making unintelligible squiggles on the floor. It was at that moment, right at the beginning of his tenure, that he lost the changing room and as the season progressed a form of self-management evolved among the players. Frequently, Mourinho would translate the words of Robson, then add extra, clearer instructions – quite a lot extra sometimes. Pep and José quickly identified each other as football people and the pair connected, talked and took coaching decisions among themselves. Quite possibly it was something that happened less frequently than José likes to admit it did, yet perhaps happened more often than Pep is prepared to own up to these days.

Guardiola has written in *My People, My Football*: 'Charly Rexach always said that in order to be a trainer you have to think 30% about football and the rest about everything surrounding the team: about the environment ... And I only understood it the year Robson was with us. I came from another school of football. I was so used to Cruyff's methods that I assumed all the coaches were like him. Robson thought we had to be different and it wasn't what I expected. He was right though, but in the process we lost three or four months. It was too late. In football you have to be brave. Always. If we just complain, we're dead. Action must be taken, always bearing in mind commitment to the common goal. Both Robson and the players were fighting for the same cause: Barça. But by the time our thoughts and his met along the way, it was too late. That synchrony was interpreted as self-management.'

Pep might call it a synchrony and claim that the suggestion that it was a case of 'self-management' was only one interpretation of what happened under Robson. But that is misleading, because that is exactly what took place. At half-time in the 1997 Spanish Cup final against Real Betis, Sir Bobby Robson sat in a corner of the changing rooms at the Bernabéu. The score was level at 1–1 and the Barcelona players wanted to seize the initiative and capitalise on the weaknesses the players themselves had spotted on the left of the Betis defence, while exploiting the gaps present between their opponent's midfield and defence. The players, not the coach, gave each other the instructions combined with interventions from Mourinho. The game was won in extra time, 3–2, the third title – Spanish Cup, Spanish Super Cup and European Cup Winners' Cup – in a season that remains etched in the memory by the images of Ronaldo powering past, round or through La Liga's defences.

Guardiola's confidence was growing both in terms of asking questions (why are we doing this? Why don't we start building that way, this way? Why don't we move those players in that direction when the ball is in that other direction?) and advising his team-mates. 'I was up to my balls with Pep, all day: this and that and this and that in the dressing room. He made my head spin!' says Laurent Blanc who played for Barcelona in the team during Sir Bobby Robson's reign, and at the time was not particularly impressed by Pep's 'perseverance' – a polite way of describing his obsessive nature.

The league title eluded Barcelona and celebrations were muted as the season drew to a close, the mood not helped by the fact that Sir Bobby Robson had learnt, as far back as April of that year, that the club had already reached an agreement with Louis van Gaal to take charge at the Camp Nou the following season.

For Guardiola, this represented an opportunity to learn from the architect of the extraordinarily successful Ajax team that he admired so much. But then a personal sporting tragedy struck.

Early the following season, in an August Champions League encounter versus Latvian side Skonto FC, Guardiola picked up a muscle injury that went undiagnosed until it was far too late. He realised something was wrong when, on his way to a delicatessen, he struggled to sprint across the road before the traffic lights turned red. What had at first appeared a fairly innocuous calf muscle injury would eventually lead to Pep missing most of the 1997–98 campaign as he visited one specialist after another in a seemingly interminable quest to find out exactly what was happening. It was not until the end of that season – in which Barcelona won a league and cup double under their new manager – that Pep was finally able to receive the necessary treatment and underwent an operation in the summer that would also see him miss out on Spain's disastrous 1998 World Cup campaign in France.

The injury required a slow and arduous period of recuperation and it would not be until some fifteen months after that fateful sprint to the shops that Guardiola would be able to play an injury-free game of football for the Barcelona first team, almost halfway through the 1998–99 season, making his return at the Riazor stadium against Deportivo La Coruña on 5 December.

There were those at the time who mischievously suggested that Guardiola's prolonged absences and mystery injury that coincided with van Gaal's first season at the club were no mere coincidents and that the player was deliberately avoiding working under the Dutchman. While it is true that, despite winning two league titles and a Spanish Cup during a stormy three-year first spell at the club, van Gaal often found himself at loggerheads with the local media, the assumption that the Catalan local hero, Guardiola, shared an uneasy relationship with the Dutch coach is incorrect. Van Gaal quickly identified Pep as a natural successor to Guillermo Amor as club captain, with Pep eager to learn from the coach whom he greatly admired, and the pair constantly discussed football, tactics, positioning and training exercises. 'He is, alongside Juanma Lillo, the manager whom I talked to most. Especially at the beginning, because in the end the contact diminished, both in quantity and content,' recalls Pep.

It is testimony to the mutual respect that the pair hold for each other that, when I approached van Gaal to request an interview asking him to reveal as much as he could about his personal relationship with Pep, the Dutchman – operating under a self-imposed media embargo at that time – was more than happy to chat about Guardiola, his former player and pupil.

According to van Gaal, it quickly became apparent to him, back when Pep was a relatively inexperienced young player, that he possessed an innate ability to lead a group of his peers and superiors: 'I made Guardiola captain because he could speak about football. You could see then that he was a tactical player. He could speak like a coach, even then – not many players can do that. Guardiola's best position was as a number four, that is in the centre of the midfield, because from there he can see the game and he had the personality to dominate it. He was younger than Amor and Nadal, but he was my captain. I told him in a meeting that I had chosen him and he said, "It's not how it happens at FCB, the oldest player in the team is usually the captain here." But I insisted, "No, you are the only one I can speak to on my level, you are my captain." He used to tell the other players like Figo where they should be: ahead of him, out wide, where he could play the ball. Pep is a very tactical guy and also a good human being, and because of that he could persuade his fellow players.'

As the Barcelona captain and his coach's relationship developed, Pep grew in stature and did more than just disseminate van Gaal's instructions to the other players out on the pitch, frequently suggesting an alternative approach if he felt it was for the benefit of the group.

Van Gaal gives one such example of the way the pair would work together to try and achieve a solution: 'Pep was always modest. Yes, we would talk and he would suggest ideas but always in a modest way. For instance, I will tell you what happened with Stoichkov. Hristo didn't want to accept my rules. Discipline is key, very important. If there is no discipline off the pitch, there is none on it. I always had to tell the Bulgarian in front of the other players, "You don't obey, I cannot keep you in the team." I even forced him to train with the reserves. But the players thought that was not such a good idea, so Guardiola, already captain, told me I should give him a second chance. I said to him, "OK, it's not about me, the team is more important. But he cannot fail again." So Hristo trained with the first team but he failed me soon after and I had to correct him again. Pep came to me and said, "Go ahead, we have given him a chance and he didn't take it." He knew how important Stoichkov was to the side but also that there are rules, limits. That the team comes first.'

That requirement, to put the team before the individual, was something that Pep would experience first hand when, during his second spell in charge of FC Barcelona for the 1999–2000 campaign, van Gaal edged Pep one step closer towards the end of his playing career and inched him towards the next phase in his journey from player to manager. 'By the way, I put Guardiola out of the team for Xavi,' explains van Gaal. 'I think Pep understood. Players must understand that you make changes not just because of talent but because of the future. You have to think about development and if you see a player dropping in form and the other improving, you have to act. That's hard for a player to understand, maybe deep down Guardiola couldn't. But it has turned out good for the club that Guardiola progressed, that he eventually moved aside as a player and returned as a manager. Everything goes full circle. The culture of the club, of any club, is essential; and it's very important that the institution teaches the footballers the need to preserve that. You now have key players – Xavi, Iniesta, Puyol – who are applying to their leadership things they learnt from Pep as a player and leader.'

Van Gaal's legacy at FC Barcelona is perhaps one of the most misunderstood elements in the club's history, largely a consequence of his uneasy relationship with the local press, which constructs and disseminates the popular memory of the club to the public, converting perception into fact for future generations. For example, the Catalan media frequently positioned themselves in favour of talented yet troublesome players like Stoichkov and Rivaldo, while simultaneously portraying van Gaal as a cold, ruthless individual who completely failed to grasp what FC Barcelona stood for as a club and a national institution. Yet the reality is altogether different and, while it's true that the blueprint for the club's playing traditions was established by Johan Cruyff, it is van Gaal who deserves much of the credit for building upon those foundations and advancing the methodologies and systems upon which much of Barcelona's current success has been based. What van Gaal might not be aware of is the influence his teachings had on Pep who today, as we shall see, recognises him as a key figure of the recent success of the side. 'I am not sure he is the best coach in the world, as he keeps saying,' Guardiola points out, 'but certainly one of the best. I learnt a lot with him. I would have to ask him, though, would you do things the same way if you had to do it all over again?'

His time under van Gaal was not without problems, however, and Pep's lengthy injury lay-offs led to some uncomfortable contract negotiations that distanced him from the board and afforded him some bitter experiences in just how unforgivingly and cruelly the football world can treat those who earn their living from it.

It was while Pep was sidelined with injury during van Gaal's tenure that the club president, Josep Lluís Núñez, enquired as to the player's well-being with one of the doctors – and when the physical report was positive, Núñez persisted with his enquiry, asking: 'OK, but what about his head? How is his head? Isn't he a bit sick in his head?'

Pep found out that his president doubted him, but, worse still, there was a spiteful rumour circulating on the streets of Barcelona that Guardiola's 'mystery' injuries were connected to the lamentable suggestion that he had contracted the AIDS virus. Pep has his suspicions as to the source of these unfounded rumours: they didn't come from the squad, from colleagues or even from journalists; nor even from rival fans. Yet it was apparent that the board did nothing to silence the gossip and protect their captain.

For Pep, it became difficult to enjoy his football at a club without the support and respect of the board. The atmosphere around the team became increasingly negative and the mood soured further when his close friend and Barcelona team-mate Luís Figo stunned the football world by moving to Real Madrid. It was a further symptom of the ruptures and divisions separating the club president and his board, the dressing room and the supporters. The club had gone from being an environment that celebrated football at the height of the Dream Team's successes, to an institution enveloped by pessimism and recrimination. The supporters poured their frustrations into an overt expression of anger at what they perceived to be Figo's ultimate act of betrayal and treachery, turning the Camp Nou into a cauldron of hate upon the Portuguese winger's return to the stadium where, just several months earlier, he had been worshipped as a hero. The noise that greeted Figo as he stepped out on to the pitch in Barcelona wearing the white of Real Madrid was likened to that of a jet aeroplane and the hostility generated by the Barcelona supporters may have sent the desired message to Figo but did little to improve the mood at a club mired in negativity.

Pep struggled to come to terms with the sheer force of hatred levelled at the Portuguese star, the godfather of one of his children, and the atmosphere surrounding the whole affair added to his growing sense of unease. He finally felt that enough was enough and took the decision, approximately twelve months before his contract ran out in the summer of 2001, that it was time to leave FC Barcelona. 'When he has made his mind up, there's no changing it,' says Pep's agent, Josep María Orobitg, whom he instructed not to open negotiations with Barcelona regarding his contract renewal. Needless to say, it was not an easy decision: but as Pep described it, 'I weighed up the bag of things I gain if I leave, and it was fuller than the one containing things if I stay.'

Pep said goodbye two months before the season finished at an emotionally charged, packed Nou Camp press conference. He took his place in front of the microphone alone, without the customary presence of a representative of the board. The president at the time, Joan Gaspart, someone who seldom missed an opportunity to share the limelight, was conveniently away on business. Pep, his voice cracking with emotion, announced: 'I came here when I was thirteen years old, now I am thirty and a father of a family. My career is slipping through my fingers and I want to finish it abroad, experiencing other countries, cultures and leagues. I feel quite liberated: a little calmer, a bit more comfortable.'

On 24 June 2001, after eleven seasons in the first team, Pep Guardiola, Barça's captain, the most decorated player in the club's history and the last iconic symbol of the Dream Team still playing at the Camp Nou, walked away from the club he loved. He had played 379 games, scored just ten goals, but won sixteen titles, including six leagues, one European Cup, two cups and two Cup Winners' Cups. He also departed as much more than just another great player: he left as a symbol of the team's Catalan identity in an era defined by an influx of foreign players.

After his final match at the Nou Camp, the return leg of the semi-finals of the Spanish Cup against Celta that saw Barcelona knocked out, Pep waited until everyone else had left the stadium. Cristina, his partner, came to support him, just as she had done from the day they first met when he walked into her family's store in Manresa – when a simple shopping trip to try on a pair of jeans led to a relationship that would become a source of strength and comfort to Pep throughout the toughest moments of his career. Moments like this. The couple, alongside his agent, Josep María Orobitg, made their way from the dressing room, down the tunnel and up the few steps that lead to the Camp Nou touchline; where he stood, for the very last time as player, to say goodbye to the pitch he'd first laid eyes on as a ten-year-old boy sitting behind the goal in the north stand some two decades earlier. He soaked up the silence in the empty stadium, but he didn't feel like crying. The overriding emotion was that of a great weight being lifted from his shoulders.

An Italian village, the dining room of a house. Luciano Moggi sits down to lunch surrounded by bodyguards. Midday, summer 2001

'When Pep left, it was a difficult time,' recalls Charly Rexach. 'They called him everything imaginable, he got a lot of stick without being to blame for anything that had gone on. The home-grown players were always on the receiving end. He was burned out and he suffered a lot. Guardiola suffers, he's not the type of person who can shake these things off. He was overloaded, he felt a sense of liberation when he moved on.'

Pep was thirty years old when he played his last game for the club and was still in good shape, so it was inevitable that people expected him to move to one of Europe's leading clubs. Offers started pouring in. Inter, AC Milan, Roma, Lazio, all came calling from Italy. Paris Saint-Germain and even a couple of Greek clubs expressed an interest. In England, Pep's availability aroused the interest of Tottenham, Liverpool, Arsenal, Manchester United, Wigan, West Ham and Fulham. But Pep wanted to play for the team that had captured his imagination as a small boy kicking a ball around the village square. He wanted to sign for Juventus, just as Platini had, his idol on the poster on his bedroom wall in Santpedor.

According to Jaume Collell in his excellent biography of Guardiola, Pep's negotiations with Juventus played out like something from a mafia movie. The tale begins with a phone call to the player's agent, Josep María Orobitg, informing him that somebody from Juventus wanted a secret meeting with him. Consequently, a car arrived to collect the agent in Barcelona and took him, via a number of B roads, to Turin. Barely a word was spoken in the car until they finally arrived at a modest hostel in a remote spot. 'Orobitg went up the stairs and Luciano Moggi came across, the general director of Juventus,' Collell explains. 'He was sitting at a round table, surrounded by shaven-head bodyguards, wearing the typical dark glasses. A chubby waitress served abundant amounts of pasta but said little. Suddenly, the bodyguards left together. Alone, Moggi and Orobitg reached an agreement in less than three minutes.' Orobitg says it took forty-five minutes but agrees with the description of the scene. The fact of the matter is that nothing was signed on paper.

Manchester United had been interested in him while he was still at Barcelona, but his agent could only listen to what they had to say at that time because Pep refused to allow him permission to negotiate with another club while he was still wearing a Barcelona shirt. Sir Alex Ferguson put a lot of pressure on the agent, as he was planning for the season ahead and saw Pep as a key player in his plans. Ferguson even presented them with an ultimatum: he wanted a face-to-face meeting with the Barcelona midfielder. Guardiola was hesitant and he turned Sir Alex Ferguson down. That was the end of the matter. Ferguson was angry but Pep had no regrets. 'Maybe the timing I chose was wrong,' Sir Alex says now.

In the press conference ahead of the 2001 Champions League final at Wembley, when Pep said Ferguson had done the right thing in not signing him, he was really hiding the reality of that failed transfer: after six or seven months of negotiations, meetings with Ferguson's son and the agent Francis Martin, and after the player rejected huge financial incentives, Manchester United moved on. In his place, Ferguson signed Juan Sebastián Verón along with Ruud van Nistelrooy and Laurent Blanc. And United went on to finish third in the Premier League that season.

Inter, Arsenal, Liverpool and Tottenham pressed on with negotiations. Inter showed considerable interest, but Juventus remained Pep's preferred club. Yet, three months after the afore-mentioned trip to Turin and continuing contact between the Juve president, Umberto Agnelli, Moggi and Pep's representatives, something strange happened: the Italian club denied that the secret encounter – even the pasta, the bodyguards and car ride from Barcelona – had even taken place and that no agreement had ever been reached.

The logical explanation for Juve's U-turn was that Moggi had just dismissed the coach Carlo Ancelotti, who had given the thumbs-up to Pep's signing, and replaced him with Marcello Lippi. Juventus sold Zinedine Zidane to Real Madrid and suddenly their objectives changed: with the €76 million from Zidane's transfer fee – then the most expensive in history – the Italians decided to build a younger team, bringing in Pavel Nedved, Lilian Thuram, Marcelo Salas and Gianluigi Buffon.

As the summer passed, opportunities and options from some surprising corners emerged. Real Madrid even sounded him out in a meeting in Paris. 'Have you gone mad!?' Guardiola replied in a conversation that lasted all of two minutes.

The deadline for Champions League registration came and went, making it increasingly difficult for Pep to join one of the biggest clubs. He had even come close to signing for Arsenal, but, the day before the deadline, Patrick Vieira's proposed move to Real Madrid broke down and the deal taking Guardiola to north London collapsed.

It was a difficult time for Pep, not least because the Catalan press were asked by some enemies of the player to publish that no other club wanted him so the club would be protected from criticism that they had lost a good player.

With the possibility of playing in the Champions League now no longer an option, Pep accepted an offer from Serie A side Brescia. The team coach, Carlo Mazzone, made a point of telling Pep as soon as he arrived that he was there because of the president, not because he wanted him. Guardiola was determined to prove his worth with his work on the pitch and accepted the premise. He signed a contract when the season had already started, on 26 September 2001, but his debut wasn't until 14 October against Chievo Verona.

A month and a half after joining Brescia, coach and Pep's friend Juanma Lillo remembers, 'the Italian team was already playing the way Pep, rather than the coach, wanted but Mazzone was shrewd enough not to object to the ideas Pep introduced to the squad. One day, Pep asked for videos of the forthcoming opposition for the players and staff to analyse, something that had never before been done at the club.' The fact is, instead of viewing the move to Brescia as a step down in his career, Pep saw it as a way of getting to know a new style of football and consequently a way of enriching his tactical knowledge: at this stage he had decided he wanted to continue to be involved in the game when his playing career ended. Football was his passion, his obsession, the thing he knew best, and Serie A was considered the league that practised the most advanced defensive tactics since Sacchi. His Milan of the eighties were regarded as having set the benchmark in terms of work rate and defensive strategy over the previous two decades – and Pep was determined to learn as much as he could from his time in Italy.

Brescia training ground. A cold November morning, 2001

The lengthy periods of injury, his departure from Barcelona or sporting defeats pale into insignificance compared with the emotional ordeal Pep suffered after failing a drugs test during his time at Brescia: firstly, after a game against Piacenza on 21 October 2001 and then, two weeks later, against Lazio on 4 November. The results of further analysis of the samples sent to a laboratory in Rome supported the accusation that Pep had taken nandrolone, an anabolic steroid that is said to improve an individual's strength and endurance and has similar properties to testosterone.

Guardiola received the news about the supposed positive result while practising free-kicks in a training session. 'I saw Carletto Mazzone speaking with the team doctor. That moment, that conversation, changed my life, but I only knew that later,' Pep recalled recently. 'They came over to me and told me the news. When I went back to the changing room I knew from the missed calls on my phone that the world had already judged me.'

That same day, Pep called Manel Estiarte, in his day the Maradona of water polo, Olympic champion and friend who played in Italy and with whom he had forged a close friendship. 'Do you know a lawyer? I'm going to need one,' he asked Manel. His friend went to see him the next day and he expected to find the footballer depressed, in need of a hug, and he had already prepared some reassuring words; but when he arrived, he found Pep to be his usual self: stoic, pensive, obsessive. Guardiola had been up all night, researching every other incident similar to the situation he now found himself in: reading the legal arguments and poring over case studies. Pep threw himself into finding a solution, rather than rolling over and accepting his fate. He was going to fight, and he wasn't just going to leave it in the hands of the lawyers. In typical fashion, Pep was taking this personally and he was determined to be in control of his destiny rather than leave it to others to decide his fate.

Despite Pep's determination to fight back, there were always going to be moments that would test his resolve, and Manel Estiarte was there to support him and help him avoid sinking into despair, as Pep himself explains in the introduction to *All My Brothers*, the former water polo player's autobiography: 'For seven years I simply maintained that I had never done anything wrong. From the first day when someone pointed me out and told me "Guardiola is a bad person", you were on my side and stayed with me. When these things happen to people, they don't forget. It was you and your blessed luck that pressed that button on teletext and showed me the way to go so that, seven years later, the person who had pointed the finger at me would change his mind and would say that "Guardiola is not a bad person", that I was a good person. Yes, it was fate, I'm sure it was, but you believed in me and that's why I was lucky. You brought me luck. Much needed luck. That good fortune is a gift, the best title that I have ever won in my sporting career. I will never achieve another quite as important, I can promise you. I held myself in too high esteem to take substances that could do me harm.'

What, you may be wondering, did teletext have to do with any of this …? Pep Guardiola is referring to a call he received from his friend Estiarte one Sunday, months after the Italian National Olympic Committee had announced the positive result in the nandrolone test. Pep was dozing on the couch when Manel called, shouting down the line, excited. Estiarte went on to explain that on Italian teletext he had accidentally stumbled upon a story referring to a new discovery related to positive testing in nandrolone cases. The World Anti-Doping Agency (WADA) had ruled that a result of less than two nanogrammes per millilitre of urine sample was an insufficient quantity to indicate substance abuse, because, they had now discovered, the human body is capable of producing up to the nine nanogrammes per millilitre they had found in his body (in contrast, the Canadian sprinter Ben Johnson was found to have two thousand nanogrammes per millilitre). It was a coincidental yet key moment, part of a long judicial process that was a test of Pep's mental strength.

'I am convinced I will win,' Pep said many times during that process to the Italian press. He was hit with a four-month suspension, but from the moment that the National Olympic Committee sentenced him, Guardiola launched a legal battle that went on until he proved his innocence. He never accepted the allegations, nor any consequent sanction. He even said 'The Italian justice system cannot look me in the eyes. I am innocent.'

In May 2005, the Tribunal of Brescia fined him €2,000 and sentenced him to seven months' imprisonment. The verdict was suspended because he had no criminal record but it was a tremendous setback for Guardiola. 'Do you think I need an illegal substance to play against Piacenza?' he repeated to everyone.

For Pep, this was an issue related to human values, truth and lies. They were accusing him of something he hadn't done and he was prepared to spend every penny fighting to prove his innocence. The lawyers could indeed take every penny, but he would never give up his reputation. His allies, including Estiarte, saw him as being fixated by the issue. Perhaps obsession is his most natural state, but it took him to the point of exhaustion. 'Leave it, it's done, no one remembers it,' his friend told him afterwards. 'I remember it and I know that it was a lie, that it's not true,' Pep would answer. He had to persevere until he had cleared his name.

Collell explains an incident in his biography that illustrated the farcical nature of the process. In the spring of 2005, Guardiola's agent, Josep María Orobitg, excused himself from a judicial hearing relating to the case to go to the toilet. A mature gentleman entered the bathroom and took his place alongside him, then muttered mysteriously: 'Sometimes the innocent have to die to win the battle.' It was a very senior person involved in the process.

Finally, on 23 October 2007, an Appeals Tribunal in Brescia acquitted Pep Guardiola of any wrongdoing, after it was scientifically proven that the test results upon which the accusations were based lacked credibility, a development that had started with Estiarte's chance discovery on teletext. 'I have closed the file and will leave it in a box. I don't want to talk about it but if one day someone wants to investigate, it's all filed and it can be checked out,' Pep told his good friend the journalist Ramón Besa.

The overwhelming feeling was a mixture of relief and happiness, of course, but much more than that. Guardiola had been carrying a huge burden on his shoulders and now felt suddenly weightless. We are never far from the glare of public scrutiny, from the feared question, 'What will people say?' Suspicion and doubt assailed him during that period, and he wanted them gone. He just craved confirmation of his innocence and demanded that the judicial system admit its mistake. A mammoth task which was inevitably doomed to failure – no one embarks upon a judicial case without the stigma of suspicion remaining, without a trauma of some kind enduring. It's the accusation that's remembered, not the final judgement.

Yes, he had proved his innocence, and had fought hard to do so. He was cleared finally, and his reputation and integrity restored, but he was determined to ensure that no one close to him would ever undergo a similar ordeal. So, in a way, the battle continued.

The captain of the Barcelona B team he was coaching at the time came to his office on behalf of the whole squad to congratulate him on the tribunal's decision. While he was listening to him he realised that he had, unconsciously, developed a very close bond with his players, a safety net he applied to his pupils and one that would eventually become all-consuming, a fatherly feeling that probably originated from the isolation and sense of abandonment he had felt during that long legal process.

The Italian federation took until May 2009 to officially accept the tribunal's acquittal ruling, when Pep was already enjoying success as manager of FC Barcelona. The beginning of the doping case had been a front-page story, but was only a brief side note when he was cleared.

After a season at Brescia and while the court case was in progress, Guardiola signed for Roma in the summer of 2002, motivated less by the opportunity to play for a bigger club than to be coached by, and to learn from, Fabio Capello, a manager he greatly admires despite their differing approach to the game. Pep was eager to experience Capello's defensive rigour and discover his secrets in terms of how to apply pressure upon an opponent. While he played little during his time at Roma, he learnt a great deal. 'He didn't play much because, by then, he was coming to the end of his career,' says Capello. 'He was a very well-behaved player. He never asked me for explanations as to why he didn't play. He knew what my idea of football was, but he was slow, he had some physical problems. He was a quick thinker, he knew what to do before the ball reached him and was very clever with positional play. And he was a leader.'

A lack of playing time in Rome eventually saw Guardiola return to Brescia in January 2003, where he shared the dressing room with Roberto Baggio and Luca Toni.

As his second spell at Brescia was coming to an end that same year, Pep received a call from Paul Jewell, the Wigan manager at the time. 'He'd always been one of my favourite players,' Jewell says. 'I got his number from his English agent. I called and left a message, "Hello, Pep, it's Paul here", something like that. About ten minutes later he called back. He knew all about us. He'd watched us on TV and talked about our midfield short passing. He knew [Jimmy] Bullard and [Graham] Kavanagh. His wages were £10,000 a week. Then he got this mind-blowing offer from Qatar. He could have played for the mighty Wigan, but ended up in some poxy job in Barcelona.'

In the meantime, before his move to the Qatari side Al-Ahli, Pep was presented with an opportunity to work alongside Lluis Bassat, a candidate in the 2003 FC Barcelona presidential elections with the backing of some of the most influential political and financial Catalan powers. Bassat approached Guardiola, asking him to become the sporting director of his project and Pep agreed under the condition that they would not use the names of potential signings to win votes, as so often happens in Spain – instead he wanted to sell a vision for the club to the fans.

Ronaldinho was offered to Bassat and Guardiola as a potential signing, but Pep wanted to focus upon a football project that could have included his former Dream Team colleague Ronald Koeman as coach, or, if Ajax refused to release their Dutch manager, Juanma Lillo.

Even though the subjects of potential transfers were never publicly disclosed to bolster the electoral campaign, Guardiola was planning to build a side that would include the likes of Iván Córdoba, Inter Milan's Colombian centre back; Cristian Chivu, Ajax's captain and defender; Emerson, Roma's Brazilian midfielder; and Harry Kewell, Liverpool's Australian winger.

In the end, Joan Laporta won the elections, with the support of Johan Cruyff and the promise of bringing David Beckham to the Nou Camp – the use of the Beckham name was no more than a marketing ploy, but one that worked for Laporta. The Manchester United website announced that his candidacy had made an offer for Beckham, a leak orchestrated by agent Pini Zahavi which included an agreement that Barcelona would sign one of his players, the goalkeeper Rustü Reçber, which did indeed happen a month later.

When Bassat's campaign defeat was confirmed, Pep told him, 'I know we approached things differently, but … we would do it again the same way, wouldn't we?'

The decision to side with Bassat would come back to haunt Pep several years later, as there were those, Laporta among them, who would not find it easy to forgive him for 'betraying' Cruyff, his mentor, by siding with an opponent.

After the failed electoral campaign, the decision to play in Qatar was just about the only step in Guardiola's career motivated by money: the move would earn him US$4 million in a two-year contract. The journalist Gabriele Marcotti travelled to Qatar to interview Pep in 2004, and encountered a player in the wilderness at the end of his career, sad, but not bitter. 'I think players like me have become extinct because the game has become more tactical and physical. There is less time to think. At most clubs, players are given specific roles and their creativity can only exist within those parameters,' he told Marcotti.

Pep was only thirty-three.

The game had been transformed, reflected in the European football landscape of the time that was dominated by a powerful

Milan side, a physically strong Juventus, the Porto–Monaco Champions League finalists, the arrival of Mourinho at Chelsea and his faith in athletes as midfielders. Pep was correct: 'pace and power' was the dominant footballing ideology of the day, but it was soon to be challenged, firstly by Rijkaard's Barcelona and, latterly, by Guardiola himself.

After playing eighteen games for Qatar's Al-Ahli and spending most of his time lounging by the pool in the complex where he lived alongside Gabriel Batistuta, Fernando Hierro and Claudio Caniggia, and after asking the former Santos winger and now coach Pepe Macia hundreds of times about the Brazil of Pelé, he went for a trial at Manchester City, spending ten days under Stuart Pearce's eye in 2005.

Eventually Pep turned down a six-month contract in Manchester, wanting a longer deal than the City manager was prepared to offer. In December 2005, he signed for Mexican side Dorados de Sinaloa, taking the opportunity to be coached by his friend Juanma Lillo. There, he learnt a new type of football, but also deepened his knowledge of other aspects of the game, especially in terms of administration, physical preparation and diet. Pep's managerial education would often continue into the early hours of the morning, as he and Lillo sat discussing tactics, training and techniques throughout the night.

Late at night in an apartment in Culiacán, north-west Mexico, 2005

After dinner over a glass of wine, Pep and Lillo would stay up until the small hours of the morning discussing the beautiful game even if they had training the following day. Pep sometimes worries that he can bore his friends to tears with his one-track conversations about football, football and more football. He had no such fears when it came to his relationship with Lillo, who had always been at the end of the phone to discuss the finer details of the game and had been a frequent visitor to Pep's house while he played in Serie A. Pep hasn't talked football anywhere near as much as he has done with Lillo – who, along with Johan Cruyff, represents the biggest influence upon his evolution as a manager.

Pep used to feel unprepared when it came to certain topics like defensive concepts or particular training methodologies. When he needed answers he would turn to Lillo at any time of day: 'How do you solve this type of situation?' 'If I do this what will happen?' According to Pep, Lillo is one of the best prepared coaches in the world and a leader in his field when it comes to developing a vision of the game, despite the fact that the world of elite sports hasn't been kind in rewarding him.

Guardiola's Mexican adventure finished in May 2006 when he returned to Spain, to Madrid, to complete a coaching course, and in July of that same year he had earned the right to call himself a qualified football coach. So, on 15 November 2006, Guardiola confirmed via a radio interview on the Barcelona station RAC1 that he had retired from professional football. He was thirty-five years old.

Unlike many former professionals, Pep had no desire to walk straight into the role of first-team coach at a big club and, as he said at the time, he felt he still had a great deal to learn. 'As a player, the fuses have finally blown,' said Pep, 'but sooner or later I will be a coach. I'll train any level offered to me, someone just has to open the door and give me the chance. I'd love to work with the youth side, with the kids, because I've no pretensions that I'm ready to work at a higher level yet. You have to respect the fact that this is a process, a learning curve. The first steps are vital and there are no second chances once you step up.'

In that public and emotional farewell as a player, he paid homage to what football had given him. 'Sport has served me as my influential educational tool; I learnt to accept defeat; to recover after not having done things well. It has taught me that my team-mate could be better than me. Taught me to accept that my coach can tell me I'm not playing because I've behaved badly.'

Pep may have finished his playing career but he wanted to continue learning about the game. It wasn't enough for him to have had first-hand experience of the methods of Cruyff, Robson, van

Gaal, Mazzone or Capello, so he travelled to Argentina to deepen his knowledge. There, he met Ricardo La Volpe (a former Argentine World Cup-winning goalkeeper and the former coach of the Mexican national team), Marcelo Bielsa (the much admired former Argentina and Chile national coach, and Athletic de Bilbao manager) and 'El Flaco', César Luis Menotti (the coach who took Argentina to the World Cup in 1978) to talk at length about football. Menotti said after his visit, 'Pep didn't come here looking for us to tell him how it was done. He already knew that.'

With his friend David Trueba, Guardiola drove the 309 kilometres from Buenos Aires to Rosario to meet Bielsa. The meeting between the two football men took place in the Argentinian's *charca*, or villa, and lasted eleven intense yet productive hours. The pair chatted with wide-eyed curiosity about each other. There were heated discussions, searches on the computer, revising techniques, detailed analyses and enactments of positional play which, at one point, included Trueba man-marking a chair. The two men shared their obsessions, manias and the passion for the game – and emerged from the *charca* declaring eternal admiration for each other.

Pep and Bielsa have much in common: they love teams that dominate, that want to be protagonists on the pitch, to seek out the opposition goal as the main priority. And they can't stand those who resort to excuses when they lose: even though losing is, for both of them, a debilitating sensation that depresses and isolates them because they cannot bear the shame that comes with defeat – they feel they have let the whole group down when they don't come out with the points. Bielsa's teams 'can play badly or well, but talent depends on the inspiration and the effort depends on each one of the players: the attitude is non-negotiable', Marcelo, '*el loco*', told him, adding that his sides cannot win if he cannot transmit what he feels. Pep agreed, taking notes all the time.

It is no mere coincidence that Pep used many of Bielsa's ideas, methods, expressions, philosophical nuggets in two key moments of his own career as a coach: in his presentation as a Barcelona first-team manager in front of the press and also in the speech he gave on the Camp Nou pitch in his last home game as manager. 'Do you think I was born knowing everything?' he answered when someone pointed out those coincidences.

Before leaving the villa, Bielsa posed Pep a challenging question: 'Why do you, as someone who knows about all the negative things that go on in the world of football, including the high level of dishonesty of some people, still want to return and get involved in coaching? Do you like blood that much?' Pep didn't think twice – 'I need that blood,' he said.

At the end of his spell in Argentina he felt that he was better prepared than ever before; not totally, because Pep will never allow himself to be completely satisfied, but he felt ready enough to start putting everything he had learnt to the test.

Upon his return to Spain, Pep was linked with a position at another Catalan club, Nàstic de Tarragona, then struggling in the first division, where he would have been Luis Enrique's assistant. The names of both Pep and Luis Enrique were discussed by the Nàstic board but both were ultimately considered too inexperienced, with neither having managed at any level before, and a concrete offer never arrived.

Instead, another opportunity arose: FC Barcelona wanted to talk to Pep about bringing him back in some capacity to the club he had left seven years earlier.

Monaco. UEFA Club Football Awards. August 2006

While Pep Guardiola was trying to discover himself, learn new tools for his managerial career, his beloved Barça had become the fashionable club of the era. The 2006–07 season kicked off with a show of appreciation for Frank Rijkaard's side, which in a couple of seasons had won two league titles and a European Cup in Paris against the Arsenal of Arsène Wenger, Thierry Henry, Robert Pires and Cesc Fàbregas. Many felt in fact that that team was on the brink of becoming the greatest in the club's history. As the influential Catalan journalist Lluis Canut explains in his book *Els secrets del Barça* at the UEFA Club Football Awards ceremony, on the eve of the European Super Cup, Barcelona captain Carles Puyol won the award for best defender, Deco the award for best midfielder, Samuel Eto'o the award for the best forward and Ronaldinho was recognised as the best player of the competition.

Yet that coronation of the team's achievements paradoxically heralded the beginning of the end for Rijkaard's Barcelona, as the first signs of indiscipline became apparent.

The Monaco trip had been a case in point.

Back at the hotel where Barcelona were based before the European Super Cup final against Sevilla, the coach had, to the astonishment of many, invited a Dutch pop group to join him at his table for dinner the evening before the game. After the meal, instead of enforcing a curfew, Rijkaard allowed the players the freedom to go to bed at a time of their choosing, inevitably resulting in a late night for the usual wayward suspects. 'The following day, on the morning of the match,' Canut explains, 'Ronaldinho was authorised to leave the hotel to attend a photo-shoot with one of his sponsors, while the rest of the squad were left to their own devices, effectively given the morning off to wander the designer boutiques of Monaco.' It was in stark contrast to Sevilla, their Super Cup opponents, who, under the direction of Juande Ramos, spent the day preparing for the game according to the Spaniard's usual discipline and order. The end result of the respective teams' preparations was self-evident and reflected in the scoreline at the end of the match: a 3–0 victory for Sevilla. That defeat served as the first warning sign of the many that were to surface throughout the following season.

In that summer of 2006 the dynamic had shifted in the Barcelona dressing room, triggered by the departure of assistant manager Henk Ten Cate, who left for the job of first-team coach at Ajax. With a reputation as Rijkaard's sergeant major, Ten Cate's absence served as the catalyst for a complete breakdown in discipline within the Barcelona dressing room. The Dutchman had always kept Ronaldinho on a tight leash and every time the Brazilian star put on a few pounds – something that happened all too often – the outspoken Ten Cate would not mince his words, letting him know exactly what he thought of his expanding waistline, putting him in his place in front of the rest of the squad and yelling that he was showing a 'lack of respect towards his colleagues'. Ten Cate had maintained a love-hate relationship with Samuel Eto'o, but the Cameroonian remained determined to win his respect and prove his worth. Rijkaard and Ten Cate made the perfect double act; the ultimate good cop/bad cop routine, but without Henk banging his fist on the table, Rijkaard's nice guy routine led to chaos.

Johan Neeskens followed Henk as Rijkaard's new assistant, but didn't have it in him to play the tough guy and, consequently, it was difficult to control the process that was causing the team spirit to disintegrate. In fact, nobody suffered more as a consequence of Ronaldinho's subsequent drop in standards than Ronaldinho himself. Here was a player who in the space of nine months went from being applauded off the Bernabéu pitch by Real Madrid fans in appreciation of his unforgettable performance in a Barcelona 0–3 victory on their rival's turf, to a figure of ridicule for the press who grew more accustomed to seeing him 'perform' in his own personal corner of a nightclub in Castelldefels than on the Camp Nou pitch. It was his waistline, rather than wonderful football, that caught the eye these days. Meanwhile, Eto'o suffered a knee injury and, in a decision that was to have serious consequences, was allowed to recuperate away from the club, distancing himself from the day-to-day life of the team.

Rijkaard was aware of the stars' behaviour, but indulged them, ever the optimist that the players were mature and responsible enough to know when to draw the line. It was a mistake. And, by the middle of the 2006–07 season that started poorly in Monaco, it was a trend far too late to reverse as Barcelona's results and their performances reflected the breakdown in discipline. The December defeat in the World Club Cup to International de Porto Alegre (featuring a magnificent seventeen-year-old Alexander Pato) was symptomatic of the declining standards among players and staff – Rijkaard had not even shown a video of the opposition to the players when preparing for the match. After Christmas, the South American players (Rafa Márquez, Deco, Ronaldinho) were given a few extra days off but, even so, the three of them arrived late for training. There were no sanctions.

The director of football Txiki Beguiristain faced a conundrum: halfway through that season, going into the Christmas break, Barcelona were second in the table, just two points behind Sevilla and three above Madrid in third. Txiki was aware of the indiscipline behind the scenes, but felt reluctant to intervene when the team was fighting for the lead at the top of the table and, like everyone else, hoped that it would rediscover some of the old magic.

After four months recuperating in isolation, Eto'o returned to an undisciplined dressing room, and was so appalled by what he found that he informed president Joan Laporta, his main ally at the club. Laporta sided with Eto'o and even offered him a captaincy role, so he felt reassured but, not long after, Rijkaard accused him of not wanting to play against Racing de Santander (the player was warming up but looked as if he didn't want to come on after being instructed) and Ronaldinho suggested in the mixed zone after the game that Eto'o had let them down because he should have been thinking of the team. Eto'o, impatient and not known for being diplomatic, exploded a couple of days later at a book presentation: 'He's a bad person' – in reference to Rijkaard: 'This is a war between two groups: those that are with the president and those that are with Sandro Rosell.'

Rosell, the former vice-president, who also happened to be a close friend of Ronaldinho and was responsible for persuading the Brazilian to sign for the club, had recently resigned following a number of disagreements with Laporta. Eto'o also sent a message to Ronaldinho, without mentioning his name: 'If a team-mate comes out saying that you must think of the team, the first person who should do so is himself.'

Given the less than harmonious atmosphere in the dressing room, the team went into a downward spiral towards the end of that 2006–07 season, resulting in their failure to win any of the titles or cups they had been competing for in the new year. Madrid finished the season level on points, but secured the title courtesy of their superior head-to-head results: the unanimous verdict was that Barcelona had thrown their title away as a consequence of complacency and lapses in concentration.

Those twin vices were never more evident than when Barcelona threw away an opportunity to reach the final of the Copa del Rey after inexplicably throwing away a 5–2 semi-final first leg lead over Getafe. Thinking that the game was won, Rijkaard left Messi in Barcelona for the second leg in Madrid. Barça were soundly beaten 4–0.

Despite the pressure for a change within the first team, Laporta thought that the protagonists of that historic Rijkaard side deserved another season. After all, at the peak of their powers this had been a magical and mesmerising group of exceptional talents that had secured the club's first Champions League trophy in fourteen years. 'The Dutch coach,' Canut continues in *Els secrets del Barça*, 'assured Laporta that he was strong enough to take control of the situation and recover the best of Ronaldinho, whom the club were considering offloading. In a visit by Laporta to Ronaldinho's home in Castelldefels, the Brazilian, who admitted to having been distracted, promised a return to the player he had been before.' He begged for the opportunity to prove that he could change his ways.

Meanwhile, Pep Guardiola, recently returned from his trip to Argentina, received that phone call from FC Barcelona.

A beach in Pescara. Just before lunchtime, beginning of summer 2007

Watching a match with Pep is an enlightening experience, a football master class. If you are lucky enough to be sitting next to him while a game is on it becomes apparent that he cannot help sharing everything he sees. 'The ball runs faster than any human, so it's the ball that has to do the running!' which, in seventeen words, just about encapsulates his philosophy.

'Look at him! Him, that one there! He's hiding! Your team-mates need to know that you are always available!' he'll shout, pointing a finger at the culprit. 'Before passing the ball, you need to know where you're passing it to; if you don't know, it's better to keep it; give it to your goalie, but don't give it to your opponent'; it's simple common sense, yet at the very core of a successful doctrine. 'Football is the simplest game in the world – the feet just have to obey the head,' explains Pep, yet he is more aware than anybody that it is anything but simple. And one more thing that Guardiola started saying while watching football: 'One day I will be the coach of FC Barcelona.'

Manel Estiarte heard those words more than a few times, muttered along with the rest of Pep's footballing theories during their long conversations at Manel's house in Pescara, Italy, where the two friends and their families would spend a few weeks together almost every summer. Pescara might not be the most beautiful place in the world, but Estiarte, whose wife is Italian, has had a house there since playing for the Pescara water polo team in the mid-eighties. After he retired, Manel escaped to the house whenever he could.

During those summers, the hot, fourteen-hour July days of sunshine would pass slowly for the two friends and their families who slipped into a simple daily routine: eight hours on the beach, home to freshen up before dinner, wine and hours of good conversation long into the night before finally heading off to bed for a good night's sleep in preparation for doing the same thing all over again the next day. It's what holidays were made for.

Of course, these days it's more complicated to remain anonymous, as other tourists can't help but notice that the most popular club manager in the world happens to be sitting on the beach a few yards away from them, and they will inevitably approach him, perhaps to share their memories of a game. But until recently, Pescara provided a sanctuary where the friends could quietly share their dreams, plans and set the world to rights.

At the start of their summer holiday in Pescara in 2007, Pep was out of work; the experience in Mexico and his Argentinian trip had finished and he had announced his retirement as a player. He and Manel were walking along the beach when Pep dropped a bombshell.

'I've been offered a job at Barça, if I want it.'

'Wow, Barcelona!'

'Yeah, they want me to work as technical director of the youth categories.'

'Well, you like to organise things and you're great working with kids.'

'Yeah, yeah; but I don't know. I don't know ...'

'What do you mean you don't know!? You are going back to FC Barcelona!'

'It's just that ... I want to work with the B team, the second team. I see myself coaching them. I want to start off there.'

'But didn't they just get relegated and are now in the third division!!??'

Manel remembers that conversation vividly and recalls thinking that there was no point trying to convince his friend that it was, perhaps, a bad idea to start his coaching career with a team on the slide on the wrong end of the Spanish league system (four divisions below La Liga) because once Pep had made his mind up, there was no turning back. Nevertheless, in this instance it didn't stop others from trying to persuade him he was about to make a mistake.

From a little village square in Santpedor, football had taken Guardiola all over the world. It had been a lengthy education; starting with tears at La Masía, coping with criticisms and defeats, failed dreams, incredible highs and lows, periods of reflection, study; encouragement from family, friends, and mentors; lengthy coach trips around the Catalan countryside, a footballing odyssey that would take him to Wembley, to Italy, to the Middle East, to Mexico and Argentina. It involved a great deal of observing, listening, watching and playing an awful lot of football.

By the summer of 2007, even though always learning, Pep felt ready – he wanted to coach and he knew how to do it and with which resources.

Txiki Beguiristain, then director of football at Barcelona, had other ideas, seeing Pep as the perfect fit for a more logistical role than a hands-on coaching position, which is why he called Pep offering him the job as director of youth football at Barcelona. Txiki saw Pep as a coordinator, an ideologist, with a capacity for teaching and communicating the 'Barça way' to the youngsters coming through the ranks. As director of the junior categories, Pep would be responsible for organising the youth set-up, selecting the players and their coaches, overseeing training methods and playing a key role in designing the new systems and the building where they would all be based, replacing the old Masía. Beguiristain had wanted to leave the club that same summer, a year before his contract ended, but when he learnt that Pep might consider coming back to Barcelona, he was prepared to continue for another season, with Guardiola as his right-hand man and understudy, grooming him as his successor in twelve months' time.

Before Txiki could even think about proposing Guardiola's return to Laporta and the board, Pep needed to build a few bridges, starting with some repairs to the two former Dream Team players' own relationship that had been practically non-existent for at least four years. Pep and Cruyff were also distant for a while: the pair hadn't quite seen eye to eye, back when Pep was still playing for the club, over an incident that occurred just after the Dutchman had left the team. Cruyff's successor in the dugout, van Gaal, had got rid of several home-grown players – Oscar and Roger García, Albert Celades, Toni Velamazán, Rufete – and Cruyff couldn't understand how Guardiola, the captain, let that happen without saying anything. When he told Pep, 'Come on, help out the guys from the youth teams', Pep said he wanted 'nothing to do with this managerial stuff', that he couldn't intervene in the decisions of the coach. Cruyff was not impressed.

But there was something else that divided the former Dream Team coach and captain. When Pep accepted the proposal of Lluis Bassat to become his director of football should the 2003 election campaign be successful, it came as something of a surprise to a group of former Dream Team players – Txiki, Amor and Eusebio – who had made a pact, with Johan Cruyff's blessing, that they would not publicly back any candidate ahead of the vote and would offer their services to the eventual winner. The former players were under the impression that Pep was part of the group and felt a degree of betrayal upon discovering that he had opted to publicly support Bassat. Laporta (with the backing of Cruyff behind the scenes) was victorious, leaving Pep somewhat isolated from the group and, as a result, he didn't talk to Txiki or Johan Cruyff, or even Laporta, for a few years afterwards.

A dental appointment made Evarist Murtra, one of the club

directors and a friend of Guardiola, arrive late to the board meeting where his name was put forward to become the new manager of the Academy together with Alexanco. Murtra missed Txiki Beguristain's presentation and the proposal included the election of Luis Enrique as a coach of the B team. The director asked politely to be given a brief resume of what had been said and grimaced when he heard what Txiki had in store for Pep. By then the former captain had already got his coaching badges and had told Murtra that he wanted to coach. Beguiristain left and Murtra excused himself to go to the bathroom. Just before Txiki got in the lift, Murtra asked him to reconsider. 'Do me a favour and give Pep a call first, just in case what he wants to do is coach,' the director told him.

So, in the summer of 2007, a meeting between Txiki and Pep was arranged in the Princesa Sofía Hotel near the Camp Nou in order to discuss Guardiola's potential return to the club. Beguiristain walked into that hotel willing to forgive and to forget – and with a particular proposal and a position in mind for Pep. Despite the suggestion from Murtra, he wanted the former captain to become the future director of football.

Guardiola: Thanks for the offer, but I want to be a coach.

Beguiristain: Where? There is no vacancy for you in the first team, even as an assistant to Rijkaard …

Guardiola: Give me the B team, in the third division.

Beguiristain: What?! You must be crazy. It's a no-win. It's easier to win the league with the first team than to gain promotion with Barça B.

Guardiola: Let me have control of the B team; I know what to do with them.

Beguiristain: But the job we're offering you is much better than just the B team, on a financial level as well. Being in charge of the academy is more prestigious. The B team is in the third division!

Back in 2007 the B team was struggling and not considered the talent pool it now is: it had just suffered relegation to the English equivalent of League Two for the first time in thirty-four years.

But Pep was insistent.

Guardiola: I want to be a coach, to train. Let me work with whatever team, whatever level you want: the juniors, or the infants, anybody. I will even work with the toddlers on a potato field, but I want to become a 'hands-on' coach.

Beguiristain: You could get your fingers burned trying to rescue that B team, you must be mad. And another thing; what will it look like if we dump Pep Guardiola, the club's icon, in the third division side? It doesn't make sense!

Pep proceeded to explain what he wanted to do with the team in great detail, how he planned to design the squad, what kind of training sessions and what kind of regime he wanted to implement. 'I want to work with these kids; I know they don't ask for anything and give you everything. I will get that team promoted,' Pep repeated.

He took some convincing, but, eventually, Txiki was won over by Pep's enthusiasm and ideas for the reserves. The director of football went away and started doing some digging around, gathering second opinions about Pep's qualities as an actual coach. He spoke to members of the academy set-up who had been on coaching courses with him, his tutors, too, and they all agreed that Pep had been one of the most brilliant students they had ever worked with. So the decision was taken soon after that meeting.

It was typical Pep Guardiola: a blend of boldness and genius. There can't be too many former players who have turned down a director's role overseeing an entire academy set-up, in order to beg for the chance to take over training a failing reserve side.

'Are you sure you know what you're getting yourself into, Pep?' his friends would ask him repeatedly once they had heard what had happened that afternoon. 'Four divisions down, that's hell: it has nothing to do with the football that you know. You're not in for an easy ride, more like a bumpy one! Are you really sure about this?' Oh, yes, he was sure. 'I just want to coach' would be his answer. As David Trueba wrote, 'Pep had always been very clear that life consists of taking risks, making mistakes – but wherever possible, your own mistakes rather than those of others.'

However, there was another stumbling block to Pep's wish that he be given the opportunity to coach and that was the fact that someone had already been chosen for that job: none other than Guardiola's friend and former team-mate Luis Enrique. The former Spanish international had been told by an enthusiastic Barça director that his approval as B team coach for the 2007–08 season would be unanimously accepted by the rest of the board. Pep's appearance on the scene suddenly changed all of that and Txiki had to let Luis Enrique know the decision had been reversed.

So in many ways, life had now gone full circle for Pep. The boy from Santpedor who had been lucky enough to get a phone call from La Masía some twenty years earlier was now coming back to where it had all begun. In putting some distance between himself and the club in the interim, he had more to give than if he had stayed.

On 21 June 2007, seven months after retiring as a footballer, Pep Guardiola was unveiled as the new coach of Barcelona B.

Camp Nou. Press conference room, afternoon of 21 June 2007

'I hadn't had any other offers, nobody had phoned me. For this reason I am so grateful to the club, because for me it is a privilege to be able to train Barça B.' That is what Pep told the media that had assembled for his presentation at the Camp Nou on that summer day in 2007. The season that was about to start turned out to be more than just a privilege; it evolved into a campaign that would define his abilities as a football coach.

At that press conference, Joan Laporta, who at that stage was beginning to resemble what the Americans refer to as a 'lame duck president', had salvaged a degree of credibility with the appointment of a former player, symbol of the club and nation. At that moment in time, seated beside Guardiola, Laporta needed the benefit of Pep's halo effect. The president's tenure had previously been a success, making Barcelona a force in Europe again with two league titles and a Champions League trophy delivered in swashbuckling style; but as time went on, the president's image had been tarnished by internal divisions at the club and accusations from a number of former members of the Laporta board – including Sandro Rosell, who had resigned – accusing him of becoming authoritarian and, some suggested, out of touch with reality. And of course, a trophyless 2006–07 season didn't help. Power is a strange thing and Laporta was the perfect example of the way it can transform even the most idealistic individual.

'All my life I wanted to be Guardiola,' said Laporta that afternoon, basking in the reflected glory of an idol to a generation of Barcelona fans. Cruyff was nowhere to be seen, despite the fact that he approved Guardiola's appointment, preferring to remain pulling the strings behind the Laporta era, just as he had always done.

The level of risk that was being taken by the club with regard to Guardiola was on a par with his notoriety – but he wasn't scared of a fall. His speech during his presentation to the media came like a cascade of words that he himself had repeated many times in bed, when in the pool in Doha or walking around the beaches of Pescara, daydreaming. 'I am no one as a coach, that's why I face this opportunity with such uncontrollable enthusiasm. I've come here prepared to help in any way necessary. I know the club and I hope to help these players and the idea of football that you all have to grow. In fact, the best way of educating the players is to make them see that they can win. I hope the sense of privilege I feel is felt by everyone in the team,' he told a full media room.

Guardiola likes to repeat that his real vocation is teaching: he dreams that, once he gives up the professional game, he'll be able to train kids, youngsters who 'still listen and want to learn'. It was to an audience of attentive youngsters eager to learn that he gave his first speech as a coach a few days after his presentation. He recalls that he chose a selection of ideas that represented, as well as any others, his footballing philosophy.

He could live with them playing badly now and again, he told them, but he demanded 100 per cent on the pitch in every single game. He wanted the team to act as professionals even if they weren't yet considered so and to be competitive in everything they did. 'The aim is to gain promotion and in order to do that we have to win and we can't do that without effort,' he said to them. He also pointed out that the attacking players would need to become the best defenders; and the defenders would have to become the first line of attack, moving the ball forward from the back.

And that no matter what happened, the playing style was non-negotiable: 'The philosophy behind this club's style of play is known by everyone. And I believe in it. And I feel it. I hope to be able to transmit it to everyone. We have to be ambitious and we have to win promotion, there's no two ways about it. We have to be able to dominate the game, and make sure that we aren't dominated ourselves.'

The club had bagged a prize asset. He was useful for the institution, and not just because he won games but also because he understood and applied what La Masía had taught him; La Masía, the academy that had shaped him and made him strong, that had accentuated his strengths and hidden his weaknesses, ultimately leading him to success.

Pep settled into his new role by surrounding himself with a team of assistants whom he knew he could trust, a group of colleagues who had been inseparable since the time they had first met at La Masía: his right-hand man, Tito Vilanova; the rehabilitation coach, Emili Ricart; and the fitness coach, Aureli Altimira. The group quickly became aware that the technical quality of the players they had at their disposal in the B team was never in doubt: because of the selection processes involved, every player at La Masía had above average technique after more than two decades favouring intelligent youngsters who could play the ball rather than being considered for their physiological characteristics. However, Pep realised that in order to make the team a success he needed to add intensity and an increased work rate to their technical abilities.

And, above all else, they had to learn to win. Instilling a fiercely competitive, winning spirit into a team, an academy already blessed with an abundance of talent, represented something of a watershed for grass-roots football at FC Barcelona.

The B team's relegation to the fourth tier of the Spanish league was symptomatic of a club that had prioritised its philosophy, but lacked the skill to implement it competitively at youth level. Pep set about disbanding the Barcelona C team, which had been playing in the third division, combining the pick of the players from the squads and taking the revolutionary step of allowing players over twenty-one to join the new B team structure for a maximum of two seasons before being sold. In allowing older footballers to play alongside the under-21s in the B team, Pep was breaking with tradition in the hope that he would raise standards and make them more competitive.

In combining the B and C teams, Pep had to trim a group of fifty players down to just twenty-three, resulting in a great number of players being released from La Masía – an unenviable task, as described by David Trueba: 'Pep wanted to find teams for the players he was letting go; he had to arrange meetings with their parents, holding back tears, dissolving the childhood dreams and vocations of those boys who thought that football was more important than life itself, who had put their studies on hold because they were boys who were called to succeed. Creating that squad was a "bricks and mortar" job, of intuition and strength, a dirty and thankless task. From one day to the next you had to decide if you were letting a lad called Pedro leave the club to go to Gavá or if you were keeping him.' The decisions also had to be made quickly, after only half a dozen training sessions: a risky business, with the potential for mistakes. But, again, Pep could live with the mistakes, because they were his mistakes.

Guardiola immediately set about introducing a series of habits, working practices, systems and methodologies acquired after a career working with a variety of different managers. 'He paid particular attention to detail', Trueba recalls: 'From control of the players' diets, rest and recuperation time; to scouting opponents by recording their matches and using his assistants and staff to compile detailed match reports … in the third division!! On occasion, if Guardiola felt that he didn't have enough information on a particular opponent, he would go to their matches himself.'

He became as demanding of himself as he was with his players and staff but, in everything he did, he always made it a priority to explain why he was asking them to do something. He was always the first to arrive and the last to leave, working mornings and afternoons at the training ground. Every aspect of running the team had to be under his control: he demanded daily reports and updates from all his staff. Nothing was left to chance.

And, if necessary, albeit rarely, he would remind those around him exactly who was boss.

Midday on 6 December 2007. Barça B were playing at Masnou's ground and leading 2–0 going into the second half; however, Barcelona threw away their lead and allowed the opposition to salvage a point: 'The telling-off was tremendous,' one of the players recalls. This is how journalist Luis Martín remembers that day in *El País:* 'Normally, Guardiola gives himself time to analyse the game and talks it through with the players the following day, but that afternoon he made an exception. "He closed the dressing-room door and told us that many of us didn't deserve to wear the shirt – that these team's colours represented many people and feelings and we hadn't done them justice. We were terrified," the player insists.

'The most severe reprimand the team received was for an indiscretion,' Martín continues. 'In October 2007, the daily newspaper *Sport* revealed what Guardiola had said to the players in a dressing-room team talk. According to the paper, Guardiola referred to the kids competing in *Operación Triunfo* – the Spanish equivalent of *The X Factor* – as an example for the players: "He told us that the kids are given an incredible opportunity and that they do everything they can, giving their all to make the most of what may be a one-off opportunity – and that we had to do the same," explained one of the players. "And later, when he saw his words repeated in print, he went mad and said that divulging dressing-room tales to the press was betraying team-mates."

On another occasion, Guardiola dropped Marc Valiente, one of the team captains, making him watch the game from the stands, simply for leaving the gym five minutes earlier than he was meant to. According to Luis Martín, Guardiola justified his decision by saying simply: 'No weights, no games.'

Sporadically, his players would join Rijkaard's team for call-ups or training sessions. However, their elevated status did not prevent Guardiola from making an example of them. Just three games into the season he hauled off former Glasgow Celtic player Marc Crosas in the forty-sixth minute of a match. According to one of the players, 'Crosas got a right telling-off at half-time for not running. As soon as he lost the ball in the second half he was taken straight off.' Perhaps Guardiola was aware of the effect that this would have upon the junior players in the B team, as one of them explains: 'We saw him doing that to a first-teamer and thought "what would he do to us?"' The senior players, meanwhile, understood perfectly well, and as one recognised: 'He always used us as an example, but he was always fair with us and everyone else.'

Pep was finding solutions to the team's problems, relying on instinct and experience to motivate, inspire and get the best out of the youngsters. When the team qualified for the promotion play-offs, he told them: 'We've made it this far together, now it's time for YOU to win promotion.' But one of his motivational methods proved quite expensive. 'He told us that every time we won three games in a row, he would take us all for lunch. He took us out three times, he's spent a fortune!' one player recalls.

But club lunches weren't his only expense: Guardiola also had fines to pay for having been shown three red cards. Occasionally the mask slipped from the cool, calm, collected Guardiola. He quickly decided that instead of trying to bottle up his emotions on the touchline, he would let rip in Italian so that match officials couldn't understand the tirade of four-letter abuse that was being directed at them from the Barcelona dugout.

His motivational methods frequently took the form of challenges. When Gai Assulin returned from his debut with the Israeli national side, Guardiola, reminiscent of something Cruyff had once said to him, set his player a test: 'This weekend – go out and score a goal.' He set up two and scored the third. 'He does it a lot – he challenges us – if you push yourself you're rewarded,' as another player remembers.

'This isn't the third division, this is the Barça reserve team – not just anyone can be here,' he told his players once, as Martín recalls in *El País*. Yet the honour of playing for the club went way beyond pulling on the shirt on match days and, as a consequence, Pep demanded high standards from his players at all times, both on and off the field. He banned the use of mobile phones at the training ground and on the team coach. Players were fined €120 if they were late for training and had to stick to a twelve o'clock curfew – if they were caught breaking it once they were fined €1,500, twice and it rose to €3,000. If you were caught three times you were out of the door. He also had strict policies regarding the procedure leading up to games: team strategy was practised on match days. If it was an away game, the team ate together at La Masía; if they were playing at home, in the Mini Estadi, each player ate at home.

The reserve team goalkeeping coach, Carles Busquets, was once asked by a former colleague what it was like having Guardiola as your boss: 'Pep?' he responded. 'You'd be scared!' In fact, only now will Busquets admit that he used to sneak round to the car park for a crafty cigarette as Pep banned everyone from smoking in or around the dressing room.

One of the reasons that Guardiola had been so eager to test himself and his ideas with a team in the lower divisions was because he wanted to confirm a personal theory: that a reserve team, like any other, could serve as a university of football; because all teams behave, react and respond the same way. Whether superstars or Sunday league, there's always a player who is jealous of a team-mate, another who is always late, a joker, an obedient one fearful of punishment and eager to please, a quiet one, a rebel ... It was also educational because it helped prepare for the fact that every opponent is different: some are offensive, others timid, some defend in their own box, others counter-attack. Working with the B team gave Guardiola the perfect opportunity to try and find solutions to the kinds of problems he would encounter working with a higher profile team; yet enabled him to do so away from the spotlight and glare of the media.

At the same time, he was humble enough to recognise that he wasn't sufficiently trained in certain areas, mostly defensive work. His friend and coach Juanma Lillo saw all the games of the Barcelona second team and, when they had finished, Guardiola would ring him to express his doubts to him, whether they be about the use of space by his players or the behaviour of those off the ball. Rodolf Borrell, now at Liverpool FC, was a coach with one of the Barcelona youth teams at the time, and each week Guardiola went to his defensive training sessions to observe and learn.

Pep's enthusiasm proved contagious and his presence a breath of fresh air at the training ground; at the same time he also gave the B team a degree of credibility. After all, if Guardiola was involved then, everybody figured, it must be important. If the B team had been neglected in recent times, then Guardiola's influence saw it transformed and given a makeover, blowing out the cobwebs and raising its profile, while instilling a new regime of professionalism that was missing even from the first team.

Especially from the first team.

The B side may have been the old workshop round the back of the club, but Guardiola was determined that it would lead by example. So when the new Barça B was ready for the season, Pep led them with pride.

They lost their first friendly under him, against Banyoles, on a small artificial pitch. It only took that one defeat and a stuttering start in the competition to herald the first murmurings of dissent in the media. Guardiola 'had more style than power', wrote one journalist. It became a popular cliché to say that Pep, who as a player read and distributed copies of *The Bridges of Madison County* to his Dream Team team-mates, couldn't possibly possess the strength and authority to mould a winning team on the Astroturf and cabbage-patch pitches of the Spanish third division.

Pep went to see Johan Cruyff soon after the stumbling start to the season, something that he would repeat frequently whenever he needed advice over the coming years. 'I've got a problem,' he told his mentor. 'I've got these two guys who I don't know if I can control, they don't listen to what I say and that affects how everybody else receives my messages. And the problem is, they're two of the leaders in the dressing room and the best players. I will lose without them on board.' Cruyff's response was blunt: 'Get rid of them. You might lose one or two games, but then you will start winning and by then you would have turfed those two sons of bitches out the team.'

Pep got rid of the pair, establishing his power in the dressing room and sending a clear signal to the rest. The team did start playing better and winning, especially after Pep signed Chico, now at Swansea, a player identified by Tito Vilanova as the central defender that the team needed. It was a B team whose line-up also included Pedro and, in the latter half of the season, Sergio Busquets, who worked his way from the bench into the team to become their best player. From four tiers down in the Spanish league, Pedro and Busquets would become household names and world champions within two years under Pep's guiding hand.

Txiki Beguiristain was a regular visitor to the Mini Estadi to watch Pep's B team throughout the season, following more reserve games than he had ever done in his four years as director of football at the club. He believed in Guardiola and realised he was watching the development of something that could be used in the first team: variations in formation, for instance. Instead of playing the most common 4-3-3 system at Barcelona, Pep occasionally used a 3-4-3 that had hardly been used since the days of the Dream Team and subsequently only very rarely by van Gaal. At other times, Pep would play with a false number nine; even sometimes deploying Busquets, a central midfielder, as a striker with three playing behind him. Pep's do-or-die attitude from the sidelines (constantly correcting and signalling during games, treating every match as if it were the last, intensely focused on the job, passionate and occasionally over-exuberant) as well as his off-pitch behaviour (making the team eat together, scouting rival players and teams, unheard of at the time in the third division) suggested he was a leader, ready for management. Ready to lead at any level. Any team.

As the season went on, Txiki became convinced that everything Pep was doing could, if necessary, be applied to the first team. Barça B finished the season as league champions, automatically sending them into the play-offs to be promoted into the Second B division. People were starting to take notice of Guardiola's achievements, not just within the club, where he was acquiring a rapidly growing legion of admirers, but beyond Barcelona. Juanma Lillo was one of them: 'What Pep did with Barça B is still of greater merit than what he did later with the first team. You only have to see how the side played at the start of the season in the third division with "terrestrial, earthy" players, and how they were playing by the end. The group progressed as a whole, but also the players as individuals. I still laugh when I remember that people said he was too inexperienced to take over Barça B, let alone the first team.'

And, of course, while all of this had been going on, as the B team was improving and behaving professionally, the first team had been declining. It wouldn't be long before FC Barcelona would be looking for a new manager.

Front seats of a plane taking the first team to China, summer 2007

For Rijkaard's team, the 2007–08 season that was witnessing a revolution at the reserve level had started in a similar depressing fashion to the previous, trophyless, campaign. Criticisms were mounting from all quarters and as the season progressed the coach gradually lost the respect of the dressing room.

Meanwhile, Ronaldinho was becoming increasingly introverted and had ceased taking orders from anyone. Behind medical reports stating that he had 'gastroenteritis' the club started to hide his absences from training sessions. By the middle of the season he had been 'in the gym' or 'indisposed' more often than training.

Often the Brazilian arrived at the dressing room wearing the same clothes from the day before after being out all night partying, as Lluis Canut explains in his portrait of the era *The Secrets of Barça*. Frequently during training, he could be found sleeping on a massage table in a darkened room at the training complex and, to make matters worse, a relationship between Ronaldinho and one of Rijkaard's daughters became common knowledge.

On more than one occasion, Deco turned up to training without having slept because he had taken his sick child to hospital. While prioritising the health of his children over his job may not be the greatest sin, his separation, one of ten marital separations or divorces within the squad, did not help him focus. Rafa Márquez would also nip off and visit his girlfriend Jaydy Mitchell, often after training and occasionally staying over – which wouldn't have been a problem if she didn't live in Madrid. Thiago Motta had such a great night out on one occasion that one night became two and the club literally had to send out a search party to find out where he'd got to. On that occasion, the Brazilian didn't escape punishment – becoming something of a scapegoat for someone else gaining a reputation for his 'samba' skills: Ronaldinho.

After losing 1–0 to Real Madrid at the Nou Camp, Barcelona were seven points behind the leaders halfway through the season and by the autumn there were murmurings among senior board members that drastic action was required, that the best thing to do would be to get rid of the undisciplined Ronaldinho, Deco and Eto'o – shifting the dynamic towards a younger, hungrier, more ambitious generation led by Lionel Messi. They also doubted whether Rijkaard was the right man to lead the new order. The president, however, publicly and privately backed the Dutchman.

Off the record, Guardiola was being briefed on the situation by first-team players and Laporta's allies. One even hinted to Pep in October that the prospect of him becoming first-team coach was gathering pace behind the scenes: 'Your name hasn't come up officially at a board meeting, and you haven't heard this from me, but you're going to be the head coach of Barcelona next season.' In early November, Pep's name was eventually raised at a board meeting by one of the directors, proposing that Rijkaard be replaced by the B team coach. However, Txiki Beguiristain was opposed to plunging Pep into the middle of a crisis at the halfway stage of the season: too much too soon for a relatively inexperienced coach.

Not everyone agreed with Txiki. Johan Cruyff became convinced that there was no way back for the first team and that a change was needed. After ruling out Marco van Basten – who was about to sign a contract to take over at Ajax – Cruyff met with Txiki to discuss Pep's potential. The former Dream Team coach then went to see how Guardiola was doing, visiting him at the Mini Estadi to take the measure of Pep and the B team, before having lunch with him to talk football. Later, Cruyff sent a message to Laporta: 'Pep is ready. He sees football with absolute clarity.' The president remained uncertain, however, believing, hoping, despite all evidence to the contrary, that Rijkaard could turn it around and resurrect some of the old magic from Ronaldinho and Co.

As the first team's complacency and indiscipline became apparent to all, certain directors and a growing press contingent began to insist that there was only one man capable of restoring order at the Camp Nou. Not Pep Guardiola, but José Mourinho. They argued that the Chelsea boss had the unique force of personality and courage to take the necessary but painful decisions. If that meant a shift in the club's footballing philosophy, some argued, then so be it: drastic times, drastic measures. And, after all, Mourinho had always dreamed of returning to Barcelona.

On 27 November 2007, Barcelona drew 2–2 with Lyons, scraping through to the knockout stage of the Champions League in less than convincing fashion, conceding after some shambolic defending at a set piece and giving away an unnecessary penalty. An anxious, agitated Rijkaard was sent off for the first time in his tenure at Barcelona.

That day the football department reached a significant conclusion, deciding that Rijkaard, with a year remaining on his contract, had to go.

Laporta continued to dither but, to be prepared, Marc Ingla (vice-president) and Txiki Beguiristain set about drawing up a Plan B. Ingla, a successful businessman with a background in marketing, wanted to approach the recruitment in the same way that any other major corporation would set about hiring a senior executive: utilising a methodical and analytical selection process followed by an interview stage, before finally making an appointment. This was a novel approach in the world of Spanish football.

As Luis Martín of *El País* explains, 'A profile of the new manager was drawn up, including a set of criteria that the candidate had to fulfil: he should respect the footballing style inherited from Rijkaard; promote a solid work ethic and group solidarity; supervise the work of the youth teams; place an emphasis on preparation and player recuperation; maintain discipline in the dressing room while being respectful of all opponents and possess a sound knowledge of the Spanish league. Furthermore, the next manager of FC Barcelona would have to have a feel and understanding for the club, its values, significance and history.'

Ingla and Beguiristain began with a long list of potential candidates. Manuel Pellegrini, Arsène Wenger and Michael Laudrup did not survive the cut when the names they had written down were reduced to their final preferences. They were left with a three-man short list containing the names of the Espanyol coach and former Barcelona player Ernesto Valverde, Pep Guardiola and José Mourinho. Valverde's name was soon erased from the list once it became clear that too few board members were prepared to back him. It came down to Guardiola or Mourinho.

One lacked experience, but was performing miracles with the B team and was very much a 'Barcelona' man; the other might not have had the club's DNA coursing through his veins, but he ticked just about every other box and had the support of several key board members – including another marketing man and economic vice-president, Ferran Soriano, who said privately at the time: 'The Mourinho brand, added to the Barça brand, has the potential to make our product enormous.'

In January 2008, Marc Ingla and Txiki Beguiristain insisted upon arranging a meeting with Mourinho, and travelled to Portugal to interview him and his agent, Jorge Mendes, who had a good working relationship with the club because he also represented the Barcelona pair of Deco and Rafa Márquez.

The meeting took place in a branch of a famous Lisbon bank, a venue suggested by Mendes to avoid any unwanted attention. Txiki's flight was delayed and when he arrived he found Ingla had already begun interviewing the Portuguese manager. Mourinho presented the Barcelona directors with a memory stick, containing a summary of his football philosophy and a strategy for Barça.

It revealed how he planned to evolve their classic 4-3-3 using a different midfield – similar to the one he left at Chelsea with players like Essien, Makelele and Lampard. It also included a list of potential recruits and the names of those who would be first out of the door at the Camp Nou. He had even drawn up a short list of names he proposed as ideal candidates for the role of his number two at the Camp Nou: Luis Enrique, Sergi Barjuan, Albert Ferrer or even Pep Guardiola. It became very clear that Mourinho had been very well briefed about every aspect of Barcelona's current malaise, unsurprising once it transpired that his assistant, André Villas-Boas, had become a regular visitor to the Camp Nou and had been compiling detailed reports for him.

Mourinho told the Barcelona envoys that, while he wasn't always comfortable with the ill feeling generated between the Catalan club and Chelsea throughout their recent clashes in the Champions League, he explained that elements of his behaviour in front of the media were a necessary evil: a vital cog in the psychological machinery that he used to win football matches. Mourinho explained how, for him, a game starts and frequently finishes at a press conference.

It was the first time that Ingla and Beguiristain had ever sat face to face with José Mourinho and the pair were impressed by his charisma and his clear football methodology. They returned to Barcelona feeling positive in spite of Mourinho's financial stipulations: he wanted a two-year contract at €9 million per season and €1 million for each of his assistants.

There was one 'but' – the issue of José's behaviour in front of the media. The two Barcelona representatives were left with a sense of unease about Mourinho's admission that he would continue to fight his battles in a psychological war on and off the pitch. They were torn: they liked Mourinho face to face, but found his double identity unsettling – struggling to come to terms with how he could be utterly charming in private, but happy to cultivate such a 'disrespectful' public image if he felt that was called for when fighting battles for 'his' team. His previous wrongful accusations against Frank Rijkaard – that the Barcelona coach had visited referee Anders Frisk's dressing room during half-time at the Nou Camp, in the first leg of the Champions League knockout stages that Chelsea went on to lose 2–1 – were still fresh in the memory.

Yet, despite the good vibes at the meeting with Mourinho, Beguiristain had come to the conclusion that Guardiola was the right man for the job and he gradually managed to persuade his colleagues, including Marc Ingla, that Pep's inexperience should not be an obstacle. Some people didn't need convincing: Johan Cruyff had never wanted Mourinho at the club and Pep's old friend and board member, Evarist Murtra, was already on board.

The nail in the coffin for Mourinho was when word of the meeting was leaked by his inner circle, providing Barcelona with the perfect excuse to rule him out. Nevertheless, it had never been a straightforward decision, as Ingla admits now: 'We weren't entirely conclusive with Mou when it came to ruling him out as Barça coach.' The Portuguese manager, after waiting for a proposal from Barcelona that never came, signed a deal with Inter Milan that summer.

Txiki, allied with José Ramón Alexanko, Barcelona's academy director, informed the other directors that his first choice was Guardiola. 'I explained to the board why I wanted Guardiola, rather than why I didn't want another coach,' Beguiristain recalls. He told the board that he was aware of the risks when it came to Pep's managerial experience, but that, as a successful former Barcelona player and captain, Guardiola understood the club and the players better than anyone else; that he had a grasp of how to work with key sections of the media; he understood the Catalan mentality and could deal with the internal and public disputes. And if that wasn't enough, he was displaying all the signs of developing into an outstanding coach.

Txiki, confident the board would eventually back him, even told Rijkaard that Mourinho was not going to be the chosen one, as the media had predicted; that he would be very surprised when he found out who it was going to be.

By March 2008, the football department and key board members had made their minds up: Rijkaard had to go – and the ideal replacement was right under their noses. Guardiola was their man.

Now they just had to convince Laporta, the president.

From January of that season, Joan Laporta accompanied Txiki and Johan Cruyff to a few Barcelona B games. Pep sensed that all eyes were on him but he was not even sure himself if he was necessarily the best solution for the first team. In fact, after witnessing Barcelona beat Celtic in a deserved 2–3 Champions League victory in Glasgow in February – where the Catalans displayed their class to end Celtic's formidable European home record – Pep wondered if that might prove the turning point for Rijkaard's team. He even told people close to the Barcelona board that he thought as much, that the team was getting back to their best and that they ought to stick with the Dutch coach.

But, soon after, Deco and Messi got injured and the team started to decline once again. Then the unthinkable happened, the nightmare scenario for every Barcelona fan and player: fate decreed that the first game after Real Madrid mathematically became La Liga champions would be against their bitter rivals. It meant that the Barça players would have to suffer the ultimate humiliation and form a *pasillo* – a guard of honour – to welcome the Madrid players on to the pitch in front of an ecstatic Bernabéu. In an act that was seen as an abandonment of their team-mates, Deco and Eto'o made themselves ineligible for the Clásico by deliberately picking up two seemingly ridiculous yellow cards in the previous game against Valencia, their fifth of the season that led to a one-game suspension for each footballer.

The key players in the side, the Catalans and home-grown talents, had had enough: they wanted a change, they wanted Guardiola, who was an icon for their generation. On several occasions, senior footballers visited Joan Laporta to describe to the president the unsustainable situation in the dressing room.

Their intervention in day-to-day life at the club helped prevent the dressing room from completely tearing itself apart and, alongside Puyol and Xavi, players like Iniesta, Valdés and even Messi stepped up to the plate and worked hard to restore some pride and order. It was a significant moment in the career and development of Lionel Messi who started out in the first team being seen as Ronaldinho's protégé, but, as the Brazilian became increasingly wayward, Messi avoided the threat of being dragged down the same path by seeking out more responsible mentors in the forms of Xavi and Puyol. It was the right choice.

Guardiola could not help but witness the real depth of the disarray within the first team. He was aware of the situation; he was being informed by senior players and some of the evidence started leaking into the press. He finally also came to the conclusion that Barcelona needed a change the day his youngsters played behind closed doors against the A team. Guardiola discovered Rijkaard smoking a cigarette, something of a habit for the Dutch boss. Ronaldinho was taken off after ten minutes, Deco was clearly tired and the reserve boys, still in the third division, were running the first team ragged. A member of Rijkaard's staff approached Guardiola and asked him to tell his players to ease off a little. Pep had doubted if he was ready to manage the first team, but this told him one thing: he could do a better job of it than was currently being done.

With Pep now finally on board the Guardiola bandwagon, there was still the president to convince.

Joan Laporta wasn't just wrestling with his loyalty to Rijkaard and the star players who had brought him so much joy, the culmination of a dream, at the Champions League final in Paris a few years earlier, the second European Cup for the institution. He wanted to be remembered as a president who had kept faith with a single coach throughout his tenure. There was also the perfectly understandable fear of handing over control of one of the biggest clubs in the world to a man whose managerial experience amounted to about eight months with a team four divisions down from the top flight. And while all of the board were now convinced, there were just as many friends and journalists telling him, 'Don't do it, Joan, it's suicidal, it's reckless.' And then, of course, in a city as political as Barcelona, there was also the fact that Pep had backed his rival in the 2003 elections. Nevertheless, Laporta finally relented and at least agreed to take Pep out to dinner and discuss the future.

In February 2008, they met in the Drolma restaurant of the aptly named Majestic Hotel in the centre of Barcelona, a Michelin-starred venue that was to provide the setting for one of the defining moments in the history of the club.

After the pair had worked their way through a bottle and a half of fine wine, Laporta finally felt ready to tackle the elephant in the room. According to the Barcelona journalist and expert on the club, Jordi Pons, the conversation went as follows:

'In principle, if everything goes well, Frank Rijkaard will continue managing the team, but if not; well, we've thought about you. You could be Frank's replacement,' suggested the president, testing the water.

'If Frank doesn't continue ...' Pep mused out loud.

'As it stands right now, Rijkaard will carry on if the team qualifies for the Champions League final. But if he goes, you will be the coach of Barcelona,' Laporta clarified.

'You wouldn't have the balls to do that!' blurted Guardiola at his purest, most honest. And those words would become the title of a fascinating insight into Pep written by Jordi Pons.

Pep recalls that the wine might have played a small part in his reaction.

'But would you take it or not?'

Pep gave Laporta one of his trademark cheeky grins – the kind we've frequently seen in press conferences and that many a time got a skinny lad out of trouble in a village square in Santpedor.

'Yes,' Pep said. 'Yes, I would do it because you know I would win the league.'

The day after that meeting, Pep's alcohol-inspired boldness was turning into self-doubt. He confided in his faithful assistant, Tito Vilanova, repeating to him the previous night's conversation he'd had with the president: 'If they dismiss Frank, they want me to take over the first team. Do you think we're ready?' His friend didn't hesitate to answer: 'You? You're more than ready.'

Laporta – as he had told Pep over dinner – presented Rijkaard with an ultimatum: he needed to bring home the Champions League trophy to save his career at Barcelona. At that moment, the Dutchman, aware that Guardiola was the chosen one to replace him, responded with a selfless gesture that illustrates perfectly why he has retained the love and respect of so many, including his president. Rijkaard suggested that, for the good of the club, it would be a great idea to include Pep immediately as a member of first-team staff to smooth the transition and prepare for the following season. Pep preferred to stay put and finish the job with his B team.

Nevertheless, Ingla and Txiki set out a plan for the rest of the season which saw them working and consulting simultaneously with both Rijkaard and Pep, talking about players, injuries and recoveries and principally how to shake up the working model of the club. The primary goal was to professionalise the first team. With the approval of both coaches, negotiations intensified for the purchases of Seydou Keita, Dani Alves, Alexander Hleb, Gerard Piqué and Martín Cáceres.

Not much was improving behind closed doors at the first team, though.

Ronaldinho had disappeared from the line-up and didn't even make the bench these days. He played his last game in a Barcelona shirt, the 1–2 defeat to Villarreal, two months before the end of a second trophyless season. A series of suspicious injuries were to blame for Ronnie's absences and, during that period, he was more of a regular at the Bikini Club than at the Camp Nou.

He also missed the semi-finals of the Champions League against Manchester United at the end of April. Barça were held to a 0–0 draw at home against United and then lost 1–0 to a Paul Scholes goal at Old Trafford. Immediately afterwards, in Manchester airport's departure lounge, on the way home from the match, the imminent departure of Frank Rijkaard became clear. On one side of the lounge was Laporta, visibly worried and deep in discussion with Ingla and Beguiristain; and on the other side, isolated and alone, was the Dutch coach.

Five days later the board made the formal decision that Pep Guardiola would be the new coach of FC Barcelona. Remarkably, it was to be the first time that a kid from La Masía had progressed through all the junior categories to finally end up as the boss of the first team. On Tuesday 6 May 2008, Laporta asked Pep's friend and club director Evarist Murtra to accompany him to the Dexeus clinic in Barcelona to congratulate Guardiola on the birth of his third child, Valentina. There he told Pep that he would be the next Barcelona coach.

Cristina, Pep's long-time partner, was concerned. 'Don't worry,' said Pep. 'It'll all turn out fine, you'll see.'

Guardiola, in typical fashion, kept the big news of his promotion to himself, not even warning his parents that he was about to fulfil his dream until a few hours before Laporta made the official announcement two days later. 'The day that the deal is done you will be the first to find out', Pep kept telling his dad, Valentí, who, like all Barcelona fans, had heard the rumours. 'In the meantime, just worry about Barça B.'

So, on 8 May 2008, with the season still not finished for Rijkaard but with the Dutchman's blessing, Laporta released an official club statement: Josep Guardiola i Sala would be the new first-team coach. It was the morning after the guard of honour for Real Madrid at the Bernabéu.

'We went for him because of his football knowledge', Laporta told the press. 'He knows a lot about this club and he loves attacking football. In fact he is the Dream Team in one package. He has a football brain – but at the same time he's educated, always alert, always curious, always thinking football. The imprint we have always liked at Barcelona.'

Curiously, Pep was not even present during Laporta's press conference and the club had publicly announced their deal with him without ever having finalised the details of his contract. Not that the issue of money was ever going to stand between Guardiola and the Nou Camp. He was offered a two-year deal and he accepted. His agent, Josep María Orobitg, tried to negotiate a third year and a single bonus for winning the three main titles but they didn't reach an agreement. 'Whatever you do is good for me', Pep said to his representative. He just wanted a fair deal and agreed a modest fixed sum plus variables. In fact, if he failed to secure the bonus, he'd end up being the fourth worst paid manager in La Liga. Not a problem. 'If I do well, they should pay me; if I don't then I'm no good to them, I'll go home and play golf', Pep told Orobitg.

There was going to be an official media presentation once the season had finished in June, this time with Pep Guardiola present as he'd insisted upon waiting until he had finished what he had started with Barça B. They had beaten Europa 1–0 at home in their final game and were proclaimed champions of regional group V of the third division; but they would still need to secure a place in the national Second B division via the play-offs. After impressively overcoming the two ties at El Castillo in Gran Canaria and at Barbastre, promotion was assured.

On 17 June in the Paris Hall of the Camp Nou, Pep Guardiola, at thirty-seven, was officially unveiled as the new manager of FC Barcelona. On the way to the room a confident Pep told an anxious Laporta again: 'Relax. You've done the right thing. We are going to win the league.'

The president had every reason to be worried. Despite Guardiola's self-belief, in spite of the faith placed in the new coach by the football brains at the club, it was still a huge gamble and these were troubling times for the president of an institution in the doldrums. A team that had dazzled Europe a few seasons earlier had collapsed spectacularly, the squad needed a major overhaul, brave decisions had to be taken over some of the biggest stars in the game and Laporta's popularity was at an all-time low. Barcelona were in turmoil. Nothing seemed to work, even reliable sides of the club like the basketball and handball teams, were failing. The football team finished 18 points behind Madrid in La Liga and Laporta couldn't stop a motion of censure in the summer – fans had had enough of his arrogant style. In fact, 60 per cent of the 39,389 votes were against the president. But the motion didn't go through because to succeed two-thirds majority was required. So Laporta didn't stand down. He survived. Just.

'That summer nobody outside the club had any faith in Pep, nor the team,' Gerard Piqué, one of Pep's first signings, recalls now. The papers were full of negative opinions about Pep's controversial appointment: 'it was too soon for him', 'surely he was too inexperienced' went the consensus. But then again, FC Barcelona and Pep Guardiola didn't do things like everyone else.

Part III

Pep, the Manager

1
THE BEGINNINGS

The gift of opportunity – you either have it or you don't. And Guardiola's appointment had it. It had been a hard few years for the Catalans. The debate over the new Catalan Constitution, that demanded more independence from central government, exposed the lack of enthusiasm the rest of the country had in understanding the Catalans' need to differentiate themselves from the rest of Spain. Rijkaard's Barcelona was suffering an unstoppable decline into decadence, the dressing room lacking discipline and team spirit. The star of the team, Ronaldinho, had lost his status as the most exciting player on the planet. The president, Joan Laporta, facing a motion of censure, had only just survived in office. Catalan self-esteem was at its lowest ebb for decades.

At that point Pep Guardiola was appointed first team coach of FC Barcelona.

Pep lacked the complete support of the Barcelona fanbase. Some of those who did back him felt that his status would at least make the wins sweeter and the defeats easier to swallow; after all, never before had a ball boy from the Camp Nou progressed through the youth ranks, captained the first team and then returned to the club as coach. Pep understood the Barcelona mentality perfectly and he knew what was being taught at La Masía. As well as a symbol of the club and a son of the Cruyff school of thought, he represented a way of understanding football as an educative process. On many levels, it was a match made in heaven.

On the day of his official presentation as coach of Barcelona, Guardiola made it very clear that he knew what he had to do and, with his parents looking on, he outlined his project.

However, in the minds of the many onlookers – even his supporters – was the nagging doubt that, after just twelve months in charge of a reserve side, his extremely limited experience as a coach was inadequate preparation for the colossal task ahead; and there were many who suspected that his appointment by Laporta was little more than a cynical ploy to boost the president's popularity and an attempt to exploit the club's prodigal son as a shield against the growing criticism of his tenure. There were also those who questioned whether Pep, as much as they had adored him as a player, was simply too fragile, too sensitive and lacking in the strength of character required.

Pep was aware of the doubts, but he never asked for a honeymoon period, patience or time to make mistakes: it was clear to him that he had to hit the ground running and get off to a winning start. Guardiola knew as well as anybody the expectations that come with the territory at a big club, where winning is an obligation, defeat always the fault of the coach.

'I feel strong,' announced Pep. 'I'm ready to overcome this challenge and believe me: if I didn't feel that, I wouldn't be here. It will be a tough journey, but I will persevere. The team will run, in case you are worried about that. I will forgive them if they don't grasp it at first – but I will not forgive them for not trying. Absolutely not.

'I am the leader, they follow me and we will achieve. They should follow me.

'I know that we have to start work quickly and intensively, whoever wants to be with us from the start will be welcomed. And the rest, we will win them over in the future.'

Tito Vilanova, his former La Masía stable mate and assistant with the B team, would be his right-hand man with the first team, too: 'At the start of the season he told me, not as advice, because he isn't the type of person to give advice, that we should do what we believe we should do. We have to apply our own idea, we'll see if we win or lose, but we'll do it our way.

'There is not a single trainer, nor player, that can guarantee success at the start of a season,' Guardiola wrote a decade ago. 'Nor are there magic formulae. If there were, this game of football would be as easy as going to the "solutions shop" and buying them all. And in our house, because it is strong, we would pay whatever the cost for Barça to be unbeatable. But, clearly, as that is impossible, each club searches for the way to reach their initial objectives, and applying a dose of common sense should be enough. Therefore, it is about knowing what you want and what type of players you need to reach your goal. Because Barça is such a big team, it is in a position to have both things: it can choose the way it plays and what type of players it wants.'

To begin with, this meant two significant things: continuing and persisting with the model of play and getting rid of Ronaldinho, Deco and Eto'o.

Armchair fans might think that managing a team of superstars, with the best players in the world at your disposal, is about as straightforward as picking the biggest names in a video game. But managing the egos and personalities in a dressing room at the Camp Nou, under the spotlight of the world's media, with the weight of expectation of an entire nation upon your shoulders must be overwhelming for a thirty-seven-year-old in his first job managing a first team. And that thirty-seven-year-old was about to sever his ties with three of the greatest footballers to have played for the club in recent times.

'We're thinking about the squad without them,' Pep announced during his presentation, flanked by the club president, Joan Laporta, and sporting director, Txiki Beguiristain. 'That's the way I think after analysing questions of performance in the time they have been with the team, and also less tangible questions. It is for the good of the team.

'If they stay in the end, I will give everything so that they join us at the right level.'

It was a revelation. Pep's common-sense approach, his communication skills and the feeling of authenticity you got from his talks, was just the tonic for a club that had, once again, demonstrated its ability to hit the self-destruct button when all seemed to be going so well. Pep Guardiola's press conference conveyed a message of stability, integrity, commitment and responsibility. In the end, Pep won most of the doubters over with a clever ploy, a few well-chosen words and a single bold decision.

Txiki Beguiristain agreed with Guardiola and the decision was agreed with Rijkaard. Pep had been informed of squad movements from the moment he was chosen as a replacement for the Dutch coach. Ronnie had been given one last chance the previous summer – and he'd blown it.

Having decided to get rid of Ronaldinho, Pep now had to tell the Brazilian face to face.

When Guardiola and Ronaldinho met, the conversation was short and swift. Guardiola told him that it wasn't an easy decision to make as he believed there was still an extraordinary player under the puppy fat. But he also felt that his recuperation was not possible at Barcelona, that he would have to return to form somewhere else. Ronaldinho offered no resistance and accepted Pep's suggestion. Within weeks, he was transferred to AC Milan for €21 million, Barça having rejected offers in the region of €70 million the season before. At around the same time, Deco was transferred to Chelsea for €10 million – despite the fact that José Mourinho, who had coached him at Porto, wanted to link up with him at Inter Milan.

Pep possessed genuine self-belief when it came to his capacity to get the message across to his players. Barça had finished the league eighteen points behind Madrid the previous season and, at times like that, sportsmen typically need somebody to show them the way, point out to them how to correct mistakes. He cleansed the dressing room of players who were uncommitted and oblivious of the club's core values: prioritising good football and hard work ahead of individual talent. Before they met for pre-season, Pep received messages from key players in the squad backing his bravery; the squad's leaders were effectively opening the door to the dressing room for him.

Iniesta, for one, could not wait to work with his all-time hero. 'When I was fourteen, I competed in a Nike club competition, which we won, and Pep presented me with the trophy. His brother had told him about me and when he gave me the trophy he said, "Congratulations, I hope to see you in the first team, but wait until I've left!" He was my idol, an example. He represents the values and feelings of Barcelona. Attacking football, respect for team-mates, respect for the fans. And now he was going to be my coach!

'I remember when he greeted us on the first day in the dressing room. He shook my hand and it was something really special because he was a reference for me. I was immediately struck by the confidence he had and that he transmitted to us, he was convinced that everything would go well, he had a lot of faith.' The admiration was mutual. Pep often remembers a conversation he had with Xavi, while they were both watching Iniesta play when he stepped up to the first team. 'Look at that guy. He is going to force us both into retirement!'

In Pep's first summer in charge, Barcelona signed Dani Alves, Cáceres, Piqué, Keita and Hleb, injecting new blood into the team.

With Deco and Ronaldinho gone, Eto'o's situation took a significant twist. Seeing that his two main antagonists had left the club, he rejected all offers and made a pledge of commitment to his new coach. With the Brazilians out of the way, he saw his big opportunity to be the standard-bearer of the team. The leader. Eto'o had always considered that he wasn't getting the recognition or credit he was due and stepping out of Ronaldinho's shadow to take centre stage was one of his obsessions.

The striker exerted a fair amount of influence over Abidal, Henry and Touré, who had the potential to help him flourish, and now – with Messi still developing – Eto'o might finally get to play the leading role he craved. In the dressing room there were certain characteristics of his that would need to be tolerated – the same things that had convinced Guardiola to get rid of him in fact – but he had now been handed a golden opportunity and pre-season would determine his future.

It feels strange to think back to a time when Messi had yet to consolidate himself as the key player in the team, but at that moment, despite his obvious talent, it was felt that handing the baton of responsibility from Ronaldinho to a twenty-one-year-old still nicknamed 'the flea' was too much too soon. As Pep said at his unveiling: 'We can't allow Messi to carry the weight of the team, I don't think it would be good for him or the club.' In the wake of Deco's and Ronaldinho's departure, Guardiola wanted to hand the lion's share of the responsibility over to players who had come up through the ranks, from the youth teams, who had become the standard-bearers of the values of the institution: Puyol, Xavi, Iniesta. Messi, who had previously been at risk of being led astray by the Brazilian group and was going to be fostered into the axis of the team, fitted that same profile.

By giving the power and captaincy to the home-grown players, Pep had, almost seamlessly, even before pre-season had begun, overseen a transition and sent out a clear signal of intent, mapping the way forward for years to come. He also achieved something essential that hadn't been seen at Barcelona for a long time: the club was now in the hands of those who understood it and truly cared for it. It also meant that Guardiola was giving the home-grown players and the academy set-up a boost: a vote of confidence. He'd worked and even played with many of them, others he was friends with. Now they had to repay his trust and faith in them through their performances, hard work and their commitment.

Johan Cruyff was among the first to endorse the new coach's policies: 'Guardiola knows what Barcelona is all about, you need twenty eyes. Guardiola can control these things because he has been through them. I can see that he is capable of doing it because he has made a great deal of decisions in a short space of time.'

When he was Barça's captain under Louis van Gaal, Guardiola once said, 'We always have to respect the guidelines set by the coaches – but it is brilliant for a team that a player can get involved and take on a role on the pitch.' Van Gaal refused to allow the players a free rein to take the initiative and he was unable to rectify things that were going wrong as they were happening. Guardiola believed in handing greater responsibility to the footballers, trusting that their intuition could help solve a great amount of their problems. As a coach, Pep remained true to this idea and was determined to let his charges take the initiative.

Pep also promoted Pedro from the B team to the first team. He needed him for his style of play, a winger who ran into space but who understood the need to give his all at all times, both in training and during matches. Pedro's parents, as Pep often reminds people, had a petrol station in Tenerife and they could rarely see their son play because they didn't have a television in the shop. At the beginning of the summer, Pedro was preparing to go out on loan, but a player who had his feet planted firmly on the ground suited Pep's vision perfectly.

Pedro was moved to the first team alongside Sergio Busquets, another footballer who had shown in the B team the previous season that he had intelligence, focus and a fundamental understanding of his role as a central midfielder. For Pep, it also helped that he didn't have a ridiculous haircut or tattoos – and the new first team coach believed that 'Busi' would at some point prove to have the character to continue in Xavi's and Puyol's footsteps as captain of the team.

Busquets and Pedro were the first of twenty-two players promoted from the youth system to the first team during the four years with Guardiola at the helm. The pair went from playing third division to Champions League football in a matter of weeks, and went on to win the World Cup the following season.

The squad was complete, the balance re-established in terms of authority and credibility. But there was to be an interesting contrast in terms of salaries.

Guardiola would earn one million euros a year gross plus bonuses, nine million less than Eto'o and seven less than Messi. Pep had agreed to join the first team without negotiating his contract. When he signed it, he was the fourth lowest paid coach in Spain. He didn't care.

And finally the first day of pre-season arrived. As Xavi recalls: 'The holidays really dragged out because I wanted to join up with the team.'

Two trophyless years had passed them by. A change was needed. Important decisions had to be made. But, first and foremost, Pep had to get the team on his side. A face-to-face meeting with the squad as a whole was still pending.

It took place on the first day of training at the world-famous St Andrews, in Scotland, in a basement conference room of the hotel where they were staying during the first week of pre-season. It turned out to be the day he set out his stall and transferred his philosophy to the group.

As he made his way to the room, Pep repeatedly told himself: 'Be yourself. Be yourself.' He felt that he had been through a similar experience at least once before, with the B team: the faces were different, new people, there were new objectives – but the ideas that were going to be put across were practically the same. And he had the same nervous feeling in the pit of his stomach.

The squad filled the room in seats set out in rows facing the front, like a classroom, with little room to spare. The medical staff, the assistants, the press guys, everybody who had travelled to Scotland was invited to hear what he had to say. In the following half-hour he put across a message that mesmerised the group, hypnotised as they were by his concepts, requirements and expectations, his sharing of responsibilities and, above all, by his ability to generate a new-found feeling of team spirit.

The players sat in silence, listening to Pep as he paced the room, making eye contact with his listeners, first one, then another, showing a mastery of communication skills. He gestured and chose his words well, finding the right tone, emphasising his ideas.

According to the recollections of many of those present (Xavi, Iniesta, Piqué, Tito, Henry, Eto'o, Messi, fitness coach Emili Ricart, club media staff Chemi Terés and Sergi Nogueras among others) we are able to piece together Pep's words from that pivotal moment.

'Gentlemen, good morning.

'You can imagine what a huge motivation it is for me to be here, to coach this team. It is the ultimate honour. Above all, I love the club. I would never make a decision that would harm or go against the club. Everything I am going to do is based on my love for FC Barcelona. And we need and want order and discipline.

'The team has been through a time when not everybody was as professional as they should have been. It is time for everybody to run and to give their all.

'I've been part of this club for many years and I am aware of the mistakes that have been made in the past, I will defend you to the death but I can also say that I will be very demanding of you all: just like I will be with myself.

'I only ask this of you. I won't tell you off if you misplace a pass, or miss a header that costs us a goal, as long as I know you are giving 100 per cent. I could forgive you any mistake, but I won't forgive you if you don't give your heart and soul to Barcelona.

'I'm not asking results of you, just performance. I won't accept people speculating about performance, if it's half-hearted or people aren't giving their all.

'This is Barça, gentlemen, this is what is asked of us and this is what I will ask of you. You have to give your all.

'A player on his own is no one, he needs his team-mates and colleagues around him: every one of us in this room, the people around you now.

'Many of you don't know me, so we will use the next few days to form the group, a family even. If anyone has any problems, I'm always available, not just in sporting matters but professional, family, environmental. We're here to help each other and make sure there is spiritual peace so that the players don't feel tension or division. We are one. We are not little groups because in all teams this is what ends up killing team spirit.

'The players in this room are very good, if we can't get them to win anything, it will be our fault.

'And let's stick together when times are hard. Make sure that nothing gets leaked to the press. I don't want anybody to fight a battle on his own. Let's be united, have faith in me. As a former player, I have been in your shoes, I know what you are going through, what you are feeling.

'The style comes dictated by the history of this club and we will be faithful to it. When we have the ball, we can't lose it. And when that happens, run and get it back. That is it, basically.'

The squad, the group, was seduced. Not for the last time; far from it.

Upon leaving the room, Xavi commented to a team-mate that everything that they had needed to know was there in that talk. A breath of fresh air, order and discipline. A reminder of the style he wanted to reinforce. All that was established from day one.

There would be many more team talks, but the one at St Andrews laid the foundations for the new era at FC Barcelona.

'There are talks that just come to you and talks that begin from a few ideas based on what you have seen,' Pep said later. 'What you can't do is study the talks, learn them by heart. Two or three concepts are all you need ... and then you have to put your heart into it. You can't deceive the players, they are too well prepared, intelligent, intuitive. I was a footballer and I know what I'm saying. In every talk, from that one in St Andrews to the last one, I have put my heart into them. And when I don't feel it, I don't speak, it's the best way. There are days when you think that you have to say something, but you don't feel it, so at times like that it is better to keep quiet. Sometimes you show them images of the rivals, and sometimes you don't show them a single image of the opposition because on that day you realise, for whatever reason, that in life there are more important things than a football game, you tell them other things, unrelated to the game. Stories of overcoming difficulties, of human beings acting in extraordinary ways. This is the beautiful thing about this job, because each rival, each situation, is different to the previous one and you always have to find that special something, to say to them "Guys, today is important ..." for such and such a reason. It doesn't have to be tactical. When you have been doing it for three or four years it is a lot easier to find. When you have been doing it for four years, with the same players, it is more difficult.'

At St Andrews, Pep knew that his job would consist of reminding the players of some basic, fundamental truths and principles. He knew that many of them had lost their love for football, their hunger – and that it was necessary to create the best conditions for them to return to the pitch. Guardiola, after spending years asking so many questions, had learnt what he had to do from some of the greatest minds in the game.

In terms of the playing staff, after putting his faith in the home-grown players, the coach chose professionals he could trust. And the same principles were applied to his backroom staff, where he decided to go one step further and professionalise the entire set-up: introducing a hand-picked team of specialists to include technical assistants, fitness coaches, personal trainers, doctors, nutritionists, physiotherapists, players' assistants, analysts, press officers and even handymen. The control and evaluation of training sessions and competitions was exhaustive, both at an individual level and as a group; recovery work was individualised and personalised.

All of them shared one thing in common: they were all *culés* (Barça fans). Xavi explains that this simple yet rare common attribute at a modern club was central to the group's ability to unite and feel that they were pulling in the same direction from day one: 'We're all *culés*. We give it our all and we all share the glory.'

Pep's right-hand man, Tito Vilanova, is a friend but also an exceptional match and team analyst. Notebook in hand, in the first season in the reserves he surprised people with his talent for strategies that turned out to be key to the team's promotion to the Second Division B. Such was his rapport with Guardiola that there were no doubts as to his selection when Pep was offered the job with the first team. And they became a tandem. 'I would mention something to Tito,' Pep says. 'If he keeps quiet, I know I have to convince him. If his face doesn't change it is probably because I got it wrong.' Always in the corner of the shot when the cameras zoom in on Guardiola during matches, Tito was there in his tracksuit, giving opinions and advising Pep on the bench. They complemented each other perfectly, as Tito points out: 'I am really at ease with Pep because he gives me a kind of lead role, he listens to me and gives me a voice within the team.'

Watching the players train one morning while still in Scotland, Pep pointed at Puyol and asked Tito, 'What do you make of what he did just then?' 'First, we need to know why he did it,' Tito said.

Pep halted play. 'Not like that!' Pep Guardiola, 'the coach', took over. 'Puyi! You shouldn't leave your marker until the ball is released for the pass.' But Barça's captain did what no one else did. 'I did it because the other forward had managed to pull away from his marker,' he replied, while inviting Tito to join in the debate: 'Isn't that right, Tito?' Pep listened to the reasoning and then went on to explain: 'You're right, but ...', proceeding then to give Puyol a lengthy, profound talk about how he should position himself on the pitch. A talk like so many others he would give during his first pre-season at St Andrews.

'We all know how to play football, but very few of us know the type of football that the coach wants us to play,' Dani Alves said at the time. 'At first, he would halt many training sessions to correct us, to explain what he wanted from us,' Piqué recalls; 'but we are grateful to him for that because we'll soon be coordinated and we will be able to transfer his ideas on to the pitch.' With a special focus on Messi (Pep spent a great deal of time working on his defensive game), the new coach had one overriding message he wanted to transmit to the entire squad: 'I want them all to understand that they can be much better as a team.'

Although he wanted an element of democracy within the group, with players using their initiative, making suggestions and keeping an open mind to new ideas, Guardiola did not delay in imposing a number of strict rules in his first few days in charge: such as insisting upon the use of Castilian and Catalan as the only languages spoken among the group, arranging a seating plan at meal times to encourage the players to mix and to prevent the team forming up into different cultural or national groups and cliques. However, his rules and the imposition of fines for those breaking them were not introduced as a measure to keep the players under strict control, but, rather, as a means to encourage a stronger sense of solidarity and responsibility. Two years later, Pep abolished his own system of sanctions and penalties, feeling that they had become unnecessary with the group exercising an impressive degree of self-discipline.

In life there are two ways of telling people what to do: either give them orders or set an example and encourage them to follow it. Pep is very much of the latter school of thought. In the modern game, if a coach does not know how to handle the different characters and varying individuals' needs, then he will struggle to lead. Guardiola has a psychological edge, experience and intuition, which helps him detect any problem and in Barcelona's dressing room he surrounded himself with people he could trust who were capable of helping him intervene at the right moment.

'I didn't know the boss or how he worked,' Eric Abidal remembers. 'The first month was difficult, because I'm a father, I'm thirty years old, and you don't speak in the same way to a young player who has just started in professional football, as you would to a veteran. And he was doing exactly that! He made us change who we sat with at meal times and he made me speak in Castilian with Henry when we were with the group. I went to speak to the president, Laporta, to tell him that I wouldn't tolerate it, that I wanted to leave, but he told me to calm down, that it was his way of doing things and that everything would go well. Now, I still laugh with the boss when we think about it.'

Pep continued the methodologies and practices introduced at St Andrews when the team returned to their base in Barcelona, where he went even further in overhauling the daily habits of the players and the club. The new training complex was shaped very much according to Pep's instructions, to such an extent that today it epitomises Barça's philosophy. Guardiola changed things so that the players felt like employees of a football club and not Hollywood stars, in the knowledge that success was achieved through hard work, not just having fun. A dining room was designed to encourage all the players to sit down at meal times together, something commonplace in Italy but previously unknown in the first team at FC Barcelona.

Whereas previous training sessions that used to take place on a training pitch next door to the Nou Camp had a fairly high-profile feel about them because of their location, the Joan Gamper Training Ground, to which the first team had moved in January 2009, was strictly off limits to press and public on a daily basis. It was such a revolutionary step that the media christened it 'La Ciudad Prohibida' – 'The Forbidden City'.

During their eleven-hour chats in Rosario, Argentina, Marcelo Bielsa told Pep all about his thoughts on the media – as well as everything else – and insisted that it was wrong to give priority access to a big television company over a small newspaper. Pep followed suit and introduced a new rule at Barcelona whereby he refused to give one-to-one interviews so as to avoid favouritism and getting drawn into media politics. From day one, Pep decided that he would speak to the press, but only at press conferences. He stopped taking calls from local journalists and avoided meeting them in private.

He also bucked the Spanish tradition of getting the team together in a hotel the day before a match. As Guardiola explained at the time, 'People don't spend the day before they go to work locked up in a hotel. We just try to make things the same for them. If they don't rest, they're not looking after themselves and that means they'll play worse and lose their jobs. I judge my players on the work they do, not on their private lives. I'm not a policeman. I'm in bed at ten o'clock and I've got no urge to go and check up on my players. That's why I'd rather have them at home and not cooped up in a hotel with nothing to do. We're just trying to use common sense.'

Pep's line of thinking was clearly the experience of a former top player at one of the world's biggest clubs, now capable of empathising with the modern star as a manager, or so Xavi thinks: 'For me, two of the most important novelties were the move to the training ground and getting rid of the hotel meetings. Working at the training ground gave us a lot of peace of mind and allowed us greater co-existence. It helped too that he made us eat together after training sessions. What is more, that way we watch our diet. I recognise that, at the start, it was a bit of a pain for me because I couldn't make plans, but you get used to it straight away and you realise that it is of benefit to you. With the meetings it was the same. I wasn't used to being at home a couple of hours before the match and at first it was very strange for me. I felt like I wasn't well prepared. It felt like I was too switched off. I even thought that fate would punish me with a bad game for not giving 100 per cent of my time to it beforehand. But I soon realised that, with these new rules, I would also benefit. Thinking too much can put too much pressure on you; this turns into nerves and I have learnt to analyse what is really important. Minimising the meetings reduces our stress levels all year round.'

'I can't promise titles but I am convinced that the fans will be proud of us,' he said on 17 June 2008 in the press conference at which he was presented as the new manager of FC Barcelona. 'I give you my word that we will put in an effort. I don't know if we'll win, but we'll persist. Fasten your seat belts, you are going to enjoy the ride,' he said on 16 August 2008 at his presentation at the Camp Nou in front of a stadium full of fans.

Guardiola's first competitive game as first-team coach of FC Barcelona had arrived. Because of the team's third-placed finish the previous season, the opening game would be in the third qualifying round of the Champions League. Barça comfortably beat Polish club Wisła Kraków 4–0 at home. They then lost 1–0 in Kraków, but progressed with a 4–1 aggregate victory. The Pep era had begun with qualification for the Champions League proper.

'I was an unknown quantity when I came in, and the first thing I asked the team to do was to put their trust in me,' Pep remembers. 'I told them everything would work out fine. I wanted the fans to see that the team was going to work hard, run, play good football, and take pride in their work on the pitch. People want to be entertained. They don't want to be cheated. The fans can accept a poor performance but they won't take it when you choose not to put in the effort. The team's come on and we've made changes and tweaked a few things here and there. The idea is still the same as it has always been in this house, though: to attack, score as many goals as possible, and play as well as we can.'

A coach is everything and nothing at the same time: nothing, because without the right tools at his disposal he's unable to achieve greatness. But he's smart enough to know that his job is vital to create the right environment and conditions for his players to fulfil their potential; it is what makes the difference between converting a good group of players into an excellent team. And that was something that Pep managed to achieve from day one, without allowing nagging doubts and questions such as 'what if it this doesn't work?' to interfere.

On one occasion Guardiola explained that there are two types of coaches: those who think problems solve themselves and those who solve problems. Guardiola belongs to the group that seeks solutions. That is his real passion.

The game. Seeing what the opponent does. Deciding the players you will use. That is the moment that 'makes sense' of the profession – the search for the solution, the decision that will change a game, that will win a game.

Often for Pep, the moment when it all becomes clear in his head occurs to him in a subterranean office in the Camp Nou. Pep's office is not much bigger than four square metres, receives lots of direct light and contains a handful of books and a table lamp. There is also a plasma screen to analyse both his team's and their rivals' games, which he paid for out of his own pocket.

If, in the middle of the almost spiritual process, engrossed in his analysis, somebody knocked on the door of his office, they would find it impossible to get his full attention. Some brave soul might try to talk to him, but he would look through them rather than at them. He wouldn't be listening. In his mind he would still be watching the videos of the rivals even if his eyes were not on the screen. 'OK, let's talk later,' he'd say, politely ushering his visitor out. And then Pep would turn his attention to visualising the game that would take place a couple of days later. Searching for that flash of inspiration, that moment, the magical moment: 'I've got it. I've got it. This is how we are going to win.' If it were up to him, he would get rid of everything else in football except that spark.

For Guardiola, tactical concepts are taken in if the players have the right attitude and understand what they are doing. The essence that he transmits is that the team should be in order, and ordered, through the ball. He talks to the players about position, imbalance, balance, circulation – ultimately, the desire to win, working to be the best.

'In the world of football there is only one secret: I've got the ball or I haven't. Barcelona has opted for having the ball although it is legitimate for others not to want it. And when we haven't got the ball is when we have to get it back because we need it.'

Since his coaching debut, Guardiola has never tired of repeating that Johan Cruyff was the inspiration for his approach and this sense of continuity has been a good thing for the club. It's allowed several factors to become well established so that, in the future, projects won't have to be started from scratch. 'We are a little bit like disciples of the essence that Cruyff brought here,' said Guardiola, who wrote more than a decade ago that 'Cruyff wanted us to play that way, on the wings and using the wingers, and I apply that whole theory ahead of everything. It was he, Johan, who imposed the criteria for quick movements of the ball, the obligation to open up the field in order to find space. To fill the centre of the pitch in order to play having numerical superiority, and, I don't know, introduce a lot more things so that everybody knew how Barça played and, above all, so it would be known how to do it in the future. And that, in short, is the greatest thing that Cruyff left us. The idea of playing in a way that no team has done before in Spain seduces me. It is a sign of distinction, a different way of experiencing football, a way of life, a culture.'

But Cruyff was not the only influence upon Pep's footballing philosophy. Louis van Gaal's Ajax was a team that hypnotised him and he admitted to applying some of their methods. 'The question is that that Ajax team always gave me the impression that they tried to and could do all of the following: play, sacrifice themselves as a team, shine individually and win games. All the players, of different quality, without exception, were aware of their mission on the field of play. They demonstrated a tactical discipline and enormous capacity to apply all of that at just the right time.'

As Jorge Valdano says, Pep is 'a Catalan son of the Dutch school of football'. But Pep isn't a simple transmitter of ideas, as journalist Ramón Besa explains: 'Rather, he takes the message, improves it and spreads it with greater credibility.'

According to Víctor Valdés: 'He insisted a lot on tactical concepts, on the system of play. His philosophy is clear: first we should have the ball. With it, the opponent suffers and we have everything under control. Secondly, we try not to lose the ball in compromising positions since it could cause a dangerous situation. If they take the ball off us, it should be through the opponent's own merits, not through our mistakes. The third aspect is the pressure in the rival's half. We must bite, be very intense. We already did that with Rijkaard, but he put more emphasis on it. Each player has a zone in which they should apply pressure. We should all help each other. You can't lose concentration ever. Guardiola says that these three concepts are our strong point, one of the things he repeats most in the dressing room. When we apply all three, everything works.'

'While we attack, the idea is to always keep your position, always being in the place you have to be. There is dynamism, mobility, but the position has always got to be filled by someone. So if we lose the ball it will be difficult for the rival to get us on the counter-attack – if we attack in order it becomes easier to then hunt down the opposite player with the ball when we lose possession.'

He gave a different edge to the defensive side of the game and that is where Barça became strong and attractive: losing the ball but then, within five seconds, trying to win it back. The principle is simple and comes from as far back as van Gaal: after losing the ball there are five seconds of pressure to win it back; if it isn't recovered, the defensive phase would begin and players should quickly drop back.

'The better we attack, the better we defend.'

Remember how football was played when Guardiola arrived as the first-team coach of Barcelona – generally with a double defensive partnership and six players behind the ball. Pep, taking advantage of the talent at his disposal, looked for a braver approach: he preferred a system with a single midfielder and two wide men. That way he liberated Messi and, in search of the ideal footballers for the other roles, he discovered Pedro and Busquets.

As the coach and journalist Lluís Lainz writes, 'In his first season, Guardiola radically altered concepts such as starting moves from the defence, using the centre backs as creators of moves; he gave the team greater depth with the constant incorporation of the wingers; he increased the rhythm of the movement off the ball; he worked tirelessly on creating space via the constant movement of players; he developed the concepts of numerical and positional superiority to the maximum level.' He ultimately knew how to manage the concepts of time and space with such ease and fluidity that many observers were under the impression that what the team was doing was easy, when, in reality, there is nothing more difficult in the modern game.

'Discover constantly where the free man is and through passing, passing, passing, work the ball into forward positions.'

The high technical quality of Barcelona's players enabled them to make passes that other teams simply could not even attempt; Xavi, Iniesta, Messi could receive the ball and pass or move out of the tightest of corners. But Guardiola revolutionised football because he used a Cruyff idea and made it a method: always accumulate more players than your rival right from the start of a move to gain the initiative. So, having three players near the ball if the other team have two, or four players if they have three. This is how Ricard Torquemada explains it in his superb *Formula Barça*: 'This formula of numerical superiority doesn't guarantee anything, because in the end everything depends on the ability, precision and concentration of the 'artists', taking advantage of space and making the right decisions, but there will always be an unmarked player and, therefore, a safe 'pass line' that can be used. In this way, football becomes a sport with a ball and spaces.'

As time went on, Pep's first-team squad was increasingly in a position to go out on to the pitch with a clear idea of what the game was going to be like, the characteristics of the rivals both individually and as a group, and what had to be done to beat them. Yet within that meticulous preparation there co-existed a high degree of expression, always bearing in mind that this is football, that players must think in tenths of a second and that there should be some freedom to show on the pitch, to do things that weren't planned off it.

'The players need to know that they mustn't be scared of trying, nor of losing the ball because that is what football is like. Messi knows that he can always make moves because he knows that he has ten players behind him to help him out if necessary. When both the defender and the forward feel important, we are with a winning team.'

'He went through all the mechanisms that bring the game plan closer to the rival's goal,' explains Martí Perarnau in his exceptional analysis of Barcelona, *The Champion's Path* (*Senda de Campeones*).

'Xavi, Iniesta and Messi began that stage with the orders of staying close to the area. Xavi didn't sit very deep so his participation with Messi on the right, Eto'o in the middle and Iniesta on the other side took place often. Little by little, the plan changed because one of the pillars of Pep's methods is based on the evolution of the process. Guardiola has never believed in absolute truths, which gives him flexibility when it comes to interpreting life. So Xavi moved into a deeper position with the intention of bringing back his direct opponent, distancing them from their centre backs and, in that way, creating more space for Messi in the back of the midfield.'

'To avoid losing the ball and being caught on the counter-attack, the concept of the "third man" is useful: throw the ball long and in front of him in a wide area. You avoid risks. Cruyff used to tell me, "when you have the ball, the first thing you have to do is look who is further away from you. He probably has some space in front of him. Normally play to the man closer to you or available, but if the first thing you can do is to play long, play long. That way you avoid counter-attacks."'

When Barcelona concede a goal in a counterattack the accusation against the team is always the same – the defenders were exposed. But it is a risk taken willingly and avoided with keeping possession. In any case, the defenders were protected by a defensive midfielder who helped with the build-up from the back but also could sit next to the two centre backs if the full backs have decided to go forward, which happened almost in every move. Keita and Sergi Busquets filled that role till it became clear that the latter was born for the job. In the eyes of Pep and even Vicente del Bosque, he is the best in the world in that position.

'The right attitude is the most important thing when defending. We can talk about a thousand concepts but what unites a team, what helps players defend, is the right attitude. If you want to, you can run for your team-mate because doing that he would improve; it is not about making your team-mate better, but making yourself better.'

To the man in the street, the mention of Barcelona was always synonymous with attacking football, and one of the great misconceptions about Pep's Barcelona was that their football was entirely focused on scoring at the expense of defending. But Guardiola's thinking would surprise many. For example, when Barça failed to score, the first thing he looked at was how his side were defending. Again, counter-intuitive and in defiance of conventional wisdom. So, for example, Abidal explains that before he arrived at Barcelona, every time he was called into action on the pitch, as a defender he'd been taught to focus on winning the ball. As soon as he arrived at Barcelona, he was taught to think one step ahead about what he could do with it once he'd got hold of it. 'Now, every time I get the ball I know what I should do because I have learnt to understand the game.'

There is a final tactical insight that is fascinating.

'One of the best things that FC Barcelona do is run with the ball to provoke or tease, not to dribble.'

A trick to test an opponent, to pull them out of position to create space, leads them where you want them. In a chat with Wayne Rooney, the Manchester United forward told me that he watched Xavi doing that often: 'He waits for one of us to get close to make the pass.'

André Villas-Boas is fascinated by it, too. 'There are more spaces in football than people think. Even if you play against a deep-lying team, you immediately get half of the pitch. You can provoke the opponent with the ball, provoke him to move forward or sideways and open up a space. But many players can't understand the game. They can't think about or read the game. Things have become too easy for football players: high salaries, a good life, with a maximum of five hours' work a day and so they can't concentrate, can't think about the game.

'Barcelona's players are completely the opposite,' continues the former Chelsea coach, 'Their players are permanently thinking about the game, about their movement.

'Guardiola has talked about it: the centre backs provoke the opponent, invite them forward, then, if the opponent applies quick pressure, the ball goes to the other central defender and this one makes a vertical pass – not to the midfielders, who have their back turned to the ball, but to those moving between lines, Andrés Iniesta or Lionel Messi, or even directly to the striker. Then they play the second ball with short lay-offs, either to the wingers who have cut inside or the midfielders, who now have the game in front of them. They have an enormous capacity not to lose the ball, to do things with an unbelievable precision. But Barça's 4-3-3 wouldn't work in England, because of the higher risk of losing the ball.'

The possibility of making it work in England is something that Pep Guardiola often wondered about. He has asked at least two Premier League players if they could start a move as his players did at Barcelona, despite the risk of losing possession close to their own goal. Does the Premiership, he asked, have the quality of footballers with the confidence and understanding of the game necessary to play that way? 'It depends on the team,' he was told. 'And not all sets of fans would accept that style.'

As a coach, a teacher, Guardiola believes that when one of his pupils truly understands why they are required to act in a specific way, they believe more in what they are being asked to do. It also means that this increases their capacity to take the initiative, or question what they've been told to do, in a more responsible way when the need arises.

This is how one of his pupils, Gerard Piqué, put it: 'The coach makes us understand football. He doesn't just give us orders, he also explains why. That makes you a better player, since you know the reasons behind the instructions. That way everything has a meaning.' While at FC Barcelona, Guardiola introduced a new approach to coaching and learning; he paid a lot of attention to detail. Piqué goes further: 'He has absolute conviction in what he believes and the team has taken on a rich football manual, from a tactical point of view, with pride.' On the field of play, in the heat of the action, it enabled Guardiola's Barcelona to switch formations or positions as many as five or six times in the same game. When players understand why,

Above After the first season, Pep tried to reinvent the team with Ibra. It didn't work

Right Pep tried to squeeze the very best from Thierry Henry as he approached the end of his career

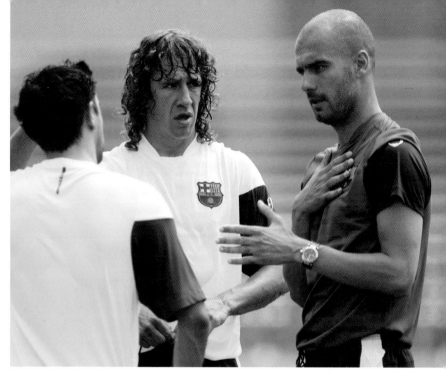

Above From the moment he arrived, Pep encouraged the home-grown players to lead the group

Above left Pep won the group over with his leadership qualities and charm, and despite the obvious frailties

Below left … and in the first season, three major titles, for the first time in the history of the club (League, Champions League and King's Cup)

Right José Mourinho, who shared the changing room for four years, presented Pep with his most difficult challenge

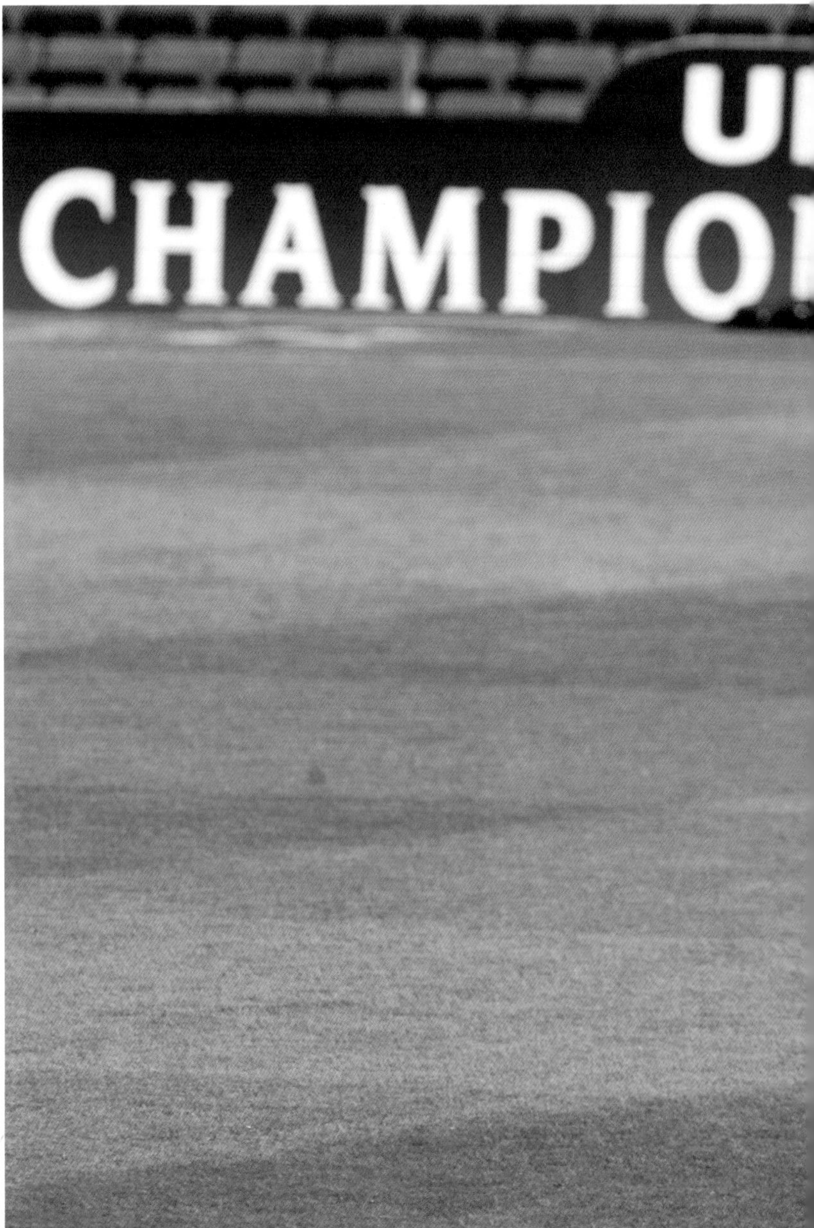
CHAMPIO

Left Manel Estiarte,
his right-hand man,
brother-in-arms

Pep lives every second of the
day thinking about how to
improve the side. Every second!

Left Andrés Iniesta learned
massively from Pep but was
also a great shoulder to cry
on in the difficult times

The ill-health of Eric Abidal has been the hardest episode of Pep's managerial career

it is easy to react to what is being shouted from the touchline in the heat of battle.

However, Guardiola also drilled patience into his sides, because, despite that ability to get his team to react, he and his players also had enough faith in their strategy to know when to avoid a knee-jerk reaction to a tough passage of play or an opposition goal. In his own inimitable way, Charly Rexach has a peculiar analogy: 'sometimes there are games where in the sixth or seventh minute you say "that plan is not working". But it is like preparing a plate of beans, some are hard, some perfectly tender, badly placed. Then you move the dish and the beans start falling into place gradually. Patience. Football is the same. You see the game and you see that a player isn't working. And you say, "relax, give it time to fall into place."'

Evolution, as opposed to revolution, is a word we've used many times so far. Because, for all of Pep Guardiola's innovation, he was also very careful not to start out by tearing down all that had gone before. Many of the foundations for success were there already, and he knew that a process of gradual adjustment was necessary, of fine-tuning, coaxing the best out of what was frequently already in place. Step by step, he introduced mechanisms and alternatives, subtle adjustments and repairs to what Cruyff had set in motion a generation or so earlier. Pep was very careful to preserve the model and its spirit (pressure, position, combination, go out to win every game) but evolving and expanding its possibilities and potential to previously unimaginable extremes.

But new things have certainly been created on the pitch since his appearance on the scene. Villas-Boas compares Pep Guardiola's Barça to the celebrated chef Ferran Adrià: but rather than gastronomic experimentation, we are witnessing molecular football. Their recipe for success is innovation: they defend with three at the back in an era when everyone has signed up to the back four doctrine; they pioneer diminutive players in the centre of midfield when the rest of the world has tilted towards the pace and power principle in the engine room. What others might perceive as weaknesses, Barcelona have provided as solutions: tiny midfielders mean you cannot win the ball, so you make sure you always have possession.

Frequently the logic might appear counter-intuitive. For example, according to widespread conventional logic, without a six-foot-four powerhouse striker you can't score from headers. Barcelona turned that theory on its head: so the wingers still provide crosses, but it's the positioning and timing of the attacker that makes up for their lack of physical presence.

And the player on the receiving end of a cross may not even be a striker, because Barcelona frequently play without one. And then there's the added ingredient of a goalkeeper who touches the ball with his feet as often as a centre back – and frequently more often than an opposing midfielder. In fact, you might describe Valdés as a centre back who occasionally picks the ball up.

Yet Barcelona's most outstanding innovation has perhaps less to do with their constant breaking of convention, or even the creation and selection of such wonderful players with the technique and vision to make it work – or even the realisation that beautiful football is such because it is effective, not vice versa – but, rather, the fact that they have found a way to use the spaces on a pitch that seem to be almost impossible to beat or counteract. Yes, Pep was beaten by Chelsea and Real Madrid in different ways in his last season; but in the years Pep was in charge Barcelona have the highest ratio of victories in crucial games in history. And not by chance.

Iniesta tells us that Pep was always explaining things to him about his positioning on the field. 'He'd correct me, help me to improve, he'd tell me to enjoy what I do, have fun and love this profession and this club.' Xavi Hernández insists that Pep 'is always two or three moves ahead of the rest'. Javier Mascherano will always be grateful to Messi 'for having recommended me and to Pep for making me see that football can be played another way'. It must be easy to train and compete if all the players had this level of analysis, humility and passion for what they do. A credit to their profession.

And all of them, no matter how many times they won, carried around one commandment: 'I am in a huge club even in the hard times. I try not to betray the club's principles nor the idea of team play nor the legacy of my predecessors.'

*

An away trip to newly promoted Numancia provided the opening game of the 2008–09 La Liga season.

The tactical chat at the hotel two hours before the journey to the stadium confirmed there were no surprises and all the big names were in the line-up: Víctor Valdés, Dani Alves, Puyol, Márquez, Abidal; Yaya Touré, Xavi, Iniesta; Messi, Henry and Eto'o.

The instructions were clear and simple: open up the pitch. Numancia will defend deep. Circulate the ball quickly. Be patient.

On the way to the tiny Los Pajaritos stadium (capacity just 9,025), Coldplay's 'Viva la Vida' blared from the speakers on the team bus. That song, a favourite of Pep's, would become the soundtrack to the rest of the season – the anthem for Guardiola's era, even. When that song played, the players knew the moment had arrived. It was a warning. The call to action.

The last rituals took place after the warm-up but by then Pep had disappeared from the players' view. His preparations were over.

Both teams came out on to the pitch. The new La Liga campaign had started.

On the bench, Guardiola gesticulated, appearing angry. Tense. He'd sit down, stand up again. Anxious. He couldn't sit or stand still. More instructions. Fists in the air, arms wide. He transmitted and exuded pure passion and energy. That is Pep, as a player and as a manager. Even as a spectator!

He had not promised titles. Rather, that each game would be treated as a final and that every minute of every game had equal importance. He doesn't understand or accept a group that doesn't shout, hug, give their all. All of that was noticeable in the first Liga game of the season.

He even smacked Dani Alves on the back of his neck after a quick instruction. Alves turned round bewildered and surprised. It was only a gesture to connect with them, of appreciation. 'But one day they will turn round and smack you back,' Estiarte warns him, laughing.

What Pep was doing, right from the beginning, was establishing a camaraderie, forging a bond, an unspoken code between football people. The players are made of skin and bone and they too like this contact. Even if it is a slap. Pep touches constantly, hugs, pushes them, to motivate them, to keep them on their toes, to make them feel loved. And his experience as a footballer allows him to decide when to do it or when not to do it.

Barcelona attacked through the centre far too much, their movements funnelled into a congested area in front of goal. Too narrow. But one element was a sign of things to come: they had almost all the possession and the chances. Twenty shots on goal from Barcelona, three from Numancia, one of them a goal from Mario, a defensive mistake that left him unmarked at the far post.

Barcelona lost.

1–0.

Beaten by a modest club with an annual budget of €14.4 million compared to the €380 million of FC Barcelona. The shock result of the weekend. Of the month. Of the season, even.

At the end, Guardiola set his doubts, disappointment and frustration to one side and approached the rival coach, Sergio Kresick, to shake his hand and congratulate him on his success.

'When we lost that first game in Soria, we weren't in a good mood in the dressing room,' Iniesta recalls. 'But Pep appeared straight away to control everything, to help us to accept the result.'

The pre-season had given the players their hunger back, they knew the path they must take, the reasoning and challenges. They were receptive – well, most of them – and they started to understand what Pep wanted of them. But they had lost their first league game to a side that everyone thought they should have thrashed. Straight after the game, Guardiola made the effort to get it into the players' heads that they needn't change anything because of the defeat. They had made mistakes and these were pointed out to them in the immediate aftermath, but they should also maintain a very clear idea about where they were going. That August evening at Los Pajaritos, *el mister*, as coaches are known in Spain, told his players something that he has repeated several times since.

'We shouldn't lose sight of the target.'

And the target wasn't to win titles, but to achieve a certain way of playing. If they stuck to their principles, titles would be the most logical consequence. Never losing sight of their goal would be one of the keys to success.

In the days after the game, during hard training sessions, Guardiola pulled his players up on many things. He insisted that they hadn't played well in terms of positioning. In future they must place themselves more cleverly to receive the pass, and to start pressuring their opponents more quickly. Not once did Pep point the finger of blame, instead putting all his efforts into finding solutions. More than training, it felt like teaching. The players were learning.

It is important in football, as in any walk of life, to appear calm in times of crisis. To hide weaknesses. Pep told them with conviction that they were on the right path. Not a complete lie but he confessed to people at the club that he had slipped up: 'The pre-season was great, but now the league has begun I've let the players fall back into their old ways of playing, their former tactics, playing down the centre.'

The international break meant that two weeks would pass before the next league game. It was to be among the hardest fifteen days of his regime.

Pep Guardiola's managerial debut at the Nou Camp came against Racing de Santander, another modest team whose target was to avoid relegation. Pep made two significant changes to his line-up. Pedro and Busquets were included, with Yaya Touré left on the bench and Henry injured. Under pressure, as he would do repeatedly throughout his tenure, Pep looked for solutions in the youth system.

The visitors held Barcelona to a 1–1 draw.

Pep's team paid the price for not converting their chances in front of goal and had to settle for a share of the spoils against a very defensive Racing side that scored with their only clear chance of the game. A hugely frustrating result.

In the dressing room, Pep did not need to point out mistakes, as there were few. It was during that post-match reflection that he really discovered himself as a trainer. He was grateful for having prioritised and trusted his instincts about the game, ahead of what any amount of reading could have advised him. Yes, there was more soul-searching to do, more convincing to do, more work on the ideas that he wanted to instil at the club: but against Racing he had seen a team play as he had asked them to play.

There was certainly an improvement and any dissent or unrest was external – in the media and on radio phone-ins – rather than inside the dressing room. Some reactionary pundits even called for Pep's head.

Just before the next training session, Andrés Iniesta, who had started the Racing game on the bench, went up to Pep's office, knocked on the door, stuck his head through the opening without entering and said:

'Don't worry, *mister*. You should know, we're with you until the death.'

Then walked off.

Other key members of the team reacted in their own ways. Xavi felt there was no need to say anything, just to win the next game. He could see that the team was playing 'bloody brilliantly, like angels' but had one point out of six. He couldn't believe it. He'd experienced days in the past when he knew that the team had played pitifully, but managed to sneak a win. This was the reverse.

He had seen the media reaction in similar situations. After a victory, the headline was going to be 'Barça are a marvel' no matter what the performance was: 'What people want are results, and from the results they analyse if you're playing well or not. If you lose, the headline will always be "Barça is a disaster".'

Xavi, Henry, Valdés, Busquets all realised that Pep was nervous behind his calm façade. He won't admit that a match can be lost without explanation. He has to find a reason for everything. In this respect he watches football from a scientific perspective and appreciates the lessons a defeat can teach you: 'What makes you grow is defeat, making mistakes. It is what keeps you alert. When you win you think: "Great, we've won." And we'd have surely done some things wrong, but you're relaxed. The only thing that winning is useful for is a good night's sleep.'

Guardiola was well aware that two years without trophies caused a certain sense of urgency and that a defeat against Sporting de Gijón the following week could leave Barcelona at the bottom of the table, but was convinced that they would soon reap the rewards of their work in training. At the same time as receiving criticism for the results, there were a number of influential voices in the media arguing that Barcelona were playing well and they had got their title-winning hunger back. Johan Cruyff wrote in *El Periódico* that it was 'the best Barça side that he had seen in many years'.

Despite his confidence, Pep was in need of someone to reinforce his belief that all was well. He decided to chat to Cruyff.

Guardiola has been fascinated by the figure of the coach since before he even realised he wanted to be one. Of the many managers who have influenced Pep, few have had quite the profound impact upon him as Johan Cruyff, the man who took his convictions to Barcelona and changed the whole structure of the club. Cruyff introduced a bug that infected Guardiola and many others of his generation and his impact upon FC Barcelona went far beyond that of simply a player or football coach. Guardiola considers that Cruyff's biggest miracle was to change a country's mentality, convincing the whole of Catalonia that his was the way to play.

'Football is played for people,' Cruyff often said. And more: 'I want my team to play well even if it is because I have to watch all the games and I don't want to get bored.'

Johan needed to be arrogant to win over the sceptics so he developed a love-hate relationship with his pupils, the board and the media. Not everybody accepted what he was proposing and there was even opposition to his ideas within factions of his early squads. A young Pep didn't comprehend every decision taken but wanted to understand the thinking process behind it, and soon, once convinced, became an evangelical follower of Cruyff.

For the Dutch coach there were three principles that were non-negotiable: firstly, on the pitch events were not casual occurrences, but consequences of your intentions. You could play the ball with advantage not only because of the pass, but because of your positioning on the pitch and even the way your body was placed, for instance.

Secondly, you should be able to control the ball with one touch. If you needed another one, you were not one of the best players, just a good one. If you needed an extra touch, you were playing badly.

Thirdly – and crucial for Pep's position as the midfielder in front of the back four – he had to dispatch the ball to the wingers to make the pitch bigger, wider, to create spaces all over the pitch.

Cruyff didn't comment on each position, but gave general instructions invariably full of common sense: when talking about passing lines he would warn players that they didn't need to position themselves in the corners because that reduced the angle of the passes. Regarding positional play, he insisted on making sure the player stayed in his corresponding area, especially when the ball was lost.

But Cruyff didn't manage to convert all his ideology into a working methodology. Louis van Gaal helped with that. And Pep Guardiola added a new twist to his version: 'I steal ideas, ideas are shared, they go from one person to another.'

Consequently, for Pep, a meeting with Cruyff would give him an opportunity to seek guidance from his mentor: a chance to listen to some new ideas and to seek reassurance for his own. After overcoming some initial hesitation for having supported Lluis Bassat in the 2003 presidential elections, Guardiola knew, as we have seen, that he had bridges to build with the Dutchman – and what better way to make him feel important and demonstrate all the respect that he had for him than by coming before him as an apprentice?

Guardiola always addresses Cruyff in the '*usted*' form – the formal 'you' in Spanish, a very rare, old-fashioned habit these days. During the initial approach, be it at Cruyff's house, at Pep's, at a meal, a meeting or whatever, the pupil will always show the utmost respect and humility towards his former coach. Once the opening formalities and small talk are out of the way there's suddenly a spark and, BANG, they start talking about football. Arms are waved around energetically, the arguments are passionate, the ideas clear. They speak and act from their hearts and everything from then on is football, football and more football. You would never hear Pep disagree and say, 'You're wrong' to Cruyff. Never. But they will discuss and debate for hours, trying to convince the other of their own views. When it comes to football, they both talk the same language. If football is a religion, they both worship at the same shrine.

On that occasion, though, after the Racing draw, the pupil met the master mostly to raise concerns and to listen to answers. Cruyff had already given Guardiola some advice in the summer that the young coach took to heart: 'You should know how to avoid problems, handle journalists, rumours, even the news that is unrelated to football. You must know how to make risky decisions given little time. You've had a lot of influences throughout your career, now evolve in your own way. You must have lots of eyes, good helpers, good players, mark the path and those that don't follow it.

'Each player must be convinced that what he does is the best thing for him, for his team-mates and for the general idea. The goal is to pass the "ABC" of football on to each player. For example, you are an inside player, you must do this and not that, and nothing more. Once you learn what an inside player must do, you can then think of variations. And when it doesn't work, you must go back to the "ABC". The main thing is to have rules. You can only ask a player to do something that he knows and nothing more. Ask for his quality. A footballer should have faith in what he does. It is better for a player to lose the ball when he is dribbling, feeling over-confident, than for a blunder, a mistake due to being scared of getting it wrong.

'The whole team – coaches and players – should share the same idea. And don't forget about authority. If you don't want to crash like other coaches, you must have control of your players. In order to be coach of Barcelona, it is more important knowing how to manage a group of stars than knowing how to correct a mistake made on the field. You have to have an influence over the group, to be able to seduce and convince them. It's necessary to take advantage of the "idol" image that players have of you as their coach.'

The level of demands, Cruyff reminded him, should match their possibilities – technical, sporting and economic. Cruyff never asked for the impossible, but he was capable of facing up to any of the stars of the team – in front of the rest of the squad – to tell them things such as 'Your performance doesn't match the wages you get, so what you are doing is not enough. You must give more.' Cruyff knew how to deal with players, well, with most of them, cooling the excitement of the regulars and looking after the egos of the ones who were often on the bench. But he had a look that could kill and some of his posturing could leave the players unsettled for weeks. 'Cruyff is the trainer who has taught me most, there's no doubt about it,' says Guardiola. 'But Cruyff is also the trainer who has made me suffer most. With just a look he gave you shivers that could chill your blood.'

Pep told his mentor that there was one thing that Johan could do, but that it would be a mistake for him to imitate. 'Johan, you used to call some of the players "idiots". I cannot do that. *Usted* can, but I cannot. I suffer too much. I cannot tell them that.'

Pep remembers on one occasion how Cruyff insulted Txiki Beguiristain and Bakero, two of his key players in the Dream Team, and an hour later asked them to organise a meal for all of them and their wives the following night. Pep envied that ability, but admitted that he is not made of the same stuff.

Subsequent meetings between the pair became frequent. Pep would visit Cruyff at his home or they would visit restaurants of well-known chef friends. Where possible, about once every six months, a group that would consist of Cruyff, Estiarte, chef Ferran Adrià, former journalist and now consultant Joan Patsy and Guardiola would meet for a meal. After Pep left Barcelona, Adrià planned to reopen the world-famous el Bulli restaurant just so that they could spend the day there.

But in that meeting a few months after Pep became the manager of Barcelona, and after two disappointing results, the message from Johan Cruyff was as clear as it was simple: 'Keep going, Pep. It will happen.' Guardiola himself had come to exactly the same conclusion.

Two games. One point. Barcelona in the bottom three.

That week, Pep Guardiola met director of football Txiki Beguiristain. Scratching his head as he often did during the games, an unconscious nervous gesture that has always been apparent in moments of doubt, Pep could not mask his anxiety. 'If we don't beat Gijón then I'll be the first coach in Barça's history to be bottom of the league,' he told Txiki, half joking.

'The players haven't been getting into the positions where we want them to be and the positions are dependent upon where the ball is and we haven't respected that. We haven't done that well yet,' Pep kept repeating and Txiki agreed. 'Txiki, the best way of defending well is attacking well and I have to get the players to see that.'

Nobody within the club was demanding Pep's head just yet. Externally there were those who saw the results as evidence that his promotion from the B team had been a mistake, the sign of a board in turmoil that wanted to paper over the cracks with the appointment of a legendary player but an inexperienced coach. Joan Laporta was holding his breath and repeating that Pep just needed time, hoping that all that was wrong with the side was that he couldn't handle more pressure.

Third game of the season. Barcelona lie in the bottom three of the domestic competition and have to face Sporting Gijón. The scenery, the legendary Molinón. Sporting have just been promoted and, in fact, the last time they hosted Barcelona in 1997, Guardiola was their captain. There were long silences on the team coach that took them to the stadium but the technical chat had already been given in the hotel. Despite victory being essential, nothing changed the coach's ideology and its practicalities. He would give his all for this cause, he knew the truth – he had the line-up and the tactics that guaranteed control and pressure high up.

Just before kick-off, Pep Guardiola crossed paths with Manuel Preciado, the Sporting coach, who sadly died of a heart attack in the summer of 2012. The older, more experienced manager had already heard the changes Pep wanted to make to the first eleven and had some warm words of comfort for the novice, and understood the enormous pressures faced by his younger opponent on that day: 'Stick to your principles, Pep. If Busquets or whoever needs to be brought on, they should be brought on. You must be brave in order to defend your ideas.'

Sergio Busquets was named in the line-up for the second game running.

Piqué smiles when he remembers where Barcelona's fortunes were about to change. 'I treasure a lovely memory of the encounter with Sporting in the Molinon. That day signified the takeoff.'

The game started. From the kick-off, ten players touched the ball, all except Messi. There were thirty passes in two minutes that terminated near the corner flag and with a foul on Iniesta. Those opening exchanges were a statement of intent. The team kept jabbing away at Sporting like a boxer: two consecutive corner kicks, two balls recovered near the rival's box, a Xavi shot on goal. Only four minutes gone.

The team used the space patiently and cleverly, Xavi found many lines of passing, the ball fizzed about at a high tempo, every touch of it was sharp and positive. Henry was ill and Iniesta played on the left. Eto'o started as number nine but he often appeared on the right wing, allowing Messi to move freely in the centre. Those tactics were to be repeated during the season.

Sporting thought that using a close-combat style against a faltering Barcelona team was going to give them a chance, but once the first goal arrived there was no way back.

When the team filed into the changing room at half-time, already 0–2 up, Pep demanded a moment of attention. He needed to give only one instruction, a simple reminder but a key instruction: 'We will continue pressing high up,' he said. The order was followed. In the second half, Sporting found that the Barcelona half was much further away and beyond their reach than the naked eye would have you believe.

Barcelona beat Sporting 1–6.

'You've surpassed us,' Manuel Preciado conceded when, at the end of the game, he met with Guardiola on the way to the dressing rooms. 'We've taken a step forward,' replied Pep.

The next day, at the training ground, one of Pep's assistants gave him a photocopy with some of the stats of the game. Pep's smile was difficult to control. Apart from Messi, who scored twice, all the forwards had recovered possession at some point, suffocating

Sporting. Barça had a total of 22 shots, 9 on target and 14 corners, compared to Sporting's 5 attempts. But there was something else that gave Pep a lift: defensively, the young Busquets, promoted from the B team, had been the best player on the field. He had recovered 10 balls. And 48 out of his 50 passes had reached their intended target.

Without Henry, there were seven players involved in the game who had progressed through the academy system (Valdés, Puyol, Xavi, Iniesta, Busquets, Messi, Bojan), two less than the previous game against Racing. Xavi was involved in all the goals.

It was the third game of the season and Barça had already established themselves as the La Liga side with the most shots on goal and received the fewest.

The result did more than present the team with a much needed three points. It also showed Guardiola was right. It showed that they had to give it time, that there were tactics and rules to follow: a philosophy that could succeed.

'Where would we be if we hadn't beaten Sporting?' Iniesta says now. The victory proved to be a sign of things to come.

2

THE EXTRAORDINARY
2–6 AT THE SANTIAGO
BERNABÉU

'Being a coach is fascinating. That's why it's so difficult for some to give it up. It's sweet, a constant feeling of excitement, your head is going at 100 mph all the time' – Pep Guardiola, 2008.

Pep could only see the positives in the early days of his coaching career, embracing the moment; there was always his inner voice reminding him that he was there for the short term. Methodical with a passion, Pep thrived on organising, making decisions, sharing experiences, applying what he had learnt over the years. His life centred on becoming the best manager he could be and tales of his dedication to the job and attention to detail started to spread around Barcelona.

He had already shown that he was more than a coach who believed his job began and ended with giving instructions to a group of players out on a pitch, and repeatedly demonstrated an empathy and ability to understand the needs of those around him; taking responsibility for the welfare of anyone related to the sporting side of the football club.

Before being appointed first-team coach back in May 2008, Pep was focused upon getting the reserve team promoted to the Second B division when he took time to visit Gabi Milito. The Argentinian centre half was a regular in Rijkaard's first team and was recovering from an operation on his knee. Despite the fact that Pep hardly had a moment to spare – not least because his daughter Valentina had just been born – he surprised Milito with a visit that lasted more than three hours to encourage and offer moral support to the player. Pep also spoke of his love for Argentinian football, of his admiration for Menotti and Bielsa. Milito was won over by Pep's charm and was especially surprised when Pep told the media: 'I'd prefer to see Gabi playing football again than win a title.'

After the final whistle in a cup match at the Nou Camp against Second B minnows Cultural Leonesa, Guardiola bumped into a group of the modest players hovering around the door of the Barcelona dressing room, hoping to swap shirts with their Barça counterparts. Pep greeted them all with a warm smile and threw open the door to the first team's sanctuary, telling the star-struck opposition players to 'go on in, please, and make yourself at home'. Cultural's players couldn't believe it.

Now that he was a manager himself he soon discovered the solitude of the job and made efforts to be included as a member of the coaching fraternity. Emulating one of the more courteous traditions of the English game, Pep spent his own money on making sure that there was always a bottle of wine ready to share with the visiting coach after a match. If a fellow manager at another club was sacked, he would send him a message of support, even once cancelling all his own prior engagements to organise a private meal with one individual to offer him encouragement only days after his dismissal.

He has an incredible capacity for hard work: upon returning home from Milan after a Champions League encounter at around 4 a.m., Pep found that he couldn't sleep, so he went to the training complex to watch a video or two of their next rivals. He would increasingly have to turn to sleeping pills throughout his tenure, particularly in his final season in charge.

One of the first decisions that Guardiola took was to make sure that all the money collected from fines that were imposed on the squad went to a charitable organisation, instead of going towards team meals, as was the custom. The sanctions couldn't contribute to a reward for the team, hence he thought of a much more supportive use for them. At the start of his first season, he donated the proceeds to the Sant Joan de Déu Foundation, which investigates Rett's Syndrome, a serious mental illness.

When Pep signed a marketing agreement with Sabadell Bank, committing to a number of lectures and personal interviews as part of the deal – while still refusing to give one-to-one interviews to the media – he was initially labelled a money-grabber by some of his critics. However, he was soon vindicated when it emerged that he had shared out all the money he received from the bank between his staff as a way of acknowledging their dedication to a project in which each person had done his bit. Meanwhile, the bank was delighted with an upturn in their number of clients, a 48 per cent increase in Catalonia and 65 per cent in Madrid.

At the start of the season Audi, as they do every year, presented a car to each first-team player as well as the coach; Pep, however, refused to accept his: if there were no cars for his technical staff, then he would not take one either.

In November of Pep's first year in charge, the goalkeeping coach, Juan Carlos Unzué, lost his father after a long illness. Guardiola didn't have to think twice – despite the fact that Barça had a game the following day, the first-team coach rearranged the entire pre-match schedule to take the squad to Orkoien in Navarra, 223 miles away, to attend the funeral.

The season was going well. Aside from a poor run of three draws in March (against Betis, Lyon and Mallorca) and two defeats (against Espanyol and Atlético de Madrid) that led to some reactionary criticism from certain quarters, the overall feeling among the supporters was one of euphoria. There was a sense that, under Pep Guardiola, something special was happening at the Nou Camp.

Their football seemed to dominate the opposition, with a high percentage of possession and effective pressure high up the field; Xavi, Iniesta, Eto'o and Henry seemed entirely different players from the season before and the new additions to the team were an improvement. 'I feel strong and optimistic,' was how Pep described his feelings around that time. Barça bounced back from their mini crisis in that spring of 2009 by going on a run of nine consecutive wins. This spell was followed by two draws – against Valencia (2–2) in La Liga and Chelsea in the 0–0 first leg of the Champions League semi-final) – that made the end of the season run-in tense and unforgettable.

The Clásico at the Bernabéu that May would be decisive. Going into that match, Barcelona were top with five games remaining and, with the two arch rivals separated by four points, a win for Guardiola's side would effectively guarantee that the title would be heading back to the Camp Nou.

Pep treated the game against Real Madrid like a cup final and demanded the same bold approach that he had seen from his team throughout the season. 'We want to be champions, don't we?' he asked his players in the days leading up to the visit to Madrid. 'Now is the time to take this step. I only ask that we go out there with our heads held high because these are the games that define us, they are what do our job justice.'

For such a pivotal match, Guardiola was considering handing Messi the tremendous responsibility of playing as a false striker for the first time. Guardiola had already won the confidence of the little Argentinian and had started the process of building a team around him at that stage. But the relationship between coach and player hadn't always been that easy.

At the beginning Pep was worried. He wanted to get Messi on his side because he had a feeling that the lad, who at the time was just twenty-one years old, was a diamond in the rough. He foresaw that Barça would depend on him and he was scared of losing him. So he had to establish with Messi a dynamic, a relationship formed on common ground before they could work together. To do so, the coach had to adjust his idea of the team to include an extraordinarily gifted and hungry individual, while at the same time convincing the player – shy, quiet, even distant off the pitch – he had to accept his leadership.

Unmoved by the status of legends or even the credit that an exceptional career in football gives former players, in Messi's eyes Guardiola was little more than just another coach. At the time of Pep's appointment, Messi was drifting into melancholy, having become increasingly disillusioned during the last few months of the undisciplined Rijkaard regime.

The beginning of Pep's tenure was a period of uncertainty for the young Messi. For all the faults of the former regime, it must be remembered that Rijkaard had given Messi his debut and the Argentinian felt protected under the Dutchman. Then along came Pep, a new boss, new regime, and instantly got rid of Ronaldinho, Messi's friend, mentor and neighbour (three houses away) in Castelldefels. Messi understood the reasons for the changes and had recently grown closer to Puyol and Xavi as he saw the damage Ronnie was doing to himself, but, nevertheless, it was a period of change in the youngster's life and he needed to establish a connection, the right one, with the new man in charge.

Pep had wanted to impress upon Leo the idea of a group above everything else, not just because he had been a midfield general but also because he understood that it was necessary for the type of football that he wanted to put into practice. Guardiola had identified Leo's drive but, crucially, he had misunderstood it, mistaking it for selfishness. 'I wanted to make Pep understand that it was ambition, not selfishness. Leo is so self-demanding, wants to play every game, win every title, to such an extent that he transmits that to others and it becomes like a tsunami,' reveals Manel Estiarte, the 'Messi of water polo' in his day, and a man brought to the club by his friend Pep as player liaison. Leo always wanted the ball, to be the main protagonist, to finish a move. 'It's like a demon inside you that you don't know you have, and you can't control it. That is what has made him become the best football player of all time. And I tried to explain all that to Pep.'

In contrast, Guardiola believed that the coach has to make the really big decisions every single day on behalf of every player in his squad. This creates a false sense of power because you realise that, in the end, the footballers are the ones who go out and follow your instructions. The coach's ideas and Messi's talent and desire had to meet somewhere in the middle.

Deep down, Pep had never forgotten the lesson he learnt on that day that he missed out on Michel Platini's autograph. Now he reminded himself that it would be useful in this case.

Guardiola's boyhood hero, it will be remembered, had been allowed to remain in the dressing room while the rest of his team-mates warmed up. It confirmed that the greatest lie in football is that all players are treated as equals. Later, when Pep was a teenager, Julio Velasco, the successful volleyball coach, taught him that your best player could often be both your greatest asset and your heaviest burden at the same time: 'You must know how to seduce him, trick him into getting the best out of him, because in our job we are above them, but we're also below them because we depend on them,' he told Pep.

Guardiola understood what he had to do, knowing that he intended to love all his players equally – but he wasn't going to treat them all exactly the same.

Johan Cruyff had harboured just one doubt about Guardiola: 'As a Catalan, would he be able to make decisions?' The Dutchman considers Catalonia a nation that is often lacking in initiative. Initiative would be key, in Cruyff's eyes, because in his experience he had seen that every team in the world had its own Messi (that is, a star player, although clearly not at his level); but not all coaches knew how to get the best out of him.

Guardiola pretty much answered Cruyff's concerns on his first day in the job, at his inaugural press conference, when he announced that Messi would be liberated from the shadow of Ronaldinho. But this had other implications, effectively ensuring that Messi wasn't going to be the focal point through his actions but by default, because Pep would get rid of anyone who could overshadow him. Although he had to keep Eto'o for a season longer than he initially anticipated, Ronaldinho and Deco were moved swiftly out of the club and out of Messi's way. Of the stars who remained, Henry was made to play on the wing when the Frenchman wanted to play as a number nine. There was only one ball and that belonged to Messi.

Guardiola knew that it would become impossible for anybody to try and compete with his star; he had never, ever, seen anyone like him. From very early on in his tenure, Guardiola recognised that, while it was true his Barcelona team represented an array of talented individuals who were combining to form an outstanding football team, Lionel Messi was going to take that group to another level. In subjugating every ego under one individual, by making just one player the focal point for a team that otherwise defined itself as a true collective, Pep was asking others to consent to something that could only be accepted by those who had lived and grown up alongside Messi and who knew, better than anyone else, that this was not simply the whim of some star-struck coach. It was a decision based upon the knowledge that the star of this team would be someone truly, truly special.

So Pep took another step that delighted Messi. While he would be given the opportunity to lead the way through his football, the burden of leadership in other areas would not fall on his shoulders. At just twenty-one, the weight of responsibility would be too much. Instead, the captaincy would be shared among the core of home-grown players. Not only would Pep give the youth team footballers the chance to progress to the first team, but he would also give them the chance to become captains, role models and representatives of FC Barcelona. It was a responsibility shared by Puyol, sometimes Xavi, Valdés or even Iniesta. They would captain the ship: Messi would be the wind in their sails.

It was in stark contrast to Messi's position with the national team of Argentina: there he was not only expected to lead the way and make decisions on the field, but also to captain the side. The armband imposed a burden on Messi, who just wanted to get on with playing his football, not to have to argue with the referee in defence of his team-mates, nor to be anybody's role model, nor give inspirational speeches.

In the same way that the coach, after some reflection, started understanding what made Messi tick, so Pep was convinced that he would understand everything that he would ask of him, and, if not, he would charm him into understanding. However, Pep also knew that he needed something that would win the player over completely. And he found it, even though the new coach had to convince the club that it was the right thing to do.

During Pep's first few training sessions with the team in Scotland, Pep and Messi had two public confrontations.

In the first, Messi reacted angrily to a Rafa Márquez tackle. The players squared up to each other and Pep rushed over to them and reprimanded them. Messi wanted to avoid him but the coach took him to one side. The Argentinian stared at the ground and backed away from Pep.

A similar scene was repeated two days later. Guardiola approached Messi to ask him to explain his cold attitude during training. He told Messi that, if he had a problem, he should tell him to his face but he knew exactly what was going on: Messi was sulking because he wanted to go to the Olympic Games in Beijing with Argentina – but Barcelona were against releasing him as the dates coincided with the first round of the Champions League qualifiers against Wisła Kraków. The matter had gone before a sporting tribunal, where it was established that the club was within its rights not to grant him permission to go, despite FIFA's demands to the contrary.

However, while the club and Argentinian Federation locked horns, the player felt like a pawn in a dispute in which he had little interest. All he knew was that he wanted to play football for his country in the Olympic Games – and Barcelona were denying him that opportunity.

It provided Pep with the chance he had been looking for.

The coach sat down with president Laporta, Beguiristain and Estiarte in the suite of the hotel in which the team were staying in the United States for a pre-season tour. He explained that if the club could ignore the ruling and let Messi go to the Olympics, the long-term gain outweighed the short-term loss: it would allow him to get the best out of Messi. Nobody dared tell Pep that he was a novice, that this was a decision that should be made by the club. Champions League football was at stake, after all. Pep asked them to trust him.

A little while later he had a chat with Messi. 'Leo,' he told him, 'I'm going to let you go because I have been an Olympic champion and I want you to be one too. But you owe me one.'

It proved to be the first building block in the construction of a relationship that grew stronger and stronger during the four years the pair were united at FC Barcelona. Pep's gesture brought them together at a time when they could have been driven apart before things even got going. Pep had decided again that, if mistakes were going to be made, they would be a consequence of his own decision-making and not those of others.

Later, Pep would make Messi a promise: 'Listen to me, Leo, stick close to me. With me you will score three or four goals every game.'

Before he made his debut in an official game with Guardiola, Messi travelled to the 2008 Olympic Games in Beijing. He returned to Barcelona an Olympic gold medallist – and he understood that it would not have been possible without the intervention of his new boss.

'If Leo smiles, everything is easier,' Pep repeated often.

It was time for the showdown against the old enemy, in a match that could effectively seize the La Liga trophy from Real Madrid and hand the title to FC Barcelona in Pep Guardiola's debut season as a first-team coach. A win for the visitors to the Bernabéu would virtually guarantee them the championship, giving them a seven-point lead with four games remaining; defeat would leave them just a point above their hosts. It was a genuine 'six-pointer'.

Pep and his boys were facing the biggest challenge and the most high-pressure game of their time together so far, at the end of what had become an exemplary season.

Standing between them and glory were Real Madrid: not only their eternal rivals, but an outfit in extraordinary form, even if their football was a little dull. Juande Ramos' team had enjoyed a phenomenal second half of the season, collecting fifty-two out of a possible fifty-four points, drawing just one game, against Atlético de Madrid, after having lost at the Camp Nou (leaving them, at that stage, twelve points behind Barcelona). 'We haven't been playing to our highest level in every game so that we can give our all when the time comes to have our shot at taking the lead,' said the Madrid coach.

The Catalan press was encouraging supporters to settle for a draw, trying to manage expectations ahead of a match in which the Barcelona fans were allowing their natural pessimism to creep in and suspect that the worst might happen. But Pep was not only calling the changes on a footballing level, he was transforming the way the *culés* felt about themselves, restoring their pride and injecting optimism into a culture that always anticipated that things would go wrong for them in the end. On the eve of the game, Pep was having none of this talk of a draw. He was going to the Bernabéu to win: to take the game to the home side and to beat them playing it his way. 'We won't speculate or leave it to fate. We will not relinquish all that we have been this year. When we return from the Bernabéu, I want it to have been all about us,' Pep told his squad.

If Madrid's run of form had dictated that the league was going to be decided at the Bernabéu, Barcelona were going to accept the challenge. Their arch rivals were breathing down their necks, piling the pressure on the novice coach and his emerging team; but it was a scenario that Guardiola relished rather than shirked: 'I want the pressure. It is ours and I want it. And if something happens and we lose, so be it: it is a final and finals should be played with ambition.'

As the Barcelona players made their way down the tunnel, towards the short flight of steps that would take them up and out on to the Bernabéu pitch, and into a cauldron of noise and unbridled hostility, they had Pep's final word's ringing in their ears above the din: 'We have come here to win! And at the Bernabéu there is only one way of winning: be brave!'

Earlier that season, in the first Clásico of the 2009 campaign, Guardiola's Barcelona had beaten Real Madrid 2-0. But the victory had not been as comfortable as the scoreline suggests: Drenthe had a chance to score the first goal before Eto'o and then Messi sealed the win for the hosts. It is still remembered as a special night, not only because it was Pep's first Clásico as coach, but also because of his reaction to the victory. The expression on Pep's face told the story – he had momentarily become a player again, basking in the euphoria of an adoring Camp Nou. He could not hide the fact that his eyes had welled up with the emotion of it all, while the enduring image of Víctor Valdés and his coach locked in bear hug summed up the bond that was being forged between this extraordinary group of players and their manager.

However, if that moment was special, it was merely a warm-up for the performance at the Bernabéu the following May. A night that would surpass all expectations.

The stifling early summer heat in Madrid that Saturday afternoon was particularly unbearable when the teams arrived at the Bernabéu. Pep's preparations were complicated by the loss of Rafa Márquez to injury and the impending trip to Stamford Bridge just three days later for the second leg of the semi-finals of the Champions League that would follow a frustrating 0–0 at the Camp Nou. With a win at the Bernabéu significant, but not essential, speculation was rife that Pep might even rest some players with an eye on the game in London.

No chance.

Pep had made one thing clear all week: the league was going to be won that night, in the enemy's backyard. And, to do that, Guardiola selected his strongest line-up available: Víctor Valdés, Abidal, Dani Alves, Piqué, Puyol, Xavi, Touré, Samuel Eto'o, Henry, Messi and Iniesta.

Pep had analysed Real Madrid in detail and, an hour and a half before the game, he got Messi, Xavi and Iniesta together: 'You three against Lass and Gago have got the game. If you do it right, three against two, we've beaten them.' Lass and Gago were going to find a third man to defend, Messi would position himself as a false striker in between the centre backs and those two.

Barcelona controlled the game from early on. Twenty minutes into the match, Xavi had a clear shot and Eto'o had another a few minutes later. But Madrid scored first. Higuaín found himself in space, unmarked – and seized his opportunity. Guardiola was undaunted. Barcelona persisted with the game plan. Their manager had made them believe in what they were doing and they just had to go along with it. As Cruyff had told Pep right at the start of the season, and Pep repeated to his pupils: be patient.

The *culés* didn't have to wait long. Almost immediately after Higuaín's goal, the score was brought level by Thierry Henry. Soon after, Xavi pulled the rabbit out of the hat with a free-kick. Before it was taken, the midfielder started making curious hand signals to Puyol, repeating them insistently as if possessed. A second later, he stopped. He turned his head, he seemed to see something that made his mind up definitively and went back to the job at hand, again making those curious hand signals. The next thing, Puyol was leaving the pitch, only to come back on and catch the Real defence unaware. 1–2.

In the celebrations that followed the goal, the rest of the Barcelona players learnt that Xavi, Puyol and Piqué had been practising that move alone, and that they had kept it a secret until that day. Four years later they would repeat the exact same set piece in South Africa while playing for Spain against Germany, the only goal of the semi-final of the World Cup.

Barcelona were in charge of the score and the game. Cannavaro and Metzelder did not know what to do. If they both moved forward to try to help Gago and Lass against the three Barcelona players who occupied the central positions, they left their back exposed to the movements of Eto'o and Henry cutting in from the wings. If only one of the two centre backs moved forward, that gave Messi the option of playing a one-on-one with a lot of space against a much slower defence outside their area. Before the match, Juande Ramos had a plan to counter Messi – involving Heinze, the left back – but on the night the Argentinian full back instead had his hands full dealing with Eto'o.

Xavi, Iniesta and Messi were quick with their decisions and passing, tempting the opponent towards the ball then passing before contact. The game was becoming the perfect example of technique, tactics and belief. It also heralded the beginning of the 'Messi explosion' that accompanied his move from the wing to playing as a false number nine. It was a tactical switch that was going to destroy opposition defences across Spain and Europe – and revolutionise world football.

And the key to all this lay with two gifted and privileged minds of this game, Guardiola and Messi, both of whom understood the importance of positioning and the needs of the individual.

With Pep's help and his own intuition, Messi started playing football with an accordion-like movement: the further the ball was away from him, the more distance he would put between himself and the ball. The closer it was to him, the closer he would move to get involved. Messi always wants the ball and in order for him to receive it in the best circumstances, Pep has made him understand that looking for the opposition's weaker side, where there are fewer opponents, behind the line demarcated by the deep-lying midfielders (*pivotes*) and distancing himself from the centre backs, the ball will find him. Furthermore, in those areas, he will have a bit of extra space to rev his engine, to work his way up through the gears, before hitting the opposition in full flow. And all this with very little effort: he only needed to work up through the gears when he received the ball. Without it he was allowed to take time to recover, to rest while he played. It sounds simple enough, but in mastering that positioning and timing, Messi has shown a thorough understanding of the game and an ability to learn in record time what many players take years to understand.

Barcelona grabbed their third just before the break. Messi. 1–3.

At half-time Guardiola warned his players not to get carried away by the scoreline nor the fact that they had an important match three days later. Madrid had managed much more incredible comebacks in the previous weeks and they were, after all, playing at the Bernabéu.

The second half kicked off. Madrid scored their second. 2–3.

It was the moment when many sides would have panicked, allowed the momentum to shift in favour of the hosts. But Guardiola and his Barcelona players were not about to let that happen.

Thierry Henry made it 2–4.

Then came Barcelona's fifth. The most magical of them all: Xavi performed a fantastic turn to lose his markers, then passing to Messi who, with a feint, sent Casillas diving to ground prematurely, before slotting home with a shot that passed the helpless keeper. 2–5.

And then there were six.

Messi released Eto'o with a ball into space out wide on the right, who fired in a cross that was met by Gerard Piqué. That's right: a centre half leading a counter-attack when his side had a three-goal lead. 2–6.

Superiority in midfield, as predicted by Pep, was the key to the game. It was the happiest day of his regime up to that point. The squad celebrated and hugged each other like never before. Xavi remembers all the players bouncing around looking like a bunch of 'teletubbies', childish, uninhibited exuberance in victory. Players took photos in the dressing room to immortalise the greatest moment in a century of Madrid–Barça games. It was Barcelona's very own cannon shot heard all around the world, the moment when the football fans, players and pundits across the globe took notice that something very special was taking place in a corner of Spain.

In the press room at the Bernabéu, Pep appeared more emotional than ever, truly moved by the historic event that had just taken place. 'It's one of the happiest days of my life and I know we have also made a lot of people happy.'

Iniesta remembers the celebrations well: 'The craziest, as always, was Piqué, he didn't stop jumping and shouting. One of his favourite rituals is to connect his MP3 player to the aeroplane's loudspeaker on the way home and put music on full blast – 'techno, ska, dance or whatever type of loud music appeals to him at the time.' Needless to say, the flight back to Barcelona that night was an impromptu Piqué-inspired disco.

The crowds awaiting the players at Barcelona airport in the early hours of Sunday morning greeted their returning heroes as if they were bringing home the trophy from a major cup final.

Guardiola, however, had to bring the players back down to earth almost immediately. He knew that he would have to calm everybody down, then pick them back up for another monumental and season-defining challenge: a Champions League semi-final against Chelsea at Stamford Bridge just three days later.

3
THE SIX TITLES IN ONE CALENDAR YEAR

During the four years that Pep Guardiola was in charge of Barcelona he did not give interviews for publication, with the exception of one that was supposed to end up on the history of Brescia DVD and somehow 'mysteriously' found its way on to the Italian television channel RAI!

Talking to Pep for this book was the only way I could open a hitherto closed window on his private world; to reveal what motivates him, what took him to where he is now, what fed his intuition to make the right football decisions; ultimately to try to comprehend what was taking him away from all he adored, or had once adored.

Before I met him privately, I felt like a naughty kid peering over a high wall to try to catch glimpses of a life, a mind, that, I was certain, was not exactly the same as the one that was discussed frequently and analysed to death. Clearly, as we all know, there are many Guardiolas: the public Pep, the passionate Pep, the fragile Pep, Pep the leader, visionary, role model and so on. In order to convey anything close to the real Pep Guardiola, it was important to try and peel away the layers, to work around the public profile and understand the man behind the finely tailored suits and the cool exterior.

Typically, meetings with Pep would be a planned twenty-minute chat at the end of a training session. More often than not, the press officer would return eighteen minutes after I'd arrived, with a knock on the door and a 'do you want a coffee?', code for: 'time's up'! If Pep brushed him off with a 'don't worry, we are OK', it was a small success.

His private words mould this book. In any case, since the day he took over the first team at FC Barcelona, Pep has done enough talking in front of the press – at his 546 press conferences – to fill an encyclopaedia with his insights. By his own account, he has sat in front of the media for 272 hours, or eleven full days. That amounts to around eight hundred questions a month. Can you imagine? Every single word scrutinised, every gesture picked up on, every utterance interpreted and extrapolated by the world's press.

He has been asked if he believes in God, if he writes poetry, about his politics, about the financial crisis and at least a hundred times if he was going to renew his contract ('although I don't really care if you do or not,' one journalist once told him!). The pre-game press conferences, at least half an hour long, always became the story of the day, but there was more to take from them if you were an advanced follower of both the politics within the media and the character himself – you hardly ever got a clue about the team, but if you were intuitive you would find out about Pep's state of mind.

So stop leaping around trying to see what's on the other side of the wall. Take a seat, if you haven't already, in one of the front rows of today's empty press conference. You will be the only journalist present. Imagine Pep clutching a bottle of water, hurrying to the front table and eagerly taking his seat, nervously touching the microphone, prepared to offer you an insight into his mind. The answers to many of the questions you'd hope to ask might be revealed in the following paragraphs. Or maybe not. Keep reading and find out.

The press conference starts now. Pep leans forward into the microphone, and starts to speak:

'When I face the press and the players, there is always an imposing element, almost theatrical, in order to be able to reach them. But in the end I always transmit what I feel. There is an element of shame, of fear, of acting the fool that makes me contain myself a little, then there is what I have learnt from football and the thing is that it scares me to make a statement when I know that the game is uncontrollable, that tomorrow my words could come back to haunt me. That's why I always search for the element of scepticism, the "*je ne sais quoi*", a doubt. That false humility that people always say I have, always giving the players the credit, isn't because I don't want to acknowledge my own merits, I must have done something right, it is because I panic about having those words turned on me. Because by doing exactly the same as what I am doing now, I could lose tomorrow. I prefer to be wrong a million times than give my people the impression that I am sure about everything that I am not. Because if I get it wrong tomorrow through doing the same thing as I do now, they'll say, "You weren't that clever, how didn't you see that?"

'I win because I am in a team rich in very good players and I try to make them give their all and out of ten games I win eight or nine. But the difference between winning and losing is so small ... Chelsea didn't win the European Cup because Terry slipped when taking a penalty, he slipped! I've given the players that example a thousand times.

'Three or four books have been written about my leadership strategy. I look at them to discover myself and see if I really do those things, because I don't know. They come to conclusions about me that I had never even considered.

'Why am I more of a leader than a coach who has been training for twenty years and hasn't won anything? It isn't false modesty, I can't find the reason because I wouldn't have won trophies if I hadn't been with Barça.

'The players give me prestige and not the other way around.

'I would go out on to the pitch with the players and go into the dressing room. I'm still very young and there are a lot of things that I would do. I'd go and hug them as a player. But I can't do that any more.

'How do I exercise my leadership? Why do I tell players one thing or another? Nothing is premeditated; everything is pure intuition with the players at all times. When they lose they are a mess, both those who played and those who didn't. So, sometimes I turn up and hug one or tell another one something, it is pure intuition. Of the twenty decisions I make each day, eighteen are intuitive, through observation.

'Is that all true? I can't work solely through intuition, I have to work using my knowledge, I don't want them to brand me a visionary. Furthermore, if I were I would make my players play in strange positions.

'In the end we do what we can and feel, through our education, we only transmit what we have experienced. There are no general theories that apply to everything. And any one could be valid, what doesn't work is *imposing* something that doesn't work.

'As professional as they are, they are also scared of losing and they look for that figure that gives them the key, that tells them: "Hey, come this way ..." this is what we coaches have to do. We have to transmit trust and security in all the decisions we make.

'That trust, security and sincerity are the fundamental pillars for a good coach. The players have to believe in the manager's message. He must always speak to the player fearlessly, sincerely and tell him what he thinks. Without deceiving him.

'The players put you to the test each day; that's why it is very important to be convinced about what you want and how you want to put it across. They are aware that luck is an important factor in the game, but they want to feel that the coach is convinced and defends the decisions he has made. The day we played against Espanyol at home (1–2), I got it wrong at half-time. A couple of weeks later, I mentioned it to them. They know that we aren't perfect, but we are humble and sincere.

'I don't know in what aspect we are good coaches. We haven't invented or revolutionised anything. The tactical concepts that we apply have been developed here, we have been taught them. The secret is in the details and in observing a lot. You have to pay a great deal of attention, constantly, to what happens every day, more so than to the weekend's game: we are always aware of every aspect, of a player's moods, their expressions, of thousands of almost unfathomable things that could make a difference. Observation is key.

'When I lose I wonder if I am capable of being a coach, of maintaining that leadership, and if I win, the ecstasy lasts five minutes and then I lose it.

'The fans need to know that their players work hard, the same as them. It is a good thing for people to know that we can be strict with them, fining them when they turn up late. The supporters have to see themselves reflected in the players. It is a question of defence because in difficult times people have to know that they haven't lost because they are lazy, that the work has been put in.

'I only know that a good leader is one who isn't scared of the consequences of their decisions. They make the decision that their intuition tells them, no matter what happens.

'In order to make decisions, you must be really convinced, they can't be taken lightly when there is so much pressure. I don't ignore the media element.

'There are times when I am tired and I have to transmit energy and I don't know how to do so. If you transmit it you're not being yourself, and if you don't transmit it you're not being true to yourself.

'With the first team, there are weeks when you are running on empty. In some training sessions I only observe because I don't have the sufficient time or energy to direct them; Tito, Aureli or Loren Buenaventura direct them.

'The key is to have a strong dressing room, knowing that we are stronger together than one person on his own.

'My players know that it bothers me less if they make a mistake ten times, than if they ignore me or don't look at me when I call them. That destroys me.

'The substitutes would do a better job if their ungrateful manager gave them an extended run of games.

'I do more work as a team manager than as a coach, because, as there are games every three days, there are few pure footballing training sessions and there is a lot of co-existence and it isn't easy. But the lucky thing in this team is having found people with important human values.

'A column in the press, instead of a front-page headline, is sometimes more influential on the players' moods than my own opinion. I have to know which headlines have come out about a player. If I have two stars and there are three headlines about one, I'm going to approach the player who hasn't had any.

'There are things that denote how a team is. Today we planned to meet at five o' clock and by 4.30 most of us were here. They know, because I have said it and they have seen it, that when they stop doing it, anyone can beat us. If each person does their job, and they know what it is because I make sure they know, then we are a team that is difficult to beat.

'I have to conserve this passion that I have for what I do. The day that I stop feeling it, I will leave. Now I want to tell a player off and then hug him immediately after. If you lose that, that's bad ... when I stop correcting a player during training, it will mean that I have lost my passion. When I no longer get excited, I will go. That's what happened to me when I was a player.

'At another team? It would be exactly the same. My closeness to my players is lessening. This year, less than last year, it is self-defence. Because I suffer, I prefer to distance myself.'

From his very first day in the job as coach, Pep went out of his way to appeal to the feelings of his players: demanding solidarity and effort from everyone. Those values represent a reflection of himself. He knew that in order to lead the group he must be consistent, manage the little details and big egos – and convince everyone, not only to do as he asked, but to believe in what he was asking them to do.

And his ability to communicate is perhaps his greatest talent.

Imagine you are a player now. It is the day of a home game. You have trained in the morning and then eaten with the rest of your team-mates in the training complex of Sant Joan Despí and then, as usual, Pep sends you all back home, to be with your families and have a rest. You love that, you don't have to hang around for games and somehow training becomes more intense, energetic, more fun. You have to return to the Camp Nou later, two hours before kick-off.

Around an hour before the start of the game, and when you are not completely ready to warm up, Pep takes his jacket off. He wears a tight shirt, white most of the time, with a tie and the sleeves rolled up. He's at work. You all head into a large room next to the dressing room and sit down to listen to him. He claps a couple of times, 'Gentlemen,' he shouts, and at that moment silence falls and you're about to have your eyes opened by him, he'll tell you the road to success in that particular match. He will make you see it, visualise it.

You go back to the dressing room and there you won't see Pep, who hides in his office. As part of the process of becoming a manager, he began keeping his distance from the players and the changing room became almost exclusively for the players, so much so that on many occasions he could be seen waiting outside the door, shouting to one of his assistants, 'how long before they go out?' If he was told five minutes, he would linger awhile before going in and issuing rapid-fire instructions. He understands his presence could influence the footballers' behaviour on their own territory. It should be a refuge where they, you, can say what you think at any time without fear of punishment. You can talk about girls, cars, even have a go at him if you want. Ask Xavi; he'll explain it to you:

Xavi: Sure. He told us from the beginning, 'I won't go in there.' It's like a classroom without the teacher. And when the teacher comes in, there's silence and it's time to work.

Manel Estiarte: He has to go through the dressing room in the stadium because his office is at the end of it. But he will not be seen with the players unless it is to talk to them after a game, to motivate them or remind them of something, or to give them a hug before it. There is always a huddle and shout before the game. He arrives, they hug and he goes. As the ex-player he is, he always says, 'This is the place where they joke, they might laugh at me, they might criticise me.'

You will be there with your rituals, one sock on before the other and things like that, you'll talk about the match, about the team talk, about Piqué's music. Valdés is quiet in a corner and so is Messi, who looks much smaller in that environment. After the warm-up, ten or fifteen minutes before the kick-off, but not always, Pep briefly appears to remind you of the two or three key points, small comments. And then he'll disappear again.

Xavi: His presence makes you sit up and pay attention, it makes you alert. All he needs to say is 'Are we ready or not?'

Javier Mascherano: And then he would give you the keys to the game, he doesn't need a ten-minute talk.

Tito: The pre-match talks are in the hotel if it is an away game, or, if it is a home game, in the Pictures room. First of all he shows footage of the opponents, explaining their strong points and how we can hurt them. The strategy is explained, both ours and the opponents'.

Iniesta: The talks remind me of school, everyone in their place, and him in the middle talking, gesticulating emphatically, passionately, if the situation calls for it, if not, he doesn't.

Valdés: In all the conversations that we have had I have always learnt something. I am quite shy and he taught me a lot about the importance of communication with team-mates, with the outside world.

Estiarte: No player looks at the floor, they have their eyes set on him.

Albert Puig (technical secretary of the academy): Yeah, he has that something, something between shy, sure of himself and very sure of himself – which is what grips you as if we were talking about a woman, that shyness and aura. That's what he has.

Xavi: Lots of talks surprise me, lots of them. He thinks in white, you think in black; and you end up thinking in white.

Cesc Fàbregas: He sees football with an amazing clarity.

Tito: Before going out on to the pitch, the message is a motivational one, he doesn't usually shout, he doesn't need to. Pep's tactic is to convince the players that everything that is said and done is for their own good. When they see that, they apply it and enjoy being out on the pitch.

An anonymous player: Ah, yes, those pre-game talks ... I remember one day at the Camp Nou, before the return leg of the semi-final against Valencia in the Copa del Rey (we had a 1–1 result in the first leg), he gave a speech full of sentimental lessons, about the club, what it meant to wear the shirt ... The magic is that after everything that this team has won, seeing Pep work makes you go out on to the pitch remembering, 'God, I'm playing for Barça.' There has never been one of those: 'What a blow today, we play yet another game.'

Estiarte: There are secrets I will never explain. But let me tell you one of the most remarkable chats he gave. Perhaps Pep will get upset if I say it. In a period where we couldn't find our best version, we were tired, people talked about refs helping us and all that, and Pep organised a meeting. 'Gentlemen, do you realise that when you are tired and we think that life is difficult that one of your team-mates has played thirteen games with a monster that was eating him inside? OK, we are tired, we have excuses, but there are priorities: we are healthy and Abi has given us an example to follow.'

The same anonymous player: And how about what he said before going to Chelsea: 'You're all on the phone all day, well while you're at it send a message to your families and friends now before going to warm up, promising them, 'We're going to go through', because that way you're all obliged to give it your all out there as you've made a commitment to them.

And then you start shouting, 'Come on, let's go, let's beat them.' Someone else is clapping, it smells of Deep Heat and the space becomes small, all of you trying to go through the small door, all of you standing up, some jumping up and down, finalising the rituals.

The game is not always going according to plan, and Pep doesn't say anything as soon as you return to the dressing room, but he finds two to three minutes to catch your attention.

Piqué: In the second season, we were drawing 0–0 against Rubin Kazan and he told us something at half-time that really stuck with me: 'When we lose our fear of losing, we'll stop winning.'

Valdés: I remember a talk at half-time during a game in which things were going pretty badly. Very calmly, he explained to us what we should do to sort out the situation. It was just a small move that the midfielders had to carry out, positional play. He showed it to us on the blackboard and 'zas!' we won the game because of that.

Xavi: With Pep, everything is calculated, if you get me, he's always been able to see two or three moves ahead. He analyses, and tells you things you haven't thought of.

Valdés: When a player understands what the coach is explaining and realises that with his decisions things improve, the level of credibility, connection and conviction increases considerably.

Estiarte: Pep told me: 'Manel, we cannot deceive them, not once, because they will find us out. And when they do, we are dead.'

Return to the pitch, second half, and after running normally even more than the opposition, you go back to the changing room having given what Pep asked of you: your all. No more, no less.

Xavi: After the game he'll sometimes give you a hug, or there will be times when he won't say a thing. Or there are days when he'll give a team talk after the ninety minutes, and other times he won't. He does what he feels and what he feels is right at all times. And if he wants to tell you off, he does so, no problem.

Estiarte: Sometimes he would only say after a game, 'Look, in three days we have such and such a match, eat, drink and rest. Congratulations.' A subtle reminder to be responsible.

Iniesta: He knows how to control his emotions and say things at the right moment. He worries about the group when things aren't going well and when we win he takes part in the hugs and celebrations. A family, we're like a family.

The main team talk in the bowels of Stamford Bridge, Pep's magic dust, wasn't applied before the start of the second leg of the semi-finals of the 2009 Champions League, but at half-time.

After emphatically beating Real Madrid and almost bagging the first title of the season (Barcelona were seven points ahead of their rivals with four La Liga games to go), the team travelled to London after the 0–0 draw of the first leg. They were nervous and anyone who said they weren't was lying. Nobody trembled but the hours leading up to the game were tense.

Rafa Márquez (injured) and Puyol (suspended) couldn't play, so Pep had to decide on the best partnership at the back. The players were told the line-up a couple of hours before kick-off, just before leaving the hotel to get to the Bridge. The two central defenders chosen were Piqué, who had grown in stature daily since his debut earlier in the season, and midfielder Yaya Touré, a selection which took everybody by surprise. Keita was the defensive midfielder and Iniesta was used up front with Messi and Samuel Eto'o.

The atmosphere was like nothing many of the players had ever experienced before – noisy long before the game, the roar, the hunger for success that came from every corner of the stadium. Pep Guardiola was astonished and admitted after the game that the atmosphere had certainly been intimidating.

The coach had insisted in the couple of training sessions and in the tactical talk prior to the match on what to do in order to avoid problems with Chelsea's Didier Drogba: basically, it was about not sticking to him when he had his back to you. He also told his players to repeat a few moves around the same area in order to get the attention of Chelsea's defenders and then, the next time, appear on the other side to surprise them.

But it was obvious right from the start that Barcelona lacked penetration. They had the ball but didn't do anything dangerous with it. Víctor Valdés saved the side with key interventions after Chelsea counter-attacks or dangerous set pieces, but Barcelona went into half-time 1–0 down after Essien scored with a shot from outside the box.

Pep needed to intervene. He didn't speak to anybody during the short walk through the narrow tunnel that takes you to the Stamford Bridge away team dressing room. As soon as he entered, and once everybody was inside, with energy, gesticulating in the middle of the room, holding the eyes of the players, he told them they had to be true to what they had done all year, that they shouldn't be scared. 'Believe, believe with all of your hearts that we can score, because then we will definitely score.'

There was also the tactical instruction: they should play fast balls down the wings, because Chelsea allowed them to start moves from the back and neither Anelka nor Malouda closed down that area particularly well.

Chelsea, with Guus Hiddink pulling the strings, wasn't a puppet like Real Madrid had been a few days earlier: they faced Barça with defensive rigour and a superhuman effort from their players. It was a fateful night for the referee Tom Henning Ovrebo, who ate away at Chelsea's morale: he unfairly sent off Abidal but he let Barça off with a couple of penalties, four according to Chelsea's protests, the strongest call being a clear handball by Gerard Piqué after the break.

Perhaps Pep Guardiola shouldn't have sent Piqué up front to play as a striker so early in the game (with around twenty minutes left) and perhaps Hiddink shouldn't have replaced Drogba, supposedly injured, with Juliano Belletti around the same time, sending the wrong message to his players. Both managers may have got it wrong at some point, but they agreed the game was as good as over towards the end. So Guardiola hugged Hiddink, as if to congratulate him on the imminent victory, some understood.

It was a hug, yes, but it was exceptional, with a smile, too, even. It was the hug of a noble fighter recognising the merits of his opponent during the extraordinary battle.

A few seconds later, Iniesta scored.

It was Barcelona's only shot on goal of the whole game. In the ninety-third minute.

Voted the best moment of the season by the Barcelona fans. Better than any final of that year, better than Rome and Manchester United. Better even than scoring six goals at the Bernabéu. It was just ecstatic, orgasmic. Everybody, with the exception of Chelsea fans, jumped to celebrate with Iniesta.

'Things were getting worse in the game,' Iniesta remembers. 'We were tired. It wasn't physical tiredness, it was something almost psychological. Alves went up the right wing, crossed to the centre, it fell to Samuel, and from then one of the most important moments of my life arrived. I got the ball from Messi. I didn't hit it with the instep of my foot, nor with the tip nor the inside. I hit it with my heart. With all of my soul. I don't think there are many photos of me on the pitch shirtless, I don't usually celebrate that way.'

It was twenty seconds from the moment Frank Lampard lost possession. Seven players involved, twelve touches of the ball before the goal that changed the contemporary history of the club. A portrait of Pep's team that, despite walking on the edge, had created a little masterpiece.

Perhaps, if Iniesta hadn't been the author of that goal, we wouldn't have seen Guardiola's legs propelling him down the touchline, his fists clenched and his face alight with euphoria, as if he'd lost control. Till Silvinho stopped him to ask him to do a substitution to lose some key seconds. He let himself be a footballer again for a second. Suddenly he stopped, turned around, contained himself and began, once more, to shout instructions.

'Iniesta taught me at Stamford Bridge to never write anything off. Improbable is not impossible … you have to believe,' Pep recalls. 'If his kick was unstoppable it's 'cause it was loaded with the will of the whole of the Barcelona fans.'

When the game ended, he proceeded to hug everybody, all of the players, the staff. At that moment he was both player and coach. Valdés came to him and got hold of him, shook him and shouted something in his face that he cannot remember. The heart was coming out of Pep. The whole team exploded like never before, not even at the Bernabéu. Everyone was going haywire. The biggest hug was with Iniesta to whom Pep must have mentioned what he later said in the press conference: 'Bloody hell, the one who never scores was the one with the goal.'

Not long before that crucial goal, Iniesta asked Pep for a few minutes. 'Give me your opinion, boss. I don't score enough, what should I do?' Pep started to laugh: 'You asking me? Me? I didn't score more than four goals in the whole of my career! What do I know!'

There is such a fine line between success and failure, as Pep likes to repeat to his footballers. Barcelona were going to play in the Champions League final against Manchester United in Rome. They had reached another pinnacle in a year that had turned out to be a glorious one.

A couple of days later, as journalist Ramón Besa recalls, Guardiola took his children to school, as he does almost every morning. The pupils, many of whom were wearing Barcelona shirts, looked out of the classroom windows, while others went out into the school yard to applaud Pep's arrival. 'Why are they clapping, Papa?' asked his son Màrius. 'Because they're happy, son,' he replied. The Espanyol fans among the children who sometimes challenged and taunted him about the result of the next Catalan derby were suddenly nowhere to be seen.

Barcelona were leaving a lot of their complexes behind; they weren't ashamed to assert themselves and bask in their happiness. As many people noted, the supporters rarely flocked to Canaletes, the fountain where Barcelona victories were enjoyed, without having a title to celebrate. But they were rejoicing over the six goals against Madrid, Iniesta's super strike against Chelsea and their acceptance of a style of play.

It was all about being proud of what Guardiola and his boys were producing.

In 2009 Barcelona won a sextet of titles, a record that had been achieved by no other team in history. They won everything they competed for in a calendar year: the Liga, the Copa del Rey against Athletic de Bilbao, the Champions League, the Spanish Super Cup, the European Super Cup and the World Club Championship. Those victories made Barcelona, statistically at least, the greatest team of all time, ahead of the Celtic of 1967, the Ajax of 1972, PSV Eindhoven of 1988 and Manchester United of 1999. Those four teams that had previously won the treble: the league, the cup and the European Cup. Pedro ('he was playing in the third division the other week!' as Pep reminded him every week – partly said with admiration, partly with caution) scored in every one of those competitions, another unprecedented feat. In the 2008–09 season Guardiola's team played eighty-nine games and only lost eight, four of which were all but insignificant and none was lost by more than one goal.

The year had shown on occasions that everything is relative: 'By doing the same, things may not have turned out this way,' Guardiola reminded people. But one thing was clear: using Cruyff's idea as a starting point, Guardiola had given the team methods by which to practise a type of football that was as elaborate as it was effective. Barça's triumph broke with some football taboos that put the result before the play, as if they were incompatible.

Barça's style has brought admiration from sports critics, similar to that generated in their day by mythical teams such as River Plate (1941–45) who ruled with an exceptional quintet made up of Muñoz, Moreno, Pedernera, Labruna and Loustau. As well as Budapest Honved (1949–55) with Puskas, Bozsik, Kocsis or Czibor, the foundations of that Hungary team that won at Wembley in 1953. And, of course, Di Stéfano's Madrid (1956–60), winners of five consecutive European Cups, with a forward line of Kopa, Rial, Di Stéfano, Puskas and Gento. Equally as celebrated was Pelé's Santos (1955–64) and the Brazil team from the 1970 World Cup – that team that lined up with five 'tens' in attack: Jairzinho, Gerson, Tostao, Pelé and Rivelino. Or Sacchi's Milan (1988–90), twice World Club Champions with players in the category of van Basten, Rijkaard and Gullit.

In the summer of 2009 and after winning the Champions League, Pep decided to make changes to his squad. Samuel Eto'o had become one of the most consistent performers of the team even when he had to, as against Madrid and Manchester United, play on the right of the attack. He scored the opening goal of the Roma final but Guardiola understood that to continue allowing Messi to grow, he had to get rid of the Cameroon international.

That same summer, Madrid had paid €95 million for Cristiano Ronaldo, €67 million for Kaká and Barcelona were negotiating with players such as Filipe Luis and David Villa, talks which fizzled out in the end. Finally, they struck a deal with Inter to exchange Eto'o for Ibrahimović. Pep spoke about 'feeling' in relation to Samuel, an English word which when used in Spanish means 'vibe'. 'It's a question of feeling, I can't change the character. A thousand things are telling me, things that aren't football- or character-related, that this year we have to change a few things in the dressing room, not just a player like Samuel but a few other things too.' Pep accepted publicly that he could be mistaken. But, again, he prefers to make his own mistakes.

Having won the League, the Cup and the Champions League in Rome, Barça attained the Spanish Super Cup over two legs against Athletic de Bilbao, with Ibrahimović and Eto'o now departed. There were two more titles left before achieving the sextet. Barcelona struggled against Shakhtar Donetsk in the Stade Louis II in Monaco. With the score level at 0–0 after ninety minutes, the title was played for in extra time. Pep knelt down in front of his starting team and began to explain to them what had to happen, what was going to happen.

'Be sure of the pass, without taking risks at the back! Do it well! As always, play at keeping the ball and above all, move forward. In our own way. They are expecting the counter-attack and they won't change. Do it more than ever, our way, with the ball. If we have the ball we can do what we know. In thirty minutes we can score! Don't worry, eh! Do what you know! Patiently. Let's not go crazy because if we do, they'll kill us. We'll pass and pass. Don't worry! Don't worry! Patience! We will work the same as always. More than ever we must move, move, move and constantly create superiority. We'll open up the pitch and we'll look for the wings and then there will be space down the centre. OK, gentlemen? As always! Let's go, eh?!' He finished off clapping. The path to victory was illuminated once again.

In the 115th minute, Pedro controlled the ball on the left, found Messi who managed to open up a channel between the full backs with two touches so that Pedro got the ball again and finished. Barça were proclaimed European Superchampions.

Out of all the titles won in 2009, the World Club Championship, to be played against Estudiantes de la Plata in December of that year after reaching the final, was the only honour the team had never won.

Pep's anguished words before winning his sixth title in his first year as Barça's coach can explain what happened two and a half years later. 'This is unbearable,' he privately acknowledged while he reflected on the fact that people have very short memories in the world of football. It worried him that more and more was being asked of a group of players that would go down in history as the greatest of all time.

The rhythm of success had been so harmonious and so phenomenal from Barcelona's point of view that it needed a happy ending. 'Tomorrow something will end that started last year,' Guardiola announced. 'The future is bleak, because surpassing what has been achieved is impossible. We'd be wrong to make comparisons. What we must do is work so that people continue to be proud of us. It isn't the game of our lives, because family are waiting for us at home, nor will it make up for anything.'

Pep took some of the weight off the pressure the team felt as a result of Barcelona losing the World Club final in 1992 and in 2006 with Rijkaard, undervaluing the competition on both occasions. But just before the game started, in the last talk to the team, he announced, in a carefully composed and convincing statement, that it was close to being the game of their lives: 'If we lose today, we will still be the best team in the world. If we win, we will be eternal.'

The game belonged to Estudiantes – the Argentinians denied Barça and scored from their best chance. But Pedro forced extra time from the penultimate kick of the game. Then, after a brief respite, it was just a question of waiting for the appearance of Messi, who scored after controlling the ball with his chest from a cross from Alves.

Lady Luck was looking out for Pep's team that season, and they persevered, never stopped running, and never looked for excuses. And eventually, it happened for them with Iniesta's goal at Stamford Bridge and Pedro's in this final.

It had been eighteen months since Guardiola was named first-team coach. On that December night in Abu Dhabi, Barcelona had won their sixth title under their new coach: that is, every competition they had competed for.

While he waited to collect the trophy, in full view of the world's TV cameras, standing on the pitch, Pep Guardiola broke down in tears.

Manel Estiarte looked on as his friend's body trembled before he burst into tears. Dani Alves was the first to approach the coach to give him a hug. Pep regained his composure for a few seconds. He took a few steps back and found himself alone once again. He hid his face with his hands and let everything out. He couldn't stop crying. He trembled; his shoulders yo-yoed up and down like a child's. Henry embraced him, smiling in disbelief. His friend Guillermo Amor, commentating for Spanish television, was moved when he saw him: 'He really lives football, he's trained for it,' he repeated, his voice breaking. Ibrahimović took over from Henry and joked with his coach. And at that moment Pep emerged from his trance as the officials slowly took over: the awards ceremony was about to begin.

Pep's sister Francesca cried herself as she watch him break down. 'It's really moving, it really gets you,' she said when she watched the footage again weeks later. Ramón Besa, journalist and friend, understands that Pep is 'so transparent that he does everything on the pitch: there's no cheats or tricks. He is extremely sensitive.' His friend David Trueba points out that 'victory is usually something that causes a lot of wires to cross'.

Pep usually bottles everything up inside, holding back his ups and downs, the secrets, the debts, the promises. Sometimes Estiarte encourages him to let it all out: 'If you want to cry, cry; punch the wall, vent your feelings.' On that day Manel would have liked Pep to have had more time to cry; he deserved to cry more after so much self-control.

And this, the last trophy of that year, was the one that finally triggered a public outpouring of emotion. The tension in the Liga, the Clásico, Iniesta's goal in London, the Champions League final. The relief, the euphoria of winning everything mixed with the fulfilment of starting a new job and knowing that in a very short time he had surpassed a level of success previously unimaginable. And now this title, so undervalued in Europe, yet considered the climax of the season in South America. A series of images and emotions built up in Pep's head and exploded. There was suddenly an escape valve for all the pressure. Guardiola got carried away by his emotions. 'That's Pep,' many said when they saw him. Or, rather, 'That, too, is Pep.'

Nobody asked him then about the reasons for his tears although he dedicated the success to Evarist Murtra, former director of Barcelona, who had been in favour of Pep training the Barça reserve team instead of working as a coordinator in the youth categories. 'They're things that happen,' he says now. 'With time, these things, if I carry on working in this field, won't happen again to me.' The strong Pep takes over again.

'For those who are here now and those who were here last year – thank you for the wonderful past eighteen months. We have played well many times. We have earned respect and the credit goes to them. They have been very generous in their effort,' he announced in the post-match press conference.

Pep Guardiola touched the sky in his first experience as a top-flight coach. They had been unforgettable months. The long days at the training complex, spending less time with partner Cris, locked in his office, making decisions, using common sense, surrounding himself with good people, being demanding of all around him on a daily basis – it had all been worthwhile. The tears humanised both the character and football.

Guardiola's Barcelona was now a 'guarantee of origin', bearing a hallmark, a trademark that stood for something the football world had never seen before – a team that knew no limits and that, through showing faith in their style and personality, had been capable of achieving greatness. The players left the dressing room to celebrate wearing t-shirts bearing the motto '*Todo ganado, todo por ganar*' (Everything won, everything to aim for).

Guardiola had replaced Joan Laporta and even Johan Cruyff as leader of the Barcelona religion. The motto 'More than a club' didn't just make sense from the entity's point of view, but also the team's. Barcelona were now 'immortals'.

Intent on finding new challenges, on taking the team even higher, Pep renewed his contract two months later, for another year until 2011. Yet . . . 'One more year and I'm off,' he thought.

At the beginning of the following season, the village of Santpedor decided to pay tribute to its most famous son. He was honoured by the village and proclaimed 'Hijo Predilecto', the equivalent to being given the 'key to the city'. In exchange, Pep had to get up on stage, in that square in which he'd played as a kid, to say a few words. He had gone back to his village, to everything that he had left behind, to the sacrifices of Dolors and Valentí Guardiola.

'I know that my parents are very happy today, and that makes me very happy. To have been born in this village, to have played for Barça and all those things …'

And then he had to stop, because his voice wavered and broke.

4
THE TWO CHAMPIONS LEAGUE FINALS

Two training grounds. One in the north-west of England, the other outside Barcelona. Two fortresses. At the end of a narrow road, Carrington. Off a main motorway, the facilities at Sant Joan Despí.

As you enter the Carrington offices, a smiling receptionist asks you to wait and then she walks you into the press room, a small version of a school classroom. A powerful silence embraces you. It is only broken by the voices of players, a burst of sound that disappears behind doors that takes them to their isolated world. Then the door opens and the imposing figure of a seventy-year-old man appears. Alex Ferguson's frame, dressed for training, is assertive, buoyant. His eyes are penetrating as he offers a strong handshake and the smile he keeps for when the cameras are not around.

Above the changing rooms of Barcelona training ground, away from the footballer's world, is Guardiola's office. As you go in, Tito Vilanova might be scribbling some notes at his table. Behind him, a glass door gives way to the three- by four-metre space where Pep spends most of the hours of every day. Guardiola's working desk is ordered – in the centre, the notebook; on one side, some files; on the other, books on leadership, a biography, a history book. Pep briefly stands up and welcomes me into his office. He then sits in a chair that suddenly becomes smaller. In fact, abruptly the whole place looks smaller than it is – he is one of those men who fills a room with his presence.

Same as Ferguson, really.

– Pepe. Pepe Guardiola. What a fantastic job he has done.

Pep leans forward. And before he refreshes his memories of Rome and the gladiators, Wembley and Messi and Xavi, he wants to praise everything that Ferguson stands for, what he has achieved, what Manchester United represent on and off the pitch.

– Sir Alex couldn't play any other way than they did in Rome. And in Wembley. It is Manchester United after all we are talking about. They dignify football with their approach as a club and as a team.

FC BARCELONA v MANCHESTER UNITED. ROME 2009

The preparations

Sir Alex Ferguson: Ah, Rome. It wasn't a great game for Manchester United, we really should have won that game, we let ourselves down really.

Pep Guardiola: Now that time has passed, I realise we had a very positive dynamic, it didn't matter who we were playing against, we had very high self-esteem. We had won the league, the Copa del Rey, got to the final of the Champions League in the last seconds of the match against Chelsea. The team dynamic was fantastic, even though we had some injuries.

Sir Alex: On the morning of the game we had two or three footballers who weren't well, we never said it. We had a problem about the fitness of some of the players, but they wanted to play and I went along with that. It was wrong.

PG: We were helped by the confidence and form going into that game: no doubt about it. How important that is! We felt we could beat anybody even though our preparations were full of uncertainty. We were without Dani Alves and Eric Abidal, both suspended; Rafa Márquez, who was crucial to us, was injured; I had to decide who to replace him with. Iniesta had not been with us for a month and a half, Thierry Henry was also restricted to a limited programme of exercises … They were desperate to participate. Wow, so many difficult situations. If you think about it now, calmly, and remember the line-up we played against: Rooney, Cristiano … Carlos Tévez was on the bench!

Manchester United also had concerns ahead of the match. Rio Ferdinand had suffered a calf injury and missed the previous four matches, but flew out with the rest of Ferguson's squad to Rome after taking part in training that morning. The signs were good: there was no apparent reaction to the defender's muscular problem. And Rio wanted to play.

Guardiola told both Iniesta and Henry he was going to wait right up until the last minute possible to decide if they could be passed fit. Pep had been playing the final for weeks in his head, visualising every conceivable tactical scenario and permutation; calculating where the spaces would open up; where his side could gain the upper hand in two v ones; endlessly replaying the key battles. The manager's reluctance to rule Iniesta and Henry out was understandable: both played a key role in the game he had been planning.

He'd prepared for every eventuality, planned every contingency. Two days before that final, he took Xavi to one side and told him, 'I know exactly where and how we will win in Rome. I've seen it. I can see it.' The midfielder looked at his boss with a mixture of enthusiasm and, perhaps for the last time, some scepticism. 'Yes?' said Xavi. 'Yes, yes, yes. I've got it, we will score two or three, you'll see,' replied Pep with such absolute conviction that Xavi's doubts, the typical anxieties experienced by every player before a big game, evaporated.

This was Pep Guardiola's first European final as a coach. The biggest club final in world football. He had less than a year's experience as manager of a first team.

PG: On paper, that Manchester United side were dominant in every department. I was worried about everything about them: quick on the counter, strong in aerial play, conceding few goals. Sometimes the rival is better than you and you have to go out and defend, but we were going to be brave. And Manchester United knew it.

Subtle changes would have to be made – and those were the little details he had been visualising for weeks – but Guardiola told the players they just had to persist with the same things they had been doing all season. Most of the especially significant decisions that Pep had to make were related to the absentees and their replacements in the line-up. Puyol would have to move to his old position at full back, while midfielder Yaya Touré would fill in as an improvised centre half. Another midfielder, Seydou Keita, was considered ahead of Silvinho for the fourth slot in defence vacated by Dani Alves. However, when the idea was put to the player in training ahead of the final, a match that every player in the world would give anything to participate in, Keita told Pep, 'Don't play me there.'

Keita's reasoning blew the manager away, because his motives were selfless rather than selfish, as they first appeared: 'I would do anything for you, boss, but I have never played there. My team-mates will suffer,' explained Keita. The player was putting the collective needs of the team ahead of any individual desire to play: the midfielder knew that he was not going to be in the line-up unless he was the makeshift right back. On more than one occasion since that day, Pep has said: 'I've never met such a good and generous person as Keita.' That week, the coach knew that his midfielder would do the job if he asked him to – 'I can still convince Keita,' he kept saying – but, in the end, decided that Silvinho, who had participated little that year and would be playing his last game for the club, would play at left back in Rome.

'I don't know if we will beat United, but what I do know is that no team has beaten us either in possession of the ball or in courage. We will try to instil in them the fear of those who are permanently under attack,' Pep told the media, translating his prediction into four different languages himself the day before the final. 'I will tell the players to look their best because they are going to be on the telly for the whole world. Oh, and I believe it is going to rain. If not the pitch should be watered. That should be an obligation, to guarantee a spectacle. After all that, the enjoyment of fans is why we play this game.'

The British press made reigning European Champions Manchester United clear favourites to retain their title in Rome. Having also just secured their eleventh Premier League title, Ferguson's side were brimming with confidence and self-belief and the mood was reflected across the country as fans and pundits alike predicted that the Red Devils would be too powerful for the diminutive Catalans.

In Catalonia the mood was far more circumspect: United were worthy of considerable respect.

Guardiola was on the verge of possibly his third title in an incredibly short managerial career, an historic treble – the first in the history of FC Barcelona – the greatest achievement for a debutant coach in the history of the game. 'And if I win that third title, the Champions League, I could go home,' joked Pep, 'call it a day and finish my career there.' He was asked, 'What would Sir Alex make of that?'

'I am sure he will think, "Look, here goes another one that will abandon this profession before me."'

Back at the hotel after the pre-match press conference on the eve of the final, Pep organised a meeting with all his backroom staff and presented them with a photograph of them together, taken a few days before, with the inscription: 'Thanks for everything. Pep'. The staff applauded and over the noise you could hear the voice of Guardiola shouting, 'you are amazing, as good as the players, you are!'

Pep had a precious minute to reflect on the way up to his hotel room. He wanted to make sure everything had been organised according to plan. There had been, as happens ahead of every final, huge amounts of information to digest and elements to ponder apart from just tactics: such as the line-up, the state of the grass, logistical issues and even private and personal matters to take care of. It was something he had experienced many times before as a player and knew how quickly events caught up with you as time flew past in the build-up, so he began his preparations several weeks earlier.

Carlo Mazzone, Guardiola's former coach at Brescia, had received a phone call ahead of the game. At first he thought it was somebody winding him up. 'Carletto, this is Pep … Pep Guardiola. I want you to come and watch our Barcelona.' For Pep, it was important to invite those people from his past who had played their part in his journey: people like the seventy-two-year-old Italian coach, as well as other former Brescia team-mates and even others from his brief spell at Roma.

Closer to home, Pep learnt that Angel Mur, the club's retired massage therapist for thirty-three years and one of Pep's favourite members of staff from his playing days, did not have tickets, so he came as a personal guest of the manager.

All seemed in order, but, around midnight on the eve of the Champions League final, Pep lay in bed, staring at the ceiling, struggling to switch off and get to sleep.

The players had been joined by their partners the night before the final – contrary to the conventional belief that players become distracted with their wives or girlfriends around them – because Pep had experienced the excessive pressure and tension that builds to a crescendo on the eve of big games he knew how important it was for the players to relax. If having their nearest and dearest by their side helped them cope with the anxiety and even distracted them, it meant they would sleep more soundly the night before. That level of empathy with those under him became another of those little details for which his footballers are grateful to him.

As the lights finally went off in Pep's hotel bedroom, the last-minute dress rehearsal of the Champions League ceremony at the Olympic stadium in Rome was coming to a close.

The day of the final. One surprise before kick-off

Andrés Iniesta: The minutes leading up to a Champions League final are like the minutes building up to any other game. Really. I don't want to seem boring or take away any of the glamour from the world of football, but that's the way it is. And it's a good thing that it is like that. The same talks, the same customs.

However, their pre-match routine was not going to be the same as any other in Rome.

On 27 May 2009, with two hours to go before kick-off, the teams arrived at the stadium. Typically, Pep prefers to leave his charges alone for most of that time and deliberately tries to avoid going into the players' dressing room up until the right moment, when he allows himself around five, ten minutes to intervene. But that night he had a surprise up his sleeve for the players.

Guardiola has an abundance of emotional intelligence, and needs, wants, to get in synch with his players. He can communicate with them in different ways, reach them with a word, a gesture, a look, a hug – it is easier to place instructions and demands in an open heart, and even to enjoy the profession if the relationships are based on trust and – yes, why not? – love.

Throughout the season, his speeches had engaged with the players emotionally before games but on this occasion he had prepared something different, something that would not require any additional words.

Pep Guardiola: What I have learnt over the years – I am aware tactics are very important, but the really great coaches are coaches of people and that human quality is what makes them better than the rest. Choosing the right people to look up to and give them the authority in a changing room is one of the many selections a coach has to make.

Sir Alex Ferguson: Well, in my experience, human beings want to do things the easiest possible way in life. I know some people who have retired at fifty years of age, don't ask me why. So the drive that certain human beings have got is different from the Scholes and the Giggs and the Xavis, you know, and Messi. I look at Messi and I say to myself, nothing is going to stop him being one of the greats. When he gets to thirty-four, thirty-five, most defenders are going to say 'Thank fuck he's gone'. You know what I mean? Because he looks to me an exceptional human being. And Xavi, too, in the same way I would describe Scholes and Giggs. In other words, that motivation is not an actual issue for them; their pride comes before everything else. You know, you see the way Giggs and Scholes train, how they go about their life and that is a fantastic example to other people in the dressing room. I think I have a few who will follow on from that and I'll be surprised if people in the dressing room at Barcelona do not take how Puyol acts, for instance, as sort of a personal motivation.

Perhaps Barcelona, as Sir Alex is suggesting, didn't need more motivation than winning, than doing the best for their manager, than making sure they didn't disappoint Puyol or Xavi. But Pep felt that the occasion called for something out of the ordinary to help set the tone. His plan got under way a couple of weeks before the final with a text message to Santi Padró, a TV producer for the Catalan channel TV3: 'Hola, Santi. We have to meet. You have to help me win the Champions League.'

When Santi came up with the goods a few days later, Pep watched the end result on his laptop and the film the producer had put together brought a tear to his eye. Santi knew straight away that he'd achieved exactly what Pep had asked him to do. Pep then called for Estiarte to come running, telling him he had to watch this DVD. His friend's reaction was equally resounding: 'Where and when will you show it to them?'

'Just before the game,' replied Pep.

To which his friend could only add, 'Wow!'

The players were surprised when their warm-up session at the Olympic stadium was brought to an end by the physical trainer a little sooner than they expected.

But they were still in the zone. There was emotion, tension, in the air as they headed down the tunnel that took them to the dressing room. Nervous, anxious.

Occasionally, one player shouts, claps a team-mate on the back, all to break the tension. Hearts racing. The clatter of studs on the floor. Toc toc toc toc toc toc toc.

At that moment, footballers don't want to be disturbed; they want only to focus on their routine, to be left alone to get on with their last-minute preparations and superstitions. At Barcelona, Víctor Valdés is always the first to get back to the changing room after the pre-match warm-up. In Rome, he got to the dressing room, only to find it locked. He banged on the door, but was not allowed in. One of Pep's assistants came out and blocked his way, telling him he'd have to wait. Valdés was flabbergasted. Xavi was next.

Xavi: What's going on?

Víctor Valdés: He isn't letting us in!

Xavi : Why!?

Víctor Valdés: I've been told to wait.

The rest of the group arrived, and they were finally let in after being made to hang around in the corridor a few minutes longer.

Pep made himself heard above the chatter: 'Lads, I want you to watch this. Enjoy it. This is the teamwork that has taken us to Rome!'

The lights in the dressing room went off as a big screen illuminated the room and the theme from the movie *Gladiator* filled the space with sound.

Guardiola's friend Santi had produced a rousing seven-minute video montage that merged images from the Hollywood blockbuster *Gladiator* with footage of the entire Barcelona squad, all set to the film's epic soundtrack. You can see it for yourself online. Every single footballer, even those who played a more peripheral role in the season, is honoured in the film – two sub goalkeepers, Hleb, Milito, and it had been tricky finding footage of the injured defender from that campaign. It featured everyone. Except Pep Guardiola – the coach had stipulated that under no circumstances did he want to be eulogised in the footage. It was all about his players.

When the film finished there was silence in the room. Nobody moved, firstly because of the surprise, then the emotion. Players were shyly looking at each other. Tears were shed. Milito cried, he was missing the final. Unthinking, unconsciously, players had put their arms around team-mates' shoulders. It was a moment, an intense, special moment.

Unforgettable, emotive. But was it the right thing to do?

'I don't know if it was because of the feelings the video brought up or what, but our first minutes of the final were pretty awful,' Iniesta says now. Even Pep Guardiola admits that he might have moved the players a touch too much.

The game, the managers

Sir Alex Ferguson: We really should have won that game, we were a better team at the time.

Pep Guardiola: United were a fantastic team! Just look at their bench that day: Rafael, Kuszczak, Evans, Nani, Scholes, Berbatov and Tévez.

Sir Alex: I think Henry's a great footballer, Eto'o's a great footballer but they weren't players that worried us, you know what I mean? The Wembley final was different.

PG: Manchester United certainly didn't set out to defend, it is not in their genes, is it? In any case, we had prepared different alternatives depending on how the game went.

Sir Alex: So Eto'o started off in the centre and Messi right, but then it was changed around to Eto'o wide right and Messi dropping into the hole that he uses quite well now. But in the final Messi did nothing, trust me, he didn't do anything.

PG: We played Messi sporadically in that position, in the hole. We did it against Madrid, but not again until the final. Looking back, thinking about those tactics now … maybe we won because of the very positive dynamic we had.

Sir Alex: If you go back to the final in Paris, Arsenal–Barcelona, Eto'o played wide left in the game and he worked up and down, he worked his balls off in that game. He's been used to playing wide but we didn't expect him to play wide in Rome. We expected at different times that they would change, Messi and Eto'o would change in the game, but not to the point where we were worried too much about it.

PG: United put us under pressure, defended high, had a few chances to score, and if they had scored, United are a team that kills you on the counter-attack, so if they had taken the lead it would have been much more difficult for us. Especially with Ronaldo who is a wide player and in important European games he played through the middle. If you leave Cristiano as a striker and with space, nobody can stop him, it is impossible, he's unique.

Sir Alex: Conceding from a counter-attack when we were controlling the game turned out to be key, because Barcelona are not the type of side you want to be behind and chasing the game.

PG: The first team to score a goal, like it or not, in a final, makes the difference.

Sir Alex: And when Eto'o scores the first goal, then, yes, Messi became a problem as Barcelona had overloaded the midfield and it was difficult to get the ball off him but, actually, he didn't threaten us that much.

PG: I remember the final in Rome came to an end and thinking, 'God, we've played really, really well!' Then, a couple of years later, when we were preparing for the Wembley final, we watched the videos of the game in Rome and realised it hadn't been as great as we imagined. We had been very lucky to survive the opening minutes.

Sir Alex: The Barcelona midfield – pass, pass, pass – was never threatening, really. When we beat Barcelona back in 1991, in the Cup Winners' Cup final, that team did exactly the same as in Rome. Salinas was the striker and Laudrup, too, with Beguiristain wide left, but they all dropped deep into the midfield, same thing. At that time we said, 'Let them have the ball in there, keep the back four in all its positions', and we never had a problem. But, if you wind on twenty years, a different quality player makes a difference.

PG: In the end, playing against us is complicated. When we are playing well, we pass the ball and we force our opponents to drop deep bit by bit. It seems like they are sitting back but, no, we're pushing them back.

Sir Alex: And the second goal, if you think about it; Messi, five foot seven, scores from a header at the back post, against an English team. That shouldn't happen.

PG: We played better in the second half than we did in the first.

Sir Alex: Barcelona had one or two chances before Messi's goal, just after half-time, and could have killed us off then but in the last fifteen minutes we actually had five chances.

PG: Xavi hit the post with a free-kick and Thierry Henry was denied by van der Sar before Messi scored with twenty minutes remaining. Then we dug in and defended. But after I watched that final again, I looked back and thought that it was all a bit of a gift.

Scouting report: Champions League final 2009

FC BARCELONA 2–0 MANCHESTER 2009

Henry   Eto'o   Messi   Rooney   Ronaldo   Park

Iniesta   Xavi   Giggs

Busquets   Anderson   Carrick

Silvinho   Piqué   Touré   Puyol   Evra   Vidić   Ferdinand   O'Shea

Valdés   van der Sar

First half:

Manchester United had beaten Barcelona the previous year in the semi-finals of the Champions League by being very defensive. With Ronaldo up front, Tévez off the striker, Rooney very deep on the right wing. They sat back and counter-attacked. Evra marked Messi, who played on the right, with the help of a defensive midfielder. In 2008, following a 0–0 at the Camp Nou, a repeat performance at Old Trafford with a goal by Paul Scholes took United to the final. United were very happy with the performance. It was perfect.

Before the Rome final, United's mentality had changed: they were now Champions League title holders and the resulting confidence and sense of superiority were reflected in their approach: Ferguson asked the team to press high. The message was, 'we are the Champions, we can't sit back and defend deep any more.'

Manchester United got off to a great, positive start: with Cristiano as a striker up against Touré and Piqué; with Rooney on the left to work the space behind Puyol at right back. The United idea was clear: pressure high up the pitch to stop Barcelona building from the back and look for Ronaldo as soon as they recovered possession, with an emphasis on trying to find him in space behind Piqué (identified as being slower than Touré). This strategy unsettled the Barcelona defence that was placed quite high upfield.

Ronaldo also dropped deep to receive the ball, turn round and run towards goal – and he always found space as the centre backs didn't follow him closely.

Evra attacked down the left flank as he was not being tracked by Messi or, later in the match, Eto'o – so the French left back and Rooney frequently found themselves in some two v ones against Puyol.

The United forwards received the ball with their back to goal in between the Barcelona midfield and defence, and could turn easily as Barcelona didn't close them down to put them under pressure. Barça were either scared or asleep in those first few minutes.

Cleverly, Giggs defended against Busquets and made it difficult for Barcelona to build up from the back, forcing them to play longer balls than usual to the midfielders.

Henry and Eto'o didn't see much of the ball and couldn't run into defenders or in behind defenders, so they couldn't link with Messi who kept trying to dribble three, four players at a time.

Then a fantastic tactical move took place that proved key to the game.

Pep moved Eto'o wide and Messi in the centre of attack. The first Barcelona goal came soon after, nine minutes played.

Barcelona 1–0 Man United (Eto'o, 9). Barcelona scoring with their first attack. Iniesta leaves Anderson behind and passes the ball to Eto'o who is in the right wing. After cutting inside and dribbling Vidić, he touches the ball with the top of his toe to beat van der Sar. The last-ditch lunge from Carrick is futile.

In the final fifteen minutes of the first half, Messi dropped deeper into midfield to participate in the build-up and create superiority against the outnumbered United midfielders, but the Barcelona wingers didn't use the vacant space in the central striking position.

With Barcelona packing the midfield, the United players became demoralised while struggling to get a foothold. Interestingly enough, there was no fluidity in the Barcelona game, or not as much as we saw in later years, and only Iniesta tried to open up the United defence with some individual work. Barcelona didn't seem to be playing like Barcelona: they lacked aggression, didn't control the ball as much as usual, giving it away far too often. They posed little threat from the wings, playing predictable football, and were too respectful of United. Despite the scoreline, Manchester United were creating lots of problems for Barcelona.

Half-time:

Sir Alex Ferguson was very unhappy. In fact after the first ten minutes he had shown his displeasure in the dugout. 'Press high, you have to press high. You have stopped doing that,' he shouted in the changing room. The infamous hair-dryer treatment. The United players had not followed instructions in the first forty-five minutes.

Second half:

Tévez came on for Anderson and Giggs moved to the double pivot position alongside Carrick.

The second half was similar to the first. Busquets didn't participate much, Barcelona were again lacking intensity and aggression (not enough then). They made only a couple of runs down the left flank, but created little danger through the wide areas.

United continued with their plan but they found less space. Ferguson swapped Berbatov for Park on sixty-five minutes, which weakened the midfield zone. The numerical superiority in midfield became clearer and Barça seemed from then on calmer and in control.

The Barcelona defence dropped deeper and the rest of the team followed suit to avoid Cristiano finding space behind the defenders. Because of it, Barça suffered less and Ronaldo became anonymous. It was a logical move by Pep as it was a final and they were already 1–0 up; but that meant they created less pressure upfield; waiting for United and looking for isolated moves, such as the one which led to Barcelona's second goal.

Barcelona 2–0 Manchester United (Messi, 70). Evra loses possession and Xavi advances, unimpeded. He sends a perfect cross towards the far post where, unmarked, Messi steers a header across van der Sar and into the far corner. Well-crafted goal, poor defending.

Scholes replaces Giggs, Keita comes on for Henry – seventy-six minutes.

So United did play well in the first half and Barcelona was more practical and defensive than they were in following seasons, risking less than usual. On that night, individual quality made the difference and Barcelona won their first European and domestic treble in their 110-year history.

The press conference

Pep Guardiola: I'm pleased with the way we achieved the result; we took risks, we played with three upfront. Nothing ventured, nothing gained.

The Barcelona coach went on to pay homage to Paolo Maldini, dedicating the victory to the Italian legend who, just a few days previously, had played his last game for AC Milan at the San Siro but had been jeered and whistled by a section of his own club's supporters. Pep was disgusted at the player's treatment and wanted to make a point while showing his appreciation for a fellow professional from his era in the game.

Later that evening, as Pep and Manel Estiarte made their way out on to the unlit pitch of the Olympic stadium to savour the moment, the two friends paused to reflect upon what the team and coach had achieved that evening. Pep spoke to the man who had stood by him throughout the years in a way that he could only do with his closest and most trusted friends: 'We've just won the European Cup for the third time, the same number as Manchester United. We're getting closer and closer to the very top of the elite. We are the European Champions! It feels like we've just written our names in history.'

FC BARCELONA v MANCHESTER UNITED. WEMBLEY 2011

The preparations

Wembley: one of the most iconic names in world football. Possibly the best final the game could have picked at that moment: featuring two contrasting ways of understanding the game, both competitive; two clubs that have paved the way in terms of academy development, of their drive, their philosophy. And two managers who share a mutual respect, reverence and competitive instinct towards each other.

Barcelona had just won their third consecutive league title, made all the more commendable because no other European league had witnessed the same winner as the previous season – for one simple reason: the 2010–11 campaign had started on the back of the World Cup in South Africa, which is more taxing for the bigger clubs that provide the best players. Incredible, then, that Barcelona had had eight of their players prominently involved with the winners, Spain.

For the Catalan club, winners in 2006 and 2009, it was their third Champions League final in six years, and that year they had also knocked out Real Madrid in a highly contentious semi-final. After just three seasons as first-team coach, Guardiola had won nine titles out of the twelve contested and could surpass Cruyff's Dream Team by winning a second European Cup. In contrast, Manchester United, Champions League winners in 2008, had reached three finals in the previous four seasons, and had also just been crowned Premier League champions, their twelfth in nineteen years.

The numbers help set the scene: the two best clubs in recent history were clashing to decide who was the best in Europe. Both teams had won the European Cup three times; their head-to-head record was also equal – three wins apiece and four draws.

Pep Guardiola did not overlook the fact that Barcelona had built their legend in the modern era upon their first European Cup, secured in 1992 at the old Wembley stadium, and this proved to be a useful motivational tool deployed by him whenever the moment called for words of inspiration: whether whispered in a player's ear on the way to warm-up, or while taking a breather and a gulp of water during a break in training, or written on a whiteboard in the dressing room before a match. The England cathedral of football was a place of special personal significance for Pep, where he had first laid his hands on the famous piece of silverware known as 'Big Ears' – also the day almost twenty years earlier where Pep Guardiola the player had counted the steps that led up to the balcony where they would be presented with the trophy.

The overall feeling of satisfaction of lifting the trophy as a manager surpassed anything Pep had felt when winning the European Cup as a player.

In the summer of 2010, at the beginning of that season, Pep knew that to reach the same heights of his first two years in charge, with the six consecutive titles in one calendar year, would be impossible. Nevertheless, in order to overcome Manchester United in another European final, he would need to reinvent elements of his side, hence the decision to sign David Villa. Pep's interest in bringing the Valencia striker to the Camp Nou first became an issue back in 2009 when, during the FIFA Confederations Cup in South Africa, Guardiola rang the player to tell him how much he wanted him at Barcelona and the role he saw for him at the Camp Nou. The move broke down amidst competition from Real Madrid and several Premier League clubs; but the fact that Pep had shown his faith in the Spanish international a year earlier played a huge part in the striker moving to the Catalan club in the summer of 2010. 'Pep is going to call you,' Puyol told the forward. When Guardiola rings you to tell you he needs you, it's impossible to be left in any doubt that his interest is genuine. David Villa will always be grateful to Pep for his persistence.

Having won the league three weeks previously, Villa, who had settled in extraordinarily well in his first season at the club, was one of the footballers rested during the last games of the domestic campaign – with an eye specifically on the Wembley showdown. 'You will get to the final in great shape, trust me, David,' Pep repeated to him in the preceding weeks. The manager knew that his eight World Cup finalists, and the Dutch midfielder Ibrahim Afellay, had not had a break from the game for a very long time – vital both physically and mentally. Pep would prepare for every eventuality and made the following promise to his players:

'Lads, you've a commitment to the fans in reaching the final, but if you get us there, then I'm committed to making sure you win it.'

Guardiola was choosing his words carefully to sprinkle his customary gold dust on a season that was again turning out as astonishing as any other. But he was not sure how his fatigued side was going to react. The game was going to have the usual thorough analysis and preparation, but did the players have enough left in the tank to respond to the demands, physical and psychological?

Even Pep's meticulous preparation and contingency plans could not have foreseen the freak circumstances that popped up unexpectedly days before the final and that required an immediate response.

The season before, a volcanic ash cloud from Iceland had drifted into European airspace, forcing Barcelona to frantically rearrange their plans and travel by road to a Champions League semi-final against Inter Milan, wrecking their pre-match preparations.

With an impending sense of déjà vu, the news broke that another Icelandic ash cloud, spreading from the Grimsvotn volcano, was heading towards England and might lead to all flights being suspended ahead of the Champions League final weekend. Pep and his staff reacted quickly. To avoid having their plans left in tatters at the last minute, the club decided to move their flight to London forward by two days from Thursday to Tuesday; giving them four days in England to focus on the final.

It may have been a blessing in disguise. The team stayed at the luxurious Grove Hotel and Spa in Hertfordshire and trained nearby at Arsenal's London Colney facilities. The days spent in the relative seclusion of their base in the English countryside afforded them some vital R&R time as well as the opportunity to focus on the match, away from the pressures and constant media attention they would have been subjected to in Barcelona.

At that time, Eric Abidal was recuperating from the operation to remove a tumour from his liver he had undergone just two months earlier in March. There were doubts as to whether he would play again, and even the most optimistic club officials were speculating that he might return, at the very earliest, the following season. Instead, just under seven weeks later,

Abidal featured in the last two minutes of Barcelona's Champions League semi-final second-leg win over Real Madrid. As well as receiving the inevitable ovation from the Barcelona fans, Abidal's team-mates rushed over to celebrate with him the moment the final whistle went, throwing him up in the air as if it were his birthday.

The player had his heart set on making the team for the Champions League final, even if Guardiola had warned 'it will be difficult for Abidal to be 100 per cent fit'. Pep knew that the player's body might not be ready for it, but had no doubts about how much he wanted to play. Another problem was the fact that Puyol was also not fully fit, so Javier Mascherano, a midfielder converted into a centre back, would have to play at the heart of the defence.

Alex Ferguson, with no injury worries, had practically two teams to choose from. And also time to prepare the match. For two years he had been saying he hoped to get the chance to face Barcelona again in a Champions League final because he knew what he had to do to beat them. His wish was granted. But, as they say, be careful what you wish for.

For starters, Ferguson felt that he'd got it wrong two years earlier, in Rome, when he kept his players isolated for too long in the build-up, locked away in a hotel with minimal contact with the outside world. To avoid making the same mistakes again, the United manager decided that he would give his players a break from the monotony of hotel life by taking them to see a West End show on the Thursday evening in London forty-eight hours before the Wembley final. Fergie's choice of *Jersey Boys*, however, was not fully appreciated by his entire squad, some of whom joked that it might have been a good night out for someone of Sir Alex's age, but not exactly the kind of night they might have had in mind if left to their own devices in the capital. The day before the big match involved plenty of last-minute arrangements, including a leisurely morning stroll in the capital and a training session at Wembley in the evening.

The United manager also wanted to get his tactics right as well and his preparations on the training pitch at Carrington had begun two weeks earlier. Ferguson spent a week drilling his players in the game plan at their Manchester HQ and took the opportunity to put them into practice in a trial run against Blackpool at Old Trafford on the last day of the Premier League season, a week before the final. It was the afternoon in which United collected the league trophy and Blackpool's tearful and dejected players confirmed their relegation.

Ferguson instructed the United players to put pressure on Blackpool/Barcelona high up the field and, if the first line of pressure was beaten, to drop deep quickly and keep a narrow midfield, because he believed that his side could effectively surrender the wide areas to Barcelona, where they were relatively ineffectual. When Barcelona did get the ball into danger areas near the United box, the players were warned to be particularly mindful of quick one-twos.

The concept of maintaining and sustaining the pressure on the Barcelona defence also applied to free-kicks, where the United players were told to hit the ball into the box at every opportunity.

They were also coached to get the ball forward early and transition quickly as soon as they recovered possession. If that meant hitting long balls, so be it, as the priority was to get the ball forward when the majority of Barcelona players were still in the United half. By getting the ball to Hernández at the earliest opportunity, he could exploit one v ones against the exposed defenders.

In other words, with possession limited in the face of Barcelona's expected dominance of the ball, the United players were under strict orders to make every single opportunity count.

The tactical talk

For the Barcelona players in the Wembley changing room before kick-off, there was to be no epic, rousing, motivational film; just short, informative, tactical video clips. However, Guardiola's pre-match chat was so intense, so precise, that there was no need for anything else. It began with the coach highlighting images from previous matches – focusing on moves and isolated incidents involving Manchester United – alongside reminders to his own team on how to defend and how to attack, but was cleverly transformed into a passionate, inspirational speech from Pep that lifted the team and gave them the confidence to believe in themselves. Villa revealed the following day that it was a pity there was no video recording of Pep's performance in the dressing room that day, because it would make a very useful educational tool for any aspiring young coaches in how to give the perfect team talk.

No video doing the rounds on the internet, but, by listening to the footballers who were in the dressing room that evening, we are able to get an insight into what Pep told them before kick-off at Wembley.

Pep came into the room with his jacket off, rolled up his sleeves and began talking, pointing every now and again at an image on the screen. He looked into his players' eyes, speaking with intent in fast, clear Spanish. Pacing around, gesturing furiously, spontaneously, he would occasionally move up close and address one of his pupils directly, to drive home his point.

'I know we are going to be Champions, I have no doubt about it at all. Lads, I told you that you would take me to the final and that if you did that, I was going to make you win. If we do things how we are supposed to, then we will be the superior team.

'Manchester United also like to keep the ball, want to take away our protagonism on the pitch. You know we are not used to not having much of the ball, so we must keep it. And if we take it off them, used as they are to having possession against other teams, they will be uncomfortable and struggle to defend.

'Now, Eric [Abidal], have a look at this: Antonio Valencia always runs down the wing so you should play further up so Valencia feels less comfortable. Alves, listen to me: Park prefers diagonal movements instead of vertical ones, so use the outer zones. United have recently started taking short corners, so remember what we have been doing specifically for this in training. It will be much better if United didn't take a single corner today. And remember our own set piece that we have been practising all this week, we've not used it in a match for at least three games to keep it secret from United, so that means you can surprise them with it.

'You are going to be able to find and create space here and here. Right here. This is where the game can be won and lost. Keep an eye on the two v ones that are going to pop up here, here and here. In midfield we will be four against three, we'll have superiority in numbers in these central areas. Here is where you are going to win the game for me. Because I have seen it, I have analysed it and I know this is where we will win it.'

So, it wasn't the simple instructions that Cruyff gave his Barcelona players at Wembley twenty years earlier, no 'go out and enjoy yourself'. The message was 'yes, we have to enjoy this match, but we have to suffer for it too'.

Javier Mascherano cannot help being a fan of Pep, of the delivery and timing of his speeches, of the quality of the message: 'I've heard more than one player say: "Son of a bitch, he's nailed it!" That speech at Wembley was one that made the greatest impression on me. While he was talking, it wasn't as if he was referring to a game that we were about to take part in, it was as if we were actually playing it right there. He was up and down, side to side in front of the board, gesticulating; and if you shut your eyes and listened to him, you were already out there in the middle of the action. Everything that he said would happen, happened as he said it would. During the match I was thinking; I've seen this already, I've already heard all about it – because Pep has already told me about it ...'

There was one more moment of inspiration. A few words that would send Mascherano, for one, out on to the pitch with a tear in his eye.

Just after the players had warmed up, minutes before the match was about to kick off, completely unplanned, Pep decided to appeal to the players' human instincts. As the referee was trying to usher them out and into the tunnel leading on to the pitch, Pep quickly grabbed hold of them and gathering them around said, with pure determination in his voice:

'Listen, lads, we're going to do this for Abidal! He has made it here and is with us, we cannot let him down.'

Scouting report: Champions League Final Wembley 2011

First half:

Abidal was in the line-up.

Pep received a report from a friend in England that explained Manchester United had been training with a 4-3-3 but that finally they were going to play with their more usual 4-2-3-1: a formation that could convert into 4-4-1-1. 'Are you sure?' Pep had to ask till he was convinced. Barcelona came out with their classical 4-3-3.

The report from his friend was spot-on.

In the first ten minutes, Manchester United applied lots of pressure and intensity with man-to-man marking in midfield. Rooney stuck close to Busquets to prevent Barcelona building from the back, through him. Giggs was all over Xavi. Barcelona struggled as they couldn't find superiority in any part of the pitch and the game was in the hands of United.

After ten minutes, the first of two key moves of that final took place.

Xavi dropped a little deeper, to receive the ball in line with where Busquets would normally start. It meant that Barcelona effectively switched to a 4-2-3-1. United didn't feel brave enough to send any player to mark Xavi that high upfield – and if they did, they reacted too late. It enabled Xavi to see more of the ball, in space – allowing him to play with his head up, under little pressure, pick his passes and start dictating the game from deep. It was a good move; but it did mean that Barcelona's superiority was taking place a little deeper than they might have wished.

And then another tactical move changed everything.

Messi started to see more of the ball in midfield. He moved from his position higher up, in between the lines, to a midfield area where neither Vidi nor Ferdinand followed for fear of straying too far from their centre-back positions.

It effectively meant that the midfield was shaping up as Busquets, Xavi, Iniesta and Messi against Rooney, Carrick and Giggs.

From that moment on, Barcelona had control of the game. They scored in the twenty-seventh minute to make it 1–0. Rooney, however, pulled United level five minutes later and in the following few minutes Barcelona appeared to be reeling from the sucker punch. However, they soon regained composure and control.

The Catalan team was brave in their pressing high upfield, too. One passage of play highlights how high Barcelona pressed: United rushed twelve passes together with none of them crossing the halfway line, so suffocated were they by the pressure of the Barcelona players in their own half.

Half-time:

The United players didn't quite stick to the plan and received a dressing down from their backroom staff. Instructions were forgotten: like failing to get the ball into the Barcelona box from deadball situations. One player came in for special criticism from Ferguson's assistants: Wayne Rooney, who failed to track Busquets as the manager had instructed him. Yet, as a sign of what some members of the United staff took as a reluctant acceptance of Barcelona's superiority, Sir Alex was uncharacteristically subdued.

Second half:

Manchester United sporadically pressed high up, with Chicharito and Rooney running after the ball when it was passed back to Valdés, but the second line (Giggs, Carrick) didn't follow up the pressure. So Barcelona were building from the back quite easily and found Busquets often, who would then start the attack.

United did not have a solution, they didn't even take a corner all game. Barcelona continued in the same fashion and it was in that vein that Messi received a pass in midfield, unmarked, turned round and fired home a shot that made it 2–1 for Barcelona.

Messi's performance illustrates the difficulties that rivals have when they face Barcelona. Even though Ferguson admitted that they never controlled Messi, he ended up making ninety-seven runs, but 85 per cent of his moves were 'low-intensity'. His choosing of his runs was game-changing.

Barcelona were so accomplished at the basics, knowing their system and personnel so well, that Guardiola could respond to anything United threw at them. Their attack involved constant positional permutations between the front five, with the full backs often involved as well. A never-ending display of ball and player circulation.

The United wingers started joining in, in midfield, making the centre of the park quite congested, so Barcelona started attacking down the more open flanks; especially down the right with Alves.

The game was under Barcelona control when Villa scored Barcelona's third goal after seventy minutes. One minute earlier, Nani had replaced Fabio, injured, and on seventy-six minutes Scholes replaced Carrick. Now trailing by two goals, United went fully on the attack, Barcelona relaxed a bit and the game took a dangerous turn for Barcelona. Pep reacted by taking off a winger and bringing on Keita to regain control – and it stayed that way until the end of the match.

Essentially, Barcelona looked far more like the Barcelona side we will remember than they did in 2009. The attacking wide players (Pedro and Villa) were more involved than Henry and Eto'o (who were in reality strikers) were two years earlier. Busquets saw more of the ball despite the efforts of Rooney, and enjoyed relative freedom when Xavi and Messi dropped deeper. Barcelona were superior.

The final word: The lifting of the cup, the managers

Somewhat surprisingly, Carles Puyol was left out of Guardiola's line-up at the very last minute. Once the game was resolved, the coach introduced him for the final moments so that he could participate in the final and receive the trophy. But the Barcelona captain insisted that Abidal lift the silverware. 'This trophy is yours; go and get it!' Puyi told his team-mate. The French left back felt his 'second family' had given him his life back. Although he did not know it yet, his illness was to return with even more serious repercussions; but that day the recuperating star had done more to inspire his team-mates with his determination and resilience on the road to recovery than, perhaps, he ever realised at the time.

Ferguson, despite his competitive nature and instinctive desire to defend his own team, admitted that night to his closest assistants that it was impossible to compete with their current European nemesis. He could not but admire the fact that they had achieved such high standards with such an extraordinary contribution from the club's academy set-up (seven of them in the line-up), the ultimate ideal in football. Rio Ferdinand and Wayne Rooney were in agreement with their manager.

And the competitive nature of Barcelona was undisputed. Before Wembley, Pep had lost only one final, the Spanish Cup against Madrid. In fact, in his four years as a Barcelona manager all the other finals played (eleven) were won.

Pep Guardiola: We were lucky at Wembley because in the semi-final against Inter we had to go by bus because of the volcano and the threat of another ash cloud meant we had to go to London earlier. This gave us four days on our own, calm days, which was incredibly rare for us. We were away from Barcelona and the pressure of the people, friends and family. We were happy at Arsenal's ground and we had time to prepare well for the final. We could think about what we had to do to, and we prepared everything, every single bit. We didn't miss anything and in the final you can see that we played well, we were the better team. The first final, in Rome, was a lot more equal, but in the second, at Wembley, we were better prepared.

Sir Alex Ferguson: At Wembley, we had to decide how to play tactically against Barcelona because of Villa and Pedro and the way they penetrated, and the fact they had no central striker made it hard to plan.

PG: Our preparation for that game was crucial. Things like that tend to get overlooked by analysts and pundits after the match but they make the difference in big games.

SAF: In that final we were well beaten. We were playing a more mature Barcelona, the team had evolved and formed a complete unit. Piqué and Messi had matured, Xavi and Iniesta performed like the players they are.

PG: It's important to remember that finals are usually very close games, which is what made our performance against Manchester United stand out even more. There have been other games when we've played really well, but it's always more difficult to do that in a final because of the emotional factors that come into it and the quality of the opposition.

SAF: At Wembley, the two wide players were big improvements on Henry and Eto'o in 2009, in terms of penetration. This is probably because Henry and Eto'o were centre forwards rather than wide players. I remember contemplating a change of tactics and going against Messi – I toyed with the idea at half-time. But after the restart they got in front and although we took a gamble in moving Valencia to right back and Nani to wide right, Barcelona always had control of that game in 2011.

PG: In that second final my team knew each other more. We had spent a few years together and I think that we played the game being more aware of our style and United's strengths and weaknesses.

Sir Alex: I don't regret anything we did at Wembley because they were the better side. The first two goals were entirely avoidable and maybe with a bit of luck we could have won the game, but when the other team's that bit better than you, then there's not much you can do about it. You accept it.

PG: The United players said it, 'What they have done to us today, that has never happened before.' They understood it, they congratulated us on it, they recognised it – something that doesn't usually happen in football. Those 'wars' against our domestic rivals are perhaps more difficult to understand for a foreign audience but I also think it is a cultural thing. English football culture is different, they've been playing longer than us, there is a respect towards not only the coaches but also the players that we don't have here.

Sir Alex: People have asked if Pep and I spoke after the final, and the truth is we didn't. It's very difficult after a final – one team is celebrating and the other is mourning, trying to come to terms with the defeat. And then you have to deal with the media and attend press conferences, so there's not an area or time when you can have a glass of wine or talk to each other because of that divide – one is winning and the other one is losing. Sometimes you have to accept it, move to one side and acknowledge that somebody else has been better.

After the hugs and the celebrations, the dancing and the fireworks; away from the noise, in a quiet moment in the Wembley dressing room, Pep took Estiarte to one side, looked into his eyes and said, 'Manel, I will never forgive myself. I have failed.'

Manel was stunned. He would never forget how, in the immediate aftermath of such an incredible achievement, when the most natural thing in the world would have been simply to relish that moment, to bathe in its glory, Pep Guardiola was still capable of feeling that he had let everybody down. Pep explained to Manel that he felt he could have done things better. And Manel told him that, yes, it could have been a bit different, maybe; but they had won. That was what mattered. But not for Pep: his quest for perfection, for improvement, meant that as everyone around him could abandon themselves to feelings of absolute joy, he could never be truly satisfied with himself.

5

PEP AND HIS PLAYERS

The former player becomes a manager

As the leader of a group of professional footballers, Pep Guardiola had to reconcile two natural impulses: on the one hand he had to learn to restrain his instinct to act and celebrate as a player; on the other, he had to learn, as a recently retired footballer, to make the biggest number of right decisions – become a manager, basically, learn the trade. Those were the challenges. On many occasions he felt jealous of his players cocooned in a little world centred on the needs of one person, and he realised very early on that his job consisted of looking after these small bubbles of isolation, caressing the egos of his pupils and constantly directing their intentions and efforts to the benefit of the group.

Announcing his retirement on the radio didn't completely shut down the part of him that was still a footballer. Guardiola had only hung up his boots seven months before Barcelona contracted him to be the coach of the B team, but when he walked into the Mini Estadi to face the Barcelona youngsters he knew a part of him had to be put firmly in the past: he was not going to work as a former player but as a new coach. And he had to construct a barrier that separated both worlds.

After the fulfilling experience in the B team, the first team was another kettle of fish. One player experienced Guardiola's transition from player to manager up close: his move from a small world to a complex network of worlds. Xavi Hernández had been his team-mate in the late nineties and he easily envisaged Pep's transition into his new role, but was very aware that an ability to read a match is just one of the assets a manager requires. Xavi and Pep conversed at length during the Rijkaard regime about the team's shortfalls and the difficulties of dealing with players who had forgotten how to behave professionally. The midfielder also told him he would make a great manager – in fact, he wanted Pep and his values and his ideas returned to the Barcelona team.

After those talks Xavi was convinced that a dose of Guardiola's medicine was what the group needed. And Pep himself knew that it wasn't Xavi (or Iniesta, or Valdés, or Puyol) whom he had to convince from the moment he entered the dressing room, but those who didn't know too much about him. He was convinced that he could.

In order to win them over, Pep had to act without looking as if he was learning on the job: he had clear ideas of what to do and trusted his instinct and his experience as a player would help him along the way, but there were going to be unexpected turns and new lessons to be learnt. In the dressing room, though, where the player is testing the manager continuously, it was essential that he looked, at all times, as if he knew exactly what he was doing right from day one.

The decision to get rid of Ronaldinho and Deco won Pep instant authority, but it was in the day to day where he could really leave his mark. And for that, the first meeting, the first chat, was crucial. He asked Xavi Hernández to come to the office very early on and although the tone was similar to previous conversations the two had had in the past, there was something that had inevitably changed: a touch of humility in the voice of Xavi, the subtle bow of his head. Pep was the boss now.

The midfielder had just come back from winning the European Championship with Spain and there were stories in the papers about his possible transfer. It had been a difficult period in his career and he was quickly falling out of love with football: not only because of the lack of titles in the previous two seasons, but the disappointment of seeing talented players go to waste, the lack of synergy at the club, the number of years spent in an institution with huge demands. A dangerous cocktail.

Xavi needed to hear what Pep's plans were; he had no intention of leaving but if he had to, he would look at the possibility of testing himself in the Premier League. Manchester United were sniffing around.

The conversation between player and coach took place in the first days of training together.

Xavi: I won't beat around the bush, Pep, I have one question for you: do you count on me?

Pep: I don't see this team without you in it. I just don't see this working without you.

With that, Pep Guardiola had reignited Xavi's spark.

But the work to recover the midfielder mentally didn't end there. In the rare instances of a defeat or a bad performance, Xavi would carry his negative feelings to the training ground the next day. After the sessions, while performing stretches, Pep would often sit next to him, chatting about general stuff, about the weather, plans for that evening: the kind of idle talk that passes between colleagues. Guardiola would then suddenly switch into the role of manager in gesture and tone: he would switch the conversation to the next game; about what he wanted from the player; about what he had been doing right, about what could be improved. Xavi's wounds left by the defeat would heal and the mood would change – there was another target.

As we say in Spain, with the arrival of Guardiola the sky opened for Xavi and the sun shone through. The midfielder regained his sense of security and self-esteem and was about to embark on the four most enjoyable years of his whole career. The manager would insist throughout that period that he was nothing without the players, that it was they who made him good. But the footballers identified him as a leader and were thankful that he was showing them the way.

There were still many others, a whole squad, to win over.

In the first speech he gave to the whole team in St Andrews, Guardiola put forward the master plan. But he demanded mostly one thing: the players would have to run a lot, work, and train hard – every team, he believes, plays as they train. He was referring to the culture of effort, of sacrifice, and it surprised many. That was Pep; the football romantic was asking Barcelona never to stop running!

He wanted to implement a system that was an advanced version of what they had been playing, with football starting with the goalkeeper, a sort of outfield sweeper who would have to get used to touching the ball more with his feet than with his hands. Even though everybody realised the style could improve the side, the risk was immense.

'That is, by the way,' insisted Pep, 'non-negotiable.'

Goalkeeper Víctor Valdés demanded to talk to him straight away. If the new system didn't work, he was going to be the first one to be blamed. It would leave him exposed and in the firing line both on and off the pitch and he needed to be convinced: was it such a good idea to move the defensive line right up to the midfield line and ask the centre backs to start the moves? Football without a safety net? Are we sure this is the way forward? Valdés, outwardly shy but with a trademark inner blend of cheekiness and directness that has made him popular in the team, felt brave enough to see Pep a few days after the St Andrews speech:

Víctor Valdés: Can I talk to you, boss?

Pep Guardiola: My door is always open …

Valdés: I need to ask one thing: all that you are talking about is fine, but only if the centre backs want the ball …

Pep: I will make sure they want the ball.

That was it. End of conversation.

Valdés had zero tactical knowledge before Pep arrived. For the keeper the following four years would be like working his way through a degree in tactics.

In those first few days in Scotland, Guardiola asked Carles Puyol, the captain, to join him in his hotel room in St Andrews. The manager showed him a video: 'I want you to do this.' In it, different centre backs received the ball from the goalkeeper in a wide position outside the box; they connected with the full backs and positioned themselves to receive the ball again. It was stuff that defenders have nightmares about because a simple mistake can mean conceding a goal. Puyol started his career as a right winger, but was converted into right back because his skill was limited. Once, he even came close to being loaned out to Malaga when Louis van Gaal was the Barcelona manager, but an injury to Winston Bogarde kept him at the club. Now, at thirty, he was asked to add a new string to his bow.

Pep told Puyol: 'If you don't do what I need you to do, you are not going to play in my team.'

Pep's warning was probably not necessary but it was another indication of where his priorities lay.

Puyol accepted the challenge. So did Iniesta.

'When I found out Pep was going to be the manager,' says Andrés Iniesta, 'I was excited. He was my hero. I knew something big was going to take place.'

The benefits of Pep having been a top-flight player could be seen straight away. Training in front of the old Masía, near the Camp Nou, with journalists and fans watching, cameras picking up on little arguments or discussions, was far from ideal. So Guardiola, who had advised on the latest designs to the new facilities at Sant Joan Despí, a few kilometres away, pushed for the first team to move there as soon as possible. The training ground then became a fortress where they could practise, relax, eat, rest and recover in seclusion, away from the gaze of probing eyes. The footballers, surrounded by professionals dedicated to looking after them, appreciated these layers of protection and the many other necessary details that only a former professional could have forseen.

Allowing them to stay at home until just hours before a home game or travelling away on a match day, thus avoiding the almost sacred hotel stay and abrupt removal from family life, was another welcome decision. Pep thought there was no need to think about football every minute of the day and players, dining with their families the night before a match, could even begin to forget that there was a game the next day. Guardiola felt that switching them on only a few hours before kick-off was more than enough.

Little by little the press was distanced, too, with individual player interviews being reduced or banned entirely for long periods. Anything to keep the group sheltered. Not necessarily isolated, but cosy, strong in its unity. He wanted to mother them, nurture them, but not police them. Once, he himself had been denied such protection and it had left an indelible scar after the lone battle to clear his name of doping allegations.

He knew Deco and Ronaldinho had lived in disorder, and that had spread among the squad. From the moment of his arrival at the club, Pep sought to monitor his players' nutrition, timetables, preparation.

Most of his team were footballers of slight physique so they needed careful attention. All kinds of attention. If need be, he would even change identities, switch roles, on a regular basis, from manager to friend, brother, mother ...

In fact, Pep's emotional investment in his players sets him apart from most managers. While José Mourinho or Sir Alex Ferguson would get to know players' relatives or partners to find out more about their pupils; where the Portuguese manager would invite his most influential footballers and their families for private meals with plenty of wine mainly to 'casually' discover if a child had been ill or if the wife was unhappy with a new house, Guardiola established a more blurred line between the personal and the professional.

Pep knew he could not treat an eighteen- or nineteen-year-old in the same way as the superstars and he would chat to those younger players one to one in his office whenever he felt he needed to. With the star players, when necessary he'd take them for a meal. Thierry Henry was one of the first he decided to take aside.

'Henry isn't a problem,' Guardiola kept repeating at press conferences, but during the difficult start to Guardiola's first season the French forward was criticised more than any other player. His price, wages and prestige – along with his lack of empathy with the press – took their toll. And even though the team improved, the former Arsenal star was not producing his best. Two factors influenced Henry's poor form: his back injury and the position in which he was forced to play. In the summer that Eto'o was on the market, after Pep had told him as well as Deco and Ronaldinho that they were not wanted, Guardiola promised Henry, who under Rijkaard played uncomfortably on the left wing, that he would be moved into the central striker's position. However, when it transpired that Eto'o was to stay at the club for another season, Thierry had to carry on playing wide, a position in which he found it difficult to impress as he was lacking the pace and stamina of his earlier years.

When Henry was at his lowest, Pep took him out to dinner to cheer him up and tell him that he had every faith in his ability. Henry appreciated the gesture. In the following game against Valencia, 'Titi' was unstoppable and scored a hat-trick in the 4–0 victory. In the end, together with Messi and Eto'o, he formed a devastating front line during what would be an historic treble-winning season (Copa del Rey, Spanish League and Champions League). The trio scored 100 goals between them – Messi 38, Eto'o 36 and Henry, who ended up playing fifty-one games, 26. At the end of that campaign, Henry went into the 2009 summer break knowing that he had had a spectacular season.

But the following summer, after a personally disappointing campaign, unable again to return to the lead striking role in the centre – or to the form that had terrified so many Premier League defences – at thirty-two and with an offer from the MLS, Henry left Barcelona.

Samuel Eto'o and the lack of 'feeling'

Pep had given his affection, time and effort to his players in a process that began during pre-season at St Andrews. Most of it was intuitive and came naturally to him. In exchange he demanded very high standards of work but something else too, something much bigger, something we all look for: he wanted them to love him back. And if they didn't give him that love, he suffered immensely.

It was the boy in Pep who, logically, never entirely went away, that kid who wanted to impress during his trials for La Masía. The kid who, once accepted by the youth academy, needed to be liked, selected by his coaches, approved of by Cruyff. The youngster who would respectfully decide to follow the politics that came with the Barcelona philosophy because he believed in them, but also to take up a role that helped him get close to the majority of the fans: leadership with emotion again.

That need to be liked might doubtless lie dormant for a while, perhaps hidden under the shield that elite football forces you to arm yourself with. But the little boy doesn't disappear, along with the fragilities that lie at the core of every human being and which can so often be the bedrock upon which genius is built.

That kid in Pep the man found it very difficult to accept rejection, disapproval, from the people close to him, from his players. In fact, there is nothing that hurt him more than one of his footballers not looking at him or not talking to him when they crossed paths. It killed him. And it has happened.

'The most unbearable drama: I try and manage a group where everyone is a person; that comes before everything. I demand them all to think something in common, if not, you can't win it all. And that common feeling is like that of any human being: being loved. Having a job that we like and to be loved for having it. For example, how do I convince a player whom I don't love and whom I don't pick to play, that I love him? That is where the drama lies: ups and downs, ups and downs. Or do you think that all the players love me?' Dealing with the footballer and with the person behind the player, is for Pep the hardest job.

He knows that his decision-making is invariably a barrier to everyone's affection. It is certainly easier to handle this build-up of feelings when you're winning, but you don't always win. And when you lose, players tend to look for scapegoats. And in football, the guy who always gets the blame in the end is sitting on the bench.

Asked if he regrets having let Samuel Eto'o, young Catalan Bojan Krkić or Zlatan Ibrahimović go, Guardiola let his guard down and admitted the difficulties of dealing with it. 'Every day I regret a lot of things. The sense of justice is very complicated. Those who don't play feel hurt and you need them to have a lot of heart in order to avoid arguments. The closer I get to players, the more I get burned, I need to distance myself.'

On the day he announced to his players he was leaving Barcelona, he was clear: 'If I had continued we would end up hurting each other.'

But, irrespective of the emotional implications, the decisions regarding those three particular players, all strikers, were taken for the good of the group, especially to stimulate Messi's relentless progression. Guardiola's admiration for 'la Pulga', and his further decision to organise the team so as to benefit the player, was something that increased with time. It wasn't just a romantic question; it had its foundations in the laws of football. Guardiola remembers that, shortly after taking over the team, during the fourth training session, Messi subtly approached him and whispered in his ear: 'Mister! Always put Sergio in my team.' La Pulga was instantly taken with Busquets's tactical sense and he wanted him on his side in every practice, every game. Guardiola was pleased that Messi read football in the same way that he did and his faith in the Argentinian was renewed.

Pep Guardiola's players often talk highly of their coach, but still, every rose has its thorn. Eto'o, Ibrahimović and Bojan left Barcelona and not happily. All three had the same role at the club and all three ended up leaving Barcelona in order for Messi to improve. The 'number nine topic' is an extremely sensitive one in Guardiola's plan. In the Cameroon forward's case, he came within an inch of winning the Pichichi (the award for the league's top goalscorer) and was a decisive player in the League and Champions League, where he scored the first goal in the final in Rome. At the end of the season, Pep decided he wouldn't continue with him the following season. What went wrong?

After Pep effectively put Eto'o up for sale in his very first press conference, the forward completed a very impressive pre-season and once again quiet, friendly, almost unnaturally modest, had won the respect of the dressing room and of Guardiola, who spoke about him with his captains (Puyol, Xavi and Valdés): the decision was reversed; Samuel Eto'o was staying at Barça.

As the season progressed, Samuel was back to being the untameable lion, the footballer with a hunger for titles; a player who on the pitch pushes his team-mates in a very positive way and, as happened against Atlético de Madrid at the Nou Camp, is capable of body-slamming his coach to celebrate a goal. Guardiola was shocked but 'Samuel is like that'.

That version of the Cameroonian didn't last all season.

Eto'o could be inspirational at times, in training and in matches, but with the occasional temper tantrums, his impulsive nature and his inability to wholeheartedly accept Messi's leadership, led Guardiola to conclude once again that for the sake of balance among the group it would be better to move him on. An incident in training at the start of 2009 confirmed Pep's intuition. And another event later that same season, made the decision to sell Eto'o non-negotiable.

This is how the Cameroonian explains the first incident, an

insight into a brief moment that exposes what both men stood for and precisely what separated them. It is one of those instances that brought to Pep, with a rush of blood, the sudden realisation that their relationship was never going to work: 'Guardiola asked me to do a specific thing on the pitch during practice, one that strikers are not normally asked to do. I was neither excited nor aggressive, but I always think like a forward, and I saw that I was unable to do what he was demanding. I explained to him that I thought he was wrong. So then he asked me to leave the training session. In the end, the person who was right was me. Guardiola never played as a forward and I always have. I have earned the respect of people in the world of football playing in that position.'

The day after that incident, Pep asked Eto'o to go for dinner. Eto'o didn't feel he needed to discuss anything with his manager and rejected the invitation. There is a switch in Guardiola's mind that clicks on or off – if you are not with me, you shouldn't be here. Loyal, devoted, when on the same wavelength, and the coldest, most distant person if the magic disappears, if someone switches the light off. It happened with Eto'o. And later with others.

Guardiola regularly started asking him to play wide right while Messi was accommodated in the space normally occupied by a striker. During one game with those tactics, Samuel was replaced and afterwards Pep broke with his rule to give the players their sacred space in the dressing room to explain to the Cameroon striker his thinking behind the decision. Eto'o refused even to look at Pep. He ignored the coach and carried on talking in French to Eric Abidal, whom he was sitting next to.

There was no way back for him after that. The team was going to progress giving freedom to Messi, a battle lost by Eto'o. Following that clash, the forward even began celebrating the goals on his own.

Three matches before the end of the domestic season, Barcelona won the title and Pep decided to rest players from the usual starting eleven in the run-up to the Champions League final. This collective need went against Eto'o's individual interests to play in every game in order to have a chance of winning the Golden Boot for the best European goalscorer of the year. Samuel Eto'o pressured the coach to play him against Mallorca and Osasuna. Pep didn't like his attitude and had to bite his tongue when Samuel complained that, with Iniesta injured, and Xavi and Messi being kept away, who could make passes and set up goals for him? Eto'o was slowly losing it, his rage confusing the real targets of that season. In his mind, the explanation was simple: if Messi had been in need of those goals, the decisions would have been different.

Samuel started the game against Osasuna. During half-time, he had a heated argument with Eidur Gudjohnsen, almost leading to an exchange of blows: the striker thought the Icelander hadn't passed to him for a clear opportunity on goal. In the end, scoring was becoming an obsession that prevented him from winning the Spanish League's and Europe's top scorer trophy for the second time, the same thing that happened to him four years earlier in the last game of the campaign.

Despite Eto'o's decisive contribution in the Rome Champions League final in 2009 – with a goal that gave Barcelona the lead against Manchester United – and the words of Guardiola at the end-of-season lunch he organised for the squad, in which he thanked Eto'o for his commitment to the club, the Cameroonian was traded for Ibrahimović that summer.

Pep had to admit he didn't have much coaching expertise in dealing with strikers of that magnitude. Each player has a personal goal, a dream – and the coach didn't forget that. So Pep tried to find the right balance to accommodate the individual's ambitions within the team. Thierry Henry dreamed of winning the Champions League and signed for Barcelona to do so; and after he won it, his level dropped and he was happy to move on. Eto'o's vision was not just the Champions League but also the Golden Boot. He had sacrificed some personal goals in order to continue helping the team, but, like every striker in the world, he had the need to satisfy his ego. To a point set by the manager.

Pep was convinced the team was doing the right things, the success was obvious and he wanted to continue with the group's logical progression. If he had placed Messi on the wing again for the next season, he would have had to deal with an exceptional player who would lose motivation, unhappy with being relegated to a less influential position. There was vast room for improvement from the Argentinian but there was only room for one ego.

When the season finished, Eto'o went to Paris during his holidays. Pep found out and wanted to travel to France to speak face to face with him, to explain the reason for his decision. But the coach also believed that he had made a real effort to connect with the player, something he felt had not been reciprocated. Pep never took that flight to Paris. That is what hurt Eto'o most: 'As well as Guardiola and Laporta, many more people have disappointed me,' he said.

Ibrahimović and Pep on a different wavelength

Ibrahimović had filled the gap left by Eto'o in Barcelona's front line in a swap between Inter Milan and Barcelona. The Swedish star couldn't have got off to a better start: he scored in the first five games he played. He also provided Guardiola with important alternatives. 'Tactically, he is very good; physically strong, quick at getting away from defenders, and he plays well with his back to defenders. So he allows us to play with someone else with him,' the coach pointed out in one of the first press conferences of the season.

The first half of the campaign was more than acceptable, but in the second half the Swede was less than effective. He gave the impression that he hardly knew his role in the club and he seemed to be getting in the way on the pitch, sometimes appearing to be yet another defender that Messi had to dribble past.

There were soon disagreements in which he showed his strong temperament, and further signs that a difficult season lay ahead. In a Barcelona–Mallorca league encounter (4–2), the referee gave a penalty for a foul on Ibra, who had had a fantastic game but hadn't scored. Messi took it and scored. The Swede's angry reaction was astonishing. 'That penalty was mine!' he shouted at the coach. There were more such incidents to follow.

Before playing Madrid in the league at the Camp Nou, Ibra suffered a muscle injury and his ultrasound scans were inconclusive in terms of his recovery. Pep didn't want to take any risks. Zlatan was desperate to play in his first Clásico. 'I will be fit for the game,' he kept repeating. He was so tense that one day he went for Barça's fitness coach Lorenzo Buenaventura and tried to grab him by the throat. The player had got wind of a rumour that Buenaventura was telling the player that he would be fit for the encounter, and Pep the opposite: 'Don't mess with me or I'll rip your head off!' Ibrahimović screamed. In the end, he didn't start the match, but he came off the bench to score the winning goal.

The team continued channelling the ball to Messi during games and Ibrahimović didn't understand what he had to do. There's this public perception of the Swedish star, backed up by his revealing autobiography (*I Am Zlatan*) and his behaviour at times, of an arrogant self-opinionated young man who lacks humility. Yet the real Ibra is somewhat less black and white. Before Christmas, Ibrahimović wanted a discussion about his role and met Pep and director of football Txiki Beguiristain. 'Both me and Messi would be a lot better with a bit of support from everyone else; but I don't feel like anyone is trying to help me out here,' he told them. 'I need Xavi and Iniesta to pass to me, but it's as if they can only see Messi … and I'm twice the size of him!'

Pep thought he could have a word with the two midfielders, and address the situation. However, that would potentially mean taking the team in a direction that differed from the one he had envisaged.

Nevertheless, Guardiola tried to maintain harmony with Ibra in the squad.

Txiki Beguiristain found out that the player was becoming increasingly frustrated and, worse still, showing it in front of other players. He told Pep the next morning and that same afternoon Pep took Ibrahimović for lunch. The coach tried to explain what he wanted from him, how much the team needed him and vice versa. He asked Ibra not to give up trying.

But the Swedish player couldn't help feeling misunderstood. For him, lunch with the coach was not enough. So there was a change before Christmas, and Pep noticed. The humble and responsive Ibra, trying hard to behave and be more like the 'schoolboys' – his slightly patronising term for Pep's loyal home-grown students like Xavi and Iniesta. 'This is not Zlatan, he is pretending. You just wait,' people close to Pep were warning.

No, that was not him. During the Christmas holiday, as he confessed in his autobiography, he got 'depressed', even considering abandoning football because he was bewildered by the lack of understanding between himself and the coach. After the break, the player's arrogance and inner tension began to emerge.

The New Year didn't get off to a good start: Ibra turned up with burns on his face. The club found out that they were caused by the cold, riding his snowmobile without enough protection. A double breach of club rules that warranted a fine. Finally, everything changed, in February, when Pep moved Messi from the wing to the centre. Ibra thought Guardiola was asking the same of him as had been asked of Eto'o the previous season, and he was no Eto'o.

The striker suspected that it was Messi who was not pleased with him being the star during the first part of the season and that the little Argentinian had complained to Pep. And if Ibrahimović feels you have hurt him or are against him, he will never forgive and forget.

The reality was, nobody wanted to listen to Ibra because the team was moving in another direction and meanwhile, using the words of the player, 'the Ferrari that Barcelona had bought was being driven like a Fiat'. Often, Ibrahimović would start tactical discussions during training sessions and would no longer hide the fact that he didn't accept many of the coach's instructions.

Pep was beginning to lose patience, too close to that breaking point where there is no turning back, and sometimes he showed this openly, in front of his players. The relationship between player and coach turned sour and Zlatan started to see Pep as an enemy. 'He should be careful with me. Perhaps in training I'll lose control of my arm and give him a smack,' he said at the time, and later wrote in his book: 'I felt like crap when I was sitting in the locker room with Guardiola staring at me like I was an annoying distraction, an outsider. It was nuts. He was a wall, a stone wall. I didn't get any sign of life from him and I was wishing myself away every moment with the team.'

The line had been crossed.

A cold war ensued, the coach and the player stopped speaking to one another and nothing motivated Ibrahimović. 'Then Guardiola started his philosopher thing. I was barely listening. Why would I? It was advanced bullshit about blood, sweat and tears, that kind of stuff. I would walk into a room; he would leave. He would greet everyone by saying hello, but would ignore me. I had done a lot to adapt – the Barça players were like schoolboys, following the coach blindly, whereas I was used to asking "why should we?"'

'Has he looked at you today?' Thierry Henry used to ask him. 'Nope, but I have seen his back,' would answer Ibra. 'Ah, it's getting better between the two of you then ...'

At the beginning of April, Ibra had a mini revival as a player but then he got injured before the Real Madrid–Barça match at the Bernabéu. In that Clásico Messi successfully exploited the false nine position and scored the first of the two goals in the 0–2 win. That muscle injury made Ibra go into the final stretch of the season at a different pace from the rest, but Guardiola used him in the semi-final of the Champions League against Inter, a decision that was damaging for the player, the coach and the team. And one that Pep wouldn't forgive himself for.

Ibra's pitiful contribution in those two games was the straw that broke the camel's back. After the 3–1 scoreline in the first leg, he considered leaving Ibrahimović on the bench for the second leg in the Camp Nou to free up that space so that Messi could move around freely. But Pep listened to his head, instead of his heart. Ibra started the match but his minimal involvement meant that he was substituted in the sixty-third minute. Barcelona were incapable of winning the tie and Guardiola decided that never again would he let his head rule his instincts. That turned out to be one of Ibra's last games for Barcelona as Pedro and Bojan were selected ahead of him: players who were key to winning the second Liga title under Guardiola.

A few days after going out of the Champions League to Milan and after coming on as a substitute against Villarreal, Ibra lost it completely. In his biography he explains that he gave Pep a piece of his mind in the el Madrigal dressing room, and that, a prisoner of his own rage, he sent a three-metre-high locker crashing to the floor. '[Guardiola] was staring at me and I lost it. I thought "there he is, my enemy, scratching his bald head!". I yelled to him: "You have no balls!" and probably worse things than that. I added: "You are shitting yourself because of José Mourinho. You can go to hell!" I was completely mad. I threw a box full of training gear across the room, it crashed to the floor and Pep said nothing, just put stuff back in the box. I'm not violent, but if I were Guardiola I would have been frightened.'

After the Champions League exit, Guardiola decided once again to change his number nine for the following season. In reality, Pep had to admit the Swede's presence in the team delayed setting the scene for Messi's role in the centre as a false number nine. Pep also knew he had betrayed himself in not sticking to his own ideas, not just in the game against Inter, perhaps the whole season. In order to adapt both the Argentinian and the Swedish players together, he had spent the season adjusting small details to try to rescue something from an unsalvageable situation: right up to the point of partly abandoning the path the team had started to follow the previous year. Ultimately, that campaign reinforced the conviction that everything had to go through Messi.

It was a difficult time for Guardiola. To sell a player who had been signed at huge cost to the club could and should be seen as a mistake. But it was a decision that had to be taken.

Pep's second season in charge of the team was reaching its end and the moment arrived for Ibrahimović and Guardiola to have a frank and honest conversation. It finally arrived before the final league game. Pep called Ibra to his office. The atmosphere was very tense. Neither of them had spoken since the day the Swede exploded at Villarreal. Guardiola sat edgy, rocking in his office chair.

'I don't know what I want with you,' he told Ibra. 'It's up to you and Mino [Mino Raiola, his representative] what will happen next.

I mean, you're Ibrahimović, you're not a lad who plays one out of every three games, are you?'

The Swede didn't say anything, he didn't even move. But he understood the message perfectly: he was being asked to leave. Pep kept talking nervously:

'I don't know what I want with you. What do you have to say? What's your opinion?'

'Is that all? Thank you.'

Ibrahimović left the office without saying another word.

That was the last contact between player and coach that season.

After the summer holidays another chat took place. Surprisingly, having calmed down during the summer, Zlatan wanted another chance, failing to understand that bridges couldn't be rebuilt and that another striker, David Villa, had been brought in to replace him. He had been convinced that he was part of one of the most admired clubs in the world. Worthwhile giving it a second go, then.

On the first day of pre-season, Ibra hadn't even put his boots on when Pep called him to his office. Once again, the situation was uncomfortable. According to Ibrahimović, the conversation went like this:

Pep: How are you?

Ibra: Very well. Anxious.

P: You must be prepared to be on the bench.

I: I know. I understand.

P: As you'll know, we have signed Villa.

I: Good, I'll work even harder. I'll work like an idiot to win a place in the team. I'll convince you that I'm good enough.

P: I know, but how are we going to continue?

I: As I said, with hard work. I'll play in any position that you tell me. Up front or behind Messi. Wherever. You decide.

P: But, how are we going to carry on?

I: I'll play for Messi.

P: But, how are we going to carry on?

The striker didn't think that it was a question of whether he was a good player or not: 'It was something personal. Instead of telling me that he couldn't handle my character, he tried to conceal it in that vague sentence. And so I decided: I will never play under Guardiola's orders again.'

Ibrahimović didn't understand anything that happened to him at Barcelona. Pep made a mistake in signing him because he underestimated his strong personality and his high self-esteem. If someone annoys Ibra, his reaction is intense and inescapable. If someone annoys Pep, the emotional connection disappears and he treats the player like just another professional, nothing more. That relationship could never go far.

When Pep was asking 'How are we going to carry on?' he was opening the door for Ibrahimović who would have preferred a more direct approach.

When his last-minute transfer to Milan was in the balance, Ibrahimović took one Camp Nou vice-president aside and warned: 'If you make me stay I'll wait till I'm together with the coach in front of the media and then I'll punch him … I'll do it, I will!' When Sandro Rosell became Barcelona president that summer, the first issue he had to deal with was the Swede's exit. 'I regret this situation,' he told the president. 'Which club would you like to go to?' 'To Madrid,' Ibra replied. 'It's not possible. Anywhere apart from there,' said Rosell.

This is how Ibrahimović describes the moment he signed for Milan. 'Rosell, Galliani, Mino, my lawyer, Bartomeu and I were present. And then Sandro told me: "I want you to know that this is the worst bit of business I've ever done in my life." To which I replied: "That's the consequence of terrible leadership."'

Ibrahimović had cost €66 million (Eto'o, who went the other way, was valued at €20 million and Barcelona paid the outstanding €46 million in instalments) and he moved to AC Milan, at first on loan and then in a permanent move the following season for €24 million. At Barcelona, Ibrahimović won four trophies, scoring twenty-one goals and making nine assists.

After his sale, the Swede didn't hold anything back. 'My problem at Barça was the philosopher. Pep thinks that he has invented Barça's football … Mourinho stimulates me, he is a winner; Guardiola isn't perfect. I was at Barcelona, the best team in the world, but I wasn't happy.' And there was more: Ibra accused Guardiola of never having wanted to iron out their differences. 'If you have a problem with me, it is up to you to solve it. You are the team leader, you are the team coach. You can't get on well with twenty people and then, with the twenty-first, look the other way.'

Guardiola's authority had been challenged, and also his vision for the team. The emotional distance between him and Ibrahimović made the decision to get rid of him a bit easier but it came at a cost. He had let himself down by not following his instincts, and he also felt that he had let Ibrahimović down by not getting the best out of him. He just hoped his choice to allow Messi to emerge as the main axis of the team would pay dividends.

Messi, the man-eater

For Messi, football is everything and everything is football. His happiest moments were when he was little playing on a makeshift pitch with thirty others, dribbling and weaving his way past them all. 'I don't know what would have become of me without football. I play in the same way as when I was a little boy. I go out there and I have fun, nothing more. If I could, I would play a match every day,' Messi says.

There's something incredibly child-like about Messi. He acts in the same way on and off the pitch, always distancing himself from the cameras and the attention, and what you see is pretty much what you get. The club has allowed him to live as he would do at home back in Rosario, Argentina, with his family around him. Unlike others at Barcelona, he's never been forced to speak Catalan or represent the club off the pitch more than is necessary. He doesn't talk to journalists, nor does he have a manager whom he can ring directly; he's not acting out his life as part of some carefully managed PR campaign. It's all about what he does on the pitch.

At the World Club Cup in Tokyo, when Barcelona played against the Brazilian club Santos, Pep pointed something out to a friend of his, to illustrate the difference between a star and a professional. He told his friend to take a look at Neymar. The Brazilian had a special haircut for the final, he had bought a big fancy watch and had some

Japanese inscription added to his boots. 'Now, look at Messi. Best player in the world. Perhaps in history. But still just Messi.'

According to Pep: 'Messi doesn't compete to appear in magazines, attract girls or appear in adverts, but to win the match, the title, the personal challenge. He competes against the rival, against Cristiano Ronaldo, against Madrid, against Mourinho. Rain or shine, whether they foul him or not, basically he competes against himself to show that he is the best. He's not interested in the rest of it. Our obligation is to give the boy the ball in the best conditions. The rest is a case of sitting down and watching how it turns out.'

The Argentinian, who will never be able to illuminate for us the secret to his success, doesn't need to have things explained to him twice when talking about football, nor receive messages via the press, a trick that Pep quickly abandoned. He understood what Guardiola wanted from him and he applied that to his game. He'll switch wings in order to help Barça gain superiority, he will hold back or he will almost disappear from the game only to reappear again by surprise. As Pep told the Argentinian coach Alejandro Sabella, 'You don't need to talk much to him, just protect him and listen to the very things he says. And don't take him off, not even for an ovation.' Unlike the foreign players who are signed as stars, he has grown up in La Masía, immersed in the culture of the club. 'He can participate in the "musical theory" side of things, accompanying Xavi and Iniesta – and then finish off with an exceptional solo', as Ramón Besa describes it. 'He usually does what the move demands of him.' He only does his fancy tricks to solve a problem.

And if things got complicated, he would always step up to the challenge. You simply have to be clever in the way you ask things of him. So Pep would sometimes tell the players just before a game: 'You should know that Leo is going to pressurise high up and will commit himself to the cause every time we decide to press.' Indirectly, Leo, that is your order. While manager of Swansea, Brendan Rodgers said, 'Leo Messi has made it very difficult for footballers who think they are good players. If you have someone like him doing the pressure without the ball, then I'm sure my friend Nathan Dyer can do it. It is an easy sell.'

Messi has a certain freedom in attack, yet he is well aware of his responsibilities in defence. If he is distracted, the midfielders remind him of that, because the great success of teamwork is having shared responsibilities. The Argentinian knows that he can miss one or two defensive movements, but not a third. In one game against Arsenal, Xavi and Iniesta, who generally act as his guardians, had to tell him off for disappearing from the game, for not tracking back, overshadowed by Ibrahimović who had scored twice and was playing as a centre forward.

From day one, Guardiola took an holistic approach, overseeing every level of his team's preparation: physical, medical and dietary. And when he discovered that Argentinian beef – arguably the best there is – formed the basis of Messi's diet, the player having never eaten fish, the coach insisted that a special diet was drawn up for him, banning cola, popcorn, pizza, and – Messi's favourite – *conguitos* (chocolate peanuts).

The effort to understand and accommodate Messi is justified not only because of his talent, but primarily because of his behaviour; his commitment. Leo works his socks off in every training session; his team-mates see that. He has never said: 'I am Messi, you have to do this for me.' He generally recognises that there is no 'I' in 'team'. For that reason, there were occasions when Guardiola gave Messi permission to go on holiday earlier than the rest of the squad or allowed him to return later. The logic was straightforward: he was often asked to do more than anybody else and frequently Messi played more. And scored more, and won more games.

During the process of determining Messi's ideal partner in attack, Guardiola had made some big decisions but he did also have some footballing doubts: where did he want to take the team? Barcelona was experiencing unprecedented success but Pep had changed his footballing criteria from one year to the next and he needed to find, once again, the right path after deciding that Eto'o and Ibrahimović were not the right options.

Upon his arrival, Pep decided to play with a '*punta*', someone like Eto'o: a quick and incisive, highly mobile striker who is always looking to make runs behind the defenders. Then he realised that that type of play, with small midfielders and Eto'o, created problems in terms of aerial defending. With Ibrahimović's arrival another system was established with different possibilities: a more fixed forward who allowed long-ball play, depth, arriving up front from the second line. But that new idea disappeared after just one year and a third way was established. Or was it the first? He went from having the space of the forward occupied to having it free; no one would be a fixed number nine. Messi would appear there whenever he thought it convenient.

It had been seen before, that 'false striker' role, as Alfredo Relaño recalled in a memorable editorial in *AS* newspaper: 'From Sinclair's Wunderteam to Messi and Laudrup's Barça, not forgetting Pedernera's River Plate, Hidegkuti's Hungary, Di Stéfano's Madrid, Tostao's Brasil, Cruyff's Ajax.'

Those changes up front could have caused doubts, but the quality of the squad and a style that combined possession and defined positional play allowed the team to win titles while a way of attacking was being mulled over. The formula was reinvented following Ibra's departure and the arrival of David Villa. With Messi as a false nine – and Villa as a left winger. The result and the success were instant: Leo went from winning the Ballon d'Or to the Golden Boot. He proved himself to be an extraordinary goalscorer, a unique passer of the ball and a player who could open up defences when necessary: he scored in six of the eight finals he played in under Guardiola.

Pep explains what his role was in the process: 'Messi is unique and a one-off. We have to hope that he doesn't get bored, that the club can give him the players so that he can continue feeling comfortable because when he is, he doesn't fail. When he doesn't play well it is because something in his environment isn't working, you must try and make sure that he maintains the calmness that he has in his personal life and hope that the club is intelligent enough to sign the right players to surround him.' And that is one of the main reasons why FC Barcelona awarded José Manuel Pinto, Messi's best friend in the Barcelona dressing room, a new contract.

Of course, there is a lot more to it than making Messi comfortable. If the great teams in history are measured in the crucial moments, Barcelona were going to become one of the most reliable ever. The team was not only stylish, but competitive in the extreme – their players were insatiable, little despots. As Pep would say, they are easy to manage because that attitude is the foundation for everything. Among all of them, Messi symbolises that spirit better than anyone – an icon of world football but one who still cries after a defeat.

Messi's hunger to succeed brought him to tears in the dressing room in Seville when Barcelona were eliminated in the last-sixteen round of the Copa del Rey in 2010. It was the third highest priority of the campaign and, in Pep's era that was in its second year, the first trophy that Barcelona would fail to win. Messi played spectacularly and could have scored a hat-trick if it hadn't been for Palop's sensational performance in goal for the opposition.

After the final whistle, the Argentinian could not hold back; he sat on the floor hidden away from the world and started to cry like a little boy, the way he did in private, in his house, during his first months at the club, when he felt alone, small and was suffering growing pains and the side effects of the growth hormones with which he was being injected.

As Guardiola soon came to understand, there is nothing in life that the Argentinian enjoys more than playing football (perhaps his daily siestas come close); why take that away from him by making him rest? He didn't need to take Messi out for a meal; their relationship was based on the field of play, on the matches and training sessions. They communicated through gestures and silences, hugs and brief talks. Sometimes just an 'Everything OK?' and a thumbs-up and a smile in response was all it took.

But the best footballer on the planet has the odd frustrating moment that Pep knows all too well. There are many times when Leo is on top form out on the pitch, but others when he struggles to score – and the first thing Pep used to do when he saw that Leo wasn't functioning at 100 per cent was to have a good look at him after the game. If the player's head had dropped, he focused on picking him back up.

Those frustrating games bring a moody Messi. He'll stare at the ground in silence, unsmiling, sulky. Under that angelic, innocent exterior there is a predator; behind his ambition and record-breaking

Above He pushed Gerard Piqué well beyond what anybody else had achieved with the centre back

Right Pep and Messi, a special bond with a very special player

Celebrating
victory in the
Champions
League final
between FC
Barcelona and
Manchester
United at
Wembley, 2011

Left Celebrations with players became commonplace. He included everybody in his hugs

Right His second Champions League, Wembley, 2011

Below Sir Alex and Pep, a mutual respect

Left The demands of the job
start taking their toll

Pep says goodbye to the
club and the President.
A difficult moment
(Getty)

Left In his last season, Pep tried
to coach Cesc into becoming
the future axis of the team. Cesc
didn't understand everything
that was asked of him

Above Before …

Left … and after. The strain of the job as manager of FC Barcelona shows after four years (Press Association)

feats, there is also a child. And children are often unable to hide their feelings.

On one occasion, Messi took to the training pitch with a teaspoon in his mouth and kept it there throughout much of the session. He normally has a coffee or *yerba maté* (an Argentinian herbal drink) before training and has a habit of sucking on the spoon until he reaches the pitch, throwing it away before starting his exercises. That day he chewed on it while they warmed up doing a piggy-in-the-middle drill. His behaviour in training coincided with him having been subbed in the match the night before. On other occasions where he was rested or substituted, he wouldn't talk to his manager for days.

When Ibra received the plaudits during his first few months at the club, Messi spoke with Pep and said either he played as a number nine or he didn't play at all. 'And what am I supposed to do with Ibrahimović?' said Pep. Messi was adamant: 'I play here, or I don't play at all; stick the others out on the wing.'

At the end of the 2010–11 season, Barcelona drew 0–0 in the Camp Nou against Deportivo, but, with the Liga title in the bag, the celebrations started at the end of the game. Messi had been named as a substitute but hadn't played a single minute, with a Champions League final against Manchester United looming; he wanted to distance himself from the celebrations of a Liga title that belonged to him almost more than anyone else. He had found out that two goals from Ronaldo in Real Madrid's encounter with Villarreal had almost put him out of the race for the Pichichi and he wanted to go home. Juanjo Brau, the team physio, had to go and get him, but by then the official team photo had been taken without him. Upon his return, the photo was retaken.

In Pep's last year, Messi gave his worst performance, coming from the bench against Real Sociedad for the last half-hour. The next day he didn't turn up to training and he didn't get over his anger at being left out until the next game: since that encounter, at the start of September, Messi played every minute of the season. If you take football away from him, you're removing his life's motivation. You just leave him with eating and sleeping.

Had Guardiola created a monster in Messi? The Argentinian had absolute power in the coach's final season, and his behaviour was sometimes out of place. He would get annoyed if young players such as Cuenca ('Lift your head up!' Messi once shouted at him against Granada) or Tello ('Cross!' he shouted at him against Milan, when he went for goal, looking for Abbiati's near side) didn't pass him the ball. Even David Villa wasn't forgiven for having shots at goal if he had the option of passing to Messi.

Like all forwards, this shrewd and determined individual wanted to keep his place and he fought for it.

'Messi learnt to make choices depending on the requirements of each game,' Argentinian César Luis Menotti stresses, and he is right. But his influence went far beyond the pitch: the club asked Messi's circle what they would think if Barcelona signed Neymar. Messi knows the young star through Dani Alves and the three have played online football on PlayStation. The club got the answer it was looking for: 'Go ahead, sign him.'

Did Pep feel that he had given Messi too much power? When he spoke about leaving the club so as not to 'hurt each other', many interpreted that as a reference to, among other players, Messi. Would staying mean for Pep readdressing the balance of power somehow and avoiding one player scoring seventy-three goals and the rest evading responsibility?

There is an argument to be made that Pep Guardiola started his coaching career at Barcelona developing the team's collective play but that in his last season he gave in to individual quality. It is something that all managers do because the footballers are ultimately the ones who decide games and especially if the individual in question is Messi.

Getting the right balance between an exceptional player and the team ethic is very difficult and yet Pep somehow managed it for the majority of his time as a coach. But was it necessary for Pep to say so clearly and so often that Messi was special? Was that the start of something that would eventually culminate in Guardiola leaving the club, conscious of the imbalance that had been created? The coach is the equilibrium. And if he gives in to a player, according to the unwritten rules of football the scales need to be realigned.

Other victims of Messi

Fernando Parrado was one of the sixteen survivors of an event known as the 'Andes Tragedy'. In October 1972, a squad of Uruguayan rugby players was flying from Montevideo to Santiago de Chile when they crashed in the snow-bound Andes. The survivors, in a story dramatised in the Hollywood movie *Alive*, waited seventy-two days to be rescued. Low on food, with friends dying around them and the feeling that there was no hope, they eventually cannibalised the bodies of the dead in order to stay alive. Parrado crossed the Andes with his friend Roberto for ten days in search of help, traipsing through deep snow wearing a pair of training shoes. In Guardiola's last year in charge, Fernando gave a motivational talk to the whole Barcelona squad.

'It helped us realise that awful things happen that can destroy anyone, but there are people who rebel against it and fight for their lives,' Gerard Piqué commented on the talk. Later, Parrado gave an account of his impression of the Barcelona players on Uruguayan television. 'They're sensitive young men, they were like an amateur team. And Guardiola told me that if there is a hint of disharmony within the group he removes it, as he did with Eto'o and Ibrahimović, who wanted to be stars in a team where no one feels a star.'

In Pep's first season in charge, Barcelona had missed a clear opportunity on goal in a key moment during a crucial game – the coach doesn't want to remember which game nor who had the chance. But immediately after the miss he turned around to look at the bench. Some footballers had leapt from it in anticipation of the ball nestling in the back of the net, while others neither moved nor reacted. Pep is guided by many details such as this to understand the thinking of his group, and this one probably stayed in his memory. It ended up being more than an anecdote. The following summer all the players who had failed to react had left the club.

At the start of Pep's fourth season in charge of the first team, another striker had to move on. It wasn't David Villa, signed to replace Ibrahimović and with whom Guardiola was very publicly delighted. It was Bojan, the amicable, baby-faced and shy-looking boy, who won the hearts of everyone after debuting in Rijkaard's team at just seventeen when he was heralded as one of the most promising players to come out of La Masía.

Bojan was hardly given a chance to shine under Pep and a loan move to AS Roma followed. The youngster was clearly upset at not being able to triumph at his boyhood club, but he was even more hurt by how Guardiola managed his departure. 'I didn't say goodbye to Pep, only those who treated me well,' he said shortly after leaving. 'The relationship with Pep wasn't a very good one.'

Those words troubled Catalan commentators. The Barcelona sports daily *El Mundo Deportivo* wrote, 'When Pep comes down to earth, walking on the same ground as we mere mortals, he puzzles us. This is what Bojan's comments have done: revealing a side to our coach that we didn't want to discover. The tale from our young player from Linyola has shown us a cold, unflappable manager, protected by an enigmatic and impeccable image, capable of keeping complete control of his feelings.'

At the heart of that debate lay the persona of Pep, untouchable, almost mystical, for the Barcelona fans and media, a persona challenged by a former player, with emotive words that came straight from the heart. 'If Pep were to phone me asking me to return, I would tell him no,' said Bojan, in an emotional television interview made on his departure. 'It would be difficult for me to trust him. I'm not saying that our paths won't cross again, but if he phoned me I would tell him no. I've not had a good time. It wouldn't be a good idea to be under his orders again.'

Bojan had left 'primarily because I wasn't playing' and 'I wasn't happy', but also because of 'the way [I] was treated' by Pep. 'Not playing is one thing, but another is not feeling part of the group; I felt that whatever I did, he didn't see it,' Bojan said, touched by a painful sadness, powerless and resigned. 'My parents, my friends, my girlfriend, they all told me: "Speak to him" but the words just didn't come out. Perhaps because I was thinking: "Whatever you do, very little is going to change …"'

The emotion was visible in the boy's eyes. Distressed, he confessed that in the last stage of the season he 'wasn't psychologically well', he 'had no desire to train' in a successful team. 'I didn't feel loved by my team-mates and a large section of the public.' It all came to a head in the Champions League final at Wembley. 'There I saw that I had no role to play and that I had put up with not playing for a long time.' He gave himself some hope to take part in the final for a few minutes, since he saw that 'we were winning 3–1, Manchester couldn't do anything and there was still a substitute left'. But Pep preferred to reward Afellay.

After that he didn't even speak to his manager. 'I didn't think there was anything to say, and I still think that. He didn't approach me either.' Nor did he do so before going to AS Roma. 'I said bye to the people that treated me well, [between Pep and me] there was no farewell, neither on my behalf nor on his. Nor were there phone calls during the summer.' It was that raw. 'I always say that Pep is the best trainer there is. But I have been unfortunate to not form part of his plans and to receive that treatment from him as a player.'

Nobody has the God-given right to play for Barcelona, not even those who come from the lower ranks. So perhaps Guardiola should have been clearer. Bojan's difficult period at AS Roma, where he never managed to have a good run of games, suggested that it was his limitations and not a personal caprice of the manager, that stopped his career at Barcelona.

The problem with all the strikers was clear: Messi was devouring them. But in the process of improving the team, while its identity was being established other players fell by the wayside. The Belarusian Alexander Hleb was another to find himself on the outside looking in and he also believes that, in the end, things could have been handled better. 'The important meetings to decide any weighty issues were made up solely of home-grown players. Guardiola was a very young coach and in some ways his lack of experience was noticeable in some situations,' he explained. 'For example, Arsène Wenger is someone who always tries to establish very close contact with each and every one of his players. I mean that when a coach talks to you and looks you directly in the eyes, it really improves the player's perception of the coach. So you listen to him and you say to yourself, "OK, he's right. I need to work on this for myself, I need to give more."'

In other words, when Pep understood that his contribution was insufficient, when he saw that the Belarusian didn't understand what the team needed, he cut him loose before the season had even finished.

But as with other rejected players, Guardiola's attempts to build bridges slip Hleb's mind. 'I have the English I have because of Hleb,' Pep has said. He spoke on countless occasions with him because he felt that he was the kind of player who needed the occasional arm around his shoulders. Guardiola thinks now that it was wasted time that could have been spent doing other things. Hleb didn't ever comprehend what Barça was about and even the player himself admits it. 'I understand now that it was almost all my fault. I was offended like a little kid. And I showed it: sometimes I would run less in training, sometimes I would pose. The coach would tell me to do one thing, and I'd do something else in defiance. It was like kindergarten, I find it ridiculous now.'

Yaya Touré, another discarded player, blamed Guardiola for his departure: 'Guardiola, when I asked him about why I wasn't playing, would tell me strange things. That's why I went to City. I couldn't speak to him for a year,' he explained. 'If Guardiola had talked to me I would have stayed at Barça. I wanted to finish my career at Barça but he didn't show any trust in me. He didn't take any notice of me until I got the offer from City.'

Yaya Touré's agent forced the situation to such an extent, with accusations against Pep Guardiola and the club ('a madhouse', he claimed), that the relationship with the player deteriorated. According to his agent, Yaya should play every game, but Busquets's promotion to the first team prevented him from doing so. Eventually, Pep's relationship with Yaya became purely professional and the footballer felt marginalised since he could no longer be a part of that cushioned world that Pep builds around his loyal players.

It was soon very clear to him that the emotional investment Pep asks of his players, an integral part of the group's make-up, had an expiry date: the affection lasted as long as the player's desire to be a part of his vision.

Gerard Piqué, the eternal teenager

Pep recognised the need to – and indeed did – treat Thierry Henry, for instance, like the star he was, but also like the star who wanted to be treated as one. With Gerard Piqué, though, the relationship took the opposite dynamic. Pep took him under his wing, loved him and cared for him more than perhaps any other player in the side; yet that same devotion to Gerard ended up creating a tension that became one of the biggest challenges of Pep's final season at Barcelona.

Initially, Pep had not requested Piqué's signing. Tito Vilanova, his assistant and Gerard's coach in the junior sides at La Masía, was the brains behind his transfer. Pep had no problem in admitting so in the first conversation he had with the then twenty-one-year-old former Manchester United centre back when he returned to the Camp Nou: 'If you're signing for Barcelona it is because of Tito Vilanova. I've only seen you play a couple of times, I don't really know you that well, but Tito has real faith in you.'

Tito's trust in Piqué was reflected in the choice of centre back for the second game of Pep's first season, when injury kept Rafa Márquez out of the team and the former United defender was selected for the 1–1 draw v Racing de Santander at the Camp Nou that left Barcelona with one point out of a possible six. The day after the game, Pep pulled the player to one side in training and told him, 'Think about their goal, the one where the shot rebounded, you should have pushed up and played them offside; make sure you're ready for the game in Lisbon.' And Piqué thought to himself, 'Shit, wow, this guy really believes in me.' Right from the start, their relationship became special because of that immense trust.

Piqué had really been signed as the fourth centre back (Márquez, Puyol and Cáceres were in front of him, Milito spent the whole season injured) and after getting the nod against Racing came the first Champions League game of the season against Sporting Lisbon. Puyol was moved to left back and Márquez and the new guy were the centre backs. 'Damn, he must have some faith in me!' Piqué kept scratching his head. That confidence boost carried him through to April, when he got selected to partner Márquez in the centre of defence against Chelsea in the Champions League semi-final at the Camp Nou. Márquez ruptured a knee ligament in that game and Puyol came off the bench – and that was it. Puyol and Piqué formed a central defensive pairing that became first choice for years to come and went unbeaten for more than fifty games.

'My relationship with Pep is not like the friendship I have with my mates because you cannot have that between player and coach, but it is close,' Piqué remembers. 'We've only ever met once for a coffee away from training to discuss football matters. A few years ago he asked me to join him after training to chat about the team and my role in it. We met at a hotel close to the training ground and talked for an hour or so, and Pep told me, "come on, you can give us a bit more". He's done the same thing with a few players; he did it with Henry once.'

Piqué's insight is a clue as to how their relationship developed since that Racing game. Guardiola has not publicly complimented many players the way he has Piqué; but neither has he challenged them to the same extent either, on a daily basis, from day one. After seeing what he was capable of in his first season, Pep was insistent that Piqué did not waste his talent and sometimes you could sense tension in their relationship. Gerard is Pep's weakness, but he knew that the player always had more to give.

In his last season, Guardiola didn't feel Piqué was in the right frame of mind and that was a source of frustration for him. The player didn't understand why, partly because of injury and partly as a technical decision, he missed six consecutive games at one point, including a Clásico, but the manager knew it was done not only for the good of the group, but for Gerard, too. The centre back had lost those feelings a player needs to have to be a regular in the Barcelona line-up, that sense of being at peace with himself and the team when he entered the dressing room. He had taken too much for granted; he was distracted.

'When someone isn't giving their all, then I think that maybe something is wrong in their personal life or they have some sort of problem,' Guardiola explains. 'So, that's when I have to step in. When someone isn't giving everything to the team it isn't because they are bad or cheeky. If that were the case, either the player goes or I do. I get paid to manage this player, to recover them.' If they are worthwhile recovering, one might add.

Pep did everything he could to get Piqué back on track and repeatedly told him he was not making the right choices. Yet it was only at the end of Pep's final season that the player truly understood what he had been talking about. His performance in the European Championship in Poland and Ukraine was the confirmation the lesson had been well learnt.

Pep has other '*niñas de sus ojos*' ('girls of his eyes', as we say in Spanish, a 'soft spot', in other words), and Javier Mascherano is one of them. Masche swapped Liverpool's starting line-up for Barcelona's bench, and in order to get a regular game he had to learn to play as a centre back. 'What I'll take from Guardiola is admiration and love for your profession,' the Argentinian admits. 'Going to train every day and being happy with what you're doing. He made sure that in my first six months at Barça, even though I wasn't playing, I felt like I was learning. I remember that he once showed me a basketball duel to make an example of how two rivals can end up at loggerheads in a game, and that it goes beyond the collective battle, the individual battle you can have can also be special. Learning is constant with Guardiola. That is why he is one of the best coaches in the world, if not the best.'

Clearly, with the continuous success the legend that preceded Pep kept growing. His aura increased at the same rate as the club's trophy cabinet. And that would prove to be a seriously inhibiting factor for some of his players.

Cesc, the return home

From the outside, Barcelona was the reference point of world football. On the inside, players were working a system that benefited them with a manager who understood them. One who revealed his knowledge of the game and his faults, his charisma and his preferences, his football eye and his complex mind. For the Barça players, he was a coach, a very good coach, a special one, even, but a coach first and foremost. Cesc Fàbregas arrived at Barcelona to work with a legend. And there is nothing more potentially emasculating than the fear of failure before the altar of a god.

That adoration started early. When Cesc was in the junior team, he got a present from his father: a Barcelona shirt signed by his childhood idol, Pep Guardiola. Pep had hardly seen him play but was told by his brother Pere about the talents of the kid. Cesc's idol wrote in it: 'One day, you will be the number 4 of Barcelona.' Ten years later, that prediction became a reality.

But first Cesc had to emigrate. Fàbregas has always been a home-loving boy and he suffered in his first years in London. He arrived as a sixteen-year-old after realising the doors to the Catalan first team were closed for years to come but with the promise that Arsenal were going to develop him. Wenger was told by one of his assistants, Francis Cagigao, to put Cesc into the first team straight away, and the French coach didn't argue with that.

But the return home was always an attractive proposition. The first calls from Barcelona arrived after they had been knocked out of the Champions League by Mourinho's Inter and before Spain, with Cesc's help, became World Champions in South Africa. In his third season in charge, Pep imagined a team with Fàbregas in it. In fact, Barcelona went for Silva first but Valencia did not want to get rid of him just yet. Cesc was more than just another option.

Pep, as soon as he heard that Cesc was willing to sign for Barcelona, got involved in the process. Director of football Txiki Beguiristain was the one talking to Wenger, but the constant conversations that took place between the player and Guardiola helped shape the deal.

Pep explained to him the reasons why he wanted to sign him: he saw him as a midfielder who could give the side the extra ability to score from deep positions, he would make transitions to the attack quicker and he could eventually take on Xavi's role as well. But, more importantly, Pep told him, he should relax, focus on working hard for Arsenal because at some point, sooner rather than later, the transfer was going to take place.

The player desperately needed that reassurance as Arsenal were not willing to sell their asset in that summer of 2010 even after Cesc told Arsène Wenger he wanted to leave. The French coach listened to Cesc but did not promise him anything.

The then president Joan Laporta had asked Fàbregas to take that step to help the proceedings, thinking Wenger would collapse under pressure.

During the World Cup, Pep and Cesc kept in touch, and the Barcelona manager insisted he would only go for him if Arsenal wanted to negotiate. 'Look, Cesc,' the manager told him. 'Either it's you or I get someone from the youth teams to take your place, I don't mind. For me, I only want you, but Arsenal are keeping us waiting until the end of August for a resolution.'

Beguiristain talked occasionally with Wenger and told him he was fed up with hearing Puyol, Piqué and Xavi say, each time they came back from playing with the Spanish national team, that Cesc wanted to return to Barça. Cleverly implying that Barcelona were almost forced to get the midfielder, that Arsenal had to let him go – usual negotiating tricks. 'I've only phoned you because they told me to ring you, and because I know you have spoken to the player and you told him we could ring you.' Beguiristain reminded Wenger that, as it said on the official Barcelona website, the Catalan club would not negotiate till Arsenal were willing to do so. Arsène was still uncommitted.

Cesc thought this was a once in a lifetime opportunity and felt he had to do as much as he could to avoid them going for somebody else. But then politics got in the way. Barcelona were experiencing a tense change of guard, with Sandro Rosell becoming the new president, replacing his arch enemy Joan Laporta, and Andoni Zubizarreta the new director of football instead of Beguiristain. And a conversation between the new man in charge and Wenger fatally wounded the transfer that summer.

'He is not a priority.' Those were the words used by Rosell when Wenger questioned the need for Barcelona to sign the player. 'Not a priority.' Was the new president negotiating or just giving up on the player, as he perhaps felt his signature would have been considered not his success but the success of the previous president who had started the discussions?

What was concluded thereafter and in the eyes of everybody involved in the transfer saga was that Rosell was not at all attracted by the possibility of bringing back a former young player at such a huge cost. Or not at that point, as it transpired.

Wenger, who stopped taking calls from Barcelona from that same moment, seized the opportunity. The French coach told Cesc that Barcelona, or the new chairman, had reduced the pressure, that he didn't want him that much, that he was not, in Rosell's eyes, 'a priority'.

The transfer was not going to take place that summer.

Pep was the first person to ring Fàbregas when that became known. 'Listen, don't worry,' he told the frustrated youngster. 'I know you tried. We will try to make it happen next year.'

When Fàbregas gave a press conference to confirm he was staying, this is how he described his feelings: 'It wasn't possible. I had been interested in going but it didn't happen. One of the most positive things I got from the summer was that I saw there are people in football who are really worth the effort.' He was talking about Guardiola.

As promised, the next year came and Barcelona showed their intent to get him. That gave Cesc the confidence to think the deal was to take place and confirmed his view that his idol was a man of his word.

Fàbregas was so determined to go to Barcelona that he reduced his yearly wages by one million and put that money towards the transfer fee as the conversations between clubs, once started in the summer of 2011, were developing very slowly.

By then the rumours that the new season could be the last one for Guardiola had started. The conversations between Pep and Cesc resumed. The player didn't know how to ask, but he did need to find out what the manager's plans were. Not even Pep knew it at that point, so that issue wasn't dealt with properly. 'If it is not me, it will be someone else who will look after you,' Pep told him on one occasion.

Cesc was very clear to Pep: 'If I've come here it is for you, too. Barça is my dream, of course, but one of the things that has made it happen is because you are the coach. As well as the fact you were my idol as a player and I have always admired you.'

Finally, in mid-August 2011, the transfer took place. Despite a certain scepticism on the part of Rosell, who disagreed with the huge cost for a former player, Barcelona ended up paying €40 million for the Arsenal captain.

With his return to Barça, Cesc had a weight lifted from his shoulders. He felt reborn and he showed it in public and in private with his family. 'Cesc is a very shy person. He keeps everything to himself. It's difficult for him to open up when he has a problem, and during his last few months in London he had a bad time of it. We know because he hardly picked up the phone, not even when we phoned him.' The speaker is the player's father, Francesc Fàbregas. 'Obviously I'm very happy that my son has come home, but to be sincere, I'm a bit worried because I've learnt that in life you always have to be prepared for the blows, especially in the world of football.'

Straight after signing for his new club, Cesc spoke to Guardiola face to face. He wanted to describe what he had been living through in his last months at Arsenal. He didn't put it like that but he was interested in finding out if Pep was going through the same experience. In the last months in London, Fàbregas had lost the enthusiasm with which he had arrived at Arsenal as a sixteen-year-old. His lacklustre training reflected that. Eight years had passed and it felt like he needed a new challenge, something to help him rediscover that feeling in the pit of his stomach, that anxiety to please, even the pleasure of combating his doubts.

He was happy to go back home even if he was going to be on the bench first, as everybody expected. He knew, he told Pep, he wasn't going to play often: 'look at the players you have!' But he was willing to fight for his place. 'I want to be whistled, that you ask more and more from me, I want that pressure,' Cesc added. He didn't have any of that at Arsenal any more.

Pep opened up to him. It all sounded very familiar: 'When I left Barça the same thing happened, I went to train and I didn't have the same excitement, that's why I needed to leave.'

It was the first of many face-to-face chats they had in their single campaign together – in training sessions, before and after games, in airport lounges. Not much about tactics at first because Pep just wanted Cesc to rediscover his love for the game. And goals, and enjoyment, started arriving from the first day.

In fact, Cesc Fàbregas learnt more than anyone in Pep's last season at Barcelona. The manager, conscious of the awe in which the midfielder held him, wanted his new player to see him as a guy who took decisions. And from the moment the midfielder arrived, Guardiola wanted to fill Fàbregas's hard drive with as much information as possible (positional play, runs into the box, movement off the ball, link-up play) with the hope that it would make sense at some point, even if at first it didn't totally sink in – and even though he might not be there to guide him through it.

Cesc, the media and fans thought he might not play much at first, but that he would be able to adapt quickly; after all, he had played for Barcelona up until the age of sixteen, when he left to join Arsenal in 2003. However, the years spent in England had logically made a huge imprint. When he returned to Barcelona, he had left a club whose style of play gave him total freedom to move around; whereas Barcelona's play is more positional and demands other tactical obligations. Cesc found it difficult.

Although in his first few months he had the same freedom to move wherever his instincts took him – but mostly in forward areas – and he had scored with ease, from the last sixteen of the Champions League Pep began to demand more tactical discipline from him in a deeper position. He found it hard to understand what was being asked of him and, as Cesc himself admits, 'I was obsessed with it. Until I understood that if they had signed me it was because of who I was, not for who I could be. I couldn't stop being myself.'

Pep wanted Cesc to feel he was on top of him, looking after him. Demanding more of him as the player asked him to in that pre-season chat. As he did very publicly in a game versus Valencia, in that phase where Cesc didn't score goals even though he was performing well and accepting his new responsibilities and obligations. Fàbregas had played perhaps one of his best games with the team, assisting once for a goal, defending, passing, but missing chances. He forced a couple of incredible saves by Diego Alvés, the Valencia goalkeeper, and on another occasion he mishit the ball. Pep replaced him at 4–1, fans reacted well and gave him a resounding ovation.

Cesc felt happy with the game, but annoyed at not scoring. 'God, the goals just won't go in', he was telling himself. As he was walking off the pitch, he saw Pep coming over to hug him and became momentarily defeatist. 'Bloody hell, it's so difficult to score, it won't go in, that third goal took a while', he audibly communicated his frustration.

'Bloody hell …' Pep replied half joking. As he did that, he pushed the player away and shouted, 'What do you mean it won't go in? Make it go in! You should have scored!'

Pep gave him a bit of stick and carrot when he needed it. Cesc is the kind of player who responds to it. The coach applied it after a game against AC Milan where the midfielder didn't play at all. In the next training session, Pep came to him and told him, 'You'll play in your position in the next game. I want to see you playing well, OK?' When Pep talks about 'your position' he means that free role he used to have at Arsenal.

Often when Cesc played, Guardiola deployed a formation, 3-4-3, that wasn't fully convincing but the coach defended one of Johan Cruyff's maxims – if you have it, flaunt it; always use your quality players. So if he had to place four midfielders and shrink the defensive line, so be it. Cesc is an important player for his system when it works, because he gets goals coming from deep and that takes some responsibility for scoring off Messi. Meanwhile, the Argentinian was free to move about in attack and therefore it became more difficult for the centre back and opposing defences to mark.

But it didn't always work.

There was too much to learn in one season, an overloading of information while he was trying to find his place in the club and the squad that ultimately frustrated him. His game suffered as the season progressed. 'I had to take lots of responsibility at Arsenal. I need to follow more tactical orders at Barcelona,' Cesc admits. 'And sometimes I felt lost.'

In the end, he not only stopped scoring regularly but he was also left out of the line-up in some important games (such as against Real

Madrid in April). That didn't diminish his adoration of Pep. So much so that within the club it was concluded that Pep's departure could serve as a potential liberation for Cesc as he prepares to replace Xavi eventually as a leader and axis of the team.

In hindsight, it must have been difficult for the former Arsenal star when he discovered that Guardiola told the president and Zubizarreta that he wanted to leave the club just two months after the player joined Barcelona in August.

The hug that Cesc gave Pep in the Camp Nou dressing room after Chelsea knocked Barcelona out of the Champions League in 2012 was one of the longest. Fàbregas was emotional; he couldn't articulate it, but wanted Pep to continue and hoped his hug spoke for him.

But three days later, as Pep announced his exit in the dressing room, Fàbregas felt a resonance of the experience he himself had had at Arsenal only the year before.

There was another embrace at the end of the cup final after Athletic Bilbao had been dispatched in the last official game of the Guardiola era. But by then it was no more than a resigned gesture of farewell.

6

PEP GUARDIOLA AND JOSÉ MOURINHO

14 May 1997. Stadion Feijenoord, Rotterdam. Cup Winners' Cup final. Barcelona v Paris Saint-Germain. On one side, Ronaldo, Luís Figo, Luis Enrique and Pep Guardiola, coached by Bobby Robson; on the other, a French team in decline, weakened by the departures of Djorkaeff, Ginola and Weah, but still featuring the legendary Rai, as well as his compatriot Leonardo, a future star at AC Milan.

It was a tense affair. Both teams had good spells in the game, and numerous chances. A single goal proved decisive when, in the last few minutes of the first half, a penalty taken by Ronaldo – then considered the best player in the world – gave Barcelona the lead.

Robson's side clung on and when the referee Markus Merk blew the final whistle, the Catalan players celebrated with more than a hint of relief. The 1996–97 campaign, the first one without Johan Cruyff at the helm in almost a decade, had been tough.

As the players celebrated, Pep wanted to hug his team-mates – and just about everyone else connected with the club who was on the pitch. Ivan de la Peña and Guardiola were both kneeling on the grass, hugging, and as they got to their feet, Pep caught sight of a member of the club's staff. Pep waved at him and, with a huge grin on his face, ran towards him with his arms outstretched.

It was José Mourinho.

Pep Guardiola and José hugged. At that time, the future Real Madrid manager was working for FC Barcelona as Bobby Robson's translator and assistant. Mourinho got hold of Pep and locked him in an embrace, raising him up and down, three times before they both started jumping up and down again, bouncing around like two elated kids on Christmas morning.

Two friends and colleagues were rejoicing in the success of a job well done.

It was their first campaign together, and there would be three more before José departed in 2000. Four seasons during which they got to know each other extremely well.

Years later, in the middle of a series of four tense and ugly Clásicos, Pep recapped that the pair had once been friends: 'I only want to remind him that we were together for four years. He knows me and I know him. I keep that in my mind.'

'I gave my all, there's nothing left. That is the fundamental thing. And I need to fill myself again,' said Pep at the press conference that confirmed his departure. It was an open admission of his weaknesses, vulnerability, exposed to the eyes of the world.

But days, even hours, after conceding his exhaustion and inability to continue, Pep's expression changed. The sense of relief that he had felt during his public farewell was replaced by one of sorrow.

There was speculation about the reasons behind his mood swing, and whether or not it was a consequence of the press conference send-off that had been such an inappropriate ending for his illustrious career: after all, the club was announcing that the best coach in their history was leaving and they decided that it should coincide with the announcement of his replacement, Tito Vilanova. Was his melancholy due to the fact that his assistant and friend Tito was staying, a decision that surprised everybody? Was it because the boss and his replacement were still awkwardly sharing the same space? Or perhaps it was more to do with the strange atmosphere created in the dressing room from the moment of his announcement, as everybody, team and staff alike, felt they could have done more to convince him to stay?

Whatever the consequences, Pep was emotionally drained and, in exposing his fragility, he revealed the scars with which the intense pressure of football at that level had aged him so much. Perhaps it is true that four years of managing Barcelona takes the same toll as managing a quarter of a century at, say, Manchester United. Pep was telling us: I am not Superman; I am vulnerable, flawed. Pep Guardiola: the archetypal anti-hero, a man capable of achieving greatness and performing wonderful deeds, despite his own weaknesses and fears, aware of his power and responsibility but who would have been happier if he hadn't spread himself so thinly in his unwanted multiple role as club figurehead, philosopher and manager, and who, despite everything, fought against being used as an example. More of a Spiderman, then.

After all, no Superman would have burst into tears in front of the world's TV cameras as he did after the team won their sixth title in a year, the World Club Championship, against Estudiantes. Or admitted straight afterwards, in his first words post-game, that 'the future looks bleak. To improve on this is impossible.' He had asked Tito, still on the pitch, 'What else are we going to do now?', because, having to face the same challenges, Pep could only foresee the problems ahead and didn't think he was strong enough to overcome them all over again. From the pinnacle of the game, the only way was down.

Yet, astonishingly, Pep did continue and did improve the team. Once again, he had proved capable of overcoming the odds, transforming and leading a group of men into performing heroics on the football field, while at the time shaping and staying true to his own values and philosophy. He achieved the seemingly impossible, superhuman feats, but it took its toll: he may appear superhuman, but cut him and he bleeds like the rest of us – and, because of that, what he achieved was all the more impressive not despite of but because of those human qualities.

That is part of Pep's magic. The public is fascinated by such a seductive mixture: on the one hand fragile, even physically, and, on the other, strong in leadership and the sheer force of his personality. And his team is precisely that, too: extremely convincing in the way they play, with obvious cultural characteristics; but, on the other hand, lacking physical stature, weak, smaller than the average footballer – it's that dichotomy that makes Spiderman Pep and his team so appealing.

He earned his authority not just through the team's play and their trophies, but through his behaviour in the good and the bad times, in his achievements and his self-confessed errors. The cynics said that his exemplary composure and behaviour were merely a front and that we would only know the real Pep in defeat. The media loves football because it's usually black and white, about winners and losers. Good and bad. And the Madrid press wanted to believe that Pep was bad, that his public persona masked something altogether different. That tribalism came to the fore when Barcelona had to play Real Madrid four times in a fortnight in April and May 2011. That desire to oppose good and bad and portray representatives of either side of the great divide as being symbolic of either one or the other led to one of the most acrimonious periods in the recent history of Spanish football.

A couple of occasions towards the end of Pep's tenure, losing to Madrid and being knocked out of the Champions League by Chelsea, worked as a litmus test and provided a rare glimpse of the other side of Guardiola. His complaints about referees were a way of getting rid of feelings of frustration that he had felt all season.

Those moments made little difference to those who see Barcelona as more than a club, who had fallen in love with the team's style and ethos – and in Pep Guardiola saw the essence of the ideal man. Pep had been a reluctant social leader and the fans who were less intoxicated by his aura, the minority, understood. The rest spoke about a Guardiola who only existed in the newspapers and in their own heads. A Guardiola whom Pep himself never recognised. 'Who are they talking about when they talk about me?' he asked himself when he read things about his methods, his moral leadership and his supposed superhero virtues. 'There are books that say things about me that even I didn't know.'

In fact, in many senses Guardiola was the opposite of that ideal portrait painted by his fans. 'He is pragmatic, not philosophical, in the negative sense used by some, including Ibrahimović,' admits Ramón Besa. 'He is a coach more than a leader, more interested in the education than the competition. If he appeared to have another role at the club after Joan Laporta left, it is because the club has been devoid of a moral hierarchy and of authority, in the absence of which he didn't shy away from the responsibilities.' But, in the necessary duality created in the public eye to make football more striking, a hero needs an arch enemy to complete the picture. And he – the media and also the fans – found the perfect character: a powerful opponent with a shared personal history with Pep but who had eventually become a formidable opponent; who represented, in a superficial analysis, opposing values to Guardiola; who thrived on displaying a contrasting personality to the Catalan manager – and who had been recruited by Barcelona's arch rival to stop their dominance in its tracks. In José Mourinho, Pep had found his perfect comic-book nemesis.

In this drama, the characters are clearly defined. The good v the bad; the respectful v the confrontational. They are antagonists and adapt each other's role in contraposition to their rival, which helps them define the character they have chosen to play. Clearly, Mourinho did look for the head-to-head confrontation, and felt more comfortable with a constant battle that he felt was necessary to unsettle a team and a club that were making history. Pep never relished those sideline skirmishes – even though on one memorable occasion he decided to stand up to his enemy. But, at the end of his four years at Barcelona, Pep admitted to one of his closest friends that 'Mourinho has won the war': a conflict that he didn't want to engage in and one that would ultimately tarnish for him the memory of the great moments of football offered by both sides.

Yet, the most surprising part of this football operetta is that, if you look deeper, if you scratch the surface, there are as many things that connect Pep and Mourinho, supposed adversaries, as separate them.

When Bobby Robson went to Barcelona to sign his contract in 1996, a thirty-three-year-old José Mourinho was waiting to welcome him at the airport, to help him with his bags and drive him to the Camp Nou. Mourinho was devoted to the man he was going to translate for and help settle in his new club, as he had done at Sporting Lisbon and Porto. From the start, José, fluent in Spanish and Catalan, was always present at the meetings with the Barcelona president Josep Lluís Núñez or the vice-president, Joan Gaspart, helping his boss both translate and understand the context, as by then he was already more than the 'interpreter', a nickname used by some as far back as Porto where actually Mourinho had already been helping with training. Despite the initial reticence of players to accept the instructions of a young man without experience in the football elite they eventually recognised José could see football as clearly as any.

At Barcelona, Robson, who never fully managed to master the language, needed Mourinho to help him settle into his new life in Spain along with his wife, Elsie. José's own partner, Matilde, was also always on hand to help out, and dinner at the Robsons' invariably included the Mourinhos. Little by little, the manager gave his subordinate more influence in the day-to-day running of the team and even the assistant offered by the club, José Ramón Alexanko, had to share his authority and involvement in training sessions with the young Portuguese. According to some of the players who spoke English, José's instructions when translating Robson came sharper than his mentor's and sometimes with a little bit extra. His videos, exposing and highlighting the weaknesses and strengths of the opposition, were well considered and his relationship with Ronaldo also helped him win some kudos in the group. He soon became the shoulder to cry on when players were left out of the team as Robson purposefully maintained a professional distance from the squad. Astutely, José crossed that line constantly and freely.

Mourinho quickly recognised Guardiola as a natural leader and decided to get close to him, and win him over. He succeeded. The pair would spend hours together after training, chatting both in Spanish and Catalan. 'We did talk about things, when we both had doubts, and we would exchange ideas, but I don't remember it as something that defined our relationship. He was Mister Robson's assistant and I was a player,' Guardiola says now.

Guardiola at that time was, as Robson would put it, 'a big fish', and never afraid to give his opinions on the way to play, what they had to do or avoid doing. In fact, little by little and finally for large parts of the season, the so-called 'gang of 4' (Pep, Luis Enrique, Sergi and

Abelardo) established an element of self-management when they recognised that Robson couldn't quite get to grips with the Barcelona style and the demands of La Liga. It was a critical time and Mourinho had to place himself on the side of the coach

Robson won three trophies that season (Spanish Cup, Spanish Super Cup and European Cup Winners' Cup) but not the league and, by April, the club, aware of the lack of authority of the manager, had already signed Louis van Gaal who had impressed at Ajax. Mourinho had decided that he wanted to go back to Portugal at the end of the campaign, but Robson recommended him to the Dutch coach who gave José even more authority and allowed him to coach the team in a few friendlies and dispense some tactical chats at half-time. The Robsons were replaced at the evening meals by Truus and Louis, the van Gaals.

Slowly but surely, José's personality started blossoming. Away from Robson, after a few years of working in the dressing rooms of big clubs, freed from the early ties that contrived his behaviour, van Gaal discovered 'an arrogant young man, who didn't respect authority that much, but I did like that of him. He was not submissive, used to contradict me when he thought I was in the wrong. Finally I wanted to hear what he had to say and ended up listening to him more than the rest of the assistants.'

Mourinho was clearly much more than a translator at Barcelona, but that was how he was known by the Catalan media and the title by which president Núñez insisted on referring to him as such. It is easy for a Spaniard to dismiss the authority of a Portuguese, two nations with a unilateral rivalry (Spain looks beyond the Pyrenees for adversaries). That lack of respect would never be completely forgotten, or forgiven, by Mourinho.

When van Gaal was replaced in 2000, José's contract was not renewed. He wanted to leave in fact, as he felt ready to be a number one. Pep was finishing his seventh season in the first team of Barcelona when Mourinho looked for a coaching job in Portugal.

The rest is history. José became a winning coach and his success with Porto and Chelsea gave him the opportunity to replace Frank Rijkaard at Barcelona, certainly one of his biggest dreams.

But his tumultuous relationship with the Barça fans made some decision-makers at the Catalan club wary. It all began to go wrong when he first returned to the Camp Nou as Chelsea manager for a Champions League clash in 2005. In the first of many stormy encounters with the Catalans, Mourinho accused Rijkaard of making a visit to referee Anders Frisk's dressing room at half-time. Mourinho complained to UEFA and in the ensuing maelstrom Frisk announced his retirement after receiving email death threats from fans over the issue. Consequently, the head of UEFA's referee committee branded Mourinho 'an enemy of football'.

But behind that controversial mask, there is an extraordinary coach – and Mourinho had several admirers at the Camp Nou. In the meeting that took place with the Barcelona directors in Lisbon in the spring of 2008, he desperately wanted to impress them. After the encounter, he was convinced he had been chosen ahead of Pep Guardiola.

But when he was rejected, with no clear notification from the Barcelona directors for many weeks, there was a burning feeling of betrayal.

Barcelona, on the other hand, and not for the first or the last time, were unable to take advantage of what could have been considered one of their assets: after all, Mourinho had been at the club and knew it well. It is a disease of the Catalan or even the Barcelona mentality: treat as deserters those who leave the club, the nation, as happened with Ronaldinho recently or even with Pep Guardiola himself. Instead of a friend, José became and was portrayed by the Catalan media and football society as a foe – yet one with inside information and harbouring the bitterness of rejection, the worst kind of antagonist.

Following that rejection and after winning the league twice and the Champions League with Inter Milan in a two-year spell, he got the chance to sign for Real Madrid: an alternative route to a date with destiny involving FC Barcelona.

Pep's and José's first encounter on opposing benches took place in the group stages of the Champions League, 2009. Barcelona, the reigning champions, met Inter Milan in Mourinho's second season at the Italian club and drew 0-0 in Italy, but the result didn't reflect the magisterial lesson in style, positioning and possession of the Catalans. At the return leg at the Camp Nou, Guardiola decided to leave Ibrahimović and Messi on the bench for the in-form Pedro and Henry, who played as striker, and again the performance was excellent – an emphatic 2–0 victory.

'Mourinho, go to the theatre,' sang the Barcelona fans as a reminder of his comment about Leo Messi's supposed 'play-acting' in a 2006 tie against Chelsea and of his provocative slide along the Nou Camp touchline to celebrate a Chelsea goal the last time he was in the visitors' dugout. The Portuguese coach cocked his ear to the 98,000 Barça fans the second time they taunted him.

All in all, it had been an uncomfortable return for José, but he was gracious in defeat: 'Barça were spectacular,' he admitted afterwards. This first exchange of blows between both managers reflected the expected superiority in quality. But Mourinho learnt up close what made Pep's team so good.

The two managers met again in the semi-finals of the competition that same season, ideal for Mourinho, who was becoming a specialist in knockout situations. His repeated strategy included kicking off the match in pre-game press conferences, creating a hostile atmosphere and placing football traps everywhere in the match.

For the first leg, Barcelona had to make their way to Milan by coach as a volcanic ash cloud drifting south from Iceland had paralysed European air travel. UEFA never considered suspending the game and Barcelona had no option but to spend fourteen hours on a bus to reach their Milan hotel. Inter were tactically better prepared for the Catalans than earlier in the season and in the second half Pep's team didn't quite seem at the races – despite scoring first, they conceded a Diego Milito goal (although clearly offside), and finally Inter deservedly won 3–1.

As expected, Mourinho continued playing his games in the post-game press meeting: 'It is always difficult to lose, especially for those that are not used to it.' Guardiola knew the game José wanted to play and avoided being led into confrontation: 'I respect him a lot and I won't spend a single second answering things like that.'

Pep needed his team to focus on the return match. José knew that Barcelona were uncomfortable when dealing with strong emotions.

Mourinho, in his press conference before the return leg, fired another barb in Pep's direction: 'We are following a dream; Barcelona are pursuing an obsession. They have this obsession called "Bernabéu".' That season's Champions League final was to be played at Real Madrid's stadium and José had shrewdly chosen those words even though Inter had not won the European cup in forty-five years. He added: 'We are used to seeing these Barcelona players throwing themselves on the floor a lot.'

Guardiola shook his head as he was listening to Mourinho's words in a backroom at the Camp Nou. When it was his turn to face the media, he tried to find the right tone to react to José's message and he wanted to steer the minds of players in a more positive direction: 'My feeling is of huge happiness, of an indescribable pleasure. It is an honour and a privilege to play again a semi-final of the Champions League. I will enjoy the game and I want my players to do so too. I have told them to be themselves. We aren't playing against Inter, we're playing against ourselves. We are going to see if we are capable of being ourselves in the most important, transcendental game of our lives. Inter Milan don't even exist.'

Pep also felt the need to reinforce what his club were about after Mourinho's insinuations: 'We are an exemplary institution. We have lost and won a few times in the past twenty months, but we have always retained respect.'

Mourinho had picked his battleground and the rules under which this second leg was going to be fought – and it worked against a Barcelona side which acted from the first minute of the game as if it were the last. Iniesta was absent through injury and the team missed his clarity of passing and vision. When Thiago Motta was sent off after a clash with Busquets, Inter had to dig in and defend for about an hour: in many ways the perfect scenario for them because it meant they could drop deep unashamedly.

Piqué scored well into the second half and a Bojan goal was disallowed for handball – but the Italian team, defending superbly, made it to the final.

Mourinho walked on to the Camp Nou pitch at the final whistle with his arms aloft, looking to the sky – only for Víctor Valdés and the water sprinklers to bring a premature ending to his victory parade. 'It is the most wonderful defeat of my life,' he added minutes later.

Pep was magnanimous following his side's knockout from the competition, no excuses were made and he was pragmatic about Mourinho: 'Criticising him would be looking down on Inter and that is not fair.'

The next game was at Vilarreal, two days after the KO from the Champions League. There were only four games left and the title was in their hands if there was no slip-up. Pep told his friend David Trueba he needed to do something about a team that was seriously wounded: 'Guardiola noticed that his players were hurt, broken by the defeat in the competition they were anxious to win. "What do I say to them?" he asked himself out loud an hour before sitting down in the el Madrigal dug-out. Pep was obsessed with motivational messages being clear, concise, uncomplicated. He had previously used videos, even from YouTube, ideas, inspirational stories, even lectures by heroes of his to boost team morale. That day he approached his players smiling. There was not going to be a video. "Gentlemen, I can't ask any more of you. You have given me more than any coach could ask of his players. You're great. Thank you for everything. I just want to say one thing. If we go out there and we lose, and the league is beyond our reach, it doesn't matter. Not at all. Be calm. Thank you so much. For me, you are all champions"'. Valentí, Pep's dad, watched Barcelona beat Villarreal by a clear 4–0 result that helped them win the League title for the second time in a row.

In his last press conference of that season, Guardiola sent a veiled message to the Madrid press when he congratulated Madrid's players and staff for forcing them to reach ninety-nine points to win the title, 'but only them'. The assaults from the Spanish capital were harsh and not easily dealt with by Pep: 'Sometimes we felt scorned. Sometimes we were ashamed to celebrate titles. We have only played a sport in the best way we can but we have felt, for a while now, that we do things that are not being supported everywhere. So we have to do the work of an ant, of not responding to all the attacks. We know they have very loud speakers but it would only be fair if we all respected these players that have dignified their profession with their effort. In any case, nothing will change, especially if Mourinho comes to La Liga.'

Even before José's arrival, certain sectors of the Madrid press were looking for reasons to criticise and even attack Barcelona, a team that was receiving plaudits from the rest of the world. According to that media: referees were benefiting Barcelona, the Spanish FA were helping them any way they could, UEFA turned a blind eye whenever Barça were involved, the television schedule was favourable to them – and some even suggested that opposition coaches were letting Pep's team win.

That sector of the media that wanted to take the Barcelona–Madrid rivalry to extremes would join forces with Mourinho in the coming season – in what turned out to be a radicalisation of the coverage that helped paint both coaches in very simple terms: this drama was going to be, right from the beginning of the season, a struggle between good and evil in the eyes of the press.

After the summer, Guardiola welcomed the arrival of the new Real Madrid coach in his first press appearance of the 2010–11 campaign: 'Mourinho will improve me as a manager. It is important that he works in Spain because he is one of the best in the world. He will make us all better.' Pep knew José's tricks: a loyal core of players around the manager, criticisms of authority and refereeing, the 'us against the world' mentality and, ultimately, a very powerful, comprehensive method to win titles.

Pep had an idea of what was to come and his words were effectively a means of composing himself, taking a deep breath, before rolling up his shirtsleeves for the battle that would inevitably commence.

Before the season gathered pace, Mourinho and Guardiola shared a few pleasantries at that UEFA coaches meeting in Nyon – five months after Barcelona's Champions League KO at the hands of Inter. The pair were never on their own at the conference but Mourinho made an effort to make Guardiola, in his first visit to the forum, welcome. Pep, nevertheless, could not help feeling a bit tense next to the Portuguese coach.

Behind the amicable façade, José had decided that, in order to beat Barcelona, this extraordinary collection of players that stood for one particular interpretation of the game of football, he had to target their foundations, undermine and unsettle their cushioned life. Watching a Barça game just before he became the Madrid manager, Mourinho was amazed at the way the referees effectively laid out the red carpet for the Catalans, and how even opposition players and fans were in awe of their talents and superiority. Mourinho decided that this had to finish, that Barcelona needed to be knocked off their pedestal. And in order to do that, he would need to use every weapon in his armoury of words, accusations and insinuations.

It was, of course, not a new strategy for Mourinho. He had used similar approaches in England and Italy, adapting his methods to the respective countries. But the way he would execute his plan in Spain would require taking those tactics to the extreme – not least because this time his rival would be the most powerful he had ever encountered.

Two big names and strong personalities rode into town, and that town wasn't big enough for the both of them. Or, at least, that's how the media liked to portray it.

Media and fans enjoy explaining the world through a set of values, prejudices and predetermined points of view that configure the vision we have of it. That the world is becoming 140 characters long (the length allowed by Twitter) reinforces the necessity of reducing the complexities of life in very simple black and white terms.

It's the latest chapter in a very old story. Barcelona and Madrid have always been understood as two different institutional models, but, from that year, with José's addition, it became as partisan and polarised as at perhaps any point in the past. Mourinho provided the kind of theatrical confrontation that this symbolic clash thrives upon. It's a contest made in heaven because it is, without a doubt, a mutually beneficial rivalry that is nourished by preconceived ideas and fuelled by clichés that have taken hold because it's convenient, not just for fans and media, but for the clubs themselves who are happy for it to continue – it's good for business and also because they operate in a world where people need to create a sense of opposites in order to help affirm their own allegiances and identities.

It was frequently presented as a David and Goliath story throughout the previous century with Barcelona relishing their status as underdogs, while Real Madrid were more than happy to play the role of the big guy. But now they are two evenly matched Goliaths slugging it out, toe to toe, round after round after round.

Just as the world of politics shows different ways of comprehending the world, the respective styles of Barcelona and Real Madrid demonstrate two different ways of understanding the beautiful game. Madrid has always been characterised by an energetic style of play, strong, fast and competitive. Whereas Barcelona discovered, in the Dutch model, a valid alternative style to take on Madrid: effective passing and offensive play.

'That role of an antagonist fits in well in Spanish football, because Spain is always the red and blue Spain, the peripheral and centralist, the Spain of Guardiola and Mourinho. That duality is something that is received well by people. Mourinho has accentuated the division between the different ways of seeing football that Barça and Madrid have. The interesting thing is the U-turn Madrid has taken goes against their history, because Madrid has never entrusted the team to a coach.' That's how the journalist Ramón Besa, of *El Pais*, explains it.

Although the Portuguese coach claims to challenge himself more than he does others ('I always try and set my sights on difficult goals so that I am always competing with myself'), the following quote about his controversial take on rivalries gives an interesting insight into his working philosophy: 'Having enemies in order to give your all isn't necessary, but it is better. Especially when you're enjoying a lot of success and you tend to relax.'

So the ongoing historical battles between these two great sporting institutions eventually boiled down to this clash of personalities, this fight between their respective coaches. Such was the media presence of Guardiola and Mourinho, the teams almost played second-fiddle to their leaders, becoming known as 'Guardiola's team' or 'Mourinho's team'. Jesús Toribio, market expert, told Miguel Alba in an article for *El Público* that the 'clubs began to lose their own identities in the midst of the duel, much like what has happened in the technological battle between BlackBerry and iPhone – the products have devoured their brands: Rim and Apple. The leading roles of the coaches gave the coaches themselves (the products) the victories, more so than the clubs (the brands).'

And, to the casual onlooker, both of them developed a footballing project that was antagonistic.

Pep Guardiola surrounded himself with players from the youth team who shared the same values: emphasis placed on good passing, teamwork, good behaviour on and off the pitch, as well as some signings that understood the philosophy. As Eto'o and Ibrahimović discovered, those who didn't share his vision of the world and of football were soon moved on.

The Portuguese coach led a team of individuals whose loyalty to their manager was unconditional – they were prepared to give their life for him and in the name of victory. Anyone who doubted him was swiftly brushed aside. Madrid's traditionally vigorous style of play became aggressive, even violent, on occasions. Madrid were capable of humiliating rivals, they had an insatiable hunger to win and it was visible for all to see exactly how much they enjoyed doing so.

For Mourinho, press conferences were like a theatre in which he really got into character and revelled in the attention. He would claim that Real Madrid were the victims of complex conspiracy theories at the hands of the referees, FIFA, the Spanish government and even UNICEF. For him, victories were to be expected as he believed it was what the team deserved, whereas the various defeats and draws were always treated with suspicion and with accusations of foul play. He would defend to the hilt his players' often aggressive behaviour but he would cry blue murder at similar conduct of his opponents against his team.

Whether he likes it or not, Pep has become a standard-bearer for good values, in a world in which there is a distinct lack of them. Mourinho is more of a product of our society, a preacher of a modern way of thinking, who doesn't shy away from conflict and arguing with those in authority, always seeking explanations and making claims about conspiracy theories. His teams win because they do things right; they lose because someone or something has not let them win.

If Pep's greatest virtue is his sense of caution, then Mourinho's is pure excess. The Portuguese prefers to massage his players' egos and point them in the direction of achieving good results; even Mourinho himself has defined himself as a 'manager of egos'. Guardiola bases his methods on developing his players' confidence through opportunities, motivation.

Their individual styles of leadership reflect their personalities. 'Mourinho defends and enjoys his nickname "the Special One" – he feels he is different from the rest and makes sure that nobody remains indifferent to him; they either love him or loathe him. Including his players, who are all aware that there are consequences to their behaviour because Mourinho operates a system of praise and punishment,' explains Almudena López, sports psychologist. Perhaps that gives José less trajectory in a club than a team coached by Pep – it is very hard to deal with constant pressure. 'Pep prefers to appeal to the players' individual emotions in order to generate a feeling of belonging to the group,' López concludes.

It's fair to say that both coaches are right for the clubs they represent. Mourinho said that Guardiola is the best coach 'for Barcelona', a subtle reminder that he won titles in four different countries. While Pep looks for references in the club's roots and history, and tries to instil in the players a sense of belonging, 'Mourinho is' – as Almudena López describes it – 'the guru whom Madrid needed to recover belief in itself.'

Even aesthetically they are different. Guardiola feels comfortable with clothes that don't normally belong in the technical area. He even won the 'Golden Scarf' for the best-dressed coach (Mourinho ended up third) and likes to wear, both on and off the pitch, clothes by Tony Miró, Prada, Dsquared2 or Armani. The Portuguese coach prefers a more classical look. And, as with most of us, they dress to reflect their personalities. This is also the opinion of Montse Guals and Elisabeth Olivé, two well-known Spanish stylists: 'His [Pep's] style recalls a human being with diverse cultural interests, whereas Mourinho's is more similar to that of an Italian man, unostentatious apart from the way he fastens his tie.' The Portuguese likes to have an open knot, a well calculated casual look. The Catalan prefers a small and neat modern one.

The differences are to be found in their personalities, too. Mourinho knows what he wants at every given moment. With Pep there are moments when it's a yes, others a no, and he chops and changes his mind. Sometimes he'll ring a friend in the evening asking for help in one thing or another – and the very next morning he's changed his mind and rings them to tell them to forget about it.

With Mourinho, it's clear from the start. 'I'm going to win the league here in this country, then there in that country and two years later, there. Then at fifty years of age, I'll win the World Cup with Portugal.' The only deviation from the plan is in terms of age or timescale. If it doesn't happen when he's fifty, then it will happen later.

He thrives on the other stuff he gets involved in, like going to London, toying with buying a house there – keeping everyone on their toes and running around him. Perhaps a consequence of a footballer's career that never took off. Pep doesn't have the need to make it all about his choices, his next move, his arguments, his crusades: 'I have played for Barça. Everything that is used to feed an ego is unnecessary for me. Even praise makes me uncomfortable.'

Even their intelligence differs: Pep takes in as much knowledge as possible to help him with decision-making. José does the same, although he also has a cunning edge. He mischievously went out of his way to get Pep to a point when their rivalry escalated to never-before-seen levels in world football. One imagines Mourinho shaving in the morning thinking what he can come up with. 'Ah, I know!' he must have thought one morning. And in the press conference that day he threw a dart: 'There are people, much more intelligent than me, who manage to sell an image of themselves completely different to mine, but deep down, they're the same as me.' Very rarely has Pep felt the impulse to answer Mourinho, but that day, less than an hour later, Guardiola mentioned his words in his own press conference. 'We're similar in the sense that we both want to win, but apart from that no . . . If that is the case then I've done something wrong. I've never wanted to bring myself to his level. There are images that speak a thousand words. Both of us want to win, but our paths are very different.'

The roads to victory may well be very different, but the cars they drive, the petrol they use to get them there, are not so dissimilar. Mourinho is right.

The first game between Pep and José following the latter's appointment at Real Madrid took place at the Camp Nou. Mourinho had only had five months with his new squad and privately admitted that football was a 'box of surprises'. He had no idea exactly how his young team was going to react to both the Barcelona style and the pressure – only when you open it, he would say, do you know what's inside.

The Clásico was played on a Monday, a rarity due to the post-ponement of fixtures because of an election day in Catalonia on the Sunday. Madrid were in good shape, taking on Barcelona as La Liga leaders a point ahead of the Catalans – under Mourinho they had already become a solid team that conceded few goals and killed off the opposition with their quick counters: the classic Mourinho team.

As they had in their prior Champions League encounters, the match started in the pre-game press conferences: a cat-and-mouse game to see who was going to fire the opening shot. José took aim at Guardiola: 'I hope players can help the referee and that it's a game where people only talk about football.' The implications were obvious. Pep kept his head beneath the parapet.

Barcelona won 5–0 with goals from Xavi, Pedro, Villa (2) and Jeffren. 'We couldn't have played better, we could have scored more. We had them asleep, they couldn't touch the ball,' Xavi remembers.

Víctor Valdés was practically a privileged spectator in the Barcelona goal: 'I was getting dizzy following the ball. Finally I decided to stop looking so closely, my guys were the ones with it anyway.'

Unsurprisingly, typically, Pep prepared for the game with an obsessive attention to detail. Early in the match, the team performed a few of those high-speed 'piggy-in-the-middle' passings for which they are famous, in midfield areas, with the intention of keeping possession and finding a gap at the same time. The Camp Nou was ecstatic, seeing their players not only hammer the opposition, but run – or, rather, pass – rings around their rivals. Guardiola identified more than ever with what the team was doing: it was a moment of confirmation when everybody, fans, players, manager, was walking in the same direction. The big idea, writ large out there on the pitch.

The fact that this moment of affirmation, one of the best games ever seen, took place against a side managed by Mourinho was doubly satisfying. Pep admitted privately that he had betrayed himself with the line-up versus Inter the previous season: the presence of Ibrahimović mortgaged the way the team played, with less possession and more direct attacks. That admission was confirmation that he didn't have the key to success but, if he was to fail, he wanted to do it his way. He studied closely the reasons for his mistake, and in the new season Pep persisted in the idea of controlling games, of making Xavi, Iniesta and Messi the focus of the team. In the 5–0 Clásico performance, Pep saw the Barcelona he had been dreaming of.

Guardiola wanted to put the result into context: 'What will prevail in history is not just the result, but the way we did it. It isn't easy to play so well against such a strong team – a team that was killing opponents domestically and in Europe. We have to be proud. Let's dedicate this victory to Carles Rexach and Johan Cruyff who started all this, and to everybody who has participated in the process: former presidents, former coaches, everybody. It is a global victory because we have done things differently and because there is no other club in the world that trusts local people as much as we do.'

José tried to take the heat out of the result: 'It is one that is easy to accept. It is not a humiliation, only my biggest defeat.'

Of course, Mourinho was underplaying the reality – and the truth was that this match would have the most profound influence upon his professional career. He made the mistake of being too bold, of focusing his team's energy on what they would do in possession, rather than when they didn't have the ball. He went to Barcelona believing that he could take them on, at their own game, in their own backyard. The scoreline might not have reflected the actual distance between the two teams in terms of quality – it was, rather, a difference in understanding how to apply that quality to a particular situation.

And that was Mourinho's mistake. It was one that he vowed would never happen again.

José used the backlash of that humbling defeat to help him justify and argue that the supertanker that is Real Madrid needed to change course – convincing all aboard that they should follow his direction. For Mourinho, that 5–0 defeat exposed the fact that the club needed a drastic change: from one being run by the president to one run by a winning manager who could control signings, the academy, facilities, everything. In his quest to knock Barcelona from their perch, the Portuguese was going to transform, for the first time in history, the role of first-team coach at Real Madrid into a general manager – and more, into the leading light of the institution.

Pep Guardiola and José Mourinho may have different styles of leadership and contrasting personalities but they have one very important thing in common: they both love football, winning and are successful in the leadership of their respective teams. They control, plan, analyse and decide everything. They win by surrounding themselves with their praetorian guard and discard those who don't fit with their ideas for the squad. They both have superstar players whom they count on in the pursuit of silverware. A lot in common, then.

Pep wants to leave a legacy and a blueprint for the club that will last the test of time, so that the team can still keep up its winning ways long after his departure from the dugout. At Real Madrid, and having reached a position of huge power, so does Mourinho – in his eyes, one of his main targets is to bring the club to the new century and set ways to keep them at the top.

The Portuguese's charisma is preceded by his fame and success, but in Spain he had a tough challenge ahead in pleasing a fanbase with high expectations, who demanded attractive football and silverware. He started providing both very early on.

Mourinho might put on a front with the media, yet another enemy, but he is generous with his players. He transmits love and respect to them. He is actually a lot softer than he lets on, although his public persona tries to give people the opposite impression. He is honest with them: 'I'm not going to tell them they are doing things well if that isn't the case.'

Pep and José soon won their troops over.

Listen to Ibrahimović: 'José Mourinho is a big star … He's cool. The first time he met [my wife] he whispered to her: "Helena, you have only one mission. Feed Zlatan, let him sleep, keep him happy!" The guy says what he wants. I like him.'

Or to Mascherano: 'Never in my career have I seen a dressing room of players follow a coach with so much faith; what he says goes. I reckon it will be difficult to come across another. Pep has the gift of leadership.'

'He has got one thing going for him that no one can fail to notice,' Patrick Barclay writes in his enlightening *Mourinho: Anatomy of a Winner.* 'He is astonishingly good looking. Players appear desperate to win his approval, like schoolgirls fighting for an approving glance from their favourite teacher. As well as being very handsome, Mourinho is always nicely turned out, something most modern professional footballers take extremely seriously.' Pep's aura can be described in the same way: 'You just want to impress him,' Xavi says.

Mourinho is constantly making notes in his now famous notebook, something he took from van Gaal, his maestro. It was not the only thing he learnt from the Dutch coach. Or from Bobby Robson. Or many other coaches he studied carefully.

According to Juanma Lillo, 'Guardiola is a sponge, he learns from everybody because for him anywhere is a good place to talk about football, to confront ideas and turn a game into a passion.'

Mourinho gets to Madrid's Valdebebas training ground as early as seven o'clock in the morning and makes sure everything is prepared for the day ahead. Guardiola has been seen leaving the training ground at ten at night and sometimes later.

They can both be characterised by their modernity, they employ all the new technology and methods possible to help the growth of their players. But they are also delegators, they lead a great team of assistants and are capable of making their personnel feel responsible, valued, gifted. And both of them have earned themselves a reputation as being great listeners.

They know the institution and fanbase whom they are working for. They know how to direct their emotions, they can awake the enthusiasm and mobilise their players and fans to do what they want. Both are very good at absorbing all the bad vibes directed at their clubs and channelling them away from their players. 'I let people see me angry because I really am, but sometime I pretend to be angry. These days coaches should play with their emotions,' Mourinho says.

Like his Catalan counterpart, he imposed his timetable, his rules and minimal contact with the press. Both coaches are aware that they live in a complex world, almost a media bubble. News sells, and the more exclusive and explosive the story, the better. Both are masters in the science that is handling the media, the message and the art of leadership, making their players stand out among the greatest in the world by clarifying expectations, helping them get to know themselves better, motivating them to be self-disciplined.

When they close the dressing-room door and prepare to face the media, that is when they certainly do things differently.

Once Barcelona had knocked Shakhtar out of the quarter-finals of the 2011 Champions League campaign, Guardiola stopped going to the gym, where he used to spend a couple of hours a day to help him overcome a discal hernia that had hospitalised him. He swapped his exercise regime for the preparation of a programme to steer his side through a run of four Clásicos in eighteen days, starting with their league encounter, followed by the Copa del Rey final and then the home and away legs of the Champions League semi-finals.

For the league encounter, he decided to field the same team that was responsible for the 5–0 thrashing given to Madrid earlier in the season, apart from Eric Abidal who was recovering from his operation. In the run-up to it Guardiola reminded his players that this game would not be a repeat of that extraordinary result; this time Mourinho would not be caught quite so off-guard.

Mourinho is especially good at making games difficult for the opponent: for that occasion, he let the grass on the pitch grow longer than usual so the ball didn't run as much and he used Pepe as a third midfielder to detain Messi. This was the most defensive side Mourinho had fielded and one that was criticised by Madrid's honorary president, Alfredo Di Stéfano. But the idea was not to lose the first one, almost accepting the league was out of reach for Madrid, and focus on the other three Clásicos.

16 April 2011 – La Liga Clásico. Santiago Bernabéu stadium

The game finished with the teams tied at one goal apiece, practically assuring that the league title stayed at Barcelona, eight points away. The tight marking of Messi by Pepe provoked the Argentinian to respond angrily following his limited contribution to the game. When towards the end the ball went out of play, he struck it fiercely, hitting some spectators. 'He had wanted to hit the hoardings and it went high,' one of his team-mates explained. There was more tension on the pitch than in the stands, and it spilled over into the tunnel after the game, with Pepe once again a protagonist.

20 April 2011 – Copa del Rey Clásico. Mestalla stadium (Valencia)

The Copa del Rey final came four days later. Mourinho stuck with his midfield defensive trio but he moved them forward to try and create greater pressure on Barça. It was a brave, aggressive Madrid team, with Ramos as centre back, Pepe giving his all and Khedira battling. Ozil acted as a false nine which disorientated Barça. The second half was agonising and the match was finally decided by a Cristiano Ronaldo goal in extra time. For Guardiola, it was the first final out of ten that he had lost. No love was lost between the Spanish internationals on either side: Busquets aggressively tackled Xabi Alonso; Arbeloa stood on David Villa and then accused him of play-acting, which angered the forward.

It was the tensest moment between both clubs.

Messi walked into the changing room, sat on the floor and cried. Guardiola, as usual, stayed away from the dressing room and didn't say anything special to the players.

The squad were silent on the bus taking them to Valencia airport after the match. Just seven days later Barcelona and Madrid were going to meet again in the first leg of the semi-finals of the

Champions League. On the plane back home, Pep decided he had to do something to recover group morale – he wasn't sure what – but he also knew that Mourinho would try and take advantage of the pre-match press conferences to kick Barcelona while they were down.

The day after the defeat, the Barcelona manager admitted to one of his closest friends, 'you have no idea how difficult this is.' He didn't mean physically, he was talking about facing Madrid, dealing with Mourinho, and everything that had transpired that year: the provocations and comments coming from the Spanish capital. Along with the regular accusations over Barcelona's influencing of referees, the federation and UEFA – a radio station suddenly came out with an extraordinary and false allegation of doping: something that, understandably, hit Pep where it hurt.

'It is all so hard, this is too much,' Pep admitted privately.

The problem went beyond Pep's mental endurance: the constant friction made it difficult to take the right decisions, his juggling of so many roles – figurehead, coach, beacon of the club's values – was becoming too much to bear. One of his close friends heard him saying, 'I am leaving, I've had enough.' The next morning the crisis was averted but Pep kept repeating to himself that he was not going to stay in the Barcelona job for long.

When Pep talks about Mourinho, suddenly an invisible wall pops up. His neck muscles tense, his shoulders hunch and he stops looking you in the eye. Clearly, he is not comfortable with the conversation and it becomes evident that he wants the chat to move on. He feels that he has suffered personal attacks; he thinks his club and its values have been assaulted, his players have been ambushed. And he is not sure why. He can't comprehend why the rivalry could not have been limited exclusively to the sporting arena, to the action on the pitch.

Perhaps one day – and it may take a very long time for him to see it this way – Pep may be able to look back on those Clásicos against Mourinho and realise that, because they pushed him as a person and as a coach to the limit, he emerged a better manager.

Every trophy, an entire campaign, was being contested against the eternal rival in a period of just eighteen days.

In that incredibly high-pressure period of less than three weeks, Pep had to establish a routine, a way of doing things that allowed him and the players to connect and disconnect before and after matches.

He kept his preparation rituals the same, the timetables, training – but he tried to sell each Clásico to the players as a different movie. He demanded a victory in the league, gave a day off after the cup final and, after the blow to the morale to his players as a consequence of the defeat, he needed a new strategy for the Champions League.

He spent every waking hour in his office dedicated to thinking and preparing for these games. Estiarte would tell him, 'Let's go, we're not eating here today, we'll go and eat elsewhere so we don't spend the whole day here.' But when they were eating out, if a meal normally took an hour and a half, after forty minutes his friend could see Pep's mind was on other things: looking at him maybe, but not listening. So Manel would give up, get the bill and go back to the training ground.

On the eve of the first leg of the Champions League semi-final, José Mourinho unwittingly handed Pep the psychological edge he had been looking for.

On that afternoon, Mourinho burst into the press room of Real Madrid's Valdebebas training ground like a whirlwind.

His face told the story, beaming from ear to ear – here was a man who had just masterminded victory over his club's arch rivals, he had put one over Guardiola and he was about to lead Real Madrid into a Champions League semi-final for the first time in eight years.

Mourinho delivered his press conference referring to his Catalan opposition as 'Barça' for the first time since taking over at Madrid – usually it was just 'them'. Another first: he also referred directly to Guardiola, singling him out, calling him Pep.

And then he let loose. He was asked about the appointment of experienced German official Wolfgang Stark as the referee for the Champions League semi-final. Previously, before Stark was named, Guardiola said Mourinho would be 'super happy' if Portugal's Pedro Proença was chosen. When Mourinho responded, he revealed his most provocative side: 'Besides the naming of the referee and the pressure that they exerted so Proença was not chosen, the most important thing is that we are in a new cycle. Until now there were two groups of coaches. One very, very small group of coaches that don't speak about refs and then a big group of coaches, of which I am part, who criticise the refs when they have made mistakes – people like me who don't control their frustration but also who are happy to value a great job from a ref.'

And then he turned on Guardiola.

'And now, with Pep's statement the other day, we are entering a new era with a third group, which for the moment includes only him, who criticise the correct decision of the referee. This is something I have never seen in the world of football.'

Mourinho was referring to a goal by Barcelona's Pedro Rodríguez that was disallowed for offside in the Spanish Cup final against Real on 20 April, and which video replays showed was a correct decision by the referee.

'In his first season [Guardiola] lived the scandal of Stamford Bridge [in the semi-final], last year he played against a ten-man Inter. Now he is not happy with refs getting it right. I am not asking the referee to help my team. If the referee is good, everyone will be happy – except Guardiola. He wants them to get it wrong.'

The Champions League Clásico had just kicked off.

After training that same afternoon at the Santiago Bernabéu and before Guardiola's turn arrived to talk to the press, well aware of what Mourinho had just said, one of the highest ranking people at Barcelona entered the sacrosant dressing room. It surprised many.

The director told the coach to calm down, not to get involved in a war of words, to stay the usual Pep. Perhaps it would be a good idea, it was suggested, if Mascherano appeared with him, always balanced, calm. He was indeed the chosen player to accompany him in the press conference.

But Guardiola had decided to reply. Enough was enough.

In front of the media, Pep had always been the Barcelona coach, a club representative, and never just Pep Guardiola: he had had to bite his lip dozens of times. But now he'd had enough. He wanted to react as his body was telling him to, exactly as he felt.

'Let's talk football, eh Pep,' the director reminded him again a few minutes before Guardiola entered the press room at the Bernabéu. 'Yes, yes,' the coach answered. He wasn't faithful to the truth.

But a doubt assaulted him just before entering the conference area where dozens of international journalists were waiting for him. He looked around for support.

Nothing is ever lineal or simple in Guardiola's mind.

Was it a good idea what he was about to do? Manel Estiarte was next to him: 'Pep, just think about your players, about yourself, about all the Barcelona fans out there on the streets.'

That was that. Point of no return.

He sat down and took the bull by its horns.

'As Mr Mourinho has mentioned my name, he called me Pep, I will call him José.' Pep glanced around with a half-smile – in front of him rows of journalists and at the back dozens of cameramen. 'I don't know which one is Mr José´s camera. They must be all of these.'

His body language showed discomfort. He moved his shoulders, shifted position in his chair. But as the discourse progressed, the Pep of easy words, the one that always convinces you, started to take over.

'Tomorrow at 8.45 we will play a match out on that pitch. Off the pitch, he has been winning the entire year, the entire season and in the future. He can have his personal Champions League off the pitch. Fine. Let him enjoy it, I'll give him that. He can take it home and enjoy it.'

The speech, two minutes twenty-seven seconds of it, was delivered with controlled anger, with wit, without pause.

'We will play a football game. Sometimes I win, sometimes I lose, we win, we lose. Normally he wins, as his CV shows. We are happy with our "smaller" victories, which seem to have inspired admiration around the world, and we are very proud of this.'

For months he had been telling his players, 'do you think I don't want to answer back? But we can't, we shouldn't. We are Barcelona.' Everything, of course, has its limits.

'We could draw up a list of complaints of our own. We could remember Stamford Bridge or 250,000 other things, but we don't have secretaries and ex-referees or managing directors on our staff to note those kinds of grievances down for us. So … we are only left with going out at this stadium at 8.45 p.m. tomorrow and trying to win by playing the best football we can.

'In this room, he is the fucking boss, the *puto amo*, the fucking chief.

'He knows the ways of the world better than anyone else. I don't want to compete with him in this arena not even a second.'

There was something else he didn't want to leave untouched. This José Mourinho that questioned the legitimacy of the Barcelona successes is the same one that hugged him, lifted him in the air that night in Rotterdam all those years ago. Colleagues in the same dressing room. Friends, even. Employees of Barcelona. José, what happened? Pep wanted to ask.

'I'd only remind him that we were together, he and I, for four years. He knows me and I know him. That's enough for me. If he prefers to "go" with statements and claims of newspaper journalist friends of Florentino [Pérez] about the Copa del Rey and to put more weight on what they write than on the friendship, well, no, not quite friendship, but working relationship he and I had then, that's his right.'

The scene was under control, the emotions applied with the right intonation. His body was releasing an unquantifiable amount of tension, of accumulated rage. But, aware of the moment, having captured everybody's attention, and in the middle of the monologue, there was even time for humour.

'He can continue reading Albert [Einstein … Mourinho had said that he used to quote him in speeches to inspire players]. Let him do all that with total freedom, or let him read the thoughts of the journalists who suck on the tit of Florentino Pérez and then draw whatever conclusions he wants.

'I will not justify my words. After the cup final I only *congratulated* Real Madrid and that is what Barcelona do. I congratulate Real Madrid for the deserved victory against the good team I represent with a lot of pride.'

Pep felt it was all said, job done. He was by then sitting very comfortably, and looked straight into the cameras. To Mourinho.

'I don't know which one is José's camera, I don't know which one is your camera, but ...'

'... this is it.'

Gauntlet taken up.

Although the day had been tense, the preparations for the training session were quieter, with the team still recovering from the cup defeat. However, in the interval between Mourinho's press conference and Pep's, the Catalan radio phone-ins were getting heated. Relatives of the players who had travelled to Madrid and knew of the incitement of the Portuguese coach were incensed. How could he get away with it?

The players were finishing training as Pep delivered his answer. He hadn't got away with it.

Guardiola felt Madrid had taken the initiative, and he needed to seize it back. Impressions and titles could have taken a definitive turn if Barcelona hadn't reacted. It was the most delicate moment of the season, with everything on a knife edge, and Pep felt saturated and ready, consumed and strong.

Manel Estiarte puts the moment into context: 'Do you think it was a good idea to come out with all that? Was it? When you've just come back from losing the Copa del Rey and they could really hurt us in Europe, without Iniesta? If we had lost, it would have been seen as a mistake. Pep showed his strength – it was without doubt the worst moment to do something confrontational like the "he's the fucking chief" thing.'

In other words, if Barcelona had lost the next Clásico it would have been analysed as a loss of control, a rant; but it would be pure genius if it preceded a victory. Whatever way you see it, Guardiola gave his side the tonic they needed.

Xavi: Pep had told us more than once he had to bite his lip, he needed to remain in control and not react to the accusations and provocations. But on that day, the Real Madrid coach had attacked Pep directly. He had mentioned him by name.

Puyol: They say things. Then more things, and more things, all lies. One day you have to blow up.

Xavi: I was impressed when I heard what Pep did: shocked. And I liked it. I liked it a lot.

Puyol: We have been attacked; people had made things up about us. That has always hurt us and Pep simply answered all that back.

Xavi: The internal anger has to come out somehow. After we finished training, we were told that he had said all that; my mobile was hot with text messages. In the hotel we watched the news and there was Pep!

Villa: We weren't watching it live as we had finished training, got changed, went to our rooms. But by the time we went down for dinner we all knew. Before the boss returned from the press conference we were buzzing.

Piqué: I got a message about it saying 'Pep's gone and done it', and I thought, 'what's happened??' because I hadn't seen it. Spoke to my parents, who were in Madrid: 'Wow, that was brilliant! It's about time someone gave it back to Mourinho,' they said. It was a real confidence boost for the whole team.

Xavi: We started watching the images of Pep's press conference replayed on the TV and, as we walked into the dining room of the hotel, our parents were rushing up to us and telling us: 'Fucking hell, you should have heard what Pep just said!'

Piqué: When Pep walked in afterwards we gave him a standing ovation. And Pep's reaction was like 'What's up?' (as if to brush it off). His friends were there too, Trueba included.

David Trueba: Yeah, he got an ovation – which I think was more than just a show of support; it was a message to Pep telling him not to feel beaten for having been sucked into Mourinho's games.

Piqué: He must have felt bad about it because he isn't like that. But it was necessary. He attacked him directly, and this time, 'well done!' He'd thought about it and planned it. It came off wonderfully.

Villa: What Pep did, it did help the team, but I don't think he did it to motivate us, rather so that he himself felt good, got stuff out of his system and also in the process defended the players, the technical staff and everyone who works with him.

Xavi: Ah, sometimes you need to give it back and it was perfect on that occasion because it was as if Pep took the lid off a bottle of fizz and he released all the tension that had been building up; it really lightened and lifted the mood.

Piqué: Sometimes I feel like answering back too, I'm not made of stone. But Pep taught us that he prefers respect, humility, demonstrating it on the pitch, you don't need to do so in a press conference … Respect for the rival is essential, but if they are attacking you all the time, in the end you have to answer back. A line had been crossed and if you don't answer back you look silly.

Pep was feeling more vulnerable without Laporta, and with Rosell acting with discretion, but he couldn't show it. What he actually did for the first time as a coach was try and win the game in the press conference. He wanted to act upon this melancholic state the club had fallen into at that moment, to turn it around, to show people that he wasn't scared or daunted by the task of facing up to his team's nemesis after losing to them in the cup. His was a statement of intent, as if to say, 'I'll take care of Mourinho'; the players could take care of their opponents on the pitch, the directors could deal with their counterparts and the journalists could fight between themselves – Guardiola, in the meantime, knew what he had to do.

The stereotypical Catalan attitude, the idea that 'if something can go wrong, it will', throwing the towel in, generally being pessimistic, could have taken over. He wanted to transmit to his team and the fans the idea of '*Sí, podemos!*' – 'Yes, we can!' The mood changed.

After the evening meal in the hotel, and in keeping with the new-won confidence, goalkeeper Víctor Valdés surprised the squad with a home-made video filmed at the training ground hours after the Copa del Rey final defeat.

The team were expecting a motivational film in preparation for the two tough Clásicos ahead. But what they got was a series of parodies of Barcelona players and staff, from Valdés himself or

Javier Mascherano, to Manel Estiarte, portrayed in a swimming pool, wearing a tight water polo hat. Valdés was the comedian in every role. It was beyond funny, it was hilarious.

What shocked Pep most was that this home-made comedy masterpiece had been created by one of the captains, who had spent extra hours at the training ground after a demoralising defeat to give it away as a gift to his team-mates. It was a treat that was repeated before the World Club Championship Final in 2011.

The night before the most important game of the year the players went to bed crying with laughter.

Mourinho's aggressive strategy worked in Barcelona's favour; it boosted their competitiveness and warmed them up for the forthcoming clashes. José had pushed Pep into unfamiliar and uncertain territory – and he brought out the best and worst in the Catalan coach and the team. Pep had resisted succumbing to Mourinho's taunts throughout the season, but he finally broke – and revealed a more human side than many wanted to believe existed. According to Víctor Valdés, he also showed he was the leader that the team and the club needed.

27 April 2011 – Champions League Clásico. First leg. Santiago Bernabéu stadium. Real Madrid 0 Barcelona 2

Mourinho had been happy with his team set-up in the Copa del Rey final the week before, but this time around he was looking for a result, even a goalless draw. During the match, with the teams deadlocked at 0–0, something happened that left his plan in tatters: Pepe was sent off in the sixtieth minute for a foul on Dani Alves. Mourinho, angered, then got himself sent off and was forced to watch the rest of the match from the stands. Following the dismissals, Madrid made no changes to the team, they did nothing to try and salvage a result. Messi took advantage of the situation and scored two goals in the last few minutes. It was after this defeat that Mourinho had one of his more memorable outbursts: '*Por qué? Por qué?*' (Why? Why?)

He accused Barcelona of having the referees on their side: 'Why, in a balanced game, in which the score is level, has the referee done this?' He controversially went on to say that he would feel 'ashamed' to win the Champions League the way Guardiola had. 'If I were to tell the referee and UEFA what I think about what has just happened, my career would end right now,' he complained. To finish off his rant, and even more astonishingly, he wrote off his team's chances of making a comeback in the second leg. 'Madrid has been eliminated from the Champions League final. We'll go out with pride, with respect for our world – the world of football, which sometimes makes me a bit sick. It makes me sick to live in this world, but it is our world.'

The complaints continued. Barcelona reported Madrid to UEFA for Mourinho's accusations and Madrid responded by reporting Alves and Pedro for faking injuries and alleging that Busquets called Marcelo a 'monkey'.

Mourinho was punished for the following five matches in the UEFA club competition, but the fifth match was suspended for a probationary period of three years and the final penalty reduced to three games on appeal. Pepe was suspended for one match. Meanwhile, FC Barcelona goalie José Pinto, who received a red card at the end of the match, was suspended for three games.

In the post-match press conference, Guardiola went back to being his usual self – the cool, calm and composed coach to whom we are accustomed. Unlike his rival, Pep refused to accept that the second leg of the tie was a mere formality, used the press conference to remind the media not to get ahead of themselves and insisted that everybody remain respectful of exactly who his team was up against: 'A team that has won nine European Cups can never be written off. We are going to be careful and recover both emotionally and mentally.'

Later that week, Pep made another announcement to the press: 'Of course, the first bit of news is that we are playing for the right to play in a Champions League final; but the second piece of news is that Abidal is back with us. It is excellent to hear that a man who has fought a battle with cancer has been given the all-clear. He will be on the bench for the match.'

3 May 2011 – Champions League Clásico. Second leg. Camp Nou stadium. Barcelona 1 Real Madrid 1

Iniesta returned to the Barcelona side after recovering from a muscle strain that kept him out of the first leg at the Bernabéu.

With Mourinho confined to a Barcelona hotel because of his suspension, and without Ramos and Pepe, Kakà made a surprise appearance in the Madrid starting eleven. His inclusion didn't quite have the desired impact in making Madrid more of an attacking threat, but with two midfield pivots and four men in front of the ball, Mourinho had sent his side out to take the game to Barcelona. And, as always, there was controversy. On forty-seven minutes, Real Madrid thought they had broken the deadlock – but with the sides level, Higuaín had a goal disallowed for a foul committed moments earlier by Ronaldo. Later on, Pedro gave Barcelona the lead. Madrid reacted by going for broke, bringing on Adebayor in place of Higuaín and withdrawing Kakà. At 3–0 down on aggregate Real finally found the net when Angel Di María's shot struck the post and rebounded to Marcelo for the tap in.

Barcelona had qualified for the 2011 final at Wembley with a 3–1 aggregate win.

Forty-five minutes later, Pep Guardiola took up his place in the press room of the Camp Nou. Typically, he began by paying homage to his own players, and the opposition – while relishing the moment: 'This has been one of the most beautiful nights I have ever lived.

'I would also like to praise Madrid for their courage this evening, because they wanted to go toe to toe with us.

'We feel that we have knocked out a superior team, a wealthier club, that can pay whatever release clauses they want to sign a player, a team with seven strikers that anybody would love to have in their squad; a heck of a team.'

Barcelona had emerged from a gruelling twenty-day period, having won their seventh European Cup semi-final and getting a chance to win their fourth final.

Pep felt drained. The three-week period had been 'tremendously hard, with a lot of tension; very intense and very tiring'.

*

For Xavi, the wounds from those Clásicos are not yet fully healed; the memory of the emotion is not diluted yet: 'Yeah, it was hard. Those four Clásicos were hard. And when you're on your own and you get criticisms, mentally you have to be very strong. It happens to me too. There are days when you think "I can't take this any more. I'm not having a good time." But at least Pep must have felt protected surrounded by his people, he has Tito, Manel, people he has known for years. People who have shared so many things with him, who helped him feel everything was under control.'

Mourinho was not about to give up the fight. He was down but not out and saw this as merely the opening few rounds in the battle he'd come to Madrid to fight. At Inter Milan it took him until the third game against Barcelona to work out how to beat them and adapt his team accordingly. During the summer of 2011, the Real Madrid manager fine-tuned his squad and introduced new tactics that would see them play a higher line than they had the previous season, moving his players closer to the opposition area. He also spent that summer with an eye on the first official match, the season opener: the Spanish Super Cup between the league and domestic cup winners. In other words, the first game of the season against FC Barcelona. Pep, meanwhile, prepared with a focus on allowing his players ample recovery time to put them in the best condition for the arduous season ahead.

14 and 17 August 2011 – the first Clásicos of the 2011–12 campaign. The Spanish Super Cup. Barcelona 5 Real Madrid 4 (aggregate)

The first leg finished 2–2 at the Bernabéu. Three days later, Messi, who had hardly trained with the team after his holidays, scored the winning goal just two minutes before the final whistle to secure a 3–2 victory for Guardiola's side. But the match will be remembered for the toxic atmosphere in which it finished after Marcelo was sent off for a dangerous tackle on Cesc Fàbregas, the sight of friends like Xavi and Casillas rowing on the pitch and – worst of all – the sight of José Mourinho sticking his finger in Tito Vilanova's eye as players and officials from both sides argued on the touchline. The unsavoury scenes led to players like Xavi and Piqué openly criticising their

Spanish team-mates in the Madrid squad for being sucked into Mourinho's dark arts.

One Barcelona player, who has asked to remain anonymous, sums up the mood among the Barcelona players: 'Half the time, we know its only pantomime with him [Mourinho], and he's only doing it to wind people up, but it's unbelievable the way he has the press wrapped around his little finger – and even though poking an opposition coach in the eye is just about the most disgraceful thing I've ever seen in a football match, look how quickly people seem to forget about it. And if you remember, it somehow gets turned around so that we take the shit for it; the media saying, "he did it because he was provoked!" It's like fighting a losing battle all the time.'

Several months later, the two sides were to meet again, this time in the quarter-finals of the Copa del Rey, not perhaps the most important competition the two sides would be battling for – but Madrid's performance at the Camp Nou, rather than the outcome, heralded a shift in dynamic between the two sides.

18 and 26 January 2012 – Clásicos in the Copa del Rey. Quarter-finals. Barcelona 4 Real Madrid 3 (aggregate)

Following a 1–2 victory for Barcelona in the first leg at the Bernabéu, the return leg at the Camp Nou was a tense affair, with some good football played by both sides, plus the usual controversy. Barcelona looked very comfortable with a two-goal lead, but Madrid's fightback to pull the scoreline level and salvage a 2–2 draw had an effect upon the Barcelona public and players. With nothing to lose, Real Madrid seemed to rediscover themselves and had the home side anxious, denting their confidence. It finally proved that an ultra-defensive approach was not the way forward and sent a message to the Madrid players who had, up until that night, been weighed down by an inferiority complex. It was what, for a while, the Spanish players had asked the manager to do and Mourinho accepted the switch in tactics. It was welcomed by attacking players, like Ronaldo, on Mourinho's side. And it provided a glimpse of what was to come.

Half-time at the Camp Nou. Barcelona are beating Real Madrid 2–0 in the quarter-finals of the Spanish Cup. In the home dressing room, Guardiola is giving a tongue-lashing to his players.

He is not happy with the performance. He complains about the lack of intensity, the mistakes in the circulation of the ball, the poor pressure to get the ball back. Despite the two goals, Barcelona are lucky not to be behind and they are playing with fire.

Pep prefers to show his disgust when the team are in front, but on this occasion the mistakes would have been pointed out even if there was a provisional Madrid victory.

In the second half Real Madrid score twice. It proves to be the game in which Mourinho and his players feel the tables have finally been turned.

And rightly so. It is the visitors who attack, who look after the details, who seem hungrier.

21 April 2012 – Clásico in the League. Camp Nou.
Barcelona 1 Real Madrid 2

It had taken eleven Clásicos for José Mourinho to really achieve what he had first set out to do: knock Guardiola and Barcelona off their perch. The Madrid coach's side remained very much a 'Mourinho' side; but this time they were confident, full of self-belief and ruthless in executing quick transitions, utilising all their attacking flair to really hurt Barcelona. The result effectively handed the league title to Real Madrid, with the win giving them a seven-point advantage with only four matches remaining. It was a hammer blow for Pep and his side, just days before taking on Chelsea in the Champions League semi-final that would eventually be followed by Pep's announcement of his departure.

He had insisted before the Clásico that an analysis of the result was simple: lose or draw and Real Madrid would be league champions. And having been thirteen points behind their rivals, Guardiola was happy that it all became similar to a one off-final at home.

For all their possession, Barcelona struggled to get the ball to their forwards – and without Villa, and with Pedro not at his best after struggling for long spells of the campaign with injuries – they lacked a cutting edge. A similar problem would see them knocked out of the Champions League by Chelsea and fuelled Pep's doubts about his ongoing ability to find new solutions to evolving problems as other teams sought ways to minimise Barcelona's threat.

In the end, the defeat meant considerably more than just losing a title – its psychological impact was far-reaching.

In his final season, Pep had remained faithful to the style that had seen his side reach exceptional heights in the previous three seasons – playing with a false nine, applying defensive pressure high up the pitch, attacking in orderly fashion so that when the ball was lost they could immediately apply defensive work, a mobility of players that created absolute order out of apparent disorder and always with the ball as the undisputed star; building up from the back. In addition – sometimes as a reaction to opponents' reluctance to attack and occasionally because of injuries – Pep had tried a three-man defence, even in big games such as the 2–3 victory against Milan at San Siro or at the Bernabéu in the league 1–3 victory.

Yet, despite Pep's best efforts, the fissures in the armour widened, either by team erosion or by the challenge of constantly evolving and improving opponents who were finding and exploiting weaknesses. Guardiola and the team suffered.

Early in the season, his old friend Marcelo Bielsa – who had just been appointed coach of Athletic de Bilbao – provided other teams with a few pointers in a 2–2 draw in San Mamés: which required a last-gasp Messi goal to salvage a point for Barcelona. Bilbao played a very physical game, with intensity; their lines compact so that Barcelona's decisive players couldn't receive the ball between the lines. It opened the eyes of other opponents in and beyond La Liga: with Getafe, Espanyol, Villarreal, Osasuna, Levante and Milan and Chelsea in Champions League all taking a leaf out of Bielsa's book and adopting similar strategies.

Yet the opposition weren't Barcelona's only problem, and sometimes they only had themselves to blame, lacking a competitive instinct, forgetting the basic principles upon which their successes had been founded or simply making stupid errors. Away draws to Real Sociedad, Espanyol, Villarreal and the defeat against Osasuna all occurred for those reasons. In contrast, Real Madrid made no such errors that season and were far more ruthless.

Guardiola recognised the symptoms: not competing well has nothing to do with playing well or badly, it is about looking after the little details. Barcelona forgot that they needed to be Barcelona in every minute of the match; yet, often, they weren't effective enough when it was required, conceding sloppy goals because of a lack of concentration, making the transition between attack and defence too slowly, or simply starting games a little too relaxed and then reacting too late. Such attitudes and errors, to name just a few, cost points and titles. Barcelona also failed to change their style even when the conditions (pitch, weather) were against them. Is flexibility in terms of a team's primary style a sign of weakness or of strength? Isn't adapting a virtue?

And then there was Messi.

Barcelona's over-dependence on the Argentinian genius – especially in terms of scoring – became a problem. The absence of an alternative plan to his brilliance handicapped the team. The injury to Villa in December, Pedro's loss of form due to constant muscular problems and a poor goalscoring contribution from Cesc towards the end of the campaign all forced Xavi to become a midfielder who had to get into the box (he scored fifteen goals, a personal best). There was no recognised striker available – with the confidence that twenty games per season gives someone to take a lead role. The team were short in a striking position with no available youngsters in from the lower ranks who fitted the profile.

Pep identified the problem: the team was no longer as trustworthy on the really big occasions as they once had been, not so long ago.

He had never promised titles but everybody had got used to them. He felt at peace, though, content that he had fulfilled his obligations in giving everything to the team. 'I do not believe the runners-up are defeated. Manchester United were not a defeated club in Rome or at Wembley,' he said in London just before the semi-finals of the Champions League against Chelsea, the game that would define the season. He wanted people to reassess the meaning of success: if clubs like Barcelona, Madrid, United compete with a month to go, you have done what you were asked to do. The rest depends on intangibles, on posts hit, on penalties missed, deflected shots: 'Nobody can hold anything against us; we have done what we had to do,' he told the media at Stamford Bridge.

But Pep knew that the accumulation of success had a logical progression: the more you win, the less you are desperate to win. At the highest levels in sport, a moment's relaxation can expose you. The side let their guard down after three years of unprecedented success and it cost them. That war of attrition, that need to continue to fuel a competitive group under any circumstances was a lost cause that took its toll on the manager, and was possibly the fight that burnt him out more than any other: more than the exchanges with Mourinho, even. In contrast, while José was competing with Pep in Spain, the Madrid coach did not need to spend a single moment trying to deal with that same psychological problem: because his players grew hungrier for trophies the more they saw Barcelona winning.

In the end the pendulum had swung the other way.

'Two Picassos in the same period' is how Arrigo Sacchi describes Mourinho and Guardiola. The legendary Italian manager – a man who pushed football to another dimension in the eighties – feels that Pep's departure from Barcelona was a bad day for football. 'It is a shame for all those who like the beautiful game. He made football evolve and still win. I would like to congratulate him for his fourteen titles in four years. I think that everyone will remember the Barça side in twenty years' time because they revolutionised the sport.' Sacchi also reserves high praise for José: 'He is a rare guy to find. So distinct from Guardiola. You have to study Mourinho as a whole. His teams play excellent football.'

Listening to José after Pep's departure, is it possible to read between the lines a sense that he also wished Pep had stayed, that he will probably never find a more formidable opponent? 'If I say today that I am tired and I stop training for ever, my career would be perfect. I

have won everything I had to win in the most important countries.'
Perhaps that's only wishful thinking on our part.

Pep wanted to operate in a footballing utopia: a place where Carlo
Mazzone joins him for coffee, Batistuta remembers every single
one of his goals, where Marcelo Bielsa, as happened on that trip to
Argentina, lines up Pep's friend David Trueba as man-marker for a
chair in the middle of the living room of the Argentinian's house.
Pep wanted perfection, in a footballing dream world that existed on
a higher plane – a place from which he was brought crashing back
down to earth by Mourinho.

'Prepare yourself, Pepe,' Ferguson had told Guardiola when
they met in Nyon. 'Mourinho is on his way to you!' Pep wasn't that
concerned: 'It won't be so bad.' Sir Alex replied: 'I live happier now.'
The Manchester United manager was right. The fight with José's
Madrid was, according to Manel Estiarte, 'draining, because the dark
arts of the Portuguese were tiring, infuriating and so often unfair –
despite the fact that they were simply a tactic for defending his own
team and club'.

Those 'arts' had tainted Pep's recollections of the Clásicos: 'I don't
have particularly happy memories of those Barça–Madrid games of
the past few years; they're not games I enjoyed, neither in victory nor
defeat: there was always something that left a very bad taste in the
mouth.'

Pep dreamed of a competition in which football decisions were all
that mattered.

'When you play as many times against each other, it becomes
like the basketball play-offs. You do one thing; they respond with
another, you answer in another way. I remember the first game
against Mourinho: Inter played with a 4-4-2 formation. When they
came to the Camp Nou in the second leg of the group stage, they
had a diamond formation and we beat them. When we went back
to Milan for the semis, we played against a 4-2-3-1 where there was
no passing; it was all direct play from them. When José came back
here with Madrid, they wanted to play more and lost. They lost in the
Champions League even though they went back to playing directly.
They have tried to play deep, leaving space behind. In the Super

Cup, the games in the Nou Camp, they had almost lost the tie but they closed us down. The guessing, the changing, the preparing, the switches during games; guessing what formation they will play, how we can surprise them too: that is what makes everything enjoyable, what gives meaning to everything. It is the thing that made those encounters fascinating. It is, in fact, the only thing that stays with me.

'The rest? Not so much. With Mourinho, so many things have happened, so many things …'

Pep took it all personally. For José it was all part of the job.

'Our relationship has been good, is good and will be good,' Mourinho said in his first season at Madrid. 'If ever Pep and I have a footballing problem, it will never become a problem between José Mourinho and Pep Guardiola: only ever a problem between the coach of Real Madrid and the coach of Barcelona. It's something completely separate. Totally different. I respect him as much as I believe he respects me and there are no personal issues between us, quite the opposite. Right now, I can't wish him luck because we are competing for the same thing, but apart from that, there's no problem.'

Pep would never see it that way.

7

THE GOODBYE.
BUT BEFORE IT, ONE
MORE FINAL

First Leg of the Champions League Semi-Finals. Stamford Bridge, 18 April 2012.

In London, and, as expected, Barcelona fielded their strongest side possible with Alexis, Cesc and Messi upfront. From very early on, the team created chance after chance: Alexis hit the bar, Ashley Cole cleared off the line, Adriano hit the post. Once, twice, three, four times the blue wall of Chelsea blocked the way. Barcelona, Pep, Messi discovered that the English club had found a way to frustrate them. Just as Inter had done two years earlier.

The team insisted on looking for answers through Messi, always in his central position.

The little genius then lost the ball, way too close to his own goal, almost on the halfway line. Lampard found Ramires and the Barcelona players tracking back made a crucial mistake. The two centre backs (Mascherano and Puyol) followed Drogba as he was trying to find space on the right of the attack. One of them should have covered the back of Xavi who was desperately following Ramires.

Xavi was on his own defending Ramires, who crossed for Drogba. There were gaps across the Barcelona defence. It led to a goal in injury time before the break.

Based on the result and not the performance, many reached the conclusion that Chelsea had defended well.

Barcelona had twenty-four shots on goal. Chelsea scored one goal from their only shot on target.

Their dependence upon Messi, who had given his all but lacked that little spark, and their lack of alternatives was clearly becoming a problem. But Pep told the players if they had created twenty-four chances at Stamford Bridge, they would do the same at the Camp Nou.

And then, in the press conference, the coach decided to reduce the pressure on a team that had lost its cutting edge and felt the heavy burden on their shoulders of trying to win again. It was a novelty on the part of the manager, perhaps a warning. At that point, it was difficult to comprehend Guardiola's reasoning: instead of demanding more from his players, about to take on Real Madrid in the league and Chelsea at the Camp Nou for the most crucial clashes of the season, Pep seemed to take his foot off the pedal.

'In sport, only those who win stay in everybody's memory. But I have the feeling we have won already. I don't know what will happen next Saturday against Madrid or next Tuesday against Chelsea. But I have the feeling we have won this season already. After four years competing at this level and having arrived at this point with injuries, the illnesses ... I have the feeling we have won. It doesn't matter what happens next.'

Second Leg of the Champions League Semi-Finals. Camp Nou, 24 April 2012. Barcelona 2 Chelsea 2

Football is a percentage game. By defending deep Chelsea had a small chance of going through that increased slightly if they attacked every now and again with intelligence. But still the percentages, in principle, were very unequal and in Barcelona's favour: as they were going to have the ball more often and spend more time in Chelsea's final third.

But that game had been played before. Against Mourinho. Against Inter in 2010. And in the first leg in London.

It was, effectively, a replay.

Pep asked the team to play in wide positions, with a double false strike force of Messi and Cesc roaming freely, and to move the ball from side to side until the gaps appeared. Barcelona were patient, and when the spaces were created they were attacked by the home side like piranhas.

Twice Barcelona scored. In any other season, that would have been enough, especially after the dismissal of Chelsea's captain John Terry following a rash off-the-ball incident when he kneed Alexis in the back with the ball nowhere nearby. Barça were battling a formidable group of strong players, proud professionals who had a last chance of glory in Europe and the task of destroying everything proposed by their opponents: a completely legitimate proposal. Cahill got injured. Everything was going wrong for Chelsea. Yet Drogba was immense, including his stint as a second full back, and Cech was a giant in the Chelsea goal. But they couldn't stop Barcelona creating chance after chance.

Pep's team hit the post twice, had twenty-three shots on goal and six on target, Messi missed a penalty. Any other season …

And Chelsea scored, again in injury time before the break. Similar lapses in concentration that had cost Barcelona a defeat in the first leg were to hurt them again. Ramires lobbed the goalkeeper to make it 2–1. Barcelona needed another goal, but it felt as if the Catalans had run out of ideas, of belief. Possession was lost often, they lacked penetration, width.

The goal never came. And then, in injury time, Torres delivered the killer blow to Barcelona's dreams.

Chelsea had cashed in on their percentages.

Guardiola, his team, had run out of answers.

As Pep's Barcelona progressed, celebrated their successes and grew in stature during the previous four years, so did the personalities of the players. Or, better said, it became increasingly difficult to harness their instincts for the team's benefit: only natural after all. Xavi and Puyol had become the elder statesman, World Champions and a massive presence in the game – and the acceptance of all of it is always an issue that some deal with better than others. Gerard Piqué transformed himself into a multinational star with a superstar girlfriend and, while not necessarily bad, it certainly meant he was not the Piqué who had joined the club from Manchester United. It wasn't easy for a big name like the young defender to accept that Javier Mascherano had become the regular centre back while he was forced to sit out some important games. As the team grew, Pep's management decisions became more complex. It is quite different to give orders to an emerging and promising young Messi than it is to a double Ballon d'Or-winning megastar acknowledged as the best player of his generation.

At the end of that final season, the team selection became crucial, with every decision being like a chess move, every step taken with the utmost caution, sometimes excessive, and often with too many variables taken into account. In the squad, some compared it to politics. A player can take being rested against Rácing de Santander or Levante, but it is a different proposition being on the bench against Real Madrid – the match that serves as the barometer of every campaign. Any player seemingly 'dropped' for el Clásico becomes the focus of negative press no matter how many times Guardiola tries to tell everybody that they all have the right to play, that they were all equal, that it's about options, resting players, etc. They were games marked in everybody's calendar and the final selection would have repercussions upon the balance and well-being of the squad. In Rome, at Wembley, the only doubts in the line-up were related to injuries or suspensions and in those games it was always going to come down to twelve or thirteen key players. But in Pep's last season, there were always doubts and tough decisions to be taken before the naming of his eleven ahead of every big game.

At times the line-up looked, yes, political, other times logical, and on a few occasions almost Cruyff-like. That was how Pep thought he would get a reaction from his players. Creating and maintaining an atmosphere of suspense and introducing players still not versed in the most intricate games was a way of shaking the squad up and keeping everybody on their toes as Pep perceived their crucial competitive edge was ebbing away. However, the uncertainty also became difficult to control and – unlike his masterly ability to smooth things over in previous years – Pep's desire to keep everybody guessing led to a sense of disquiet, anxiety and uneasiness in the players' minds and in his own.

And, let's not forget, Pep's biggest fear since the day he travelled to St Andrews for pre-season those four long years earlier was that he might one day lose the group and be unable to connect with them.

Perhaps the lack of attention to detail and the conceding of injury-time goals were some of the warning signs he had been dreading. And when he felt not all was in order, he started pressing buttons at key moments in the season. And often, he did not hit the right ones. Yes, they remained faithful to their style against Madrid; granted, they did not have the luck against Chelsea. But . . . there was something in the way the English club neutralised Barcelona in the last twenty minutes of the Camp Nou tie that again suggested something had been lost.

In that second leg of the Champions League semi-final, Pep had decided to use the youngster Cuenca down the left flank, leaving experienced players like Pedro, Keita and Adriano on the bench. He had done something similar against Madrid with Tello, who started the Clásico while Piqué, Alexis and Cesc started on the bench. In the club offices, the analysis was a list of question marks. Those decisions reminded some of Johan Cruyff's when, towards the end of his tenure, he started to apply a very peculiar logic that suggested to his critics that he was clutching at straws. Others argued that, perhaps, Pep felt some form of 'paternal instinct' for La Masía boys Cuenca and Tello – which blurred his judgement. Could two incredibly inexperienced kids really be chosen ahead of internationals for such monumentally important games? How could Tello be considered more of a heavyweight than Cesc?

It also meant that the bigger names left on the bench, incapable of challenging a decision made by someone they admired, adored and respected – with a proven track record for making so many correct decisions – started doubting themselves: 'there must be something wrong with me if I am not playing'. Doubts create fear. And fear is a bad companion when you have to take responsibility if things are not going your way. The sudden absence of a familiar eleven – an element so clearly defined in previous campaigns – meant many were struggling with confidence issues. Pedro, for instance, went from the great discovery and hope for the future to the great forgotten man. Cesc, frequently, the match-winning goalscorer, went from saviour to sub.

They were an extraordinary bunch of players, an exceptional team. But they were human, too.

Imperceptibly, for those brief weeks Guardiola may have forgotten that football belongs mostly to the players.

Guardiola knew that the system, the style, had to become automatic, second nature, as it had been for most of his four years in charge. And, when everybody knows what to do, talent appears to enhance the team effort. But changes of personnel and of formation in the final months of his tenure had created a certain level of disorder. So if the players felt, perhaps not even knowing why, that things were not going well, they would look for Messi.

But against Chelsea and Madrid, when the Argentinian had the ball, the two centre backs and two defensive midfielders were on top of him and it became apparent that there was a way to stop him. He has talent to overcome that and more, but not every time. It had become easier than ever to contain a slow and predictable Barcelona. In those games, why didn't he try to surprise opponents by appearing in wide positions, leaving the four central defensive players marking shadows? There weren't enough players overlapping down the flanks and Cuenca and Tello rarely got one on one with the full backs in those key games – and when they did, they more often than not failed to beat them. Pep's gamble on youth over experience, his experiment, had failed.

Separated by just four days, those two games at the Camp Nou against Madrid and then Chelsea seemed to confirm that the fragile, perfect balance was slightly, but inexorably, broken.

'President, let's meet tomorrow,' Pep told Sandro Rosell the night of the KO by Chelsea in the Champions League; the next morning, the recent history of the club changed for ever.

Two days later, after announcing his departure to the players, Guardiola observed the light training session at Sant Joan Despí from a discreet distance, before jumping into his car to travel the ten minutes or so that separates the club's training complex from the Camp Nou.

The ensuing press conference, to announce to the world his imminent departure, was crammed to the rafters with local and international media; while down near the front row sat Puyol, Piqué, Cesc, Xavi, Busquets, Valdés and a few other players. Messi was not to be seen – he didn't want the cameras to capture his emotions. Sky Sports broadcasted it live. Even in the UK, where some polls put Barcelona as the fifth largest football team in terms of followers, the rumours about his future were having a huge media impact. Sky Sports announced exclusively that Pep was about to say goodbye to all of us.

The set-up of the press conference and positioning of the lead characters was a smart piece of staging. The coach was sitting to the right of the president; to his left, director of football Andoni Zubizarreta. It was an attempt by the club to show that they had taken Pep's decision well, they were showing the calm, institutional face of a club that hadn't always dealt well with change. The club was hurt by the departure of Pep, but here were its two main representatives to announce to the world that there was life after Guardiola.

Barcelona's president solemnly announced that Guardiola would not continue as manager of the club. He hugged the coach. It was an embrace that seemed a little forced; perhaps it caught Pep by surprise.

Guardiola went on to ask people to understand his decision and explained his reasons in much the same way that he had done to his players.

'I'm deeply sorry about the uncertainty that I've created. I have always thought that things are best done in the short term. Four years is an eternity and I didn't want to be tied to a contract that wouldn't allow me to make my own decisions. In October or November I told the president that the end was in sight for me, but I couldn't make my decision public because it would have been too complicated. The reason is very simple. It has been four years and that time can wear you out and take its toll. I'm drained. The reason is that I have to get my passion back. I wouldn't continue as a Barcelona coach should.

The new person will be able to give you things that I am unable to give.'

· He had no more to give and needed to recharge. Or, put differently: he could give a lot to the club if he stayed, but not everything it needed.

'I'm grateful for your patience, I know I have been a pain, here every three days with you all,' he said to the press. Now he would abandon the dugout for a time, although he pointed out that 'sooner or later' he would coach again. At the same time he tried to stop any potential rumours spreading. 'Leo is here' was the only forthcoming explanation from Guardiola about Messi's absence, a comment supported by Rosell himself.

In the dressing room, the players decided that the captains would be present in the media room; that meant Puyol, Xavi, Iniesta and Valdés. However, others joined them to show their respect for Pep – but not *la Pulga*. 'Messi is here in spirit,' Rosell insisted.

Leo cries, but not publicly. The Argentinian went on Facebook a few hours later to explain why he hadn't been there: 'I want to thank Pep with all my heart for everything that he has done for me both professionally and personally. Due to the emotional nature of the event, I preferred not to be in the media conference. I wanted to be away from the press because they were going to look for sad faces and that is something I have decided not to show.' As a thirteen year old, when he first joined Barcelona, Messi would hide away from everybody whenever he cried, especially so as not to upset his dad.

And then came the revelation that nobody had anticipated. Rosell, who was notably solemn, announced that Tito Vilanova would be Pep's replacement. His assistant had received the club offer at Guardiola's house two days earlier but had accepted just an hour before the press conference.

Pep did leave one doubt hanging in the air that appeared to go unnoticed. 'Tito's appointment wasn't my decision, it was Zubizarreta's. I have just found it out myself this morning.' Nobody guessed that there could have been any sort of conflict although soon those words would be used to create controversy that suggested that without Guardiola life at Barcelona would be more difficult.

The club, however, wanted to demonstrate publicly their commitment to Vilanova and not give any cause for speculation at a time of uncertainty and potential instability. It was Zubizarreta's chance to prove that he had an immediate solution and Rosell accepted it. With the continuity that Guardiola's right-hand man would bring, the club was giving itself time to decide if it was the right decision or whether a change of direction was needed. 'Announcing that we had chosen Tito three or four days after accepting Pep's departure would have been counter-productive for Tito. The club could have been accused of not having found a better coach, of not having a plan,' a source at the club admits.

But the replacement can be interpreted differently. Since October, when Pep began having serious doubts about staying for another season, he imagined that his departure included Tito. 'We either all stay or we go,' Pep had thought. A third option emerged when Zubizarreta mentioned Guardiola's assistant as his successor as early as November. Everybody suspected Tito would probably decline the offer. In reality, it only took him an hour to accept the promotion when it was offered to him again on the day of the press conference. It caught Pep by surprise even though they both talked about it and Guardiola accepted that it was Tito's right to take over – he was not going to interfere with that.

Zubizarreta explained the new Barcelona era to the media: 'The important thing is the idea, the principle that makes us different. We'll keep fastening our seat belts and I'm sure that we're going to have a great time.' Helped by the immediate and apparently seamless transition, the club appeared to be taking everything in their stride.

If a moment perfectly encapsulated the emotion and the feelings of the club, the fans and Pep, it was his farewell at the Camp Nou.

Pep's send-off coincided with the Catalan derby against Espanyol, but, since neither team had anything to play for, it became Pep Guardiola's leaving party from the moment the first whistle blew. Hundreds of fans left their messages of gratitude and good luck on an enormous mural that the club had set up outside the stadium. A huge banner covering an equally huge section of the stand welcomed his entry on to the pitch and showed a picture of the coach with the message '*T'estimem Pep*' (We love you, Pep).

Guardiola directed his final home game with his usual level of intensity. 'Come on, Pedro, we've been working together for five years and you're still doing this to me!' he shouted, pushing the youngster he had discovered while at Barça B. Four years earlier, Guardiola intervened when Pedro had been on the verge of being loaned out to Racing Club Portuense, turning him under his tutelage into one of the elite members of the side.

It even seemed like the referee wanted to join in the party, with a laid-back approach to some of his decisions that benefited Barcelona. The game ended 4–0 to Barça, with all four goals coming from Lionel Messi, marking yet another record, one of many: he had scored fifty league goals, beating the European league record previously set by Dudu Georgescu in the 1976–77 season with Dynamo Bucharest. After scoring his first that night at the Camp Nou, Messi pointed across to Pep, dedicating it to his mentor. The manager answered pointing his finger back at him. The ball had gone in after a majestically struck free-kick that found the net in precisely the way Messi and Pep had discussed it during the week.

After his fourth, Messi, ran over to the touchline followed by his team-mates to embrace the coach who had been instrumental in making him the player he is today. It was poignant. Theatrical, but honest. Two of the biggest characters of the biggest soap opera in the world were filling the screen with an emotional hug, a public display of affection, unashamed in showing their eternal gratitude for each other. Pep whispered in Messi's ear: 'Thanks for everything.'

And after the game, Pep was to give a speech out on the pitch. He took the microphone and shuffled around uncomfortably on his own while the players rallied round him. Standing near the centre circle, he watched with the rest of the crowd as a video montage was played on the giant screens, set to the music of Coldplay. Then, his favourite song '*Que tinguem sort*' (I hope we are lucky) by Catalan songwriter Lluís Llach was played, the words echoing around the stadium thanks to the thousands of supporters singing along.

'Si em dius adéu, vull que el dia sigui net i clar, que cap ocell trenqui l'harmonia del seu cant. Que tinguis sort i que trobis el que t'ha mancat amb mi ...'

If you say goodbye to me, I hope the day is clean and clear, that no bird breaks the harmony of its song. I hope you are lucky and that you find what you have been missing with me ...

Pep looked into the stands while everyone was waiting for his words. The stadium was near full to capacity with 88,044 spectators, sitting in anticipation. Some holding each other. Fully grown men trying to hide their tears. Young girls taking pictures on their phones to capture the moment. As everyone remained on their feet, Pep's dad, Valentí, had to sit down because his legs were trembling.

The man considered the club's favourite son was leaving home, again. It was goodbye to an older brother for some, a father figure for others, a Messiah, even, for a few. An example of comportment, a leader, a role model, courteous, the ideal husband, the fiancé you dream of, the friend you share a beer with on a Saturday, a good man, healthy, calm and alternately passionate and measured according to what the moment requires. A nation, a club and its fans were feeling orphaned.

Imagine.

Imagine having to represent all those roles. The weight of all that, the pressure. Can you understand now why he had to go?

'Pep is a privileged man. He is one of the few people that I know who in his private and professional life cultivates the urgent, the important and the essential.' Trying to work him out, Guardiola's friend Evarist Murtra read a speech in the Catalan Parliament the day the coach was paid homage to by the Catalan civil society in November 2011. Pep complied with the urgency of winning titles and matches; he related to the importance of honouring noble codes that underpin sport; and, finally, he was loyal to the institution he represented and the spirit of its founders and followers – and that was essential.

In an interview at the time, former Real Madrid director, coach and player Jorge Valdano chose well-crafted words to describe his influence. 'He believes in football as a territory where greatness is possible, because he never cheats, he is always brave, he takes away all the miseries of the game. He is an authentic example of leadership not only applicable in the world of football. Definitively a leader.'

Football, sport, is all that matters in Spain for the masses. The media ignore other walks of life (culture, formation, critical thinking) and people cling on to sports symbols as their only valid point of reference. It places a huge responsibility on those individuals and is a sign of foolishness in our culture, even though it should be asked: do the masses require it, or are the various channels of communication responsible for selling this brand of bread and circuses? Perhaps the truth lies somewhere in the middle and, probably, no one is entirely free from blame. Pep has always been acutely aware of the transcendence of his behaviour and the importance of the institution he represents, so he has moderated and modulated his conduct accordingly. Society in general has been grateful to him.

That Gold Medal offered by the Catalan Generalitat was given to him 'because of his track record as an elite sportsman, for his success in his time as a manager, for his projection of a cultured Catalunya, civil and open, that has succeeded in a very notable way, and for his values that he has transmitted in an exemplary way, such as sportsmanship, teamwork, effort and personal growth, very positive values not just from an individual point of view but also for personal progress'.

Excessive? Some would argue that on another day perhaps, but that at this moment in history, when Catalonia needs so many leading examples after falling time and time again into despair, attacked on a daily basis from so many political flanks, it was just what the doctor ordered.

But he often insisted, as he did in his own speech in response to the parliamentary homage (in front of so many members of the political and social elite, the military, finance) that he 'didn't want to be an example of anything'. Was anybody listening?

The idolising of Guardiola, some of it forced upon society by a faithful media and some genuinely spontaneous, was born of an objective reality but, little by little, it was transformed into a mass delirium that retained hardly any of the original feeling.

Success had created an image of Pep, a popular perception based perhaps upon some primary religious and churlish mechanisms, that did not belong to himself – he was not the owner of that duplicate. Adulation had created an unnecessary pedestal that Pep himself rejected.

How do you go from the humility of that Barcelona team, their constant prioritising of the principles they based everything on (work ethic, respect, collective effort) to the fanaticism of some of their followers, and even the cottage industry created around the figure of Guardiola? It is a fashion that seems to have transcended Catalonia: *AS* newspaper carried a study in 2012 that showed there were more Barcelona than Madrid fans in Spain – a first.

Is there, as many say, a Pep method that can be extrapolated? It is a good example to society in the context of difficult times and mediocrity, but perhaps his ability to create a method, a new religion, is exaggerated. If Pep had stayed and led a team that lost games and more titles, would the reverential frenzy persist? Surely Pep has changed some mechanisms of the public psychology in Catalonia, but not even he can transform hundreds of years of history and cultural thinking. Sometimes, the image of Pep's Barcelona coincided exactly with what an international audience was looking for. They embraced its success, but also its values, whether exaggerated or not. Catalan society, generally shy and allergic to role models, saw Guardiola as a throwaway Dalai Lama, a guru for the Catalan masses. Pep often joked about the articles that praised him, as if they were part of a competition to see who could be more sycophantic. And he always wondered if virtues become defects in defeat, if the praise wasn't a tool to sharpen the blades for when it was time for the slaughter.

In the VIP area at the Camp Nou after the Barcelona derby, Zubizarreta was on his feet, red-eyed and clearly emotional, but deep down scared. The leader was leaving his job so that the club could continue shaping it and Tito would follow in his footsteps. Massive, daunting footsteps.

Still on the pitch, away from his players who had gathered a few steps from him to listen to his words, Pep was checking his microphone. It wasn't working and he was nervous, wanting the moment to finish, that funeral for his public persona. Out of the ashes was going to appear the other Pep, the familiar one. But before that he had to address the fans.

'We'll do this quickly, the players need to get to the showers,' he began. And in his words there was a hidden homage to Bielsa who started his own farewell speech to the Chile national team in the same way: 'Life has given me this gift. In these five years we have been able to enjoy the spectacle produced by these guys.'

'You have no idea of the love that I'll take home with me, these past five years, you have no idea of the feeling of happiness I take with me. I am just as lucky as all of you, I hope you have enjoyed watching them play.

'Know that I will miss you all. The one who loses is me', a last reference to his admired Bielsa, words used too by the Argentinian manager in his last day as Chile manager.

And with a reference to the same metaphor he had used at his presentation as Barcelona manager, he said, 'The seat belt got a bit too tight, so I took it off. But the rest of you needn't do so because this will continue. I leave you in the very best hands. Stay with them. I wish you the very best, good luck. See you soon, because you will never lose me.'

Pep's mum, Dolors, advised fans, via radio interviews days later, to get hold of those last words, to treasure them. They weren't said by chance.

That final message hinted and foretold of a return; the ball boy, the youth team player, the captain, the coach and the man who made Messi the best player in the world, maybe of all time, would surely be back. The only thing we can't guess yet is in what capacity. After spending some time abroad to distance himself from the club, the next logical step in Pep's Barcelona career would be a return as sporting director or even president.

When Pep finished speaking, the players applauded and ran towards him to throw him up in the air, the way they had done in Rome and at Wembley. Then, they all stretched out their hands to make an enormous '*sardana*' ring of bodies – the traditional Catalan dance – and ran around the centre circle. It was another of the symbols that this Barça team will leave behind, this example of unity, spinning to the music that had started a unique cycle: Coldplay's 'Viva la Vida', the exhilaration and enthusiasm of the first year, those first tentative steps of the new project that began to take shape despite the voices of the sceptics that were gradually and systematically silenced with each victory.

Soon after that Pep needed to become reacquainted with the old Pep, to resuscitate himself even.

So when the lights went out and the public had disappeared, Pep made his way down on to the pitch with his family, brothers, sisters, cousins and friends to take photos.

That Guardiola knew that life was much more than football. That Pep was curious to discover new worlds, literary worlds, cinematographical, theatrical, musical worlds; and others geographical, at the other extreme of the globe, and some even closer to home.

Throughout the night, Pep was half smiling – it was the end of an era but also the start of a new one. What he had wanted since the previous October: a rest. A reunion with his other self and other dreams. It was time to enjoy things away from his consuming passion after a seemingly interminable four years.

One of the photos taken was with Cristina and their children opposite the bench. Màrius and Valentina ran around the pitch excitedly, but nine-year-old Maria was receiving the most attention. She knew what it all meant, she could feel the affection, the sorrow and the emotion. How different from when, eleven years earlier, he had played his last game for Barcelona and, after the game, ended up being carried off the pitch by his team-mates Luis Enrique and Sergi Barjuan. Not everybody stayed behind to see that. That night, there were no post-match celebrations, eulogies or speeches, no emotional grandfathers or excitable youths taking pictures of the moment. He had also walked around a dark, empty stadium with Cris and his agent.

As a player, he had received harsh criticism for leaving the club at the end of his contract, whistles from an unforgiving crowd unjustly accusing him of trying to cash in. It counted for little that he was the captain, an icon and thirty years old at the time. For the club that you have adored and served since childhood to turn on you in such a cruel way, and without any apparent motive, isn't something that is easy to deal with and less so for someone like Pep, sensitive to criticism and who never forgot the lesson that leaving at the right time is crucially important: just as he did as a manager.

His latest farewell at the Nou Camp, beyond its implications, was the most sensitive, most heartfelt and honest experienced on a stage that, all too often, had been unable to say goodbye to its heroes or managers. Guardiola left in a way that both Cruyff and Rijkaard were unable to, who ended their careers in sporting decline and without the unanimous consent of the fans. Strong criticisms were heard when Louis van Gaal, twice league winner, dared to return for a second stint as manager.

'The legacy? For me, the memory I have of these people, I hope it lasts for ever,' Pep said some days later. A banner at the Villamarín, in Pep's final league game, spoke for the fans who adored him: 'Pep, your football has shown us the way.'

Guardiola had defended the club's values and taught people a special way to support and feel part of Barça. Would it be the new way to be a *culé*? Or just a momentary lapse in a culture that seemed to relish the role of victim? Pep had already warned, during his final season, in a moment of doubt: 'This won't last for ever. Sooner or later we will stop winning and that is when we will have to see if we really do have faith in the way we are and the way we play. I'm not putting my hand in the fire, I have to see it. If the club is firm in its convictions, it will always progress.'

But while certain sectors remained tied to their old ways, the Camp Nou, the fans, showed signs that this team has changed history, going far beyond just the titles. The final reaction in the Clásico defeat was an impressive message. Rather than surrender and start to doubt, thousands of Catalans raised their voices to make sure Pep and the team knew that they were with them, that they deserved recognition and loyalty ahead of a result.

Perhaps the fans have changed, but the environment was still harmful. Pep's departure was enough for a sector of Barcelona to fall back upon old ways, indifferent to the massive change that the club had undergone at a sporting level. With Guardiola present, nobody dared disrupt the harmony. And he himself had always made an effort to remain equidistant from all sides – he always spoke well of former presidents Laporta, Núñez and even Gaspart – and he had always been amicable with Rosell, with whom he had a cordial relationship without ever managing to have a particularly high level of trust.

'I'm stepping aside, I don't want my name to be mentioned. I'm leaving and I want to be left in peace,' Guardiola warned. But before the last game of the season, Joan Laporta resurfaced: 'the current board is obsessed with destroying when what we did was build, including Pep ... they could have done more for him to stay.' Johan Cruyff was asked for his opinion, as was Carles Rexach. Rosell's strength was tested, Guardiola's steps were controlled. All sorts of rumours began to circulate: clashes between Valdés and Messi, separated by Keita; rumours of the Argentine star getting angry; the alleged rift between Pep, Tito Vilanova, and even Pep and Andoni Zubizarreta.

Did Guardiola leave at the right time? Would the same things have happened if he had stayed one more year? Luis Aragonés was the only football man who questioned Pep's reasons for leaving the club. 'I don't understand him,' the former Spain national coach told *AS* newspaper. 'I don't believe him when he says he is tired. I agree with Mourinho. He has only been at the job four years, he has just started. It must be something else. Don't get me wrong – what he has done has a huge merit. But I don't know why he is leaving. People will forget what he has done very quickly.'

When they meet, and Xavi Hernández has insisted to Pep they should, as he considers them two of the best brains in the game, Guardiola will be on the receiving end of some stern words from Luis and will have to hear a few home truths.

But on that line, was Pep's decision to quit really for the good of the club? Some might say that he abandoned his players and colleagues at the time when they needed him most. His nemesis, after all, was on top. The movie doesn't usually end with the arch enemy winning – not unless they're preparing us for a sequel. And the suggestion is that Pep's legacy, his bequeathing of his powers to his sidekick, Tito Vilanova, could provide us with a sequel. But has he really left his successor in an ideal situation or a no-win scenario where every victory will be heralded as another win for Pep, every defeat as the fault of whoever follows him?

Whatever the answers, nobody in Catalonia was ready to question his motives or his timing. He was protected, as José Mourinho has always said and envied, by the press, who enjoyed his successful era with that combination of devotion and blindness that often goes hand in hand.

One thing is certain. Without Guardiola, without the spiritual leader, Barça is facing a new situation, and Tito, Guardiola's best friend, a mammoth task. Does Guardiola-ism make sense without its most charismatic leader, without Guardiola? Will Tito be able to control it in the way Pep did for four years?

That is, though, another story, one still being written.

'Today, you all let me down.'

That is what Pep Guardiola told his players at the end of the last league game of the season in Seville, at Real Betis. Barcelona had managed to scrape a 2–2 draw in the last few seconds of the game after a poor performance, a reminder of the worst trips of the campaign, especially in a second half where they ran less, worked less, pressured less and just seemed generally apathetic.

Fifteen days later the team would play in the Spanish domestic cup final and that level of performance and attitude could not be accepted.

As soon as the players entered the dressing room, the manager asked for the door to be closed behind them. 'Quiet! Today you let me down,' he grievously pointed out in what probably was the worst telling off of his entire time at the helm. He didn't want to personalise the mistakes in one or two players but he couldn't ignore the signals.

The farewells, the endless rumours about dissent, the speculation about the future of certain stars had distracted and softened his team. He felt responsible.

At first nobody responded. They all listened in silence, this time looking at the floor, like scolded children: reminded that the season had not finished yet.

Then Dani Alves asked to be allowed to speak.

The Brazilian had lost focus during the season, more than most, and he had been sent off in that match with most of the second half still to be played and with the team winning 1–0. Betis scored two goals after that.

'Forgive me. I am sorry, it was a stupid sending off,' he told his colleagues.

That game, that performance, even the sending off, was not mentioned again by anybody in the following two weeks that preceded the cup final in Madrid against Athletic de Bilbao – the message had been received.

That title could become the fourth of the season after the Spanish Super Cup, the European Super Cup and the World Club Cup.

Pep had won his first trophy as manager of FC Barcelona against Athletic de Bilbao in 2009, his first final played and won as a manager. Now, it was going full circle in 2012, 247 matches later.

His last ninety minutes as a Barcelona coach were lived with the usual passion and intensity the public had grown accustomed to seeing, something that had been missing in previous weeks.

At the start of the match, Pep gave few instructions as he enjoyed a spectacular first half an hour; with his side hungry, aggressive with the ball, not conceding an inch to the admirable Marcelo Bielsa's team.

The night marked a return to common sense, a return to basics. Even Guardiola was once again more Guardiola than ever, with his energy and determination recovered, contagious.

Guardiola shyly celebrated the first goal, scored in the third minute. Pedro was the scorer, tapping in a rebound in the box. And the coach went back to his seat on the bench where he didn't move till five minutes later when he stood up to clap young Montoya, the right back for the night, after failing to cross from the wing.

Messi got the ball, around the twentieth minute and Pep, back to his privileged seat, shouted to nobody in particular, 'Look at him, look at him.' The Argentinian scored after receiving a pass from Iniesta.

Guardiola jumped from the bench, arms raised, clapped, turned around and gave Tito Vilanova a big hug.

Equally effusively, he looked for the physical trainer Aureli Altimira after the third goal. Xavi had held off a defender and left the ball for Pedro on the edge of the box, who finished with a low, left-footed strike into the left-hand corner of the net. While Pep was hugging Aureli, Tito joined them and so did other members of the technical staff – clearly transmitting an image with a message. 'What are they doing? What are they doing!!??' an exuberant Pep kept asking Tito.

The two friends were trying to kill some intentioned rumours about their relationship but it was also a celebration of a feast of football in which all the right decisions had been made – of a return to common sense, to basics. Every player was in his place. Iniesta in the midfield, Alexis and Pedro back in the eleven because they put more pressure to the rival build-up, and could help Messi more than Tello, who stayed on the bench all game, and Cuenca, who had not been called up.

And finally Pep had to give the last instructions. There was going to be no more after those. Some give it even the status of symbolic – the coach asked Pinto, his goalkeeper in the Cup competition, to look for the long ball after an Athletic corner. Perhaps the keeper didn't hear his boss but he certainly didn't take any notice – he put the ball down and played it short to the centre back on his right. And he gave it short to another player, who in turn gave it short to another one. A celebrated *toro* or piggy in the middle was played till the referee blew his whistle. It was the end. Of the game. Of an era. 3–0 to Barcelona.

The team had won the fourteenth title out of a possible nineteen in the Guardiola era (or the fifteenth, since Pep likes to count the promotion of the B team as a title – in his eyes, one of the most important). It is unprecedented.

Guardiola came out of his seat and went to shake Marcelo Bielsa's hand. He returned to the bench to hug each one of the technical staff and players. The Athletic players received his gestures of consolation and then Guardiola retreated, to allow his players to take centre stage.

He did not climb the stairs to the balcony to receive the cup. Listen to his memories of that night:

'Carles, injured, took the decision to let Xavi lift the trophy: the same as he did with Abidal at Wembley.'

'You get it,' Xavi said. 'No, you get it,' Puyol insisted. 'No, you do.' The whole of Spain was waiting and watching as Xavi finally picked up the cup, raised it and offered it to Puyol.

'Carles is a great captain, he is always proving that by example. He helped me a lot, especially with the new guys. He saves you lots of work because he explains a lot of things for you. The important thing in a dressing room is to have good people.'

Pep thanked the fans for their presence and walked towards the tunnel and to the dressing room as the Barcelona players were walking around the pitch with the trophy.

'I thought I had done enough, that the party belonged to them. I was looking forward to going inside to talk to Tito, Manel …'

A few minutes later he returned to the pitch, without his jacket, to do the '*sardana* of the champions'.

'Paco [Seirul-lo, a football veteran and the team's physical coach] always destroys our circle with his poor hip, it is not what it used to be! We used to do it much better, we would hug, arms around the shoulders and go round. Now we hold hands, we have lost faculties. But it is a lovely gesture. And in the centre of it, there was a Catalan and a Basque flag …'

After the *sardana*, the coach left the pitch, now with a big grin. It had been a good day at the office.

In the dressing room, when the players returned, Pep chatted amicably, holding the cup.

'I always find them pretty, the cups. I like them. Some more than others, but I like them. I touch them, I caress them …'

Messi crossed paths with Pep and, stepping aside from boots, plastic bottles, towels and bins filled with ice, they hugged again.

'The players wanted to give me a present, but I told them I just wanted the cup. At that point, in the sanctity of the dressing room, I have a huge feeling of gratitude, not just towards Messi, to everybody. Leo was happy, we were all happy. While hugging Messi I could see Alexis sending a message on his phone. It always happens, players want to share those moments, that happiness with their people.'

In the first relaxed chat with his people, even in the press conference, everybody could notice his sense of relief, too.

'I am very joyful. To be able to finish with a victory always gives you a touch more peace, tranquillity. Before the game I thought nothing would change my opinion of everything we have done, but ending up winning a title is better: for the next two months, for the future, because it means the team has qualified for the Spanish Super Cup ...'

And then, it was time to return to the hotel and celebrate, to enjoy a few beers with the relatives. Before closing the door behind him, people, fans, admirers stopped him for a word, to get a piece of him, to touch him. Carles Puyol, wearing jeans and a t-shirt, came to his rescue.

'When they are dressed like that, it becomes dangerous.'

When Pep returned home, for the first time in a long time there were no more games to prepare for.

The week of Guardiola's departure, Gabriele Marcotti wrote in the *Wall Street Journal* that, whatever his next destination, 'it wouldn't be fair or realistic to ask Pep to replicate Barça in another country. What has happened at the Catalan club is the perfect storm in which Guardiola has been a crucial ingredient, but not the only one.'

Pep knows that better than anyone and now felt it was time to distance himself from it all. He decided to take a sabbatical, a year that started with visits to Israel, Croatia, Singapore, Indonesia, and finally settling for a few months in New York with his young family. He knows how Barcelona views the world, but, as he did after he retired as a player, he needed to discover again how the world views Barcelona. It is true, he thinks, that the institution is more than a club; it's true and definitive that the style he believes in and has helped establish at the club is a winning one, but is any of it exportable?

In his last months at Barcelona he started talking with admiration about the German league, influenced by Raúl, who succeeded at Shalke 04 and told him all about the direct football, the big clubs, the atmosphere, the full stadiums (none of the half-empty and soulless Getafe or Zaragoza or Mallorca visits) …

When Pep left Barcelona as a player, many expected him to go to England or Italy, but he ended up playing in Qatar and Mexico. So nobody should have tried to guess his next destination. This is what he was saying before his agreement with Bayern Munich was common knowledge: 'I will let passion take me somewhere else to be able to transmit it. Without it, I cannot coach, with me you can tell. Maybe I should go where I cannot win titles; perhaps that would make me grow as a coach. I live with my doubts, I don't feel better than others only because I won titles.'

But Guardiola, as he himself has admitted, wanted to be seduced. And not with money. But just how did the Bavarian club manage to secure his services? Before closing the deal a whole number of possibilities had come up.

In the middle of his last season, Pep used a short break in the calendar to travel back to Brescia to see friends – and visited the club's Rigamonti stadium where he once used to play. A flag was hanging on the wall – 'Pep, orgoglio del passato, sogno per il future' (Pep, pride of the past, dream of the future). Brescia are now in Serie B, yet Pep did not mind admitting that he would love to be their manager at some point. He wants to pay them back for the faith they showed in him after being rejected by Juventus and others, for all their support during the doping accusations, where nobody at the modest Italian club doubted him for a second.

Italy is one of Guardiola's loves. And, as well as those long summer days he spent with his friend Manel Estiarte in Pescara, Pep has visited the country at various times. He spent his last summer holidays as a Barcelona coach in Toscana (Siena) and during the previous winter break, after wandering the medieval square in Brescia like any other tourist, he went for dinner with the club chairman Gino Corioni and met coach Eduardo Piovani, one of the best friends he left in 2001.

According to the Italian press, during his sabbatical AC Milan honorary President Silvio Berlusconi wanted to offer Pep a one-year contract, a salary of 15 million euros and a free hand to sell and buy players. The legendary club was not considered.

There is an undeniable, special attraction to the Premier League, an unfulfilled dream, as he admitted in a video made by the English FA to celebrate its 150th anniversary: 'To play in this league is something unique, the feelings of the fans, the media and the players' style. As a player I was unable to realise my dream of playing here. But I hope in the future to have the opportunity to be a manager and have the same experience that other managers and players have had here.' In his final years as a player, he was offered to every big English club, including Arsenal. Their manager, Arsène Wenger, told his agent he preferred to recruit younger footballers, and other clubs fielded other excuses, so he was never able to compete in England.

As soon as Pep confirmed he was leaving Barcelona, all sorts of rumours came to the fore. A recurrent theme was a possible contract with the English FA for the role of national coach. Although the Football Association did not contact Guardiola, an intermediary did try and broker a deal. He told the FA that Pep was interested, and told Pep that the FA was thinking about it. At some point, the intermediary was tested: let's organise a meeting, he was asked. But that did not take place.

Throughout Pep's last three seasons at Barcelona, Chelsea tried to convince him to take over at Stamford Bridge. The financial offers were growing with each attempt: €10 million a year, €13 million, even €15 million according to certain sources. But Roman Abramovich, fascinated and seduced by the football practised at the Camp Nou, soon learnt that he would have to offer something else to bring him to west London: a structure and a squad that would allow for that style of play.

Chelsea's Russian owner has met Txiki Beguiristain three times since the former football director of Barcelona left the club in June 2010. Abramovich wanted Txiki to structure the club but also to serve as a platform for the arrival of Guardiola. Beguiristain understood his role, but felt that Abramovich was mostly just looking for another adviser, not so much as a football model. There wasn't really an executive role offered, as Abramovich wanted to maintain his influence, so there was no common ground or agreement reached.

Undeterred, Roman continued thinking of ways to attract Pep. Perhaps the most adventurous proposal came in the summer of 2011, just after Barcelona had won the Champions League final. Guardiola didn't want to hear from any club at that point as he had already agreed to stay one more year at Barça – despite the growing number of doubts creeping into his mind.

But Abramovich, having decided to let Carlo Ancelotti go, wanted to talk to Guardiola face to face. The list of replacements for the Italian coach also included André Villas-Boas, José Mourinho and Guus Hiddink. But Pep was at the top of that list. Michael Emenalo, technical director at the club and friendly with Tito Vilanova – whom he once played with at Lleida – spoke with both Pep and his assistant during that summer. Finally, Guardiola was invited to Abramovich's yacht in Monaco at the end of June: a meeting that would have to take place in total secrecy.

Pep wasn't committing to a meeting. After two weeks of waiting for an answer, the Chelsea owner received the message he least wanted to hear: that the Barcelona coach has declined the invitation. Pep sensed that if he went to Chelsea, then there was a chance he could get his head turned – and why take that risk? The following week, Villas-Boas was the guest on Abramovich's yacht.

Pep's message might have included an extra. The intermediary who was putting him in touch with Chelsea thought it would have been a good idea if Abramovich appointed an interim coach for the 2011–12 season. Guardiola could then tell the Russian owner half-way through that campaign if he was leaving Barcelona – allowing him to prepare for his arrival. It's a good job that ultimately that idea was not put to the Russian owner because, up until the end of April

2012, there would have been not one but two clubs hanging on for Pep to make a decision.

Abramovich didn't give up, though. He was aware Pep was seriously considering leaving Barcelona and, after sacking André Villas-Boas in March 2012, he thought it would be a good moment to renew contact with the Catalan coach. The plan was clear: Abramovich wanted to sign Rafa Benítez for three months, rescue a season that threatened to collapse and give the team to Guardiola in the summer.

But the meeting with the former Liverpool manager, who wanted a long-term commitment, did not convert into a proper offer and the job was handed temporarily to Roberto di Matteo, and, after winning the Champions League, his contract was renewed for two more years, although Abramovich did not have much faith in him.

While all that was developing, Guardiola didn't want to hear from Chelsea or anybody else – he didn't want his world unsettled – and he made sure Abramovich got the message. He was going to tell the club, the players, the world, that he was leaving and then he was taking a sabbatical. Without having a particular team in mind, it was suggested to him that, while he was away in New York, he could at least start meeting and planning with his next club, whichever that might be, start identifying signings, planning organisational changes to lay the groundwork before he joined. But Pep, having just said his farewell to his beloved Barcelona, only wanted to detox from football. Everybody who knew him well was convinced that full-time detachment would not last long.

Guardiola measures success in different ways from most coaches. His experience as a player, his bitter departure from Barcelona in 2000 and his experience in Italy made him stronger. He values happiness above anything else but, at the same time, doesn't ignore the fact that money gives you the freedom to do whatever you want, whenever you want. His managerial career will be assessed not by titles won, but because he did it his own way.

So, in the autumn of 2012, he strolled around Central Park hoping that a new club would offer him friendship, affection, respect and commitment, the possibility of immediate titles, of competing in the major tournaments, a club with structure, laden with history and run with order and common sense. And Bayern Munich, who had been courting him for two years, offered all of that.

As a player, Guardiola learnt to hide his private life; most players do. Discovering what they like, what they do, is a little step away from using it against them. 'Public opinion is cruel, but I like the same as everybody: wine, reading, the family.' Success, extreme success, had allowed the public to think that Pep, his image, his private life, were public property. Sometimes he dreams of having failed, or tries to imagine what that would be like, even how healthy that could be.

'From failure you learn ten times more. Victory gives you ten minutes of peace, but then it makes you stupid. In victory you have to realise what is not going right. I have many fears and insecurities, I don't like people that can and offer to sort everybody's life. I want to be happy in my microcosm.'

'It can be put very simply,' argues one of the people who has had the greatest influence on Pep: 'Guardiola fights against himself in the same way that Barça fights against Barça. The club is never happy with itself, is it?' Until recently, Barcelona has always had only very brief moments of stability; the rest of its history is a succession of cycles: success, crisis, success again. The fight has been to bring about a degree of stability. Pep was cast from the same mould. He wants to be, and demands of himself that he be, the same coach who made his debut in 2008, but instead of finding answers he finds more questions, a victim of his own dedication and perfectionism, and also of his own torments and the difficulty he has in allowing people to help him.

Managing: one of the hardest and most solitary professions. Rich in victory; orphaned in defeat. Guardiola treated defeat and victory with equal respect, but always kept a healthy distance from both.

But no matter what he wants the epitaph of his career at Barcelona to read, nobody is about to usurp him from the most prominent place in Barça's roll of honour and that of world football. Joseph M. Fonalleras uses some wonderful words to describe Pep's legacy: 'The football put in practice by Guardiola stemmed from childhood romanticism, from the shots in the main square of Santpedor, and is based on a cold and detailed analysis. It is consumed by the passion of returning to his childhood and it is carried out with the precision of a surgical knife.' As his friend David Trueba wrote, 'Guardiola is always looking for "the perfect match", that certain "El Dorado", that paradise that isn't conceived without his impeccable conduct on and off the pitch.'

It is simplistic to reduce Pep's influence to mere numbers, but the stats are extraordinary: 177 victories, 46 draws, 20 defeats. He gave twenty-two kids from the lower ranks the chance to make their debut in the first team. He was the youngest coach to win two Champions League trophies; the sixth to win it as both player and coach.

Without doubt, the best coach in the history of FC Barcelona.

The style, criticised in the past for being too baroque, irregular, unbalanced and often ineffective, was still enjoyable and now also successful.

And Pep's decision-making affected the Spanish national side as well. National coach Luis Aragonés had already decided to give the team's leadership to the midfielders and Vicente del Bosque, enjoying the growth of that style in Barcelona and in Spain generally, introduced little change, paving the way for the Barcelona idea to be at the core of the national team. Eventually the side that became twice European Champions and World Cup-winners was based upon the principles introduced by the Barcelona players. It was a style Guardiola had shown could be effective, but also an astonishing cocktail which incorporated the strong characters of Real Madrid, represented by Iker Casillas, Sergio Ramos, the resilient emigrants (Alvaro Arbeloa, Xabi Alonso, Fernando Torres, David Silva, Juan Mata) and the brushstrokes of the periphery (Jesús Navas, Fernando Llorente).

Before Euro 2012, del Bosque wanted to add to the voices that were saying farewell to Guardiola: 'My regards to my colleague. It is impossible for anybody else to repeat what he did in four years. I am happy and proud that we have Spanish coaches with that much human quality. He has all my appreciation. His story is unique.'

At the successful 2012 tournament in Poland and Ukraine, del Bosque applied solutions that were successful at Barcelona, including the false striker role that became the only tactical innovation of the summer competition. And it was effective, too, despite the criticisms. Spain had been facing similar problems to Barcelona: teams defended deep, closed down spaces and tried to prevent the ball circulating quickly. It was time, then, to reinvent themselves – when Spain played with no striker, the opposing centre backs did not know whom to defend. The maximum expression of that style was the wonderful final against Italy, that explosive 4–0 that killed off so many debates.

An interesting conundrum would appear if Guardiola were offered the opportunity to follow in the footsteps of del Bosque in the future. As a player, he was once asked what national team he would choose, if he could, between Spain and Catalonia. 'I played with Spain because at that time there was no possibility of doing it for Catalonia and because I was happy to join Spain and play as well as I could as the professional I was. I was ecstatic to be able to participate in World Cups and European Championships, and I wish I could have played more. But I was born in Catalonia and if possible I would have played for Catalonia; the question answers itself.' Given the chance to coach Spain he would probably do it with the same passion he would coach Argentina or Qatar, the difference being that some of the players he will have under his orders are also Catalan or from FC Barcelona.

Guardiola was voted best coach in the world in 2011 by FIFA. 'But don't let him deceive you, he never thought all this would arrive so suddenly, so quickly,' his friend Estiarte jokes. When he received the trophy, Pep wanted to share the moment with the other two candidates, Alex Ferguson and José Mourinho. 'It is an honour to be your colleague,' he said. That was the day Sir Alex was asked if Pep could replace him at Manchester United: 'Why? If I was in his place, I would stay at Barça.'

The trophy recognised the titles but also left a question hanging. What he had done at his club: was it revolution or evolution? Changing an answer is evolution; replacing the question is revolution. Guardiola didn't start from scratch, but has evolved the style by reinforcing the idea and introducing subtle and not so subtle variations. And he did so in the middle of a successful era, which is a brave thing to do. 'He gave the team a touch more of intensity, virtue, effective. He used extremely well a great generation of players,' adds Rafa Benítez.

But Guardiola also replaced the question with a touch of boldness and imagination – no striker, sometimes defending with two, no pre-match hotel stays, moving to the new training ground, training behind closed doors, travelling the same day, analysis of players' diets and rearranging meal times and places and so on and so forth.

As Jorge Valdano says, never before have the ideas of one individual had so much influence at FC Barcelona. Pep was more than Messi, more than the president. The challenge for the Catalan club had always been to convert their irregular access to success into a methodology that guaranteed its continuity. Not only the continuity of success – that can often depend on things beyond your control – but mostly of the integral working of the club.

And with Guardiola the club became stronger. He converted an idea into method and planning, always with a flexible point of view, always based upon the central philosophy: as he repeated hundreds of times in the corridors of the Camp Nou, of the training ground at Sant Joan Despí, 'if we have doubts, we attack, we get the ball and we attack.' He knew better than anybody that he didn't know everything about modern football, so he showed the need for a powerful group of specialists who helped deconstruct the complex puzzle of this game. Another legacy: the multiple eyes.

Under Pep, football became entertaining for his players, too. Every job, when it becomes professional, loses the essential amateur feeling, the ludic sense that every occupation should have. His footballers, though, enjoyed playing as they used to as kids. Pep reminded them that the person who thinks 'I am going for a few hours of training and that is it' will fall much earlier than those who enjoy what they are doing. 'Being amateurs at their job is what makes them special,' Pep says. But it was he who made them fall in love with football again, helped them create that Corinthian spirit.

On one occasion, English midfielder Jack Wilshere revealed that the former England coach Fabio Capello had prepared a special video session: 'We paid attention to Barça and how they put pressure on.'

Similar videos have been viewed in dressing rooms of Championship teams, and other of Leagues One and Two, and clubs of first and second and third divisions everywhere.

That is the big inheritance Pep has left us with. But there are small legacies, too.

At the beginning of the press conference at Stamford Bridge prior to the first leg of the semi-finals against Roberto di Matteo's Chelsea, a translator asked Guardiola if he could have a minute with him at the end of the media proceedings. When all the questions had been answered, this slipped his mind and Pep hurriedly left the press room. The translator, a young Spaniard living in London, ran after him: 'Can I have a minute with you?' 'Ah, yes, sorry, forgot.'

'I am a coach here at Chelsea, Pep.' And Guardiola listened to him for a minute, two or three even, looking into his eyes, attentively. 'I understand now why you translated so well the tactical concepts,' Pep told him. That minute will last a lifetime for the young trainer.

The value of a minute, of a gesture.

Guardiola mixed, as Mascherano said that night, work with feelings. He wanted to transfer the indescribable pleasure of caressing the ball. Outside Catalonia, Guardiola was seen as someone who breathed life back into a game that had become stagnant and soulless.

In his last day in his office at the Camp Nou, Pep Guardiola gathered up a bunch of personal objects he had been accumulating over four years. It is the place where, on so many occasions, that magic moment appeared before him, where so many videos have been watched. Where he studied the words he would utter to the press.

The laptop, books, CDs, photos of Maria, Màrius, Valentina, Cristina, all placed in cardboard boxes. Should he leave behind the wooden table lamp, the paper one by the sofa, the rug?

As the last item went in the box, a thought. 'We have made many people happy.'

And a memory: his son Màrius repeating his gestures in the technical area on the day of the Camp Nou farewell, when all the spectators were on their way home and Pep was watching him from the bench – an arm outstretched, the hands on his little face, shouting unintelligible orders to create an imaginary attack, celebrating with similar eloquence a fantasy goal. If your son is going to copy anybody in football – and he will – Pep Guardiola is not a bad place to start.

'It was a real privilege to be under your orders. And that is so absolutely true' – Andrés Iniesta.

8
FAR FROM HOME, MUNICH

Three months after his announcement to the world that he needed rest and did not think he was capable of making further decisions at Barcelona, Guardiola sat down for a meal with a good friend, where they talked about what else but football. Pep had a thought, and once seated he started to expand on it. His friend could not believe it – or could he? This was a moment of pure Guardiola. 'What would you think if I accepted one of the offers I have received to start training again?' he asked.

'But haven't you said that you were tired, that you owed your family some time, that you wanted to distance yourself from everything?'

And that's how it was, except that by the end of November, as he strolled around the massive space that is New York's Central Park, he asked himself once again, 'What am I doing here?' Perfectly valid answers emerged. It was a year that he could devote to those closest to him, one that would give him the opportunity to get to know the MLS, another country, to perfect a couple of other languages and to be able to follow Barcelona from a distance, something he needed to do. He would think about where to go next, choose a team, prepare his landing in a new country, a new world, a new culture.

And it would enable him to sit at a table and dine anonymously, as he had done with Sir Alex Ferguson in September 2012. He listened to the Scotsman who did not mention his imminent retirement, but told him that he should not allow himself to be tempted by Chelsea, a club that lacked everything from aura to history, but mostly vision.

What Sir Alex did not know is that before that private meal the two men had enjoyed in New York, not only had Guardiola already received a number of offers, he was also seriously considering one of them. Bayern Munich were beginning to lay the foundations to a deal that would come to fruition much earlier than the Bavarian club could have imagined.

Everything began with their defeat by Chelsea in the Champions League final in their own stadium in front of their own fans, against a side the club's directors considered to be old, defensive and incapable of stringing two passes together. Consequently, they found the result humiliating, traumatic and incomprehensible. How had they failed to complete the task? How did they manage to lose that final? Was it bad luck, tactics, the performance of some of the players? Fingers were also pointed at the General Manager, Christian Nerlinger. Conscious of the fact that he needed to come up with something that would re-establish his credibility, Nerlinger devised an ambitious and cunning plan. Why not contact Guardiola and try to convince him to postpone his year's sabbatical before it had even begun?

It wasn't a completely off-the-cuff decision. Two years previously, the Catalan coach had met Bayern directors, and they were surprised to hear that 'one day, I would love to work for you'.

So, with that in mind, in May, just a few weeks after the exhausted Barcelona coach had announced his departure, the Bayern director met with Pere Guardiola, Pep's brother, to negotiate his future, only for Bayern to receive exactly the same answer as all the other aspirants. 'It's better that we talk again in six months' time. Pep only wants to rest and has asked us not to fill his head with different offers during this time.'

As an aside, the then Malaga coach Manuel Pellegrini, the successful former manager of Real Madrid and Villarreal, and league winner with San Lorenzo and River Plate, was Bayern's second choice, which is more pertinent than some people might think. Guardiola had taken a couple of tactical set-ups from Pellegrini's Villarreal side that got to the semi-finals of the 2006 Champions League: the movement of wingers and a defensive concept related to the position of the back four. The Chilean, who would sign for City the following season, and Pep are both considered by European football to be managers of exceptional quality, in their tactical brilliance and their management of players.

Anyway, Nerlinger's valiant bid was not enough to save his skin, but his replacement, Matthias Sammer, was informed of all the details of what had been discussed and planned to pursue the matter.

In the summer, Bayern explained their plans for the future with Pep and made a definitive offer, and the manager began to see a clear vision for the project. In his house in Llavaneres, Guardiola hosted the legendary Bayern directors Uli Hoeness, Karl-Heinz Rummenigge and Franz Beckenbauer. Pep told nobody about this meeting except his wife, his representative and his brother. So, it was unknown to the various clubs and national teams that approached him in the coming months. But from that moment on, his mind was made up. Using a common Spanish football expression, they had left the ball bouncing in front of him, perfectly placed for him to score a goal.

It was impossible not to be attracted to the idea of becoming a part of the historic institution that is Bayern Munich. In the autumn, a new meeting was organised between Pep and Bayern's director Karl-Heinz Rummenigge, during which it became clear that Guardiola had been successfully seduced by the German club.

That afternoon the basis of the deal was agreed.

Raúl had spoken to Pep on various occasions, extolling the virtues of the Bundesliga: packed stadiums, great atmosphere and a competitive league. A gem for all football-loving people. But Bayern was much more than a mass of statistics that filled football's history books: twenty-two league titles, fifteen major cup wins, winner of the three major European competitions and, at that time, four-times winner of the European Cup. It was also a club with a profile similar to that of Barcelona: both clubs are owned by their members, both have a distinct identity, a clearly defined structure, and both clubs look to their academies to make up their squads.

The team was used to winning, or, at the very least, competing right to the end, and for that reason the club were favourites to take the Bundesliga title before the start of the 2012–13 season, which they managed to achieve a month and a half before the campaign ended. Before that winning season, they had competed in two out of the previous three Champions League finals with two different managers – van Gaal in 2010 and Jupp Heynckes in 2012 – a sign of the quality of the squad, despite having lost both. In the Bernabéu, van Gaal's Bayern went down to the Inter of Mourinho and Diego Milito, and two years later in the Allianz Arena they came off second best against Chelsea's Di Matteo and Drogba. Bayern Munich, then, did not need any drastic changes to its competitive team, another factor that made it an attractive sporting option.

With 190,000 members, it is one of the best-supported clubs in the world, even accounting for the fact that it does not have the financial clout to make the huge-money signings that clubs such as Paris Saint-Germain, Manchester City or even Chelsea can. Nonetheless, its financial power does guarantee the club a stable future. Its accounts are healthy, even after taking into consideration the 400 million euros spent on the construction of the Allianz Arena. It is therefore protected from the predatory advances of new money looking to buy quick, short-term success. That is how Rummenigge explained the Bayern set-up to Pep – one he admired for the way they had been able, during the season, to spend a record 40 million euros on Javi Martínez yet retain economic independence, a crucial element for anyone looking to build long-term projects.

In the words of Ramon Besa, 'For Guardiola, who ironically had spent some time in Qatar, what was happening to football in England – with clubs falling into the hands of oil sheiks, Russian oligarchs and American millionaires – was worrying. There is a notable downturn in the game, and the feeling is that teams can be built with easy money.'

The appeal of the Bavarian club was obvious and also something of a safe bet, as well as offering the chance of fighting for honours from day one. There would also be the chance to learn a new league, a new language, a new club and a new organisation. In short, a whole host of things he could use should he ever return to complete yet another of his lifelong dreams: control of Barcelona, not from the touchline, but from the club's offices. And what's more, the label 'Pep man of football' would hardly be affected by his choice – quite the contrary.

From the outset, it was explained to Guardiola that his role at the club would be control of the first team. No more, no less. And that suited him just fine, especially coming as he did from a situation where there was so much more to do than just train, and watch and play matches. No longer would he need to be the very soul of a club, as he had been at Barcelona, but merely its coach, which, curiously enough, was precisely what his replacement at Barcelona, Tito Vilanova, had become. Just a coach at an elite football club. He was aware of the expectations his decision would create and the inevitable star billing, but he felt that at Munich, he would be judged soley for his decisions as a coach. That was the test. The money could find its way into his bank account from any number of places, above all from the wealthy English clubs, but no one could offer him what Bayern could.

There were, however, a couple of problems he would have to face. Bayern divides the country in two: their supporters, and the rest. 'Anyone but Bayern!' is many people's motto, and Guardiola knows better than most the consequences of being loved and loathed simultaneously, and in equal measure. But while this contempt for the club could tarnish him, he surely couldn't have imagined that it would ever be as extreme as what he had experienced in the Spanish league.

Then there was the potential problem of working with a board every single member of which has an opinion and, rather than keeping it 'in house', has no compunction about expressing it. Not for nothing has German football expert Raphael Honigstein described Bayern Munich as 'FC Hollywood': 'The biggest names have the biggest egos.' The president and impetuous father figure of this German footballing family is Uli Hoeness, who was general manager at the club for 30 years and is known for being tough on his coaches. More conciliatory is the executive director Karl-Heinz Rummenigge, who represents Bayern on the international stage, while honorary President Franz Beckenbauer, who writes a weekly column in the *Bild* newspaper, is loyal although unpredictable, but nevertheless a good and necessary influence on the club. And finally there's sporting director Matthias Sammer, who has shown himself to be ambitious, expansive and direct in all his actions.

All of them, according to Honigstein, 'provide a 24 hours a day newsletter on what's going on at the club'. Even though, as the football analyst says, the aim is merely to maintain the high profile of the club, it will be difficult for Pep to accept with good grace any judgement on the playing capability of his team. The club directive certainly made life very difficult for managers such as Otto Rehhagel, Felix Magath and Luis van Gaal, all of whom left after confrontations with the club. By the same token, however, the institution provides a variety of spokespersons who represent and protect the trainer, something that Pep missed at Barcelona.

Bayern Munich fulfilled all the conditions asked of it by Guardiola. He was seduced. They wanted him. There is nothing more important for Pep than to feel that he is wanted by his people and by a club. He said it himself in a packed press conference in excellent German on 24 June, the day of his presentation: 'I came because of the players, because of the history of the club, but mostly because you called me. I am ready, it is a new challenge and I needed a new challenge.'

So, Guardiola was making the transition from spokesman, icon, trainer, father, brother and perfect boyfriend to merely a first-team coach. Or would the Germans, too, fired with enthusiasm at his arrival, seek to set him, once again, on the pedestal from which he had only too recently stepped down?

Pep wanted to decide his future at the earliest opportunity so as to begin working on his new project after the 2012 Christmas holidays with the same Guardiola-like obsession he had always shown, whether it was coaching the Barcelona B side to the third-division championship or taking players such as Messi, Iniesta, Xavi, Puyol and co. to two Champions League titles in four years.

And, as well as Bayern, only two other clubs offered him the chance to choose his next destination halfway through a season: Chelsea and Milan.

Guardiola knew that he had only to pick up the phone to become the new manager of Chelsea. But every time they called him from London, Pep always gave them the same reply: 'Call me in a few months' time.' It was never a good day to negotiate. The English club, desperate to get their man before he chose another club, sacked Roberto Di Matteo just hours after their defeat by Juventus in the 2012–13 group phase of the Champions League, a result that saw them practically eliminated from the competition. Before appointing Rafa Benítez, Abramovich made another call to Guardiola and was told yet again that Chelsea were not the type of club he wanted to manage after Barcelona.

The decision makers at Chelsea were worried about Pep's opinion of them following the sackings of Roberto Di Matteo and André Villas-Boas. Those decisions suggested an alarming lack of vision and patience. And they were right to be concerned. Guardiola never saw Chelsea as a club sufficiently calm or solid enough, one where he would enjoy working. So they offered a one-and-a-half-year contract to Benítez, although in the end he chose to commit himself only to the end of the season.

And what of Manchester City? New sporting director Txiki Beguiristain knew that it was vital to pick the perfect moment before offering Guardiola the post. But he was also sure that there was little he needed to say to Pep. They had spoken during the 2012–13 season, but an offer was never put to the Catalan manager. All the conversations included a 'well, you know that if you fancy coming over here, there is always a possibility' and Pep would answer with a 'I know, you don't need to tell me'. Neither Pep, Txiki nor City chief executive and former Barcelona director Ferran Soriano had set any agenda to discuss their futures together.

Other stumbling blocks had appeared, too. Roberto Mancini, having won the league for the club for the first time in 44 years, had the unanimous support of the fans, and City's Abu Dhabi owners were in no mood to allow the Catalan coach to dictate the club's agenda. They decided that the time to look at Mancini's future would be at the end of the season and not before. As a result, the perfect moment to propose any new project to Guardiola never arrived. The much talked about close association between Txiki and Pep came to nothing. With everyone expecting him at City or Chelsea, Guardiola's thoughts were all about Bayern.

There was also the risk of a potential fallout between City and Barcelona, something that Pep desperately wanted to avoid during his years of voluntary exile. He could not be seen as a potential enemy in the transfer market of his old club and an ally of some of the enemies of Barcelona chairman Sandro Rosell, especially Ferran Soriano. In any case, some people who know him well are convinced that Guardiola did not consciously decide against the Premier League, but rather opted for the many advantages that the Bundesliga could offer him. In the words of Juanma Lillo, 'He did not sign for Bayern while thinking about the negative aspects of the other clubs. Knowing him as I do, I would say he did so because he liked the club more and not because he disliked the others.'

His stay in Munich will not alienate him in the eyes of his English fans, who will always welcome him with open arms, as I discovered on the tour that followed the publication of the hardback edition of this book. He has heard all about it and is aware of his popularity in the UK. But any future choice of club will invariably have to satisfy the same criteria. It will always have to be a club that wins, that has a distinguished history and that can fit in with his style of play.

Ferguson, unaware of, or hiding, the fact that he was enjoying his last season in management, told him in New York he would carry on as long as his health and his iron will allowed him to. At Arsenal, according to information that was reaching Pep, Arsène Wenger would remain as manager until such time as he decided otherwise. But, of course, after three years in Munich the situation might have changed. Wenger has had a number of conversations with Guardiola during which Pep has asked him about the Premier League, and Pep has also on occasion told him that he would like to coach in England. That is still a dream.

One day he will no doubt live in Great Britain. London would be his preferred destination, but that is not set in stone. Again, his words, when speaking to the Football Association on the occasion of its 150th anniversary in one of the few interviews given by him during his stay in New York, are clear: 'I have always been fascinated by English football because of its environment, its atmosphere and its fans. I was never able to fulfil my dream of playing there, but I hope to have the opportunity, sometime in the future, to be a trainer or manager and live the life that other trainers and players who have lived in England have.'

The financial constraints and difficulties of the Italian league do not make it as attractive a proposition as the English or German. And AC Milan, who made a concrete offer, needed much more than just a new trainer to convert itself into the club it aspired to be. It was not the time to go to Italy. Pep's agent, Josep María Orobitg, confirmed that there had been contact with clubs such as Roma and Milan, and various countries had offered him the chance to take charge of their national squads. Even the biggest nations had Guardiola in their sights: a media campaign in Brazil tried to convince the federation to approach Pep, and in Argentina a rumour started that he could be considered if things did not work out with Alejandro Sabella. It did not go any further, and in Pep's opinion a national side ought to be managed by someone of that country, someone who understands the idiosyncrasies of the nation, their media and their fans, and, in any case, managing a country's football team would actually be boring at this stage of his life – a lot of work but with very little time actually spent on the pitch. For Guardiola, who craves the day-to-day involvement, the constant decision making, the continual dialogue with his players and being able actually to watch the football every morning, it is a job for another age, another time.

Bayern for their part were able to offer him exactly what he wanted at the moment he wanted it. The contract of the 67-year-old Jupp Heynckes finished in June 2013, and, according to Bayern, he had told the club he did not want to continue, something disputed by Heynckes. In any event, that was what Bayern told Pep as early as May 2012 – they wanted him to replace the German coach at the end of a season that had not yet started.

Everything fell into place. The timing was perfect.

In December 2012, the Bavarian club received the message from New York that the time was right and the agreement put in place by Rummenigge in the autumn could now be signed. Pep had spent enough time strolling around. He wanted to start work. 'Shall we meet after Christmas?' the Bayern directors asked from Germany.

'No,' replied Guardiola. 'We'll meet before.' Hoeness travelled to New York to meet with the Catalan coach on 20 December, just two weeks before his first public reappearance at that most crowded of footballing events, the Ballon d'Or Gala.

That visit to Zurich came a full five months after his arrival in New York. Five months far from the madding crowd. Five months well spent. Pep is one of those people who firmly believe that time is a gift to us, not something that should be taken for granted but worked, enjoyed, moulded and filled with all manner of activities, both urgent and trivial.

He would walk through Central Park, close to the apartment that he had rented for a year. He would visit the theatres on Broadway, dine in the well-known and fashionable restaurants, and visit museums and exhibitions. What did he want from his stay in the Big Apple and what did he get? This is how he explained it: 'Socially and culturally, the United States is not a footballing country. There are many other sports that are far more integrated into the city. The 14 million people living here go about their own business, and we too go our own way. We live, and we get to know this way of life and to enjoy the millions of things it has to offer us.'

He was spotted at MLS matches, at NBA games and watching tennis at the US Open. He travelled around the city on the subway and often by bicycle when he attended classes at the University of Columbia given by former Barcelona treasurer and professor of economics, Xavier Sala-i-Martín. He attended as just another student, listening, taking notes and then eating in the university dining room, as shown by various photos that have subsequently emerged on numerous social-network sites. Or he could be found sharing a computer with a student to watch live coverage of the Borussia Dortmund–Real Madrid game.

He studied German so that he could speak fluently in his first press conference in Munich, took English classes, and, when time permitted, attended golf lessons. And perhaps one of his finest experiences was the time he spent alongside José María Olazábal on that unforgettable final day that saw Europe retain the Ryder Cup at Medinah.

'He was delighted,' Olazábal recalls. 'He told me that he had never lived anything like that in his life. I said to him, "What the hell are you talking about?" He insisted that closely watching developments on the 18th hole he had realised what real pressure is.' Throughout the twists and turns of that final day, Guardiola followed two matches, the second of them along with basketball star Michael Jordan.

Olazábal was returning a favour. Pep had loaned him two motivational videos. The Ryder Cup captain mixed scenes from *Gladiator*, that Guardiola had used before the Champions League final in Rome, along with speeches by Al Pacino from the film *Any Given Sunday*. There were also pictures of all the golfers at the event as well as historic images of previous Ryder Cups and moments from the glorious career of the late, great Severiano Ballesteros. In addition, there were scenes from Spain's World Cup triumph, Usain Bolt running and great rugby victories. Before the competition began, Olazábal showed his team the video. It had the same effect then as the one Pep had shown his team in 2009. I'm sure no one would admit to it, but I was told that many wept.

Pep met with Tito Vilanova when the new Barcelona coach visited New York to get a second opinion on his cancer diagnosis after it was discovered that he had a second lump in the parotid gland, which was later removed. When asked by FIFA.com about the health of his friend and colleague, Pep said, 'We have suffered a lot, as has everyone that loves him. But we know that he is strong and that medically he is in the best possible hands and with a club that will protect him, and above all with his family alongside him. I'm sure he is ready to fight and go forward.'

But those were words for public consumption. Guardiola was not entirely happy with the way the club had dealt with his replacement, how it had all come out minutes after announcing his departure. Instead of becoming his moment, it became the club's moment. Good club decision, bad management from the top of the institution in relation to the best manager in its history. Guardiola expected in the first instance to see his friend leaving with him, and his friendship with Tito died a little that day. So, when they met in New York the reunion did not take long, and the coolness was so present that, without saying it out loud, it became clear bridges had been burnt. And that it will take quite some time to rebuild them.

Time was also spent watching Barcelona games. The post-Guardiola era had a strange feeling of light and shadows: a strong start in the league, which was eventually won, but more goals conceded than in the previous five years; Real Madrid knocking them out in the Spanish cup; a bad performance in Milan in the last sixteen of the Champions League, followed by a demolition of the Italians; another poor couple of nights against PSG, who were not beaten (2–2 in Paris, 1–1 in Barcelona), rescued by a half-injured Messi in the second leg as he came from the bench to help create the Barcelona goal by attracting three PSG defenders that left Villa, with the assist, and Pedro, who scored, one on one with the centre backs; the embarrassment of losing to Bayern 7–0 on aggregate; not to mention the return of the illness of Tito Vilanova, who was absent from the team for two months and underwent a delicate operation, as well as chemo and radiotherapy, and partly compensated by Abidal's year-long recuperation from a liver transplant.

Andoni Zubizarreta explained the new era in detail in an interview with *El Pais*:

When someone so important leaves the club, with everything that they brought and left behind, a relocation takes place. It is not that the players take more responsibility, they were always responsible. But maybe decisions and analysis looked more at the players, people didn't filter everything via the manager.

With Pep we looked, or people looked, for many answers to many things: some football, but also economic, social, political answers. That put him in a certain position in a society with not many references. Pep was a huge referent, he attracted many things and it acquired a huge dimension, especially if on the other side we found Mourinho. Now the debate is more football-like: we play well or bad; we play wide or through the centre. Nobody goes to the press conference in search of answers from our coaches beyond football and that decompressed the club.

This made life at the institution more relaxing.

Some of the things Pep had seen in the changing room, in the squad, things he had predicted or that he had tried to correct, even some that he didn't feel the energy to act upon, resurfaced. Players admitted that they had lost focus, that they had not adapted as well as they would have wanted. Gerard Piqué, for instance, was honest enough to say that Pep's last season was the hardest of his career: 'Partly for the injuries, for personal questions too. We are all people at the end. The fact is that I started that season badly, injured, and it took me a while to catch up. The problem is that if you don't play, everything gets worse. You want to but you can't, and that is complicated because it is not enough to try to please the manager. He knows better than anyone how you are. What you feel inside you is what gives you the confidence you need. If you lose that feeling, and I lost it, the coach sees it. And you don't play.'

After Pep's departure, Cesc Fàbregas also explained the reasons why his best performances did not appear regularly enough: 'At first it was hard because I had the tendency to disconnect the side, to lose concentration. At Barcelona everybody has to be where they have to be – they have a position. Being responsible for my position was something I lost in England. There I ended up getting crazy. I used to move everywhere. Years ago I couldn't have coped with being a sub. I would have died! With time, I have grown up and learned to relativise it. I had the need to show that I could play in the best team in the world, to compete with the best. I tried too hard. I had no problem with Guardiola's concepts because I knew them and understood them, but there was not enough time to assimilate them. My error was to try to do things that did not correspond to me.'

'I remember Cruyff used to say, "We will play from A, then B, after, C . . ."' Zubizarreta said. 'With Pep we reached Z, and with Tito perhaps we have gone back to T.' The Barcelona director of football explains why Tito was chosen: 'The answer was in the day of the presentations. It was worthwhile to continue with a football idea that was not finished, to give more chances to winning players, to maintain a style that allows us to be a reference point as a club, singular, something that defines us in the world. And we had the perfect person to develop it: Tito. I don't value the results but how the idea was sustained and the way that good decisions have been taken in complicated situations. I feel we are in good hands. We can't forget were we come from, Pep's inheritance and philosophy. We keep it going with a person with a different personality, but when the team is on the pitch we recognise it.'

The process of keeping Barcelona at the top was becoming more and more complex and demanding, as Pep had found out. Tito Vilanova searched for simpler solutions without abandoning the Guardiola foundations. All of a sudden the team could look to Xavi (more possession, control) or to Cesc (more direct) – there was a dual focus, two ways of doing things. To avoid the mental blockage that the team had suffered at the end of the previous season, Vilanova wanted a less predictable Barcelona, one that reached the other goal quicker, and Fàbregas helped with that. At other times, Xavi would impose his tempo, which produced a more recognisable Barcelona. This combination was seen as providing a transition to a new style of play that saw the team beat records in the league and end up winning it easily after a first half of the season with eighteen victories and one draw, with Messi scoring regularly again.

But the defensive frailties, the alarming lack of attention to the little details that had taken so much of Guardiola's time and energy, the enforced lack of leadership during Vilanova's two-month absence, were abused by Real Madrid in the semi-finals of the Spanish Cup (4–2 on aggregate, with Real beating Barcelona 3–1 at the Camp Nou) and, at certain times, by Milan and PSG in the Champions League, and certainly by Bayern Munich in the semi-finals. The 7–0 aggregate scoreline was not unfair or lucky – quite the opposite. It exposed some difficult truths that could be traced back to insufficient planning and preparation: the squad was unbalanced (only three of the seven centre backs used were natural in the position); Song did not improve the midfield or the defence, despite being signed to do both; Cesc was a regular in the starting line-up but was left out in the big games; substitutions were late or inefficient in the crunch period of the season (Villa came on in the 84th minute with the scoreline already 4–0 in the first leg of the Bayern semis); the team was burnt out at the end of the campaign as the staff preferred to overuse the regulars after Christmas to guarantee the title, taking advantage of the Madrid decline and due also to the absence of Tito. Generally, the decisions that Pep had not taken regarding the squad were not considered either by Vilanova after he replaced his friend. And the muscle injury Messi suffered against PSG was so poorly managed. Did he have to play the second leg against the French? His intervention was crucial but didn't help his recovery. He scored against Bilbao, a game sandwiched between the Bayern semis, but his fitness suffered and he missed the return leg.

Barcelona had become a lovely ice cream that had started to melt in the sun under Pep. Tito couldn't stop that dynamic. Guardiola watched all this from a distance. It never occurred to him to help the club whilst Tito recuperated in New York. It was not his role to intervene, and, in any case, as far as he was concerned, the club had decided to keep assistant Jordi Roura (and the players) in charge.

He was far away from the world he had known but not completely isolated. On 11 September, the National Day of Catalonia, and a day of national mourning in America, Pep sent from his new home a video of himself backing a demonstration in Catalonia – he holds a green ballot paper in favour of independence. 'From New York, here's one more,' he says. In front of a giant screen in Barcelona, where the video was watched, banners were to be seen proclaiming Pep Guardiola's sortie into the world of politics. They announced, 'Pep Guardiola, first President of the Catalan transition'.

Pep left New York on rare occasions. He appeared as a guest speaker at different events, including one in Mexico City organized by Fundación Telmex, the charity of Mexican telecoms tycoon Carlos Slim. He also went to Barcelona a couple of times during his voluntary exile, the first of them to spend the Christmas festivities with his family, a trip that also took him to Zurich to attend the Ballon d'Or Gala.

He had been nominated as coach of the year, even though he had not managed for six months and had not achieved all of his objectives for the season. In reality what he really wanted was to witness live the crowning of Messi and the consecration of Vicente del Bosque as the best coach in the world. 'I am coming here to applaud Vicente,' he announced.

In the lounge of the Hotel Hyatt, where the players and coaches nominated for the awards gathered, he met up with the Spanish team coach and with some of his old players, including Messi, Iniesta, Piqué, Puyol and Alves. At one moment during the ceremony he crossed paths with Ronaldo, who tried to greet him. His instincts were to show him the cold shoulder. Mourinho's Madrid had prevented him from enjoying his profession in the last few months at Barcelona. When, out of the corner of his eye, he spotted Ronaldo – the living embodiment of much that had hurt him – he decided that this was neither the time nor place for an affectionate reunion. Effectively, he blanked him.

Pep did greet the President of Real Madrid, Florentino Pérez, Jorge Mendes, the agent for both Mourinho and Ronaldo, and Brazilian footballer Neymar, who has since joined Barcelona.

'I have been distanced from everything, will carry on being distanced and will remain so out of respect for the people who are doing their job,' he told FIFA.com in an interview. When asked about the possibility of joining Bayern Munich as coach, he chose to defend the club's present incumbent by saying, 'Heynckes is the trainer of Bayern. It would be disrespectful of me to talk to any team that has a coach at the present time. I have not taken the decision. I am eager to train again next year, and I will do, but no decision has been taken.'

In fact, what he was announcing to the world was his return to football. 'I don't know where it will be, but I will coach again. I am young, I am 41 years old, and I am keen to work,' he said at the official press conference in the presence of Vicente and the three Ballon d'Or finalists, Cristiano Ronaldo, Iniesta and Messi.

The time was now. He had rested enough. He was coming back.

Of course, two weeks earlier in New York, and in the presence of Bayern president, Uli Hoeness, he had in fact signed the contract that would take him to the German club the following season.

Pep could stay away no longer. He missed the game. He wanted once again to put the faces and the names in place that would bring him back to what he did best – win football matches. He was enjoying life without the endless sideshow that surrounds football, but he could not live without the game.

Speaking about his trip to meet Guardiola in the States, Hoeness explains that, 'I wanted us to meet at a place I used to frequent in New York, but he preferred to send a black limousine to pick me up at the Four Seasons hotel on Fifth Avenue. His brother Pere and I arrived at his Manhattan apartment via the underground car park.' Hoeness had brought with him the contract already signed by Rummenigge and drawn up after the meeting the two men had held in the autumn.

'He told me that since August he had seen all of Bayern's matches on television. He was very well-informed. He asked me about issues related to training and about relations with the press. He is a very open and affable person. Within a minute, I knew that this was the perfect coach for us.' Hoeness's comments are reminiscent of those made by Txiki Beguiristain when he interviewed Pep to try to bring him back to the Catalan club to be the reserve-team coach.

Talks went on for about three hours and then, during a break, an enthusiastic Guardiola asked, 'Shall I sign, then?'

Hoeness looked at Pep, opened his eyes wider and then looked at the view of Central Park through the window. Turning back to him, Hoeness said, 'What a great idea!'

So, Pep signed, as did Hoeness, and the contract, which was for three years, was kept in a safe for weeks.

Bayern's president, at Guardiola's request, was asked not to reveal the news to anyone so as not to destabilise the German club's season in any way, and Pep, his brother Pere and all those in his inner circle would deny to everyone, including his closest friends, that any agreement was in place.

Mind you, circumstances almost contrived to force Bayern to make the announcement much earlier than was planned. Hoeness explains: 'I was in a place where I should have met Pep, and the head waiter came up to me and said there was someone that wanted to say hello. It was Alex Ferguson. He asked me what I was doing in New York. I told him I was on a business trip. It wasn't a lie, because I had to go to Chicago with my son for a matter connected to the family sausage business.

'Ferguson explained to me that he had an apartment in New York, that every now and then he spent some time there. I can't begin to imagine what would have happened if he had arrived and seen me talking with Guardiola!'

Ferguson tried to arrange a meal with Guardiola, the second one after their encounter in September, but it never happened. Pep told Sir Alex that he had to go back to Barcelona for the holidays and that he was a little busy. He wanted to avoid too much explaining – and probably too many white lies.

A couple of days later, Guardiola returned to Barcelona to spend Christmas with his family. He had supper with his friend, David Trueba, but mostly he preferred to catch up with relatives in private rather than being seen in public.

Two weeks later, Pep did have to tell some white lies at the Ballon d'Or Gala.

Back in New York, he shut himself away again in his own little world, often in his office to study his new club, where things were going very nicely. By the time the winter break arrived, Bayern were well on track in the Bundesliga: top of the table and a full nine points clear of second-placed Bayer Leverkusen. What if that made Heynckes reconsider his decision to quit? What if he decided to stay on at Bayern for a further year?

Hoeness found himself facing a dilemma. A personal friend of Heynckes's from their playing days – Hoeness at Bayern, Heynckes at Borussia Mönchengladbach – he had already been responsible for making a most difficult decision regarding Heynckes during his tenure as a Bayern director. After winning the title with Jupp at the helm in 1990, the club then sold many of its best players, suffering a severe dip in form as a result. A hostile press had a major influence on the club's subsequent decision to show Heynckes the door, a choice that, to this day, still shames Hoeness, the then commercial director.

Around Christmas, Bayern leaked that Heynckes had decided to retire or leave the club at the end of his contract. True or not, Hoeness preferred to keep the secret about Pep. How could he explain to his friend that the decision as to his future had already been taken? It was essential that the secret should be kept from everyone, including the present club coach, and kept until the spring when Bayern would be on the verge of winning another league title. That was the plan.

But the bidding for Guardiola's services continued apace. Clubs received the message that Pep was still to decide his future, with the result that they persevered in their courting of the Catalan. Finally, Silvio Berlusconi and Umberto Gandini, the executive director of Milan, found out the truth. It was time to stop insisting. Pep was to become the next manager of Bayern Munich. The secret of the Central Park agreement was about to go public.

The Milan club leaked the news to Sky Italia on Monday, 14 January, and it was met by an immediate denial from the German club. Guardiola's family, trying to protect Heynckes, categorically denied that there was any agreement and asked people close to them to put it out on relevant social networks. But as the rumours grew, the Bayern board were desperate to avoid the matter overshadowing the club's season, and Uli decided to meet with his friend Jupp to explain to him the truth of the story, revealed by the Italian TV channel.

On a Wednesday, two days before the resumption of the Bundesliga season after the Christmas break, Bayern announced to the world that Guardiola would succeed Heynckes.

The announcement made a huge impact around the sporting world. Germany's *Bild* newspaper described the arrival as Bayern's 'biggest coaching coup of all time'. And the *Süddeutsche Zeitung* sent a message to the rest of the world: 'German clubs have reached the zenith. This transfer is a clear signal to the international football community'.

As far as the German press were concerned 'the Professor of Success' and the 'Intellectual of Football' was arriving in Germany, and *Das Bild* already had a new name for him. Pep, the diminutive form of the Catalan name Josep, had been renamed by them 'Sepp', the diminutive of the German name Josef.

Das Bild also talked about the 'miracle coach' and revelled in the fact that Guardiola's appointment was effectively a slap in the face for the Premier League. 'The man, as they say in Spain, has *cojones*,' wrote the newspaper with the highest circulation in Europe.

Surprised by the international repercussions when the news was finally given, the Bayern president, Uli Hoeness, now recognises that he probably made an error in the timing of the club's announcement. 'Knowing what I know now, I would probably change one thing. Had I announced our agreement at Christmas, at least the media frenzy that followed would have occurred during the Christmas break and not when the season was in full swing.'

It was clear, then, that despite Pep's earlier misgivings, the negative connotations of being head of the team that half the country detested was not, at least for the time being, going to impact on him. Instead, he was going to become the face of Bayern and its most high-profile spokesman, as well as that of a very much in vogue Bundesliga that had seen its popularity soar over the previous five years. 'The perfect solution' headlined the *Frankfurter Allgemeine Zeitung*. Rummenigge summed up the feelings of many. 'Glamour has arrived,' he said, 'not just for Bayern, but for the whole of the league.'

'Great. Congratulations for this blow struck by Bayern. It should be recognised without envy,' said Borussia Dortmund's general manager Hans-Joachim Watzke in a statement that would have been unthinkable in any other league. The words of Klopp, his coach, however, sounded out a sporting warning to Bayern's new man. 'I want to be Guardiola's new Mourinho,' he said. 'If he doesn't like it, then that's his problem.'

Jupp Heynckes, told only hours before the official confirmation of Guardiola's appointment, started his first press conference after the Christmas break in Spanish, 'So you get used to it!' he joked. In it, he resolved some of the mystery surrounding his alleged retirement after the season. He confirmed that the previous summer he had informed Hoeness of his intention to quit at the end of the campaign, while adding that he would be prepared to carry on if required to do so. 'I said to him, if you do not find the right man, ask me again.' In any case, the former Real Madrid trainer was leaving open the possibility of continuing in football. 'Am I retiring completely? Sure, I'm retiring from Bayern, but I haven't said that I'm retiring from the game.' In fact, Jupp did leave football the following summer, but he did it on a high.

This is football. The king is dead! Long live the king! But Heynckes knew how these things worked and welcomed the new coach with words as elegant as they were responsible. Pep matched perfectly the ideology and competitive demands of a club like Bayern. 'Here you will find the best club in Europe after Barcelona,' he told Pep from the seat he was keeping warm for him.

And so it was that two days later, with Guardiola now the recognised successor at Bayern, the German league, complete with packed stadiums – a reflection of the cheap prices charged at the turnstiles, but also of a football culture that puts the stadium spectator ahead of the armchair fan – resumed.

The perception and balance of world football had changed.

At the beginning of February, Guardiola rang Johann Cruyff to explain his move to Bayern. 'Proud and delighted with his decision,' was the reaction of the Dutch master, who praised Guardiola for taking the sporting challenge rather than opting for one of the many financially dizzy deals that were on the table. Ultimately, what Pep wanted to do was demonstrate his Cruyff-like understanding and style of football in Franz Beckenbauer's house. Beckenbauer, a great rival of Cruyff in the '70s and also a good friend, had been a great admirer of Barcelona since Bayern were KO'd by the Catalans at the quarter-final stage of the 2009 Champions League at the Camp Nou. Around that time, as Ramon Besa wrote in *El Pais*, 'German coaches spent fifteen days at the Sports City to study how grass-roots football at Barcelona works, so there is a history of interest between both sides that goes back some way.'

The question was, though, would arriving at Bayern after having won so much with Barcelona put enormous expectations on the new manager? 'I wouldn't swap it. I prefer to go on like this, having done what I've done, rather than starting from a position where I have it all to win, where I have to win all the people over.' That is how Guardiola answered FIFA.com when asked about his reception at a future club. Having won the world's admiration, he preferred to bank on the privileged position that his years at Barcelona allowed him despite the pressure of having to start after Heynckes's league, cup and Champions League win: 'When I began working at the Camp Nou, 80 odd per cent of the people didn't like me. These things happen in life and you can't control them. But we did what we had to do, between all of us, and now I carry with me all the memories of those years. Even now they can still say what they want to say, but what I lived is mine. It belongs to me and no one can take it from me.'

But how do you transfer Barcelona's style of play to another football team? Guardiola explained: 'The system of football played by Barcelona is a very simple one. It's about playing with the ball, doing everything with the ball. Every footballer in the world, whether from the tiniest village or largest city, has dedicated himself to a life of football because at some time in their life they once kicked a ball and they loved it. Barcelona's system, despite the fact that people say it is very complicated, is in fact as simple as that. We've got the ball. Let's see if you can get it from us. We pass it to each other as much as possible and we try to score. That is what I was taught by my predecessors and what I try to instil wherever I am. I'm not sure what they are doing at the moment since I left, but judging from what I see on television, it is not dissimilar. Wherever I go to train, I try to transmit what I feel. And what I will try to do in the future is what I did when I played, what I sensed, what I felt then or, five years ago, when I started coaching. Attack as much as possible, win the ball and pass it to someone who's wearing the same colour shirt.'

In reality, Guardiola is going to a club that has already walked much of the road. The work of Louis van Gaal in 2009 and 2011 prompted a change of style from the team. They went from being a hardened and pragmatic outfit to playing a style that was more Dutch in its outlook, more expansive. They pass more and keep possession more than any other club in the Bundesliga. Louis and Pep come together again. 'Pep follows my philosophy,' explains van Gaal. 'I began the system that is in place here, Heynckes took charge of it and Pep thinks the same and will take it in the same direction.'

In search of continued success at home and abroad, the team has been filled with talented players all over the pitch – Neuer, Robben, Javi Martínez, Ribéry, Lahm, Kroos, Müller, Mario Gómez, Schweinsteiger, all of them internationals and all of them with a tremendous understanding of the game. There are, of course, still things to do. Will Pep play with a false number nine, or was that merely a tactical solution for the team that he had? At Bayern he has the wingers that he enjoys using so much, open and decisive in one-on-one situations, but he will also have available conventional strikers such as Gómez, Pizarro and Mandžukić. And if he's looking to build from the back, he'll have to convince his defenders that they are up to the task. The arrival of Mari Goetze, for whom the chance to be coached by Pep was the main reason for his departure, will provide slower, more controlled gears to compliment the direct game of Javi Martínez and Schweinsteiger.

'Many people will wait and see how things go before commenting on whether or not his appointment was a good one.' So says Juanma Lillo before adding, 'I already believe it is a good appointment because he will have under him players that meet his football criteria and have the quality he looks for in all positions.'

Despite the constant rumours about possible signings of players closely connected with him, or others that he particularly likes, the new coach was pleased to discover that Bayern were going to take charge of changing the squad as and when it was considered necessary and his input would be solely to make suggestions.

It was reported in mid February 2013 that Guardiola had been spotted dining at the famous Kafer's restaurant, a favourite place for private meetings for the Bavarian club's board. It wasn't true and nor was it that he presented a list of potential signings mentioned in the press (Luis Suárez, Gareth Bale, Radamel Falcao). He did suggest Neymar, but the board preferred Goetze, as they felt that Brazilian players do not tend to adapt to life in Germany. Pep understood what his role would be and had no problem accepting the squad offered to him.

*

There were clubs that were prepared to pay him more, Chelsea more than any. Even so, Guardiola has become the highest-paid manager in the history of the Bavarian club. Josep María Orobitg has not confirmed the salary his client will receive, but adds that Bayern did not offer the most lucrative deal: 'He picked Bayern because, out of all the offers he received, theirs was the best. We have been passing him offers and this was not the club that offered the most money. He picked it because of the organisation in place, for the possibilities he sees with the team at his disposal.'

It is thought that a deal, assisted by Adidas, a sponsor of the club and owner of 9 per cent of Bayern shares, will allow him to earn in the region of 8 to 10 million euros a year. He will not have to deal with the media pressure that exists in England and Spain and, furthermore, José Mourinho decided to return 'home' to Chelsea after the bittersweet experience at Madrid.

Most of his assistants in Barcelona will stay at the Catalan club, but some will accompany him – Manel Estiarte will be one of them. For months Manel was in limbo before the confirmation of the destination of his new job. Before Christmas and the Hoeness meeting, Estiarte didn't know whether he should perfect his English, brush up on his Italian or start learning German. 'I'll tell you in January,' Pep told him. 'But stay calm.'

Rummenigge announced that the club wanted to present Guardiola in his 'official first day at work' at the beginning of June and that a friendly between Barcelona had been arranged. But as the time drew closer to see Guardiola in a new tracksuit, donning a new badge, many of the Barcelona faithful began to feel uncomfortable with the situation. Some understood, others felt betrayed. As Besa explains, 'Most of the decisions that Guardiola has taken throughout his career have provoked controversy and more than one interpretation. He has those who adore him without limits but also defamers who view him with concealed contempt and judge him purely in terms of his results, or at times by the way they feel he has treated them. This happens with some journalists and with the fans ever since his playing days. Some consider him to be the very heritage of Barcelona and, as such, someone who should work solely for the interests of the club without actually knowing exactly what that interest is, while there are others who consider him to be a guru who has won the right to decide on everything, and much more, about his own life.'

At the age of 42 the path he has taken has been long and complex. Who would have thought on the day that he was offered the opportunity to become the Brescia manager – before Barcelona came calling and he suggested working for the club as a football director with Tito Vilanova as the coach – that six years later he would turn out to be the main ambassador for the revitalised German league, which might soon prove to be the most powerful on the planet?

In the Barcelona changing rooms they wish him nothing but the best. Tito, in one of his last press conferences before his operation, put into words what they all feel: 'I am very pleased that he has returned to coaching. He was able to choose, and if he has decided on Bayern, it is because it will make him happy. He has had time to think about it and make his decision, which is what he wanted. He could not have made a mistake with his choice, because all the teams he could have gone to were of the very highest level.' And he added something that was very relevant. The contract his friend had signed at Bayern was for three years and not for one, as was the case with the last two deals he had made at Barcelona. 'Here, he worked at home and when you do that, everything affects you directly,' Tito continued. 'It's different. More demanding.'

'If he is happy, then so are we.' (José Manuel Pinto)

'It was always expected that he would go to one of the major clubs in Europe. There are a couple of things that fit the Pep mould: the club have got a similar philosophy to Barcelona and the team is full of local guys.' (Javier Mascherano)

'It hasn't surprised me, because it is a great club, but what concerns me is what happens at Barça.' (Carles Puyol – who else?)

'I'm happy for him because it means that he is now well and with the strength to return to this crazy world of football. That he has come back at the highest level is good news because it forces us to think and be at our best. I am not at all surprised that he chose Bayern in preference to the Premier League.' (Andoni Zubizarreta)

'So, what's Munich like to live in?' Pep asked a couple of friends who knew the city well. It's wealthy, cosmopolitan, though not as much as Berlin, and home to the famous and the artistic. You can escape into the mountains or contemplate at your leisure in one of the many expansive green spaces. No one in the street expects you to explain yourself – you can be just another Munich resident. That's what they told him as he returned to New York, where he stayed till the end of his childrens' school year.

But soon he would be returning to football. Back onto the pitch. The training ground. The challenge of managing footballers.

Strolling along one of the great avenues in the city of skyscrapers, Guardiola had rediscovered the magically sweet moment that he had missed, the feeling that he had lost at Barcelona.

Once again he looked at the ball with affection and it occurred to him that if the wings pushed forward more often and found Schweinsteiger coming from deep, then, then . . . He wasn't thinking about Iniesta, or Puyol, or Messi. And for a brief second a sense of gloom came upon him before quickly passing.

Yes, indeed. Schweinsteiger would be the key to his next team.

Part IV

APPENDICES: Pep Guardiola for Beginners

Appendix 1
LA MASÍA

The modern FC Barcelona with an idea, a philosophy, a way of playing, a particular type of footballer, started as far back as the mid-seventies.

In 1974 Laureano Ruíz became general coordinator for youth football and one of the first things he did was to tear down a notice next to the entrance of his new office that read: 'If you are coming to offer me a youngster who measures less than 1.80 metres, you can take him back.'

'Laureano prioritised the technical quality of a footballer, reaction times and, above other factors, intelligence, to learn and understand the game,' explains Martí Perarnau, former Olympic highjumper, journalist and now the leading analyst of the Barcelona youth system. 'He wanted players who controlled the ball with their first touch, who had quick feet, who retained the ball and created superiority from individual technique and group work. He said that if you pass the ball well, you receive it well and have good control; then you have far more possibilities. He stood against the established rules, which emphasised tall and strong players even if they were clumsy. Winning one battle after another, he steadily planted the first seeds of that philosophy in the club.'

The training sessions were based on the use of the ball and not on the physical exercises and continuous running that were fashionable at that time. When asked why Laureano's kids ran so little, he would explain, 'If we spend all our time running, when will they learn to play with the ball?' After all, footballers never run constantly in a game, do they? They do short sprints, stop, change direction, long sprints ... Emphasis on physical exercise alone isn't necessary; it should be incorporated into training and practice with the ball.

In Perarnau's fascinating book *The Champions Path*, Laureano explains how he introduced the drills known as '*rondos*' (a form of piggy-in-the-middle, also known as Toros) that would encapsulate and instil the essence of a club philosophy still practised by the kids at La Masía endlessly, even today: 'No one else did it in Spain, it was the fruit of hours and hours of reflecting about football. I started with three against two. I saw that way two of the three moved wide and there was always one free. I thought, why not do four against two? Or nine against three?'

The Barça of the 1970s had an English trainer, Vic Buckingham, who asked the president Agustí Montal to close the academy and invest the money in buying top-class players for the first team. Thankfully, Montal refused, so Laureano Ruíz persisted with the idea of organising and establishing a unique style of play and a common methodology throughout the club.

When Johan Cruyff said, just after becoming manager of Barcelona in 1988, 'This is what we are going to do: the ball will be the starting point, I want to dominate possession and I will always go out to win, which means it forces my players to conquer the ball, to have it and not lose possession of it', it sounded familiar to those at La Masía because they had heard Laureano saying similar things fifteen years earlier. Despite the fact that all big clubs are under pressure to win and prioritise the short-term goals over long-term gain, those ideas didn't fall on deaf ears.

Cruyff had become synonymous with the playing style of 'Total Football', honed by Ajax coach Rinus Michels who also went on to coach Johan at Barcelona. As the Wikipedia article on the style says, it is a system whereby 'a player who moves out of his position is replaced by another, thus allowing the team to retain their intended organisational structure. In this fluid system, no footballer is fixed in his intended outfield role; anyone can move seamlessly between playing as an attacker, a midfielder and a defender' all in the same game.

Cruyff felt from the start that Catalan society had welcomed him with open arms and he felt obliged to return that appreciation with a piece of his mind to the European press: he had preferred Barcelona over Real Madrid, 'because he could not play for a club associated with the Spanish dictator Francisco Franco'. His first kid was called Jordi (Saint George is the Catalan patron) and in 1974 Cruyff helped the club win La Liga for the first time in fourteen years, defeating Real Madrid along the way in a historical 5–0 at the Bernabéu that is still remembered as one of Barcelona's best-ever performances. Needless to say, he had enough credit and charisma to ensure there was little resistance to his Total Football vision when he landed the job of manager in 1988.

'The biggest problem was the Catalan character and when you try to do something new, they always have doubts: they prefer to wait and see how it goes,' says Johan Cruyff who today understands better than most the conservative and pessimistic mentality of the Catalans. He also knew that once they were convinced (by the team's continuity and success) those same people would also become the most loyal disciples of his ideas.

Cruyff introduced some passing drills into Barça's 'arterial' system. And since then, the *rondos* have been not just a method but a symbol of the club's playing style: of dominating possession and never losing the ball. Cruyff blended several ideas and concepts and converted them into a philosophy – the seeds of which were planted throughout a club in urgent need of a footballing identity. Until then, the first team of Barcelona had been comfortably living in a world of excuses and enemies, content with their role as victims when faced with Real Madrid, an institution seen from Catalonia as the club of the Establishment.

Xavi Hernández describes the style in its purest form: 'I pass the ball and move, or I pass the ball and stay where I am. I make myself available to help you; I look at you, I stop, I keep my head up and look, and, above all, I open up the pitch. Whoever has the ball is running play. That comes from the school of Johan Cruyff and Pep Guardiola. This is Barça.' Or, as Pep Guardiola put it succinctly in a press conference after one of the impressive victories against Real Madrid: 'I have the ball, I pass the ball; I have the ball, I pass the ball. We have the ball, we pass the ball.' T-shirts bearing that slogan can be seen in the streets of Barcelona.

Having the ball required technical ability, being able to control it quickly and place it well (the difference between a good and bad footballer, according to Cruyff, is how well you control the ball and where you place it with your first touch, accommodating it for yourself in the right direction or sending it accurately to your teammate). It needed players who were able to be in the best positions to receive the ball, capable of constantly assisting, of one-twos, of keeping their heads up, of looking for the next pass before receiving, of anticipating play. But, more importantly, they had to be footballers capable of understanding the game. If they had a brain, Cruyff was able to explain to them not just how but why things were done. From the moment the Dutch coach had an influence on the work and methods of the academy, there was a definitive change in the selection process of young players.

'Why do we open up the field?' Cruyff would explain. 'Because if we have the ball and we are open, it is more difficult for the opponent to defend.' Or: 'People criticised me because I played with three at the back, but those criticisms were really ridiculous: what we did was fill the zones on the field where the game required it. If the opponent played with two up front, which was common then, and my team went out with four defenders, I had one too many, so I moved him forward towards the midfield.' Or even: 'There are people that say it is very dangerous to have a corner against you. I think that the solution is not to give the corner away.' Sublime common sense.

Cruyff demanded changes at the academy and La Masía began regularly producing the players he wanted as well as providing the kids with a sound education, dual ambitions of the Dutch coach and the club. 'The player who has come through La Masía has something different from the rest, it's a plus that only comes from having competed in a Barcelona shirt from the time you were a child,' says Guardiola. He is talking not only about the understanding of the game and their ability, but about human qualities. The players who go through La Masía are taught to behave with civility and humility. The theory being that, not only is it pleasant to be unassuming, but also if you are humble, you are capable of learning – and the capacity to learn is the capacity to improve. If you aren't capable of learning you won't improve.

Since his arrival, Johan had tried and succeeded in convincing the club to train all the junior teams in the same way as the first eleven – and to favour talent over physique. Naturally, there were remnants of the traditional way of perceiving youth football and occasionally old habits persisted: 'Little by little' – said Cruyff – 'we tried to change things. In the junior categories we wanted to mould the player. You must know what his strengths and weaknesses are, work on them and correct them. Depending on how you progress, you could start your time at the club playing in one position and end up in another. The most important thing is being prepared to make the jump, understanding the game. Halfway through this process that was transforming the club, Pep appeared before us.' Cruyff called him up to the first team.

Pep, Xavi, Puyol and Messi: they all know there is a reputation to live up to, an extremely high standard of expectations to meet and an institution, a nation even, that they represent. And from the moment they walk through those doors, even the very youngest players are constantly reminded of that. When they travel to another city, when they are taken for dinner, when they go for a walk as a group, the kids are told to be respectful and have good manners every single day. Guardiola summed up those principles for the B team players when he delivered his introductory speech at the Mini Estadi: 'I like to win. I like to train, but above all, I want to teach people to compete representing universal values: values based on respect and education. Giving everything while competing with dignity is a victory, whatever the scoreline suggests.'

Appendix 2
THE STATS OF THOSE FOUR WONDERFUL YEARS

Four wonderful years in which FC Barcelona became a reference point for world football: 3 Liga titles, 2 Champions League, 2 Copa del Rey, 3 Spanish Super Cup, 2 European Super Cup and 2 World Club Championships are testament to one of the greatest football teams of all time.

2008–09 Season: Liga, Copa and Champions League

The 2008–09 was the greatest season in Barcelona's history. Guardiola's team won the Copa, Liga and Champions League in an impeccable year full of celebrations and memorable moments. It was the first treble of the twenty-first century in Europe. Highlights included the 2–6 scoreline against Real Madrid at the Bernabéu, the 5,000th goal thanks to Leo Messi and the unforgettable 'Iniestazo' goal at Stamford Bridge.

Squad: Valdés, Cáceres, Piqué, Rafa Márquez, Puyol, Xavi, Gudjohnsen, Iniesta, Eto'o, Messi, Bojan, Pinto, Gabi Milito, Keita, Henry, Silvinho, Dani Alves, Hleb, Abidal, Touré, Jorquera, Pedro, Busquets and Víctor Sánchez.

Total games played: 54 (Pre-season 5, Gamper 1, Copa Catalunya 1, Liga 38, Copa 9, Champions League 15)

Total games won: 48 (Pre-season 5, Gamper 1, Copa Catalunya 0, Liga 27, Copa 7, Champions League 8)

Total games drawn: 13 (Pre-season 0, Gamper 0, Copa Catalunya 0, Liga 6, Copa 2, Champions League 5)

Total games lost: 8 (Pre-season 0, Gamper 0. Copa Catalunya 1, Liga 5, Copa 0, Champions League 2)

Total goals scored: 186 (Pre-season 25, Gamper 2, Copa Catalunya 1, Liga 105, Copa 17, Champions League 36)

Total goals conceded: 67 (Pre-season 8, Gamper 1, Copa Catalunya 3, Liga 35, Copa 6, Champions League 14)

Titles: 3 (Liga, Copa del Rey and UEFA Champions League)

Individual awards: Zamora Trophy (for least goals conceded) Víctor Valdés.

2009–10 Season: Liga, Spanish Super Cup, European Super Cup, World Club Champions

The treble-winning season continued into the 2009–10 season, in which FC Barcelona lifted four more trophies: the Liga title, the Spanish and European Super Cups and the first World Club Championship in history. The highlight was the team achieving ninety-nine points in the league.

Squad: Valdés, Piqué, Rafa Márquez, Puyol, Xavi, Iniesta, Messi, Bojan, Pinto, Gabi Milito, Keita, Henry, Dani Alves, Abidal, Touré, Pedro, Busquets, Zlatan Ibrahimović, Maxwell, Jeffren and Chygrynskiy.

Total games played: 65 (Pre-season 5, Gamper 1, Spanish Super Cup 2, European Super Cup 1, Liga 38, Copa 4, Champions League 12 and World Club Championship 2)

Total games won: 48 (Pre-season 3, Gamper 0, Spanish Super Cup 2, European Super Cup 1, Liga 31, Copa 3, Champions League 6 and World Club Championship 2)

Total games drawn: 12 (Pre-season 2, Gamper 0, Spanish Super Cup 0, European Super Cup 0, Liga 6, Copa 0, Champions League 4, World Club Championship 0)

Total games lost: 5 (Pre-season 0, Gamper 1, Spanish Super Cup 0, European Super Cup 0, Liga 1, Copa 1, Champions League 2 and World Club Championship 0)

Total goals scored: 150 (Pre-season 12, Gamper 0, Spanish Super Cup 5, European Super Cup 1, Liga 98, Copa 9, Champions League 20 and World Club Championship 5)

Total goals conceded: 44 (Pre-season 4, Gamper 1, Spanish Super Cup 1, European Super Cup 0, Liga 24, Copa 2, Champions League 10, World Club Championship 2)

Titles: 4 (Liga, Spanish Super Cup, European Super Cup, World Club Championship)

Individual awards: Zamora Trophy, Víctor Valdés; Ballon d'Or, FIFA World Player, Golden Boot and Pichichi (for most goals scored), Leo Messi.

2010–11 Season: Liga, Champions League and Spanish Super Cup

Barça overcame the adversities encountered that season and ended up lifting three trophies, earned through hard work and good play. The team became European Champions in magnificent style and three-time Liga winners. Highlights were the second Ballon d'Or for Leo Messi and the 5–0 win over Mourinho's Madrid in the Camp Nou.

2010–11 Squad: Valdés, Piqué, Puyol, Xavi, Iniesta, Messi, Bojan, Pinto, Keita, Dani Alvés, Abidal, Pedro, Busquets, Maxwell, Jeffrén, Milito, Adriano, Mascherano, Fontàs, Afellay and David Villa.

Total games played: 65 (Pre-season 3, Gamper 1, Spanish Super Cup 2, Liga 38, Copa 9, Champions League 13)

Total games won: 48 (Pre-season 3, Gamper 0, Spanish Super Cup 1, Liga 30, Copa 5, Champions League 9)

Total games drawn: 12 (Pre-season 0, Gamper 1, Spanish Super Cup 0, Liga 6, Copa 2, Champions League 3)

Total games lost: 5 (Pre-season 0, Gamper 0, Spanish Super Cup 1, Liga 2, Copa 2, Champions League 1)

Total goals scored: 185 (Pre-season 12, Gamper 1, Spanish Super Cup 5, League 95, Copa 22, Champions League 30)

Total goals conceded: 44 (Pre-season 4, Gamper 1, Spanish Super Cup 3, Liga 21, Copa 6, Champions League 9)

Titles: 3 (Liga, Champions League and Spanish Super Cup)

Individual awards: Zamora Trophy, Víctor Valdés; Ballon d'Or, Leo Messi

2011–12 Season: Spanish Super Cup, European Super Cup, World Club Championship, Copa del Rey

Guardiola's last season at the helm of Barcelona was full of incidents. President Sandro Rosell and Pep himself talked of it having been a 'very strange season' suggesting dubious referee decisions. The team was handicapped by the serious injuries to David Villa, Abidal and Fontàs. Even so, Barça won the Spanish and European Super Cups, their second World Club Championship, and the Copa del Rey, and they made it to the semi-finals of the Champions League. Highlights included Messi's third Ballon d'Or together with the greatest Pichichi ever with 50 Liga goals and 73 in all competitions, as well as the Golden Boot and a fifth Zamora Trophy for Víctor Valdés.

Total games played: 70 (Pre-season 6, Gamper 1, Spanish Super Cup 2, European Super Cup 1, World Club Championship 2, Liga 38, Copa 9, Champions League 12)

Total games won: 49 (Pre-season 2, Gamper 1, Spanish Super Cup 1, European Super Cup 1, World Club Championship 2, Liga 28, Copa 6, Champions League 8)

Total games drawn: 15 (Pre-season 2, Gamper 0, Spanish Super Cup 1, European Super Cup 0, World Club Championship 0, Liga 7, Copa 2, Champions League 3)

Total games lost: 6 (Pre-season 2, Gamper 0, Spanish Super Cup 0, European Super Cup 0, World Club Championship 0, Liga 3, Copa 0, Champions League 1)

Total goals scored: 202 (Pre-season 8, Gamper 5, Spanish Super Cup 5, European Super Cup 2, World Club Championship 8, Liga 114, Copa 25, Champions League 35)

Total goals conceded: 57 (Pre-season 8, Gamper 0, Spanish Super Cup 4, European Super Cup 0, World Club Championship 0, Liga 29, Copa 6, Champions League 10)

Titles: 4 (Liga, Spanish Super Cup, European Super Cup, Copa del Rey)

Individual awards: Zamora Trophy, Víctor Valdés; Ballon d'Or, Pichichi and Golden Boot, Leo Messi

2008–12

Total games played: 255
Total games won: 194
Total games drawn: 52
Total games lost: 24
Total goals scored: 723
Total goals conceded: 212
Titles: 14 (3 Liga, 2 Champions League, 2 Copa del Rey, 3 Spanish Super Cup, 2 European Super Cup, 2 World Club Championships)
Individual awards: 3 Ballon d'Or (Messi), 1 FIFA World Player (Messi), 2 Pichichis (Messi), 2 Golden Boot (Messi), 4 Zamora Trophies (Víctor Valdés)

BIBLIOGRAPHY

Patrick Barclay, *Mourinho: Anatomy of a Winner* (Orion, 2005)

Lluis Canut, *Els secrets del Barça* (Columna Edicions S.A., 2010)

Jaume Collell, *Pep Guardiola: de Santpedor a la banqueta del Barça* (La Butxaca, 2010)

Juan Carlos Cubeiro, *Mourinho versus Guardiola* (Alienta, 2010)

Alex Santos Fernández, *L'entorn. El circ mediàtic del Barça* (Cossetània, 2011)

Josep Guardiola I Sala, *La meva gent, el meu futbol* (Sport, 2001)

Zlatan Ibrahimovic, *I Am Zlatan* (Albert Bonniers Förlag, 2011)

Andrés Iniesta, *Un año en el paraíso* (Now Books, 2009)

Martí Perarnau, *El camí dels campions* (Columna Edicions S.A., 2011)

Gerard Piqué, *Viatge d'anada* (Edicions 62, 2010)

Jordi Pons, *No tindràs collons de fer-ho* (Editorial Base, 2010)

Francisco Javier Garasa Sibis & Santiago Padró Navarro, *Paraula de Pep* (Ara Llibres, 2009)

Ricard Torquemada, *Formula Barça* (Cossetània, 2011)

Miguel Angel Violán, *El mètode, Guardiola* (Columna Edicions S.A. 2010)

Articles by Martín Mazur, and articles from *El País* (Ramón Besa, Luis Martín) and *El Periódico* (Joan Domenech, Marcos López, David Torras)

ACKNOWLEDGEMENTS

This book comes on the back of conversations held in the last four years with Pep Guardiola, Johan Cruyff, Joan Laporta, Sandro Rosell, Andoni Zubizarreta, Xavi Hernández, Andrés Iniesta, Víctor Valdés, Javier Mascherano, Lionel Messi, David Villa, Cesc Fàbregas, Pedro, Carles Puyol, Gerard Piqué, Manel Estiarte, Emili Ricart, Oscar García, Michael Laudrup, Joan Patsy, Txiki Beguiristain, Albert Ferrer, José Mourinho and Louis van Gaal, amongst others who are or have been at FC Barcelona.

I have to thank Pep Guardiola for his time but also for having sent an email to Sir Alex Ferguson, which then became a trip to Manchester to talk to him. Apologies to Màrius for taking time from your dad.

If it wasn't for the trust of my agent David Luxton and Alan Samson at Orion, this would have never seen the light of day. Sorry for the delay again! Thanks to Lucinda McNeile for her patience and her kind words, too.

During the years, I have chatted about Pep (and much more) with good football friends to whom I want to send a paper hug from here: Vicente del Bosque, Rafa Benítez, Mauricio Pochettino, Ramón Planes, Pep Segura, Pako Ayestarán, Paco Herrera, José Manuel Ochotorena, Arrigo Sacchi, Brendan Rodgers, Fabio Capello, Graham Hunter, Juan Ignacio Martínez, Unai Emery, André Villas Boas, Gary Neville, Wayne Rooney, Michael Robinson, Alfredo Relaño, Santi Giménez, Michel Salgado, Marcos López, Joan Domenech, David Torras, Johanna Gará, Paul Jewell, David Trueba, Sique Rodríguez, Alex Castells, Juan Carlos Garrido, Borja Valero . . .

The extraordinary hard work of Lee Watson and Elizabeth Duffy in editing this book is clearly reflected in it. Isabel Díaz was always at hand for help, so thank you! Brent Wilks – yes, I am working on the book, talk to you later – thank you, too. Jacquie Feeley injected enough confidence and energy into everybody to get to the end. Thanks to Kevin, too, for looking after her while she sorted out so many worlds. William Glasswell offered new eyes to the project and is now a mad football fan. Mark Wright was always at hand to remind me that, yes, it has to be done, keep going. Their strength helped me get to the end.

For the Spanish edition, I needed the words, work, time, and much more of Maribel Herruzo and Ladislao J. Moñino. Without you it would have been impossible.

There are some good friends who deserve much more than a word, but at least they will get a word for sure. Luis Miguel García, who always opens my eyes, Gabriele Marcotti and our arguments, Raphael Honigstein and Carlos Bianchi, Sergio Alegre, who will always wear a 6 with Barcelona and an 8 with the national team, Chus Llorente and vodka Chopin, Gustavo Balagué and culé, Yolanda Balagué and new born culé, Chris Parle and shopping, Stevie Rowe, who heard so many Pep stories, Scott Minto, who hasn't got bored of them yet, Mark Payne, who doesn't believe all of them, Damian O'Brian and his DVDs, the Revista de la Liga team for their love and passion for Spanish football, Andy Melvin, Barney Francis and Vic Wakeling for allowing me to blossom in Sky Sports, Patrick Barclay and Sitges, Peter Bennett and a window to the proper world, Edu Abascal for looking after AS while I finished this, Eduardo Rubio the coach, Gerard Nus and his lessons, Encarna Martínez and Sonia Moreno, who shared wines and stories, and I owe a beer or two to Andy Goldstein (who will never forgive me for not having added his name before! And rightly so!) and Jason Cundy.

Thank you also to Miguel Ruiz, whose fantastic photographs add a new dimension to the book.

And my parents, who will always read every book I write in English even though they don't speak the language.

INDEX